LINOCUT

for artists & designers

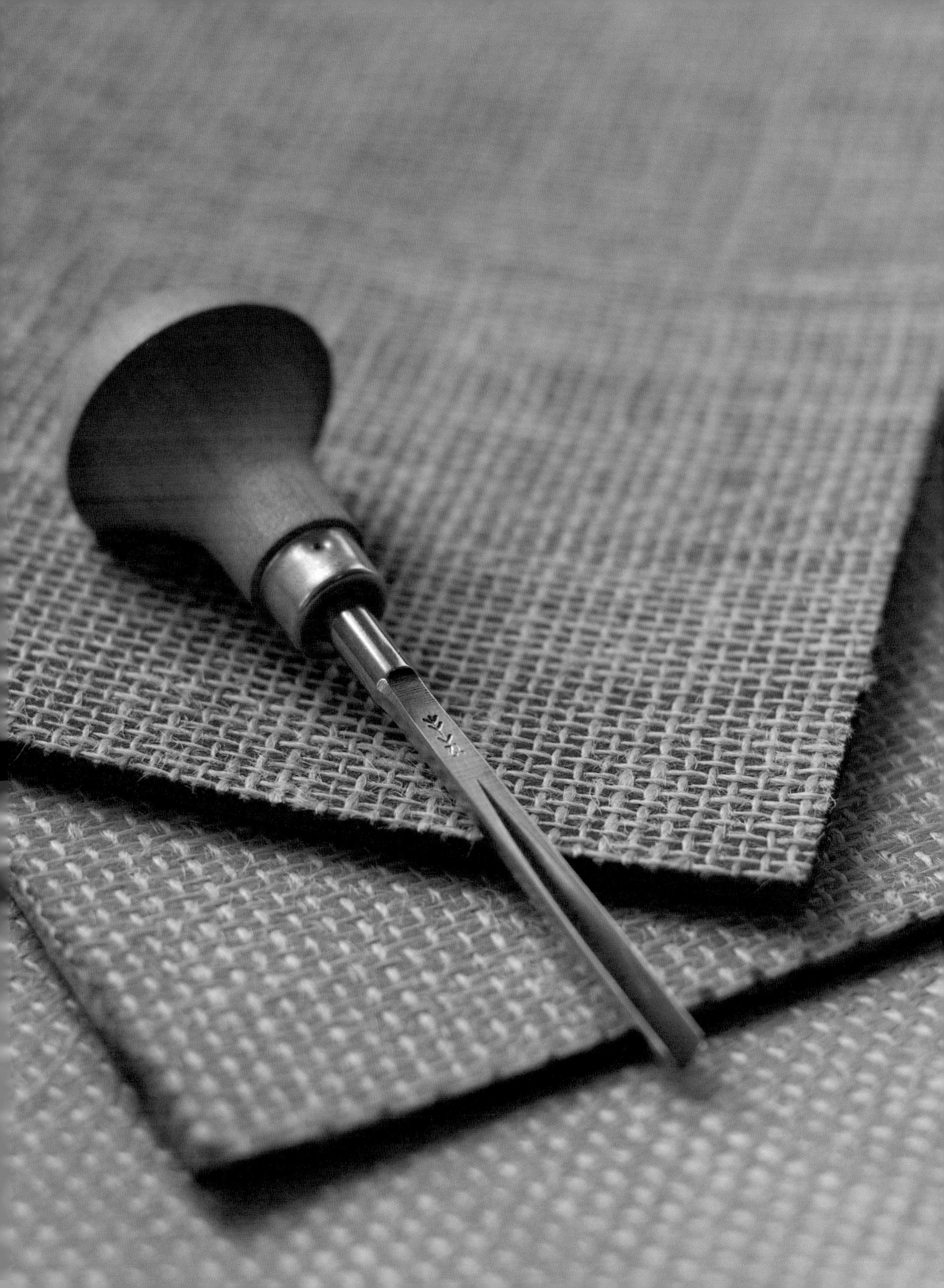

LINOCUT

for artists & designers

Nick Morley

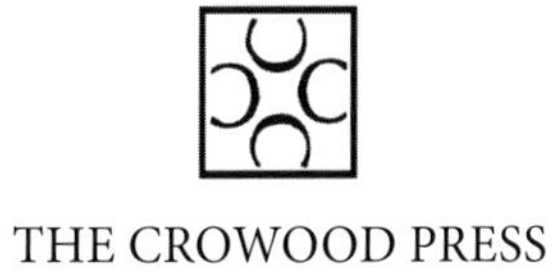

THE CROWOOD PRESS

First published in 2016 by
The Crowood Press Ltd
Ramsbury, Marlborough
Wiltshire SN8 2HR
enquiries@crowood.com
www.crowood.com

This impression 2022

British Library Cataloguing-in-Publication Data
A catalogue record for this book is available from the British Library.

ISBN 978 1 78500 145 1

Acknowledgements

Massive thanks to my partner Catherine, for her encouragement and understanding, and for laughing at my jokes and spotting missing commas. Also to my photographer Hazeleigh Prebble, for his unending patience, beautiful photographs and willingness to stand on chairs to find the best angle. To Ian Youngs for laying out the pages elegantly and juggling all the images and words to fit nicely. To Steve Edwards, Wuon-Gean Ho and Andrew Watt for teaching me new techniques. To all the artists and designers who have contributed to this book and created such inspiring works. To everyone at East London Printmakers and Resort Studios in Margate for their encouragement. Last but not least to my parents Anne and Neal for encouraging me to become an artist in the first place and supporting me every step of the way.

Page design by Ian Youngs
Photography by Hazeleigh Prebble
Printed and bound in India by Parksons Graphics

CONTENTS

INTRODUCTION

Linocut

Linocut is a versatile and popular printmaking process which attracts both professional and amateur artists and designers. It is easy to learn and simple enough to do at home. The materials you will need are widely available and can be bought cheaply. However, many people who start making linocuts give up because they cannot control the tools and are unsatisfied with the quality of their prints. In some cases they will end up with cut fingers and this is enough to put them off for life. With some inside knowledge and a few simple tips all this can be avoided and you will be able to make beautiful prints. This book will show you how.

What is linocut?

Linocut is a form of relief printing. This is the family of techniques which includes woodcut, wood engraving, letterpress, rubber stamping and potato printing. To make a relief print, ink is applied to the surface of the prepared block and then transferred under pressure onto another surface, usually paper. The print is a mirror image of the block.

A linocut print is simply a relief print made from a block of linoleum. To make a traditional linocut, any unwanted areas of linoleum are carved away with gouges and the block is inked up with an ink roller. The ink is only transferred to the raised, uncarved parts. It is then pressed onto the paper using a printing press or by hand with a tool. The block is then re-inked before making the next print.

There are many ways of making prints with lino, some of which don't involve cutting at all. These include drilling, scraping and etching the block with chemicals. This can result in a wide range of effects, some of which look very different from the typical graphic style often associated with linocut. As well as traditional linocut, this book explores some of these more unusual ways of making prints.

History

For centuries wood was the material of choice for making relief prints. It was plentiful and gave beautiful results. Then, in the late nineteenth century an Austrian educationalist called Franz Cižek began using the newly invented linoleum for his art classes. It was softer and easier to cut than wood, making it ideal for children to use. Cižek was friends with some influential artists and the use of linoleum for printing spread through Europe. The first historically important artists to make linocuts were the German expressionist artists, known collectively as *Die Brücke* (The Bridge), with founder member Erich Heckel making his first recorded print in 1903. After that such big names as Matisse and Picasso were drawn to the strong graphic qualities of linocut. In Mexico and Russia these same qualities made it the perfect medium for printing political posters. Today linocut has been adopted by artists, illustrators and designers the world over.

Linocut today

Linocut is wrongly seen by some as a slightly crude artform, lacking refinement and nuance. Much of this prejudice is down to memories of school art classes, with cut fingers resulting from the use of blunt tools and tough, old bits of lino. Dried-up, poor quality inks may also have contributed to the pain, giving patchy prints. In fact your experience of linocut needn't be like this at all. With the right tools, some helpful guidance and a little practice you will quickly learn to control the carving process. And with the right inks, roller and choice of paper you will learn how to make high quality prints, time after time.

The hands-on nature of linocut makes it appealing to a wide spectrum of creative people. In recent years it has been taken up by illustrators and graphic designers who are tired of staring at a computer screen all day. Fashion and fabric designers are making bespoke wallpapers, clothes and lampshades. Linocut elements make up animations, artists' books and installations; paste-up designs appear as street art alongside spraypaint graffiti, and a new generation of makers, artists and designers are selling their products online through sites like Folksy and Etsy to a public hungry for hand-crafted and unique items.

About this book

Recent years have seen a resurgent interest in printmaking in all its forms. Linocut is especially attractive to those with limited resources. Unlike screenprinting, etching and lithography, linocut does not require lengthy technical training, dangerous chemicals or bulky and expensive equipment. It is cheap and easy to get started. All you need are a gouge, some lino, ink, roller, paper and a wooden spoon. In an hour a beginner working on the kitchen table can carve and print a simple one-colour design.

At this stage many will believe they have reached the pinnacle of their linocut abilities. The aim of this book is to help those who want to reach the next level and make more ambitious prints. You will be guided step by-step through a series of practical projects that will give you a deeper understanding of your materials and how to work with them to get better results every time. You will be given a thorough introduction to the linocut basics: how to select and look after your tools, which materials to buy, how to perfect your carving and printing techniques and trouble-shooting guides for when things go wrong in printing. And you will be introduced to new ways of using lino to create unexpected marks, textures and finishes on a variety of materials.

As well as being a practical guide, this book will explore the myriad creative applications of linocut, from prints on paper, through illustration and graphic design, ceramics, fabrics, and street art to installation, animation, books and sculpture. You will be encouraged to experiment with new approaches to image making and new ways of thinking about how linocut can be used. To provide extra inspiration and context the book also features profiles of contemporary practitioners along with images of their work.

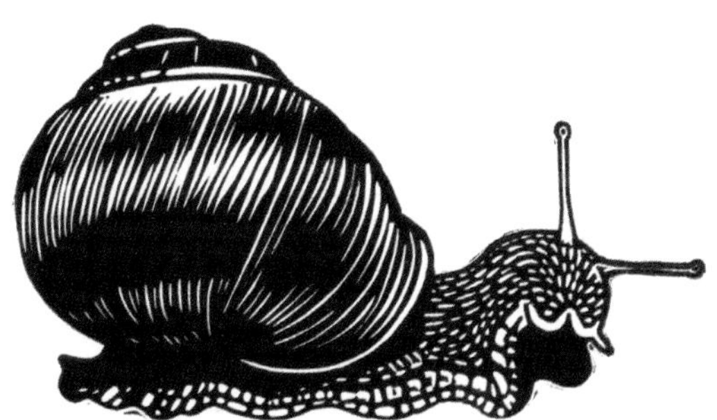

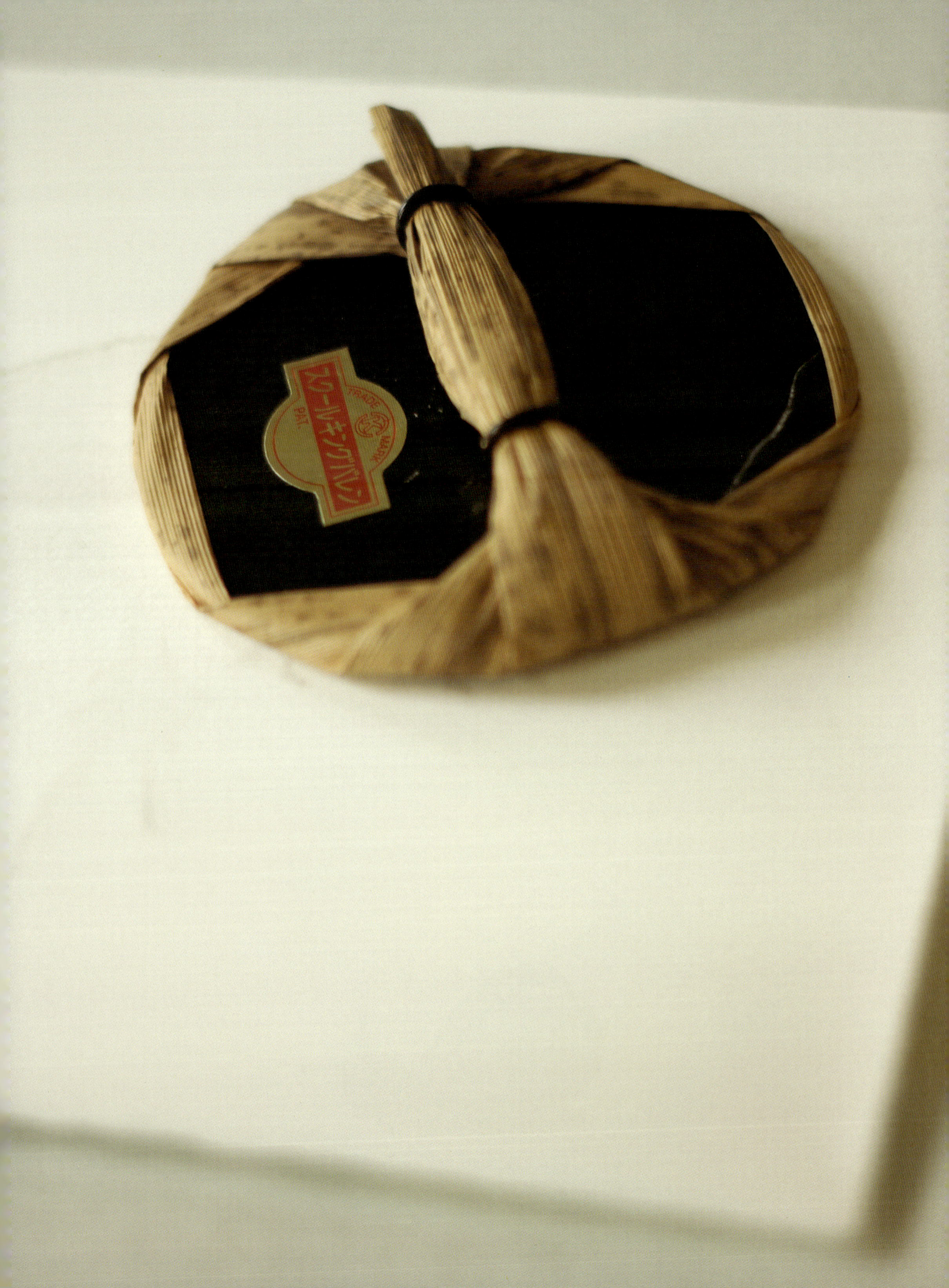
スクールキングバレン
TRADE MARK
PAT.

CHAPTER 1

MATERIALS AND EQUIPMENT

In this chapter you will learn about the materials and equipment you need to make linocuts. The quality of your carving tools, printing inks and paper will have a big effect on the quality of your prints, as well as your enjoyment of the process, so it is worth spending some time researching your options before you buy. Please read this chapter carefully so that you can make informed decisions from the start. Most art shops will sell some linocut materials but they won't necessarily be good quality. You may be better off looking on the internet for certain items or visiting a specialist printmaking supplier. A list of suppliers is included at the back of this book.

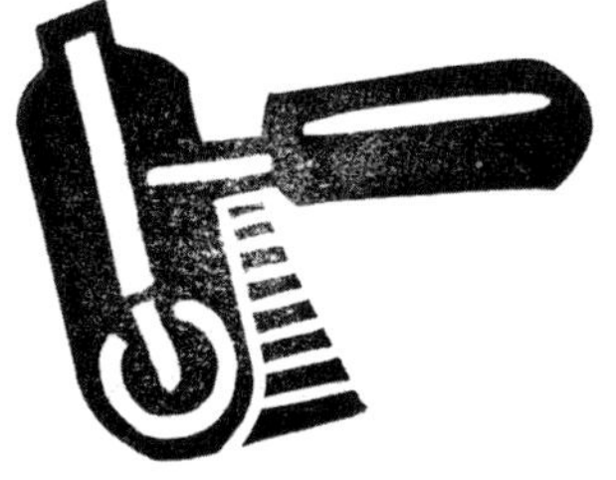

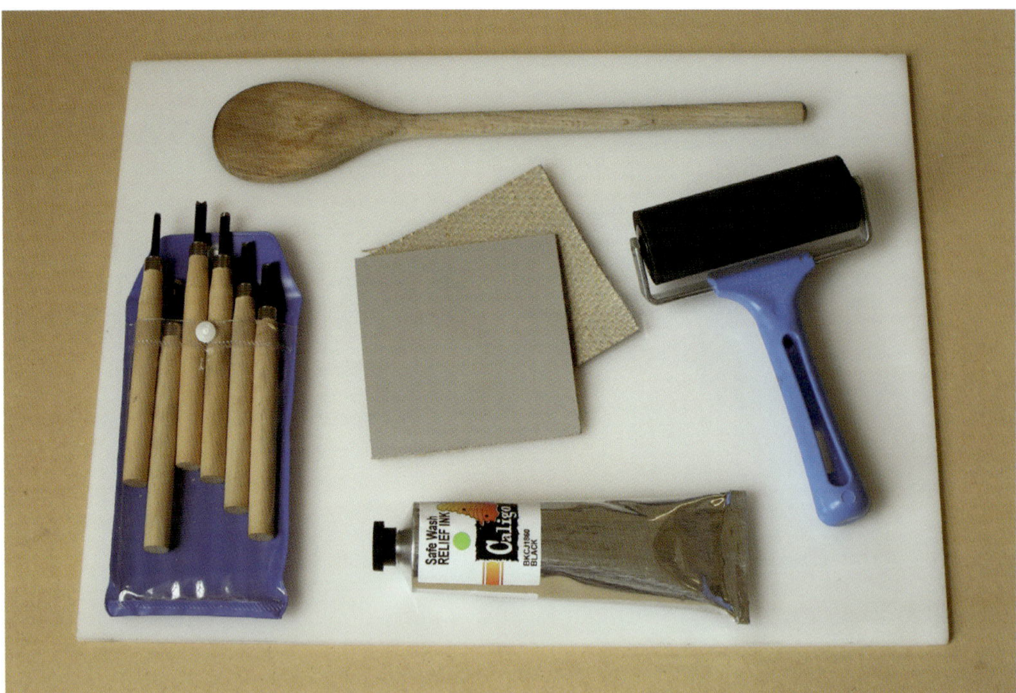

Basic kit: cutting tools, lino, ink, roller, wooden spoon, ink slab.

Basic kit

It is relatively inexpensive to buy the tools and materials you need to get started making linocuts. A basic starter kit will include cutting tools, lino, an ink roller (also known as a brayer), ink, paper and some kind of hand-printing tool. This can be a wooden spoon or similar hard wooden object. This is all you need to start with and shouldn't cost too much.

If you are becoming really serious about making prints, especially on a larger scale, you may want to try using a printing press. Although it is by no means a necessity to have a press for making prints there are certain benefits: it is quicker to make each print, easier to print solid blocks of colour and possible to print onto a wider range of papers than printing by hand. You may be lucky enough to live close to an open access printmaking studio or college where you can have access to facilities or you may want to buy your own press. Chapter 3 contains information on the different types of press available.

Other useful items

Cutting mat, craft knife, pencils (HB and 2B), marker pens, brush pen, eraser, steel ruler, set square, carbon paper, tracing paper, masking tape, non-slip mat, sheet of glass or perspex/plexiglass/acrylic, ink knife or spatula, baren (a Japanese printing tool), newspaper, rags for cleaning, water sprayer.

Protective clothing

No matter how careful you are, when you are printing you will inevitably get ink on you at some point. Because printing ink tends to be slow drying it can easily spread from your clothes to other surfaces. Keep a set of old clothes for printing or wear an apron or overalls to protect your clothes. If you are buying an apron, go for a full length one with a pocket, useful for keeping a rag handy for cleaning. Choose one made out of thick cotton as ink can seep through thinner fabrics. Art suppliers usually sell good quality aprons, or try a catering supplier, which may be cheaper. You will also need a pair of rubber gloves for cleaning up ink. Keep a pair to use just for printing, don't use your kitchen ones. If you prefer you can get a box of disposable latex or vinyl gloves.

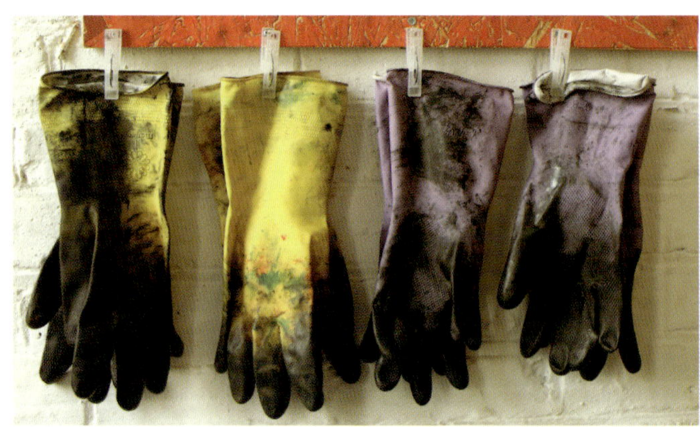

Hang your gloves up on pegs to dry.

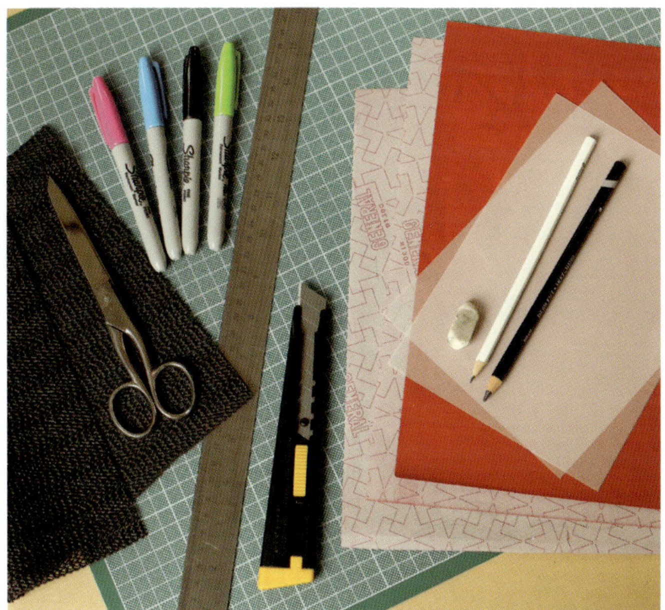

Useful items: cutting mat, non-slip mat, scissors, marker pens, steel ruler, craft knife, carbon paper, tracing paper, eraser, pencils.

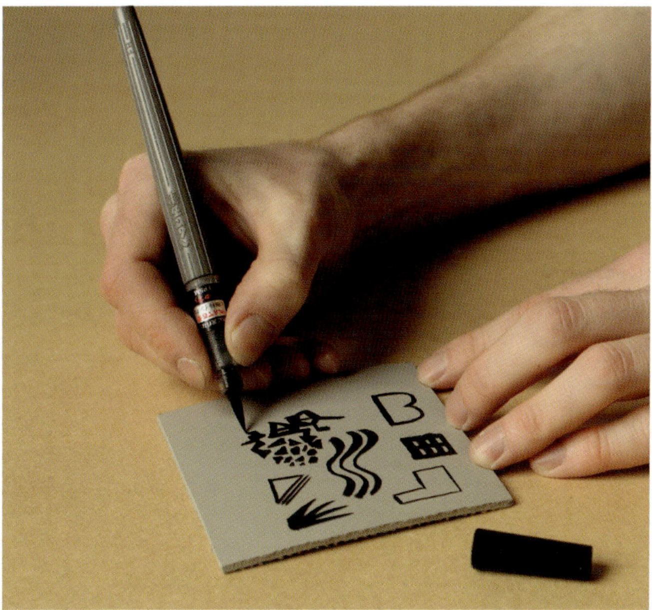

A brush pen makes a wide range of marks and is useful for developing your design.

Linoleum

History and manufacture of linoleum

Linoleum, or lino, was first invented as a cheap flooring material in 1863 by Englishman Frederick Walton. Its name comes from the Latin words *linum* meaning 'flax' and *oleum* meaning 'oil' and it was manufactured from a mixture of oxidized linseed oil, cork dust and pine resin with a backing of hessian or jute material. Following widespread use up until the 1950s, linoleum was replaced as flooring by other materials, including plastics. Today genuine linoleum is still used for flooring and is favoured by some for its ecological properties as it is made from natural, renewable materials. Be aware that some companies make products which they call linoleum but are, in fact, made of other substances. Some of these can be used for linocut but most are too hard or covered in a thick varnish which makes cutting difficult. If in doubt, ask if it is genuine linoleum before you buy. Look for the hessian backing and also give it a sniff – it should smell of linseed oil.

Where to buy linoleum

Linoleum for artists is available from art suppliers and comes in several varieties. The 'battleship grey' lino is the finest grade and is smooth and free of large particles, making it good for detailed work. When it is fresh it is very soft and easy to cut. Other available colours include tan and brown but these tend to be slightly coarser and harder to cut. All lino can be heated gently on a radiator or in the sun to soften it but it will make it slightly crumblier to cut and is best avoided for the finest detail.

You can buy lino in pre-cut blocks in most art shops but if you want to work on a large scale, rolls of grey lino up to several feet wide are available from specialist suppliers. If you are going to be using a lot it will work out cheaper to buy a large sheet and cut it to size yourself. Store your lino flat if possible and away from sunlight and extremes of temperature as over time this will make it go hard and brittle. Warm the lino gently with a hairdryer before unrolling it to stop it cracking. If it refuses to flatten out you can glue mount it onto a piece of wood. You will sometimes find tiny flecks of lino stuck to the surface. These should be removed with a blunt knife or fingernail otherwise they will print as little white halos or dark blobs.

Some suppliers stock lino blocks pre-mounted onto wood. These can be useful if you are printing on a press designed for printing letterpress type, as the extra thickness of the wood brings the surface of the lino up to the same height as the type, or 'type high'. However, it's not usually necessary and costs more than unmounted lino.

Alternatives to linoleum

Alternatives to traditional linoleum include Japanese vinyl and Softcut, both of which are manufactured for the purpose of making

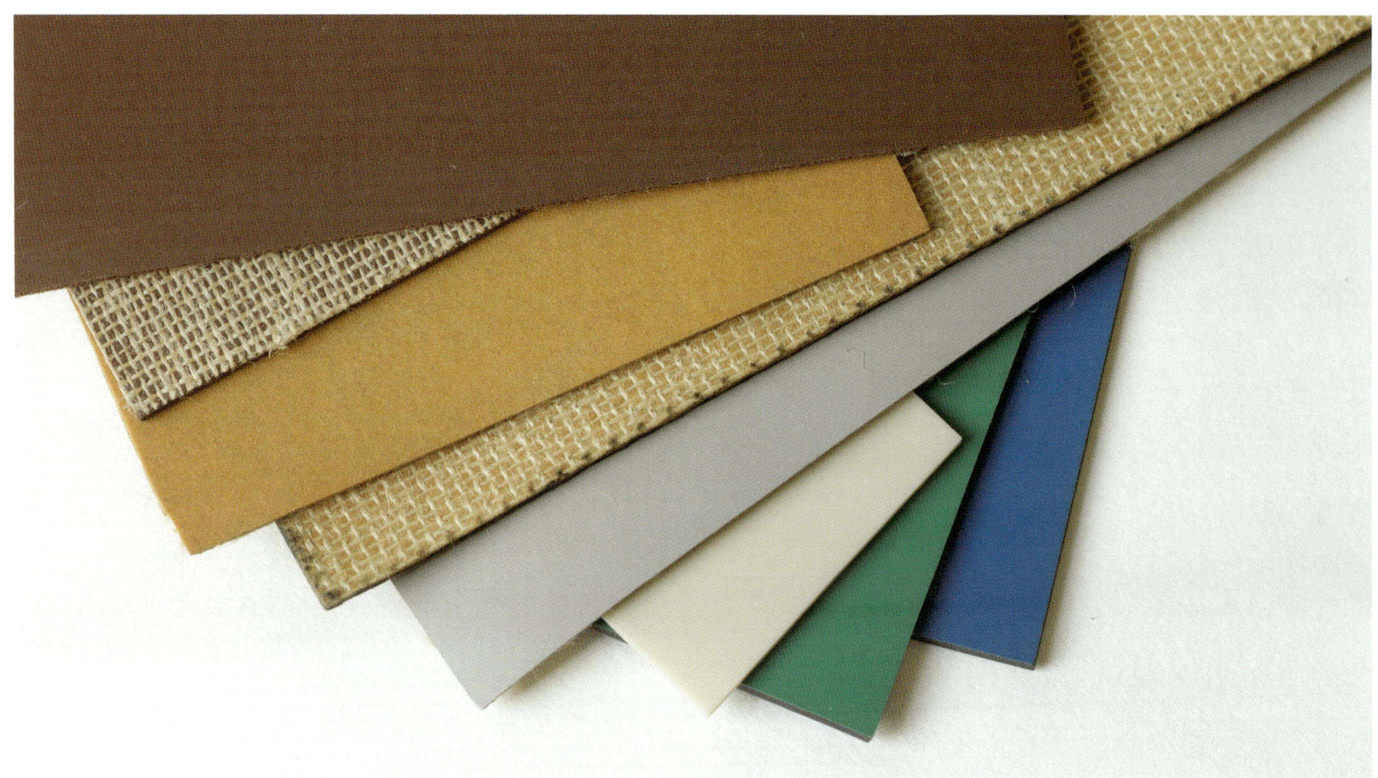

Types of lino: traditional linoleum in brown, yellow and grey.
Softcut is a yellowish white. Japanese vinyl has a blue side and a green side.

prints. Neither is available in as large a size as the traditional lino. They are possibly easier to cut but they have a rubbery, plastic quality which carves slightly differently to the crumblier lino. They also have a hard, smooth surface which prints colours flatter than lino and won't give such a range of textures. However, you may prefer them so try them if you wish. For the purposes of this book, you can use them as an alternative to lino for most of the projects, with the exception of etched lino.

Other, cheaper materials you might like to try include flooring tiles, polystyrene and MDF. Flooring tiles come in a range of materials, some of which will be easier to carve than others. Polystyrene can give some interesting printed textures and can be drawn into using a ball-point pen, to create lines that will print white. MDF is favoured by some artists but is harder to cut and will blunt your tools more quickly.

Carving wood, although closely related to linocut, is too large a subject to cover in this book. The history of woodcut is long and illustrious and it would be impossible to do it justice in a few pages. However, there are many similarities with linocut and much can be learnt by looking at the work of woodcut artists such as Albrecht Dürer and Emil Nolde, as well as the Japanese ukiyo-e woodblocks of Hokusai and Hiroshige. Wood engraving, another related artform, although it uses different tools, is also worth looking at, in particular the work of Thomas Bewick.

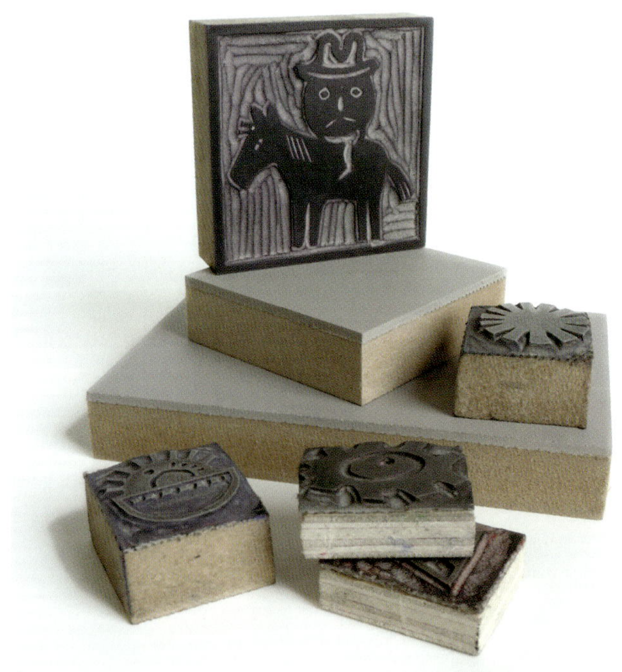

Mounted lino blocks can be bought ready made or you can mount your own by glueing the block to a piece of MDF or plywood with PVA glue.

Cutting tools

There is a large variety of tools suitable for linocut and with a little research you will find good tools that fit your budget. It is not necessary to spend a fortune on a set of Japanese tools made by ex-Samurai sword makers; at least, not to start with. You may end up buying a tool you use once and never pick up again. To start with it is better to buy a cheap set to see which tools you use the most and upgrade if and when you feel the need. Having said that, a set of poor quality tools may put you off linocut for life so it's worth knowing what to look for.

Note: Tools sold for woodcut are suitable for carving lino, but some tools sold for linocut may not be good enough for carving wood.

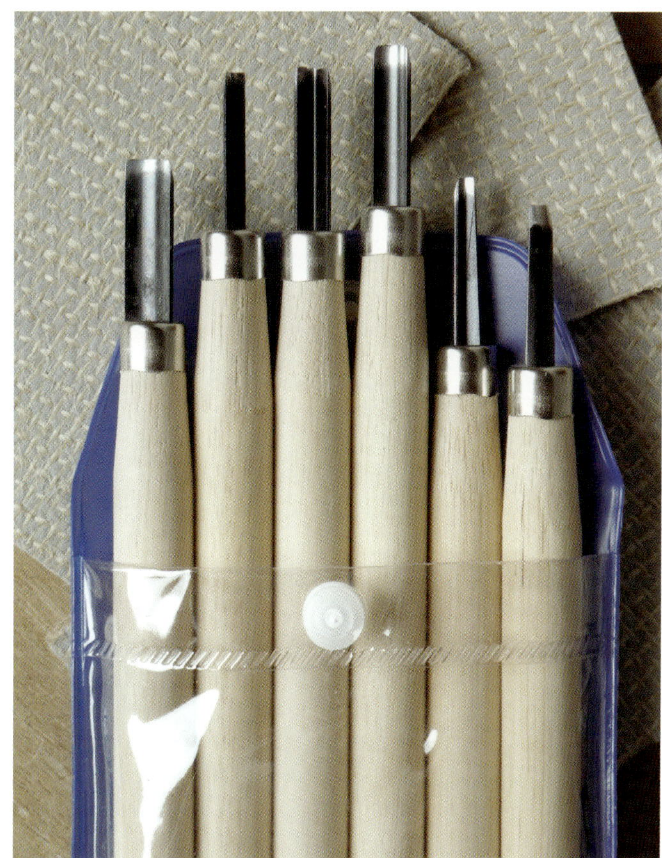

A starter set of pencil-shaped tools in a handy plastic wallet. Make sure the tools you choose are well sharpened.

Shape of handle

Carving tools come with handles in a variety of shapes. The two most common are mushroom-shaped and pencil-shaped. Mushroom-shaped handles are traditionally from Europe (Britain, Germany, Switzerland) and fit snugly in the palm of your hand. Pencil-shaped handles come from Asia (Japan, China, Korea) and are held rather like a pencil. If you can, go into an art store that stocks both kinds and ask to try them out to see which you find more comfortable.

Sharpness

Once you've experienced the difference between a sharp tool and a blunt one you won't ever want to work with a blunt tool again. A sharp tool cuts a cleaner line than a blunt one and with less effort. It is therefore easier to control your mark-making, achieve fine details and avoid straining your wrist and arm through over-exertion. Blunt tools tear the lino rather than cutting it and you are more likely to slip dramatically as you have to push harder, risking injury. For this reason, sharp tools are actually safer than blunt ones.

Finding sharp tools doesn't necessarily mean paying more, so hunt around and, if possible, try before you buy. You can tell whether a tool is sharp simply by looking at it. If it has been well sharpened it will have a mirror finish to the metal near the cutting edge and the cutting edge itself will be straight and true. Hold the tool end-on so you are looking straight at the cutting edge. If you can see light reflecting off it, it is not perfectly sharp.

Note: Most tools you buy will be sharpened but not honed. Honing is the final stage of sharpening and can easily be done at home or in the studio before you start carving. (*See* the section on sharpening tools.)

Quality of materials

Good tools cost more because they are made of better materials. The most important material is the steel of the blade. Steel can be treated in various ways to make it harder or softer, more durable or more flexible. The very best tools (including the ones made by Samurai craftsmen) use two kinds of steel laminated together, one for strength/flexibility and one for hardness. This means the cutting edge stays sharp for longer but the metal is flexible and the cutting edge is less likely to be chipped under pressure. These top-end tools are meant for cutting wood, which is harder than lino. Cheap tools are made of a lower grade of steel and may be damaged more easily or need sharpening more often.

The material the handle is made from is more of an aesthetic consideration. Whether it is plastic or pearwood doesn't make any difference to how it performs, but wooden-handled tools have an undeniable attraction, and through use over time will build up a rich patina.

Finally, when you pick up a tool, check it is solidly constructed. The metal shaft should be firmly attached to the handle and you shouldn't be able to feel it move at all.

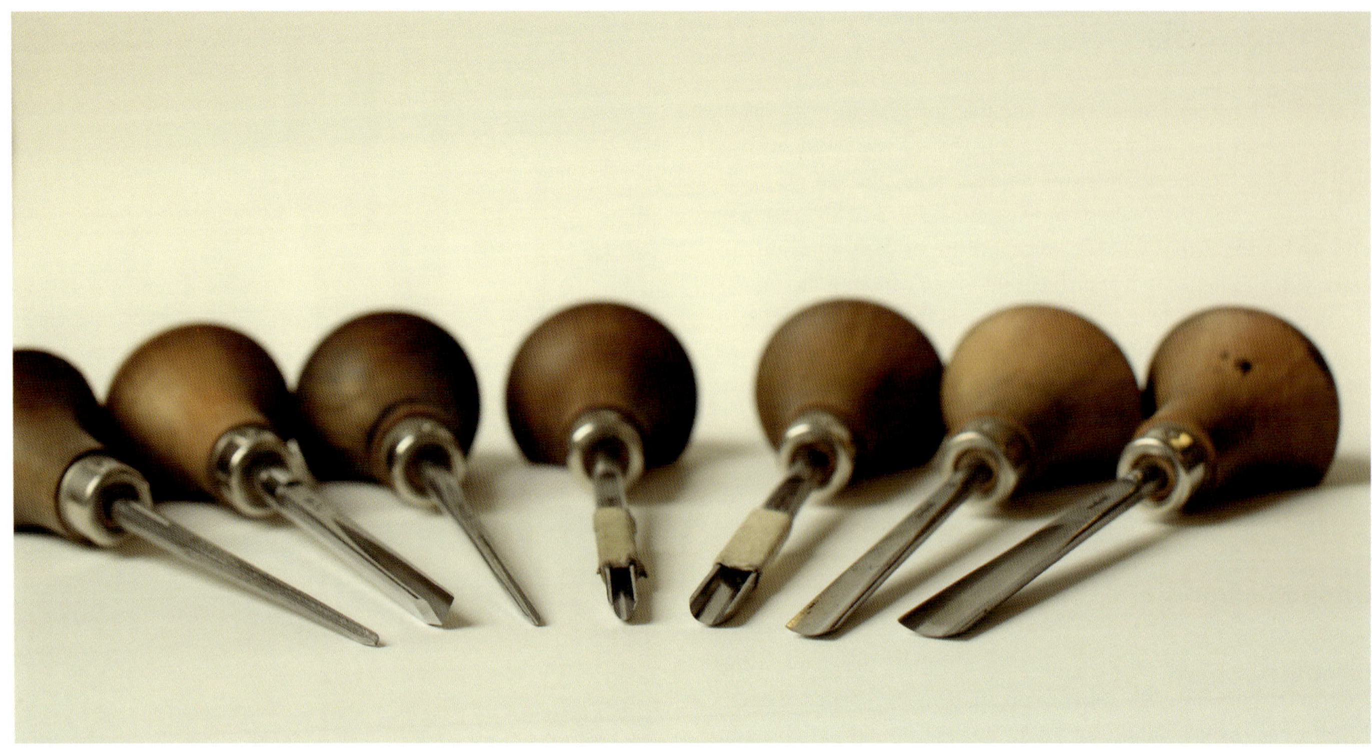

A set of Pfeil tools. Left to right: small V, large V, small U, medium U, large U, medium flat scoop, large flat scoop. Two of the tools have masking tape wrapped round the shaft to make them more comfortable to hold.

All-in-one tools

These are the most common linocut tools in art stores and consist of a handle with a variety of detachable blades. Although they are a neat idea, they tend to be poor quality. Often they are difficult to sharpen because the bevel of the cutting edge is on the inside, making it impossible to reach with a sharpening stone. In addition to this, when you are carving you will frequently want to switch tools and this becomes cumbersome if you have to unscrew the blade from the handle each time you want to change the blade. You are better off getting a set of tools with fixed handles instead.

Pfeil tools

By far the most popular tools among serious linocut artists are the mushroom-handled ones made by Pfeil. These Swiss tools are precision made, beautifully sharpened and are comfortable to hold. They are made from good quality steel with pearwood handles. They are not cheap, but if looked after should last a lifetime. They are widely available and can be bought individually or in various sets of six tools. The sets work out cheaper but you may find you don't use all the tools so it could be a false economy. You are better off starting with one or two tools and building your collection from there.

The numbering system for Pfeil tools is slightly confusing. They are coded in the format x/y where x denotes the shape of the cutting edge and y denotes its width in mm. Here is a guide to the most useful ones:

11/0.5 Tiny U-gouge
11/1 Small U-gouge
11/3 Medium U-gouge
9/5 Large U-gouge
12/1 Small V-gouge
12/4 Large V-gouge
7/10 Large flat scoop

Tool shapes

The many available shapes of tool can be broadly categorized into three groups: knives, chisels and gouges.

Gouges are the most commonly used tools. They usually come in three shapes: V-shaped, U-shaped and a wide, flat scoop shape. You may also come across a square-shaped gouge. Each will make a variety of marks and is useful for a different job. It is worth getting a couple of sizes of each tool.

V-shaped gouge

The V-shaped gouge is capable of making lines of varying width from the very finest line to a wide line. With a bit of practice you can carve a continuous line of varying width, making it excellent for expressive, gestural marks as well as very fine detail. Lines carved with a V-shaped tool will have a pointy, tapered end.

U-shaped gouge

The U-shaped gouge carves a line of more even width with a rounded end to it. The smallest variety, known as a veining tool, is perfect for fine, even lines and closely tracing the edge of shapes. The large U-shaped tool is good for clearing areas of lino, making big bold marks and round dots.

Flat scoop gouge

These are like a U-shaped tool but flatter. They create a mark that will print with a soft edge because of the shallow angle of the cut. The larger versions are perfect for clearing very big areas of lino.

Square gouge

These sometimes come in the all-in-one kits and will carve a line of even width with square ends.

Knife

Some kits come with a knife, known in Japanese as a *hangito*. This can be used to cut away areas of fine detail, making two cuts at opposing angles to remove a piece of lino. A scalpel or craft knife can be used instead but is liable to break. The *hangito* can also be used to cut the lino in two, although it is easier to do this with a large-handled craft knife.

Chisel

The chisel is probably the least useful tool. They are included in some woodcut kits and are used in Japanese woodblock printing for making registration marks called *kento*. They can also be used to bevel the edge of the block or gouged areas to give a softer printed edge.

Selecting a set of tools

A starter set might include a large and small V-shaped tool, a large and small U-shaped tool, a wide scoop and a knife. If you just want to buy a couple of tools to start with, get a large V and a medium or large U.

Not everybody uses the same tools, so try them out and see what is right for you. Once you have decided you cannot survive without linocut in your life, you can invest in better quality tools.

Looking after your tools

A sharp blade is fragile in its thinnest part so it is easy to damage your tools if you do not look after them well. This will result in hours of re-sharpening or having to buy a replacement tool. When you are carving, make sure you don't leave your tools near the edge of the table where they can be knocked onto the floor. If you are using tools that keep rolling around, wedge them up against something to stop them moving. You should also store your tools safely when not in use to avoid accidents and to avoid damaging them. Sharp tools will cut through fabric so keeping them loose in a pencil case is NOT a good idea! If your tools came in a box or wallet, use that, otherwise you can buy or make a canvas holder which rolls up, or push corks onto the cutting tips and keep them safely in a tin or box.

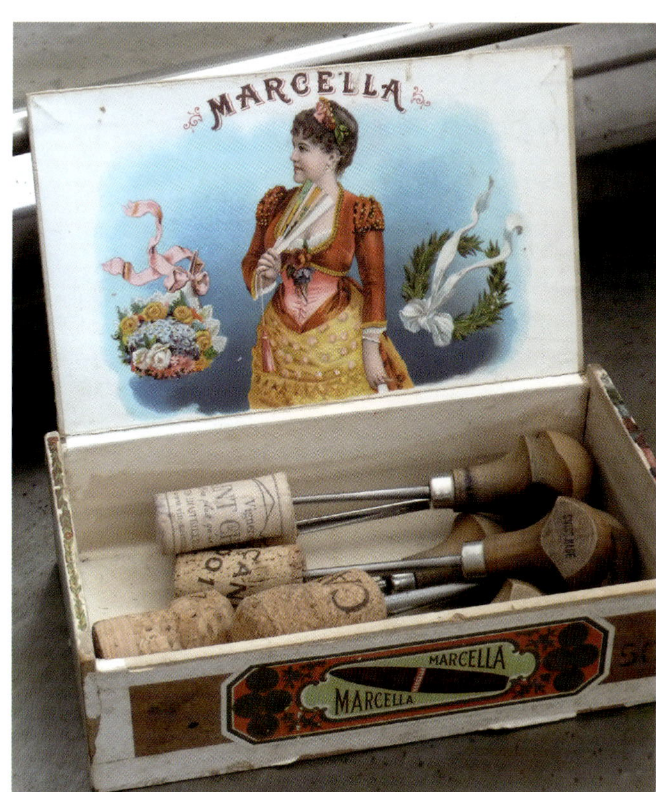

A cigar box is perfect for storing tools.
Wine corks pushed onto the tips protect them from getting damaged.

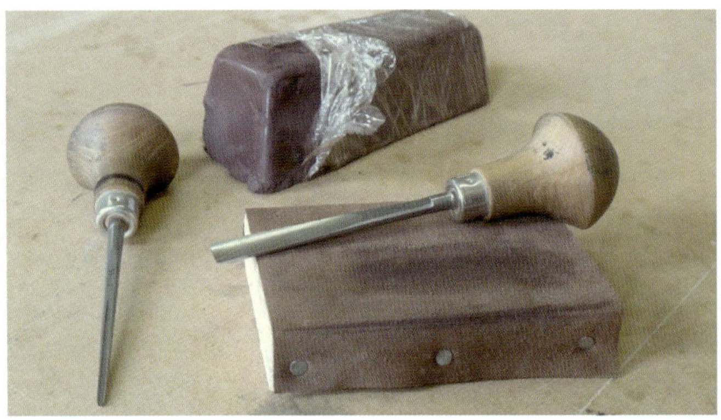

A simple honing strop made from a piece of suede leather tacked onto a piece of wood. A sharpening compound like jeweller's rouge (seen here) is rubbed onto the strop and the cutting tip of the tool is pulled backwards along it repeatedly.

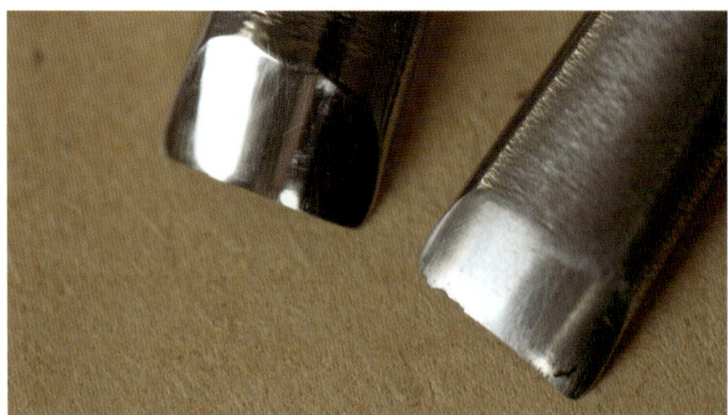

A properly sharpened tool will have a clean, straight edge and a polished bevel. The tool on the right is blunt and the cutting edge is damaged, probably from being dropped on the floor. It will need considerable attention before it cuts well again.

Sharpening tools

All tools will become blunt after a lot of use. Learning how to keep your tools sharp is easy in principle but takes a little practice to master. Sharpening is a useful skill and is definitely worth spending some time on. The rule here is 'little and often' as this will require less effort in the long run. If you let your tools get very blunt they will take a lot of sharpening to get back to peak condition.

Honing

It is a good idea to hone your tools when you start and every half hour or so during use. If you do this it may never be necessary to sharpen them using a stone. Honing is what old-fashioned barbers do with their razors when they wipe them up and down on a piece of leather. The leather is known as a strop and can be bought from a hardware supplier but it is much cheaper to use a piece of old leather like a belt. You will need a piece of leather which has a soft, suede side to it. If you want you can glue the leather, suede side up, to a piece of wood.

Before you start sharpening, apply a sharpening compound such as jeweller's rouge to the leather. Again this is readily available to buy from a hardware supplier. The sharpening compound is slightly abrasive and is what does the honing; the leather is simply to hold the compound in place and provide a soft surface. Run the tool along the strop a few times with the cutting edge pointing backwards. The bevel should be flat to the leather. After a while the strop will become blackened. This is normal and is caused by the tiny amounts of metal being removed from the tool. If you take a look at the tool now you should see a mirror finish on the bevel and when you try cutting, it should be perfectly sharp.

Sharpening with a stone

There are times when you may need to sharpen your tools with a stone: if they have become too blunt to simply hone or if the cutting edge is uneven, dented or chipped. It is worth investing in two or three stones of varying grades from coarse to fine. Use a coarse stone for reshaping and repairing a damaged tool, a medium stone for sharpening it, a fine stone for sharpening it further and a strop to give it the finished honed edge.

The grade of stone is indicated by its 'grit' number. This refers to the particle size: the higher the number the smaller the particles and the smoother the stone. Get a stone in the region of 700–1200grit for sharpening and a 4000–6000grit for finishing. If you have a very blunt or chipped tool use a rough stone of 120–400grit.

Avoid buying a tiny stone; you need a decent size of surface area to work on. Bench stones are good and chunky and heavy enough not to move around while you sharpen. You can also buy combination stones which are two grades of stone glued back to back. These may work out cheaper than buying individual stones.

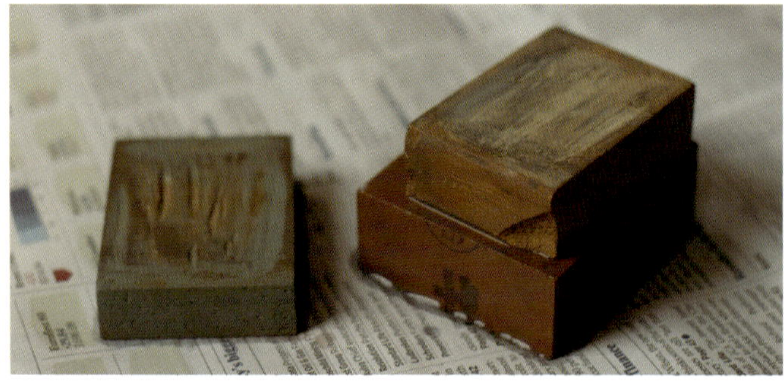

A set of Japanese waterstones. The roughest stone (left) is used for reshaping the tools. The medium and fine stones (right: bottom and top) are used for sharpening and finishing the cutting edge. They should be soaked in water before use and kept wet with a water sprayer.

Waterstones and oilstones

There are two kinds of sharpening stone: waterstones and oilstones. In Japan waterstones are traditionally made from natural stone and have been in use for centuries. They are more expensive but work fast so are worth the investment if you are going to use them a lot. Waterstones should be soaked in water before use and kept wet during use (a spritzer works well for this). They are relatively soft and as you use them you will see a slurry build up on the surface, made from particles of stone suspended in the water. This slurry speeds up the sharpening process, so treat it as your friend.

Oilstones need a drop or two of oil applied to the surface to act as a lubricant. A light mineral oil like 3-in-1 or sewing machine oil works well. Clean the stone after use with WD-40 and a clean rag to prevent the surface of the stone clogging up as this will stop it working properly.

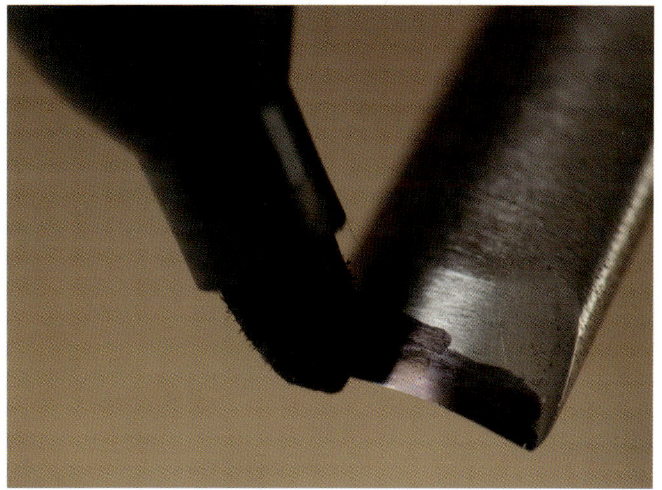

Colouring the bevel with a marker pen.

Alternatives to stones

There are a few alternatives to using a traditional stone for sharpening, including diamond stones and grinding wheels. There is plenty of information about this on the Internet including video tutorials if you want to research further. If sharpening your own tools is completely beyond you, don't worry, you can send them off to be sharpened by a professional. There are several places that offer this service for a modest fee.

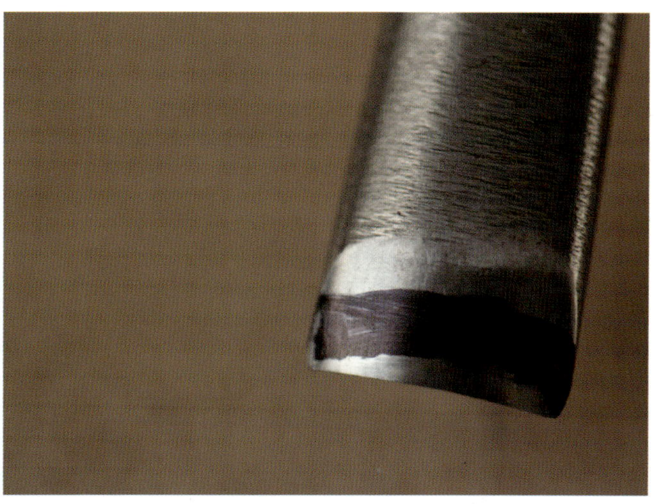

If you are sharpening correctly, the marker will be removed along the cutting edge.

How to sharpen

It is important to maintain the existing shape and angle of the bevel on each tool that you sharpen. Place the tool so that the bevel is flat against the stone and take a look at it side-on to check this. You should aim to keep the shaft of the tool at the same angle as you sharpen.

Tip: Use a marker pen to colour the bevel. As you sharpen, keep checking to see where the marker is being removed and adjust the angle accordingly. The marker ink should disappear evenly if you are doing it correctly. If you need to, you can keep reapplying the marker as you go.

The blunter your tool, the longer you will have to sharpen it but it should take no more than a few minutes unless it is damaged. If it is taking hours it is because you are using too fine a grade of stone. Switch to a coarser stone and use the finer stone to finish.

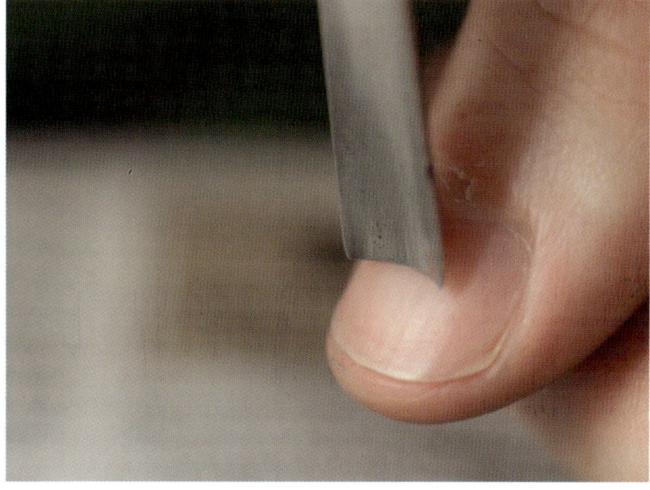

Gently rest the tool on your thumbnail to test for sharpness. If sharp it will grip; if blunt it will slip.

Sharpening a knife or chisel

Sharpening a flat tool like a knife or chisel is the easiest and if you have one you may want to practise sharpening it before you move onto gouges, which take a little more concentration. Check you have the tool at the correct angle and simply move it back and forth along the flat of the stone. Try not to rock the tool as you go, but maintain the same angle. After a minute or so have a look at the bevel and the cutting edge to check your progress. Continue until the blade is sharp. You can test it on a piece of lino if you're not sure.

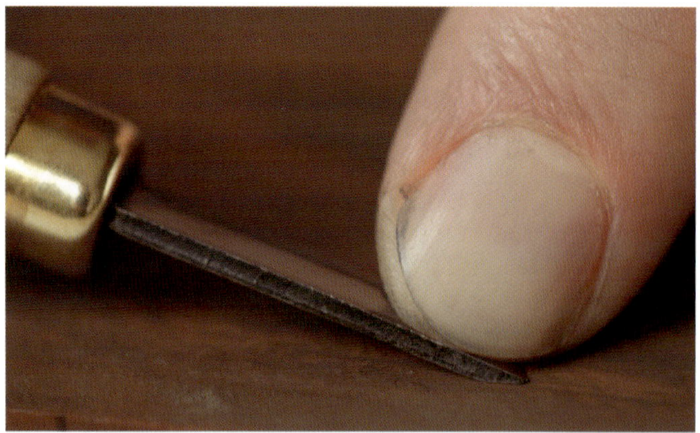

Hold the bevel flat against the sharpening stone to find the correct angle.

Removing the burr

If you have sharpened a tool for a long time you will find you have created a tiny ridge of metal along the cutting edge on the opposite side to the bevel. You may not be able to see it but you can feel it with you finger (be careful!). This ridge is known as the burr and can easily be removed with a fine stone. Place the tool with the shaft flat to the stone, bevel side up, and pull it along the surface once or twice away from the blade.

Sharpening a V-gouge

Sharpening a V-gouge is very similar to a knife or chisel except that it has two bevelled surfaces to sharpen. These must be sharpened at the same rate or the tool will become lop-sided. Hold one of the bevels flat to the stone and sharpen as before. Count ten strokes then turn the tool to sharpen the other bevel and count ten strokes and so on. Keep checking the shape of the tool, particularly the point of the V, to make sure you are sharpening the two sides evenly.

Sharpening a U-gouge

Sharpening a U-gouge is different in two ways. Firstly, instead of moving the tool back and forth as you sharpen, you move it side to side. Secondly, as you sharpen you need to rotate the tool in your hand so that the curved bevel is sharpened evenly. Start with the tool centred on the bevel and check the angle against the stone as before. Then move the tool sideways on the stone and rotate it sideways at the same time until you reach the edge. Move and rotate it back the other way as far as the other edge and so on. This does take some practice and it is definitely worth using the marker pen method to check your progress.

Removing the burr from a gouge

Once you have sharpened a V-gouge or a U-gouge there may be a burr on the inside of the cutting edge. This cannot be removed with a flat stone but if you fold a piece of fine grade wet and dry sandpaper over you can get in there to remove the burr. You can also buy specially shaped stones called slipstones for the same job. Slipstones come in different shapes so make sure you get one that fits your tool.

Reshaping a damaged tool

If you have badly dented or chipped a tool it will need to be reshaped before sharpening. Tools can also get worn out of shape over time through carving or incorrect sharpening. To reshape a tool, take a rough stone and hold the tool at 90 degrees to the surface. Move the tool from side to side, keeping it upright. Continue until the edge is worn down past the damaged area. The tool can now be sharpened.

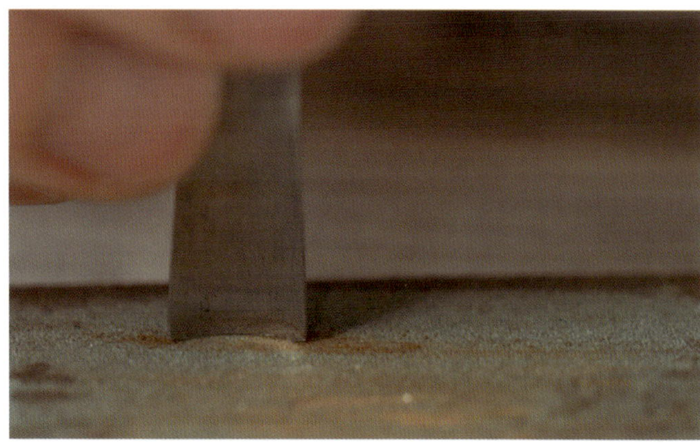

Reshaping a damaged tool on a rough stone.

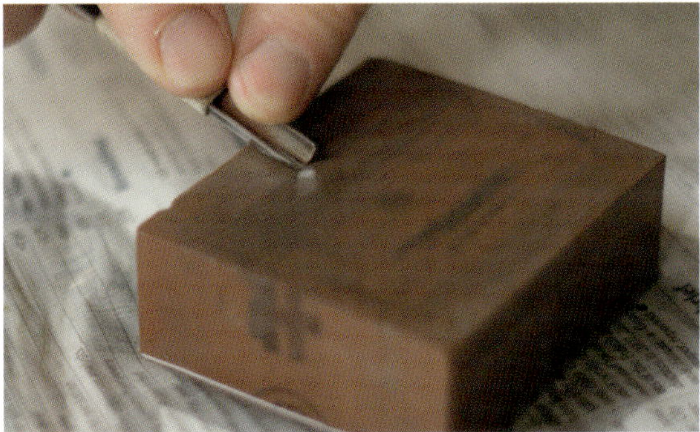

Start with the U-gouge in the middle of the stone with the bevel flat to the surface.

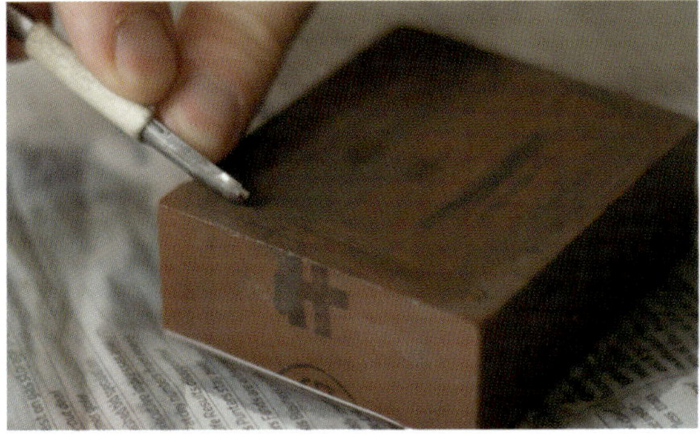

Move the U-gouge sideways and rotate your wrist at the same time.

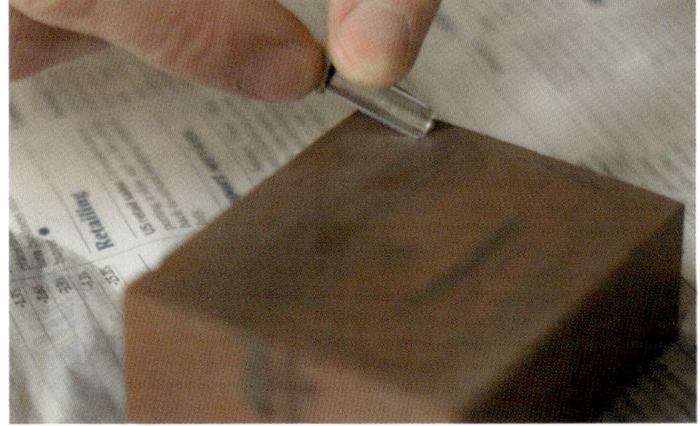

Move the U-gouge back the other way, rotating your wrist as you go.

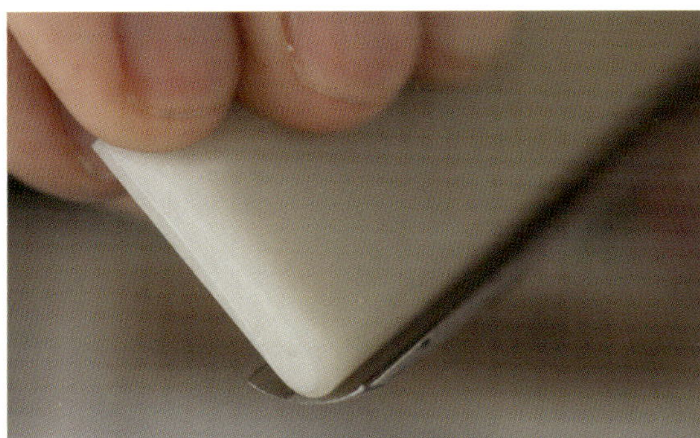

Using a slipstone to remove the burr from a U-gouge.

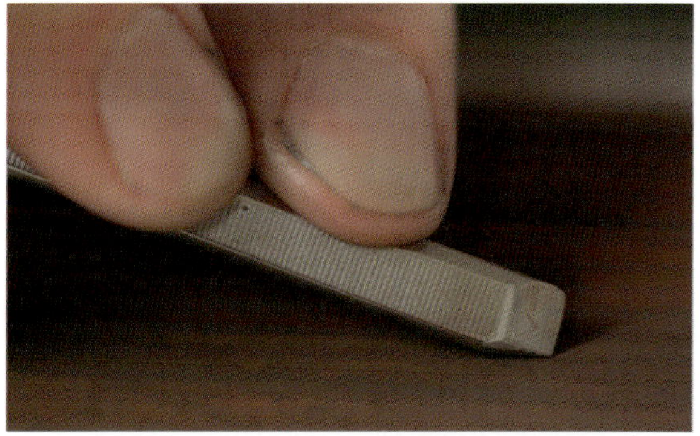

Move the V-gouge forward and back with the bevel flat to the stone.

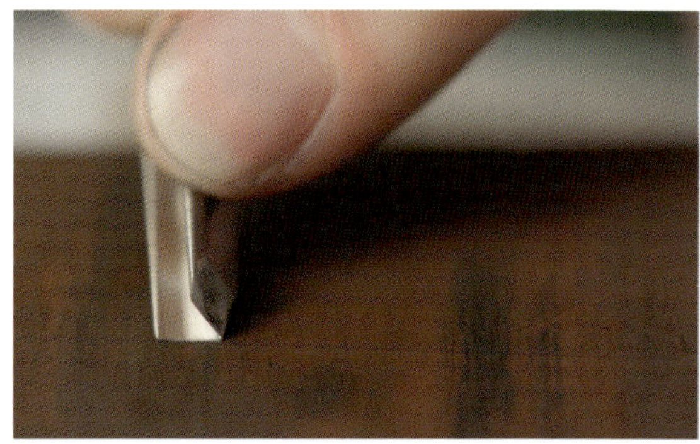

Count ten strokes on the first side.

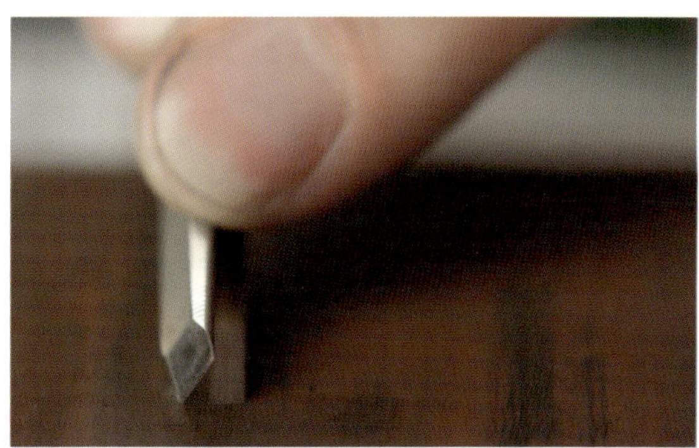

Count ten strokes on the second side.

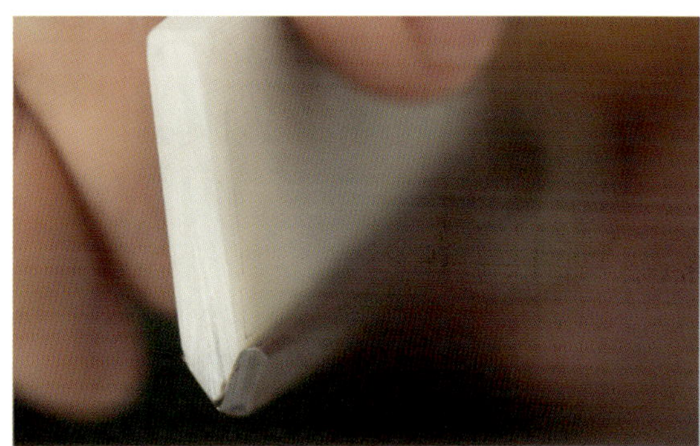

Using a slipstone to remove the burr from a V-gouge.

Inks

The ink you use will greatly affect the way your prints look. You will need to choose the right ink for the surface that you are printing onto, whether that is paper, fabric or something else. The right ink will be easy to roll up, colourfast and adhere properly to the printed surface. There are health considerations too: do you want an ink that you can clean up with water or do you have a place where you can safely use solvents? Do you want your prints to be permanent? If you are printing onto fabric does it need to be washable? Again, it is worth doing some research before you buy.

All inks are made from a pigment and a liquid vehicle. The pigment provides the colour and is held in suspension in the vehicle, which also acts like a glue to bind the pigment when dry. In relief printing ink the vehicle is of a consistency that allows the ink to be rolled evenly onto the block to print. Other ink additives, if they are present, control things such as the consistency and drying speed. Traditionally inks were made with a type of linseed oil but many new inks have been developed in recent years and this has led to an array of types and brands that can be bewildering for the beginner. The following section looks at some of the terminology used to describe inks to help you choose one that's right for you. If you're feeling experimental try printing with different things – ink, paint, melted chocolate – whatever you want. But to start with you will probably want an ink that gives you solid, even colour.

Where to buy ink

If you already know what you are looking for, your local art suppliers might have it, otherwise they should be able to order it in for you. A better bet, however, is to go to a specialist printmaking supplier. They will be able to advise you and will have a more in-depth knowledge of inks for printing and the subtle differences between one brand and another. If you don't live near one, call and ask for advice then mail-order what you need.

Tube, cartridge or tin?

You can buy inks in tubes, cartridges and tins. If you only need a small amount, buy small tubes. Cartridges and tins come in larger sizes, which is more economical if you will be using a lot of ink. Tubes and cartridges have the advantage that the ink is less likely to dry out, whereas ink in tins is prone to forming a skin where it is in contact with the air. This can be prevented by using anti-skinning spray or a disc of waxed paper on the ink surface. If stored correctly, ink will last for years.

Removing ink from a tin

Never gouge ink from the tin. Instead, skim a layer of ink from the surface of the ink using an ink knife or a square piece of rigid card or plastic. The aim is to leave a smooth, flat surface so you can place the disc flat on top without any air bubbles.

Inks for printing on paper

These are available from art shops and specialist printmaking suppliers. They may be called block printing, relief printing or lino printing inks. Some lithography and letterpress inks are also suitable for printing linocuts.

Terminology

Oil-based inks/solvent or oil clean up

Oil-based inks have been around for many years and are still used by many professional fine art printers and artists. They tend to be highly pigmented and give excellent colour strength, even when diluted. They can be cleaned up with solvents or alternatively with vegetable oil which is better for your health but will leave a residue on surfaces. Common solvents used for cleaning are white spirit, turpentine, paraffin (kerosene) and alcohol (ethanol) all of which have health and safety implications and are therefore becoming less common in schools and colleges and among independent artists.

There are several citrus-based solvents, which are less harmful than traditional solvents but are quite expensive. These include Zest-It, which is available in the UK and smells like oranges. Zest-It is useful for giving ink rollers and lino blocks a final clean after using vegetable oil.

Oil-based inks/water soluble/water washable

Water washable oil-based inks are replacing traditional oil-based inks in many studios. They print almost as well but are easy to clean up using just soap and water and so considerably reduce the risk of damage to your health through long-term exposure to solvents.

Water-based inks

Water-based inks clean up just with water and don't contain any oil. They are often made with gum arabic. Water-based inks are great for kids as they are safe and wash up easily, but tend to be fast-drying and of a consistency which doesn't roll out as evenly, leading to inconsistent prints.

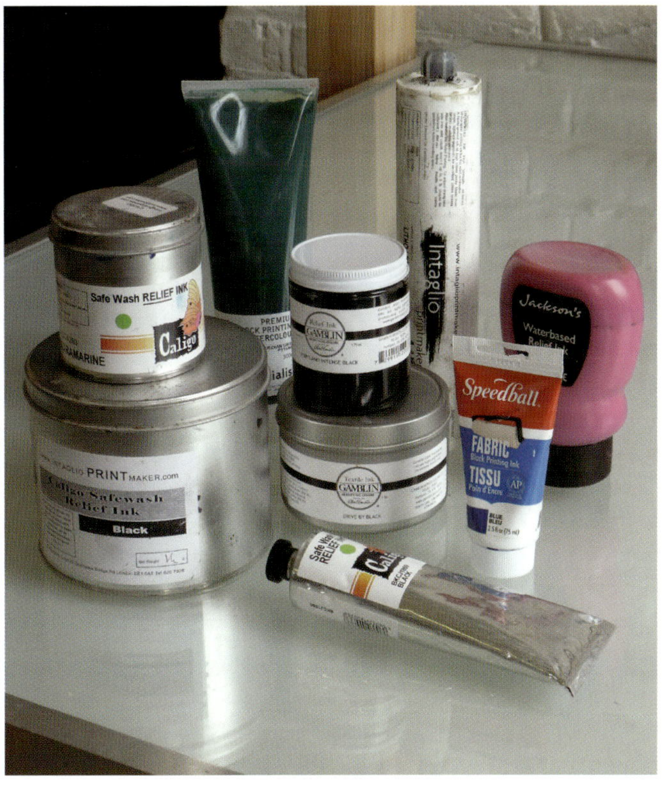

Printing ink comes in tins, cartridges and tubes.

Oil-based vs water-based

Oil-based inks have a distinct advantage over water-based inks in that they dry much more slowly. This means you can work for several hours and the ink won't dry on your roller. Water-based inks tend to dry much more quickly because the water evaporates faster than oil. Water-based inks have the advantage of being easy and safe to clean up and some will also wash out of clothes so are suitable for working with children.

Note: You cannot mix oil-based with water-based inks. You should stick to one or the other. Get a small sample tube of ink to try out if you are not sure which system you want to use.

Alternative inks

Etching ink, oil paint and acrylic paint can be used for printing and are worth trying if you already have some but their properties are not ideally suited to relief printing.

Health and safety

If you need to use solvents, ensure you do so in a well-ventilated area or outside and away from naked flames and sources of ignition. If necessary, wear a suitable mask for use with solvents (a dust mask will not work). You should also wear plastic or rubber gloves, as solvents like white spirit are absorbed through the skin.

Ink additives and modifiers

There are several chemicals and compounds designed for adding to printing ink. They all do different things. Many of them have different names according to their country of origin and brand. Make sure anything you add to the ink is compatible with the ink you are using. Sometimes it is possible to mix an ink from one manufacturer with an additive from another but it is safer to stick to one make. If in doubt, ask your supplier or the manufacturer direct.

Extender/transparent base

Extender is added to ink to 'extend' the colour. In other words it dilutes the colour in the ink without changing the consistency too much. It increases the transparency of the ink, allowing the background colour to show through. This has the effect of lightening the colour when printed on a white background. If printed over another colour, that colour will show through; the two colours will combine to produce a third colour where they overlap. Extender looks like a yellowish-white liquid, is slightly runnier than most inks and has the side effect of increasing the drying time of the ink.

Driers

Some oil-based inks contain chemicals called driers (check the label or ask the supplier). Driers speed up the drying time of the ink and can be bought separately and added to the ink before use.

Retarder

Retarder slows the drying time of the ink. This is useful if you are spending the whole day printing and you don't want the ink to dry on the roller. It will also slow the drying time of your prints.

Tack reducer gel

Reduces the tack, or stickiness, of ink. Some inks, especially lithography inks, are very sticky and are difficult to roll out. A small amount of tack reducer will help the ink to lie flat.

Anti-skinning spray

Stops oil-based ink drying in the tin by acting as an anti-oxidant. Spray a small amount onto the surface of the ink to form a barrier to the air, which will prevent a skin forming. Can also be sprayed onto ink which has been rolled out so it can be left overnight.

Plate/copperplate oil

Plate oil, also known as copperplate oil, is the oil which is used to make oil-based inks. It is a form of linseed oil which has been thickened by heating under pressure. It comes in three grades of viscosity: weak (the runniest), medium, and heavy or strong (the thickest). A drop of one grade or another of plate oil can be added to ink to alter its viscosity without affecting the colour.

Magnesium carbonate

This is a white powder, which is used to stiffen ink by mixing it in thoroughly. Used in small amounts it doesn't change the colour of the ink. Useful if your ink is very runny.

Inks for printing on fabric

There are one or two inks formulated specially for relief printing on fabric. These are discussed in Chapter 7.

Ink brands

These are some of the most popular ink brands. The brand's country of origin is given but most of these are available internationally.

Intaglio Printmaker (UK)
T. N. Lawrence (UK)
Caligo (UK)
Akua (USA)
Schminke (Germany)
Graphic Chemical (USA)
Speedball (USA)
Charbonnel (France)
Gamblin (USA)
Sakura (Japan)
Van Son (Netherlands)

Caligo Safe Wash Relief inks

Every printer and artist will have their own requirements and opinions about what is the best ink. However, one brand which is very popular among linocut artists is Caligo. The Caligo Safe Wash Relief range are vegetable oil based inks but wash up in soap and water. The majority of projects in this book were made using Caligo inks. They are widely available and come in a wide range of colours. These inks are very highly pigmented, which means that the colours are strong and vibrant even in very thin layers. This has the advantage that you can often print straight over a previous layer of ink with a new colour without problems.

Beware that some of the colours are slow drying, in particular some of the reds and yellows. Although the inks contain some driers already you may want to add an extra drop of cobalt driers to the ink. This will reduce the drying time from several days to overnight. (*See* Chapter 5 for more information on driers.)

Although Caligo inks are advertised as being washable in soap and water, it is better to clean linoleum with vegetable oil as it curls up if the hessian backing gets wet. Wipe the oil off thoroughly with a dry rag. If you want to get it really clean, use a drop of Zest-It.

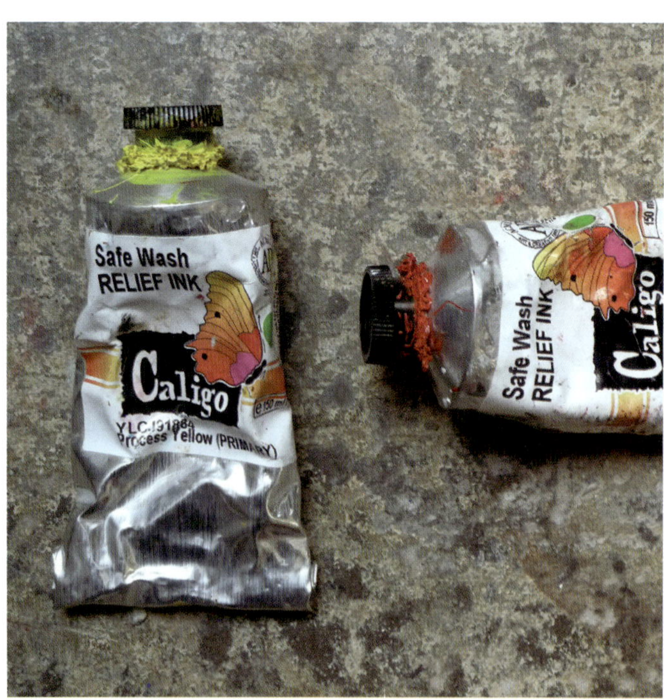

Caligo Safe Wash Relief inks.

Paper

The surface you print onto is known by the technical term 'substrate'. Paper is the most common substrate for printing onto but almost anything thin with a flat surface can be printed onto: card, plastic, fabric, cellophane, leather and wood amongst others. It is also possible to print an embossed texture onto a soft material like clay. For some this is just the start of the process and the printed materials are made into clothing, accessories, furniture, sculpture and ceramics. For many, though, paper is the only substrate they wish to print on and is probably the best one to start off with.

What is paper made from?

The obvious answer is trees, and indeed many papers come from wood pulp, but paper can be made from a whole host of other materials, usually fibrous plants. Common paper ingredients for printmaking include cotton, mulberry and hemp. Many countries have long traditions of paper making and because they tend to use the plants which grow locally they all look and feel different. If you're really into paper you can even make your own.

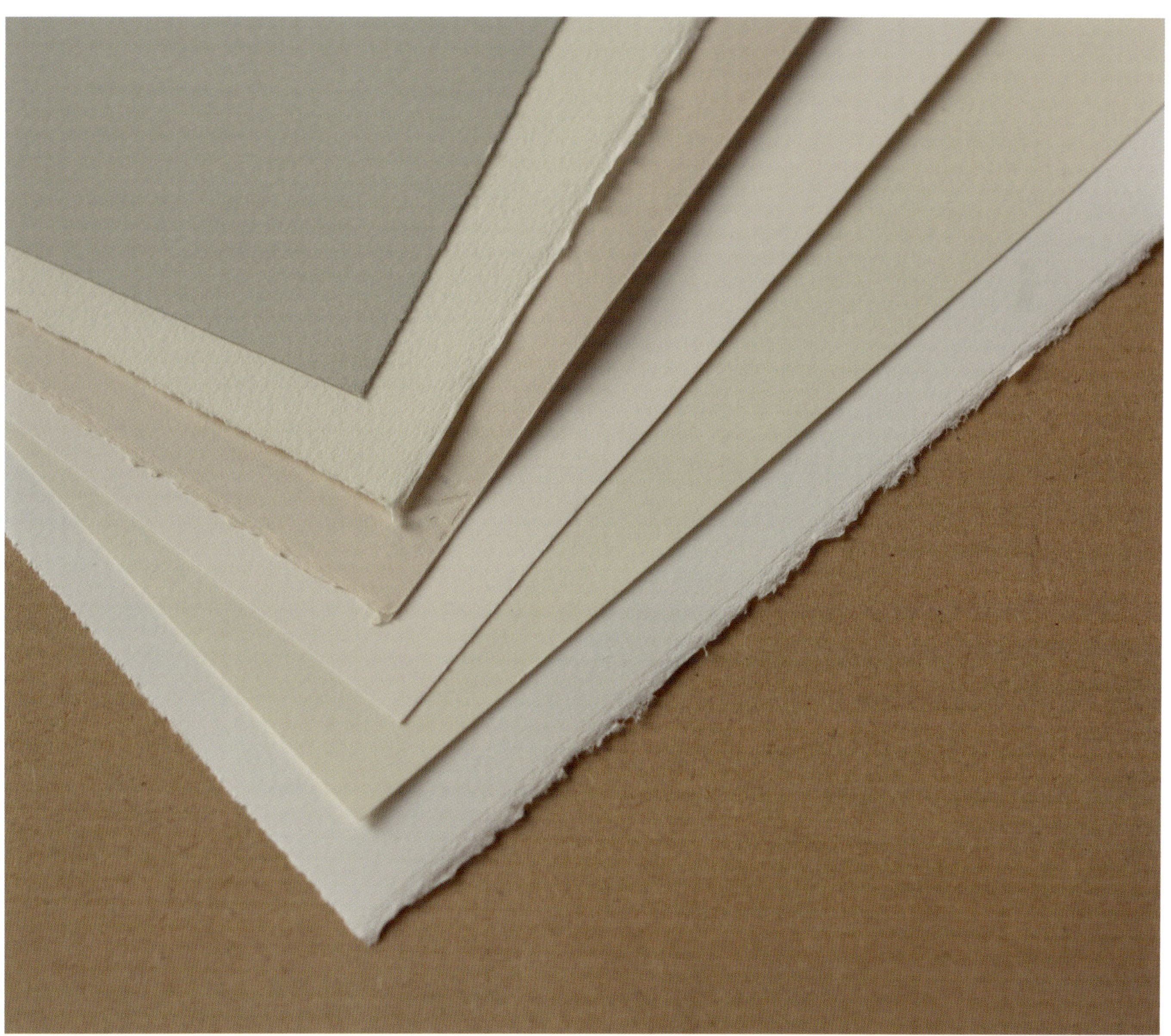

Paper for printing comes in many different shades. The colour of the paper can have a dramatic effect on how a print looks.

Paper characteristics

Whole books have been written on papers for artistic use and many printmakers have their favourite so it is worth trying a few. Different papers will give very different results when printed and there are certain characteristics which affect how a paper picks up ink. In addition to this, if you want to make prints that look professional and will last a long time you need a paper with archival (long-lasting) properties.

Coated or uncoated

Paper made for commercial printing may be coated or uncoated. A number of finishes can be added to a paper to change its absorbency, smoothness and shine. All of these things will affect how well you can print onto it, how fast the ink dries and whether the ink dries with a glossy or matt finish.

Colour

This may sound obvious, but the colour of your paper will have a dramatic effect on the colours in your prints. This is for two reasons. The first is that if you place one colour next to another it changes the way the eye perceives it. For instance, a blue next to an orange will look more vibrant than it will next to a green. The second reason the paper colour affects ink colour is that most inks are transparent to some degree and the paper colour comes through. If you print a yellow on white paper it will appear yellow but on blue paper it will often appear green. This is an extreme example but there are subtle differences even when printing on one shade of white versus another. If you've never looked closely at white paper, take a sheet of regular printer paper for your computer and hold it next to two or three other things which look white. You should notice quite a difference (printer paper is usually quite blue!).

Shades of white

These little variations in colour don't matter too much for the beginner but once you start buying specialist printing papers you will discover that different brands have different ideas of what white means! Some brands even sell multiple shades of white: bright white, soft white, ivory, antique white, etc. If you printed a single colour onto each one and compared the results it would appear brighter on the purest white and duller on shades like ivory.

Surface texture

The surface texture of your paper will determine the texture of the ink on the print. A heavily textured paper will give a mottled look, with uneven distribution of ink and possibly even flecks where the ink hasn't transferred at all. This is more noticeable when printing a flat area of colour and when printing with low pressure. When printing by hand on a very textured, rough paper it is almost impossible to get flat, solid colour. On the other hand on an etching press the pressure can be cranked right up; this will flatten any paper as it goes through, resulting in even colour. By adjusting the printing pressure you can achieve a range of printed textures. To get solid blocks of colour when printing by hand you need a very smooth paper.

Weight of paper

The thickness and density of a paper dictates its 'weight', which is measured in grams per square metre (gsm). You can use both thick and thin paper for linocut. For hand printing, thin paper works better. Certain Japanese papers are excellent because they are thin but very strong. If you want a slightly embossed look to your prints you will need a thicker paper. There is also a certain luxuriousness to thick paper, which can give your prints a look and feel of quality.

Absorbency

Ink is absorbed by different papers at different rates. This depends on the materials the paper is made from and how much size it contains (see below). Sometimes ink will be absorbed by the paper at such a rate that it bleeds. At other times it won't be absorbed at all and will just sit on the surface. This will affect the drying times and the gloss of the ink.

Strength

All paper is made up of strands of fibre. The longer the fibres, the stronger the paper. A sheet of cartridge paper is very easy to tear as it has short fibres. At the other extreme, some Japanese papers have such long fibres that they are almost impossible to tear, even though they are very thin.

Paper terminology

Here are a few terms you may come across when choosing papers.

Archival

If you look at an old newspaper you will notice it is yellowed and maybe even falling apart. This is because it has been damaged by acid present in the paper when it is made. In contrast, a good quality paper that is archival will last for decades or even centuries if properly looked after. You may not care whether or not your prints survive longer than you do but even within a few months or years, some non-archival papers will change in appearance. This is a particular issue if you are selling your work and want your prints to last.

Acid-free

Acid-free is a good thing. It means the paper is more archival. If a paper is marked as acid-free it has a neutral or high (alkaline) pH. Paper made from wood pulp contains a substance called lignin which is acidic. During the paper-making process the pulp can be treated to remove the lignin. This makes the paper slightly more expensive but it will last a long time.

pH buffered

Sometimes extra chalk is added to make the paper slightly alkaline. Over time this will compensate for any acid in the environment which attacks the paper.

100% rag

Paper made entirely from cotton, which is naturally acid-free. Rag papers are popular among printmakers because they are soft, absorbent and can be soaked in water for techniques like etching. Rag papers are more expensive than paper made from wood pulp. Some papers contain a mix of cotton and woodpulp.

Watermark

Some papers have a watermark. This can be in the form of text or a symbol and identifies the make of the paper. The watermark is usually located near to the corner and can be seen when the paper is held up to a light source. The paper in the watermarked area is thinner and can be visible if printed on, so it is best to avoid doing this if possible.

Size

The addition of a glue-like substance, called size, to a paper, either during or after the manufacturing process, is called sizing. The size binds the fibres of the paper together, giving it more strength. There are two kinds of sizing: internal and surface sizing. Internal sizing occurs in nearly all papers and is what binds the paper together. Surface sizing is added to make the paper more water-resistant. Watercolour paper, for instance, has a lot of size added to its surface to stop the paper soaking up the water in the paint and buckling. Surface-sized papers are sometimes called tub-sized as they are made by dipping into a tub of size.

Waterleaf

Paper which contains no size and is therefore extremely absorbent.

Laid

You can see the stripes in laid paper when you hold it up to the light. It is made up of bands of thicker and thinner paper. This texture will transfer to your print.

Wove

Wove paper does not have the stripes characteristic of laid paper, it is of uniform thickness. Most papers you use will be wove.

Hot pressed and cold pressed

Machine-made paper is passed through a series of metal cylinders known as a calender which press it flat. The cylinders can be hot, resulting in very smooth paper (Hot Pressed) or they can be cold, resulting in slightly textured paper (Cold Pressed).

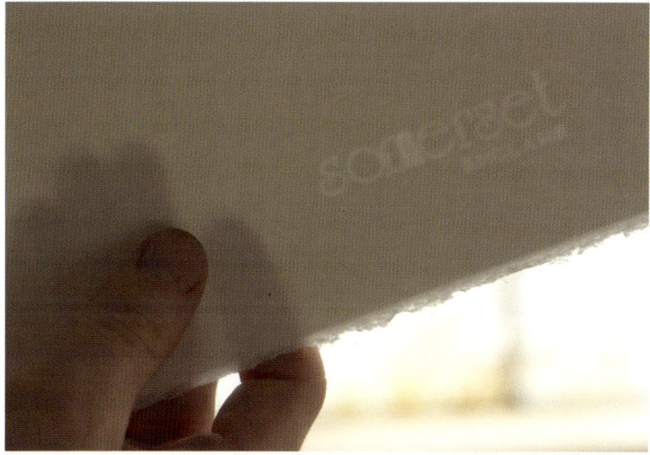

The watermark on a sheet of Somerset paper.

Choosing a paper

Handmade papers

If you get really serious about paper you can make your own, using many different ingredients such as recycled paper, fabric or vegetable matter. You can also buy handmade papers commercially in art supply stores, Indian Khadi papers being a popular example. Handmade papers tend to have quite a rough, rugged quality to them, often with flecks in, which can add interest to your prints. Because they are not very flat or smooth, most handmade papers are not suitable for fine detailed prints. Handmade paper has a soft edge to it, rather like a feather. This is known as the 'deckle'.

Mould-made and machine-made papers

Mould-made paper is similar to handmade paper in that it has a deckle edge, but it is made on a cylinder mould which gives it a very even consistency. Most specialist printmaking papers are mould-made. Machine-made papers include cartridge paper and most mass-produced papers like newsprint. These have a cut edge rather than a deckle edge.

There are many specialist printmaking papers which are great for printing linocuts. These usually contain size, so they can be dampened if desired. Brands include Rives, Somerset, Hahnemühle, Fabriano and Zerkall.

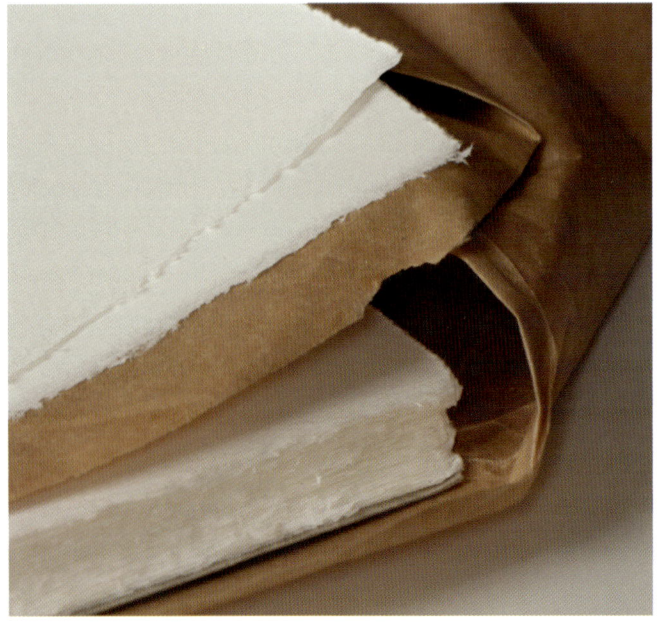

A pack of Somerset Satin, 250gsm, white. Note the deckle edge.

Somerset

An English paper which comes in a range of colours, weights and surfaces. A good one to start with is Somerset Satin white 250gsm, which has a smooth finish. Somerset Velvet is the same but with a slightly rougher surface.

Fabriano

An Italian manufacturer, as well known for their beautiful stationery as their paper. They make a few papers specifically for printing, including Tiepolo and Rosaspina. Their drawing papers can also be used.

Arches

BFK Rives is a fine printmaking paper made in France under the historic Arches brand. It is 100% cotton and comes in a range of colours including white, tan and grey. Arches also make a paper called Velin Arches, which is available in white, cream and black.

Zerkall

A lovely, very smooth German paper which picks up fine detail well. Available in a range of weights, colours and sizes. Zerkall mould-made paper is made from a mixture of cotton and woodpulp and is pH buffered.

Japanese paper

Paper, like many other things, is taken very seriously in Japan. It is used for origami, lanterns, doors, calligraphy and many other things. Many specialist papers were developed for making ukiyo-e, the woodblock prints which were huge business during the Edo period. Woodblock printing is much less widely practised today but many papers are still available, some made by hand and some by machine. Any paper made for woodblock printing will also be suitable for linocuts, especially when printing by hand.

Traditional Japanese paper is known as *washi*. It is made by hand and is something of a dying craft. Washi comes in many types but is generally made from long-fibred plants giving it both suppleness and strength, almost like fabric.

Kozo

Kozo is made from the mulberry tree (in fact, in Japanese, *kozo* means 'mulberry'). There are many kozo papers, some of which are very expensive, but there are also one or two machine-made kozo papers which are cheaper. These are made specifically for woodblock printing and are also great for linocut.

Hosho

Made from kozo, this is a luxurious, thick paper which takes ink brilliantly. Hosho is available in single sheets and also in a handy tear-off pad.

Masa

An affordable machine made paper. It is soft and white.

Simili Japon

A popular paper among linocut artists. It is actually made in The Netherlands but uses techniques adapted from traditional Japanese papermaking. Made from acid-free woodpulp.

Other useful papers

Newsprint

This is what newspapers are made of and is a light grey colour. Newsprint is great for taking test prints (called proofs) and prints beautifully by hand as it is very smooth and absorbent. This paper is not archival so it will not last; it tends to go yellow in sunlight, eventually becoming brittle and disintegrating completely. Newsprint is cheap and so is good for paste-ups and other temporary uses. Unwanted prints on newsprint can be used for cleaning up ink after a printing session.

Printer/copy paper

Useful for taking proofs of small prints. Very cheap. Good for hand printing.

Cartridge paper

A better quality paper designed for drawing on but also good for printing as it is smooth.

Tissue

Not usually used for printing on but indispensable for interleaving and wrapping prints. Get an acid-free tissue paper as any acid will slowly leach into your prints. Tissue can also be scrunched up and stuffed into the end of postal tubes to cushion your prints from knocks in transit. Usually comes in packs of 500.

Ink rollers/brayers

To apply an even layer of ink to your block, you'll need a suitable ink roller, also known as a brayer. Rollers come in various sizes and materials. To begin with, one roller is enough, but if you're printing in multiple colours you'll soon find you want one roller for each colour. It is useful to have a variety of sizes for inking large and small areas.

Size

There are two dimensions that will determine the area of ink a roller can lay down. The first is the width of the roller; the second is the circumference. To calculate the approximate circumference of the roller, measure the diameter and multiply by three. So a 3-inch-wide roller with a diameter of 2 inches will roll out an area of ink roughly 3 × 6 inches. Ideally you should be able to ink up your whole block in one roll but in reality once you start working above a certain size this is impractical. Inking up a block in one roll makes it easier to get an even coverage of ink. It also reduces the risk of roll-marks, which are made by the edge of the roller, and allows you to do a colour blend. If in doubt, go for a slightly larger size as you can use it to ink both large and small blocks.

Hardness

The hardness of a roller will determine how evenly you can ink up a block and how much of the carved-away parts pick up ink, if any. Because lino is not always perfectly flat, a very hard roller may not go into any slight dips in the surface, leading to areas without ink. For linocut a roller of medium hardness is best. If you squeeze it between your fingers there should be some give. A soft roller will go down into the carved areas and deposit ink in the carved-out areas which may come out as marks on your print. The hardness of a roller is measured in durometers, sometimes called Shore (after Albert F. Shore who came up with the system). A roller of 35–40 durometer/Shore is good for linocut.

Materials

Rollers are commonly made of hard or soft rubber, nitrile PVC or polyurethane. In the past they were also made of gelatine. Gelatine rollers work beautifully but are easily damaged by sunlight, heat and moisture so are no longer common. A soft rubber roller is an excellent choice for a beginner as it is more affordable and will give good results. However, the rubber will slowly degrade over time. A nitrile PVC or polyurethane roller is considerably more expensive but will last for many years if properly looked after.

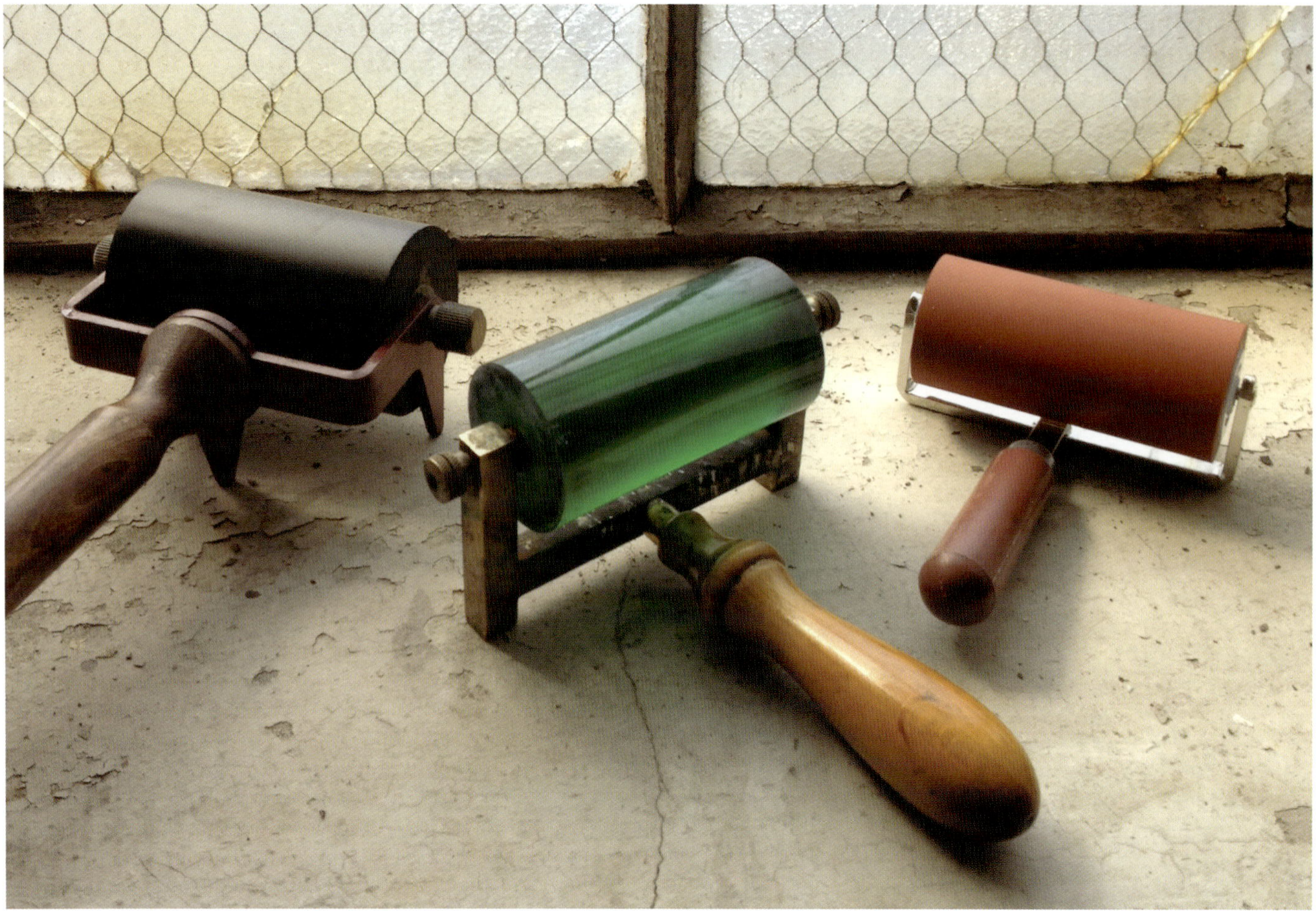

Ink rollers come in different materials. Left to right: nitrile PVC roller from Intaglio Printmaker, Durathene roller from T. N. Lawrence, Japanese rubber roller from Intaglio Printmaker.

Other things to look out for

Choose a roller that feels comfortable in your hand and isn't too heavy. The roller should rotate freely. Check the roller surface is smooth, even and free of holes or dents. Some rollers come with a stand so you can put them down cleanly. Large rollers may have two handles. Pin or spindle rollers have a handle at either end, like a rolling pin, and come in the larger sizes. They are expensive but can be re-surfaced or ground down to remove any uneven areas if the roller becomes damaged.

Roller care

Always clean your roller thoroughly after use. Dried-on ink can be impossible to remove, and can easily ruin a roller. Rollers should be stored in a dry place away from sunlight and heat sources, preferably so that the surface is not touching anything. You can screw a small hook into the handle and hang it on a nail. If you have a spindle roller you can make a stand for it with supports for the two handles. This is useful both for storage and to hold the roller in between inking a block to stop it rolling away.

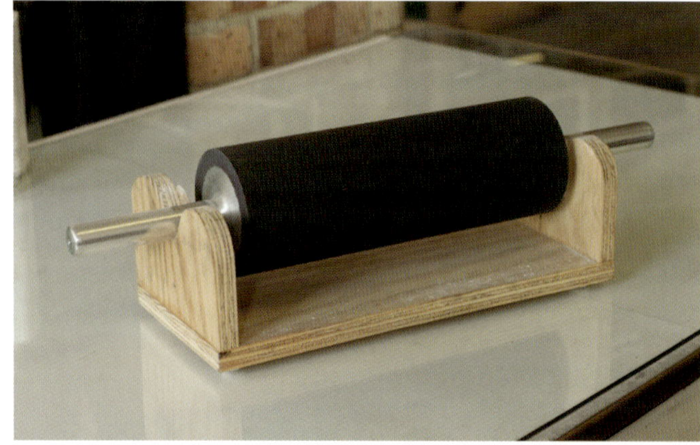

A large spindle roller. The stand, made by Martin Froggatt, protects the surface of the roller and stops it rolling around when not in use.

Hand printing tools

Wooden spoon

Many printmakers use nothing more sophisticated than a wooden spoon for printing. A hard smooth surface works best as it won't damage the paper. Over time your spoon will build up a nice polished patina. Any similar implement can be used; door knobs, pieces of antler and darning mushrooms work well. Metal spoons can also be used but the friction generated by rubbing makes them surprisingly hot. The metal can also mark the back of the paper.

Baren

The baren is the traditional tool for printing Japanese woodblocks and can also be used for linocuts. It is made of a round disc of rigid material onto which is stuck a coil of thin rope. This is then covered with a bamboo leaf. The two ends of the leaf are bound together on the reverse to make a handle. The fingers are used to grip the handle and a downward pressure is exerted onto the back of the paper. Modern versions are made of plastic. These have a surface covered in a pattern of small bumps. The most expensive barens are made by master craftsmen in Japan, and take many years of experience and skill to make. Their finely tuned printing qualities are possibly wasted on most of us linocut artists, but if you buy one you will be supporting a dying tradition. Cheaper, smaller versions, still made from bamboo, are available for the beginner and work perfectly well. The bamboo leaf on a traditional baren will eventually wear out and can be replaced. Cheaper barens can simply be replaced.

Roller, rolling pin, pinpress

A clean ink roller or rolling pin will give good results but doesn't allow the same degree of control over variations in printing pressure. A hard roller works best. You may also come across a 'pinpress' which is essentially a metal rolling pin which is aimed at the printmaking market. A kitchen rolling pin can also be used.

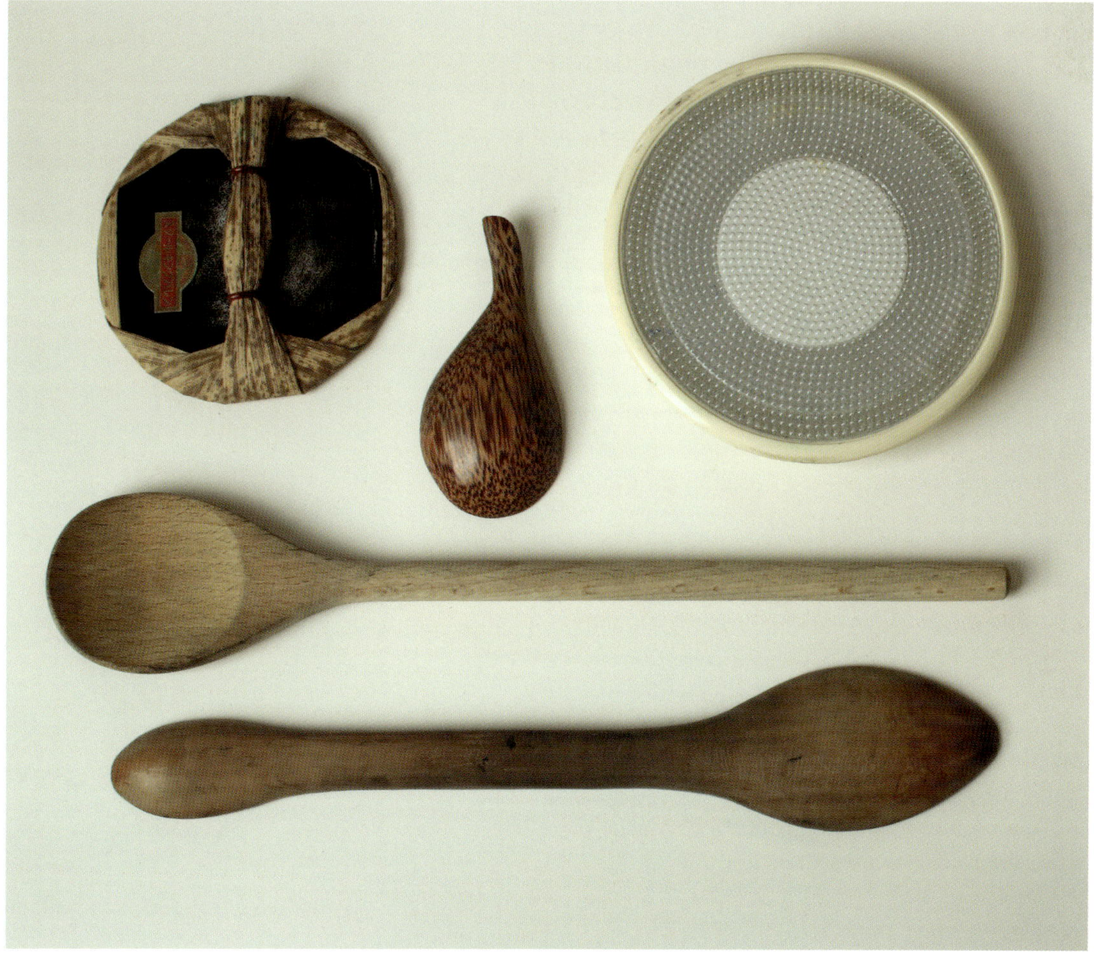

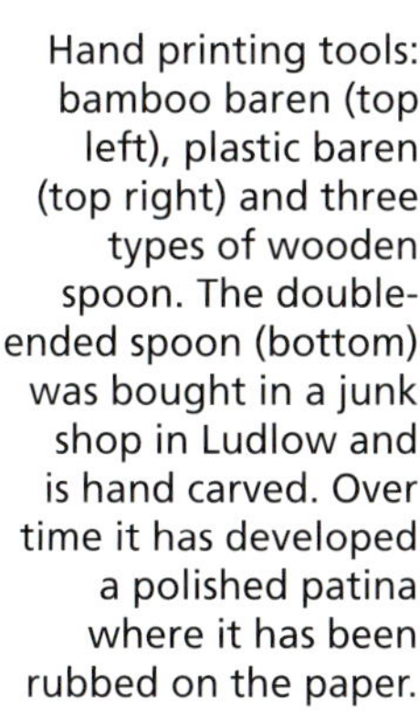

Hand printing tools: bamboo baren (top left), plastic baren (top right) and three types of wooden spoon. The double-ended spoon (bottom) was bought in a junk shop in Ludlow and is hand carved. Over time it has developed a polished patina where it has been rubbed on the paper.

Zach Medler (USA)

zachmedler.blogspot.com

Zach Medler uses linocut blocks to print onto, and emboss, his ceramic works. He works in a shared studio in Lafayette, in the midwestern state of Indiana. He has gallery representation all over the USA, mostly east of the Mississippi river, and has shown from New York to California. As well as ceramics and prints, Zach makes street art murals, assemblage paintings and interactive installations using sound, video and audience participation.

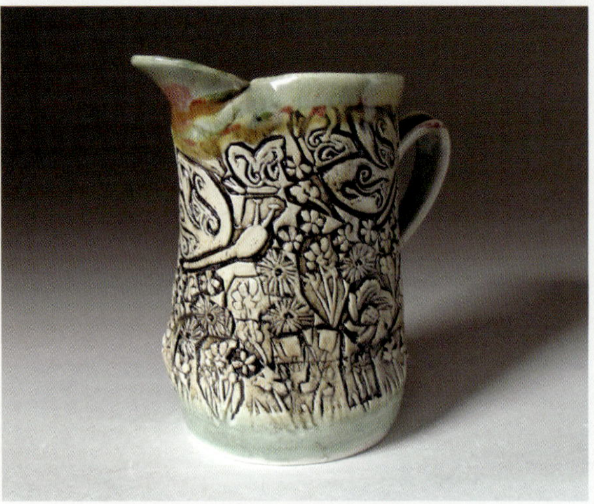

Wildflowers, Zach Medler, 9 × 8 × 5in, porcelain and linocut.

I started using linocut in 2005 after earning my MA in ceramics. I actually used linocut in clay before I used it on paper. I was trying to find my niche in the art market and was looking for a way to get repetitive imagery on the surfaces of my pottery and clay sculpture. I was mostly interested in a simple printing idea, so I remembered doing a linocut project in art class when I was a kid. It seemed simple enough, so I worked through some ideas to figure out how to make it apply to clay.

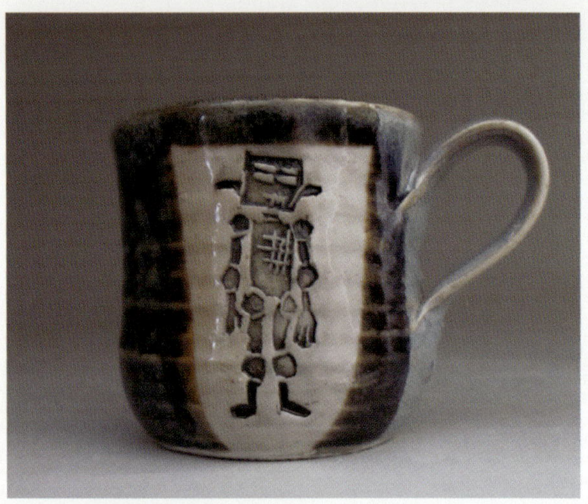

Robot Mug, Zach Medler, 4.5 × 4.5 × 3.5in, porcelain and linocut.

I like the versatility of linocut. It's a wood block with flexibility. All the different lino materials on the market allow for a lot of different uses. I use lino blocks in clay, on paper, on wood, on fabric, on metal, and basically anything else I can get the image to imprint upon.

I use a different material for whatever surface I'm working on. I use Dick Blick's Wonder-Cut linoleum exclusively in clay. Its makeup is such that it is flexible but embosses deeply without the squishing that the rubbery stuff does. On harder surfaces like metal or wood I use the rubbery lino material. On paper I use everything.

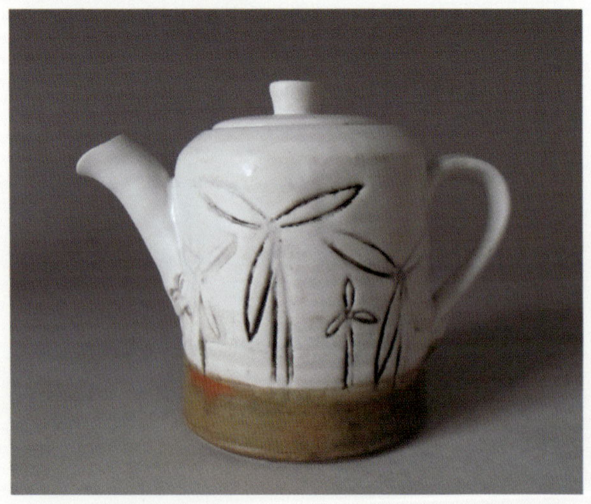

Windmills in the Snow, Zach Medler, 9 × 9 × 4.5in, porcelain and linocut.

My work is mostly influenced by place and observation of everyday life in that place. I live in the 'heartland of the US', a place mostly devoid of cities and population density. There is a lot of open space. Mostly people drive through thinking it is one of the most boring landscapes they've ever seen. I like to look for the things that everyone looks over. But it's more than just looking for the little things, it's about processing all those little things in such a way that the work feels like it came from my particular place and represents a regional aesthetic.

I work in an old garage in an industrial section of town. My studio is called Foam City and I share the space with several other creative people. We use the space to show experimental and avant garde music and sound events. There is a silkscreen printer, a digital/interactive artist, a record label, a couple of bands and a couple of performance artists. I would love to have a quieter space, but it's cheap, dirty, and has a good vibe.

I draw my designs directly onto the surface of the block, then I outline things with a Sharpie and cut away. I use Speedball's cheap-o student cutters with the plastic handle. I'm not particular about how awesome my tools are. For clay, I have to think less about positive and negative space, and more about what pops forward, and what impresses into the clay. I mostly make black outline prints. If I'm printing on something other than clay, I will make color block stencils and use spray paint for the different layers of color.

With clay, there's no ink. It'll just burn off in the kiln. I use Amaco black underglaze to stain the stamped impressions after the initial (bisque) firing. Some people will 'ink' their lino for clay, using a thickened oil-based underglaze that can be brayered onto the block. On everything else, I use Speedball's new oil-based fabric inks. They are versatile, clean up with soap and water, and don't eat the rubbery lino material.

I use a baren to print with. I don't have a press, so everything I do is by hand. On hard surfaces like metal or wood, I will use a heavy roll of plastic cling wrap as a rolling pin, and apply the pressure to the back of the block as opposed to what I'm printing on. Everything in my studio is done without proper equipment. It is all improvised and very anti-printmaking.

> “*If a printmaker walked into my studio, he/she would be aghast at how dirty everything is but I'm not a traditional printmaker and I don't think of myself as making 'prints'.*”

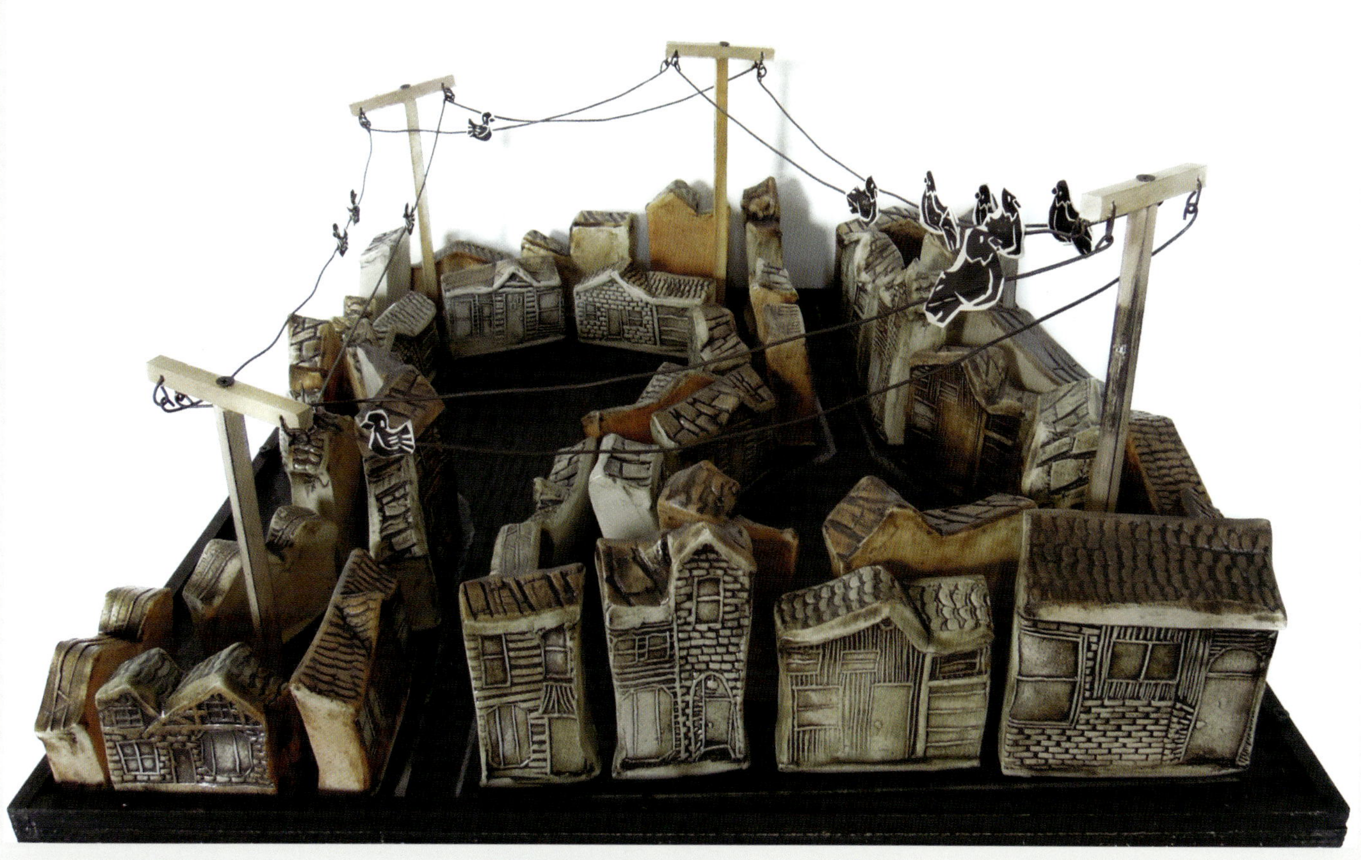

Subdivision, Zach Medler, 12 × 24 × 24in, porcelain and linocut, wood, wire, paper.

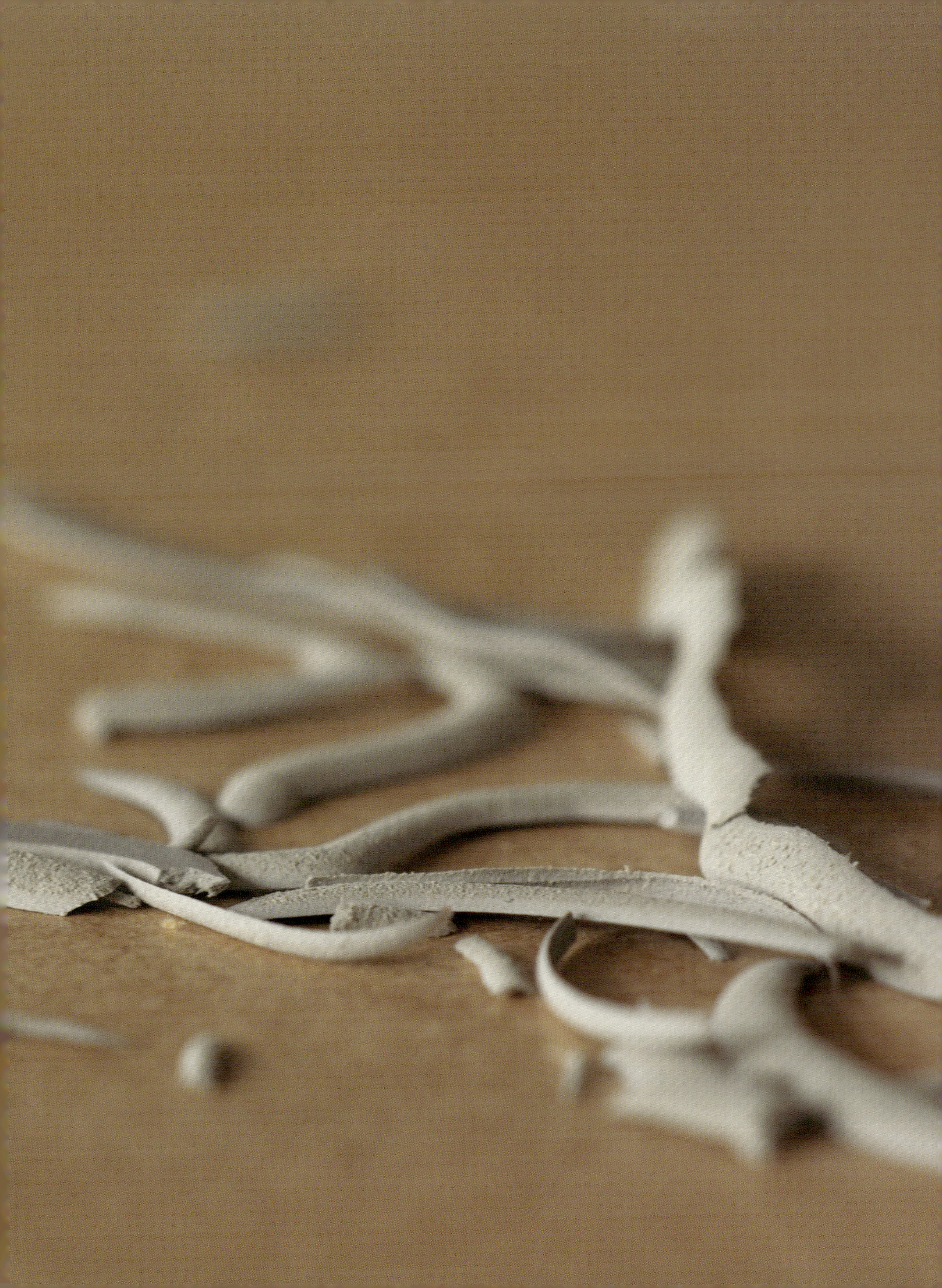

CHAPTER 2

GETTING STARTED

You are probably itching to get started. Hopefully you have bought the basic materials you need; now you need a place to work. This chapter looks at setting up a working space, and guides you through carving and printing your first test print. The simplicity of linocut makes it an ideal printing technique for doing at home on the kitchen table, but eventually you may want a more professional studio set-up. The first sections of this chapter cover everything you need to know about laying out your working space in the most efficient and user-friendly way, as well as issues like drying prints and storage. The later sections look at how to use your carving tools, what marks they make and how to pull your first black and white print.

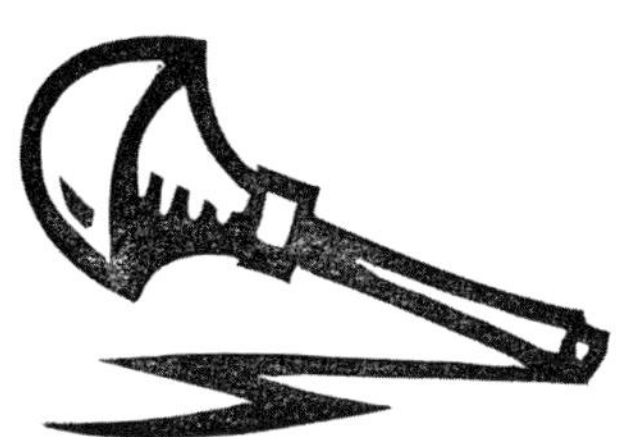

Setting up a working space

Your working space might be a kitchen table, a room in your house or your own fully equipped studio. It doesn't matter which it is, what's important is that it works for you. The size and location of your set-up will depend on how much space you have, how much you want to spend and how often you want to work. The other factor is how large you want to work. You will need a printing area, drying area and storage for materials and equipment.

The kitchen table

There is absolutely nothing wrong with working on your kitchen table. Many beautiful linocuts have been printed using nothing more technically advanced than a wooden spoon. If you are organized you can set up and clear up quickly, fitting in a quick carving or printing session when you have time. Cleanliness is important, however. You do not want to spend a morning printing only to discover you've got marmalade on the back of the paper. A flat, sturdy surface is essential, so if you have a lovely old wonky oak table you will need to put a sheet of heavy board or plywood on top. If you are a messy person, put an easy-wipe tablecloth down before you start work. Use inks that clean up with water, as solvents in the kitchen are not a good idea.

The artist's studio

If you are lucky enough to have a spare room, garage or shed you may be able to set up your own studio. The advantages of this are that you can spread out as much as you like and you don't have to clear everything away at the end of each working session. If you have small children, pets or nosey housemates it is also good to be able to lock the door, both to protect your artwork and to keep any dangerous chemicals and equipment out of harm's way. Any space you use should be clean and dry to avoid damage to equipment and paper. Natural light is great for working in although direct sunlight can damage prints over time. You can use tracing paper or adhesive frosted plastic over a window to diffuse the light. This will reduce strong shadows and make it easier to see what you are carving. Work surfaces should be a comfortable height, whether you are sitting or standing, and laid out to give maximum ease of movement through and around the space.

As well as being a practical space to work in, a studio is a focal point for your creativity. Hanging sketches, notes of ideas, prints and other images around your studio will help you to refine your ideas and come up with new ones. Sometimes just sitting and thinking about what you want to make can be a useful way to spend time and having a dedicated creative space can help you do this. For some people, the creative process is a very personal one that requires complete privacy. For others, being in the studio is a way to escape the distractions of daily life and focus on making stuff.

The shared studio

Not everyone likes to work alone or has the means to set up a studio. Shared studios come in many forms, from privately owned spaces to artist run cooperatives. Some colleges and universities also offer access to equipment through courses and open access sessions. Usually these need to be booked in advance although you may find somewhere offering drop-in sessions. By sharing facilities you will gain access to specialist equipment and knowledge. Large printing presses cost a lot, are very heavy and take up space, so if you want to work on a large scale a shared studio could be the answer. Working alongside others is great for finding out printing tips and making contacts for possible collaborations, exhibitions or support groups. Some find it intimidating at first to create prints in full view of others but it can help you get used to showing and talking about your work.

To find your nearest open access studio or printmaking course, do an online search or ask someone in the art department of your local college or university. People who make prints are usually friendly and willing to share their knowledge. You never know, someone on your street might have a press you never knew about.

Setting up a print studio

Creating a space to work in can be a rewarding experience. You can set things up just how you like them and if you invest some time and thought at the planning stages you will reap the rewards later on. A well laid out studio is a pleasure to work in and will help you to work more efficiently. Position your work surfaces, tools and equipment well and you will have everything to hand when you need it. Get it wrong and you can end up constantly looking for things, contorting your body to stretch for something or damaging your work. There are several key things to consider when making a plan. It helps to break the space down into areas, each with a different function. If you only have a small space some areas will be multi-functional. For example, you may have a table you use for drawing, carving and printing.

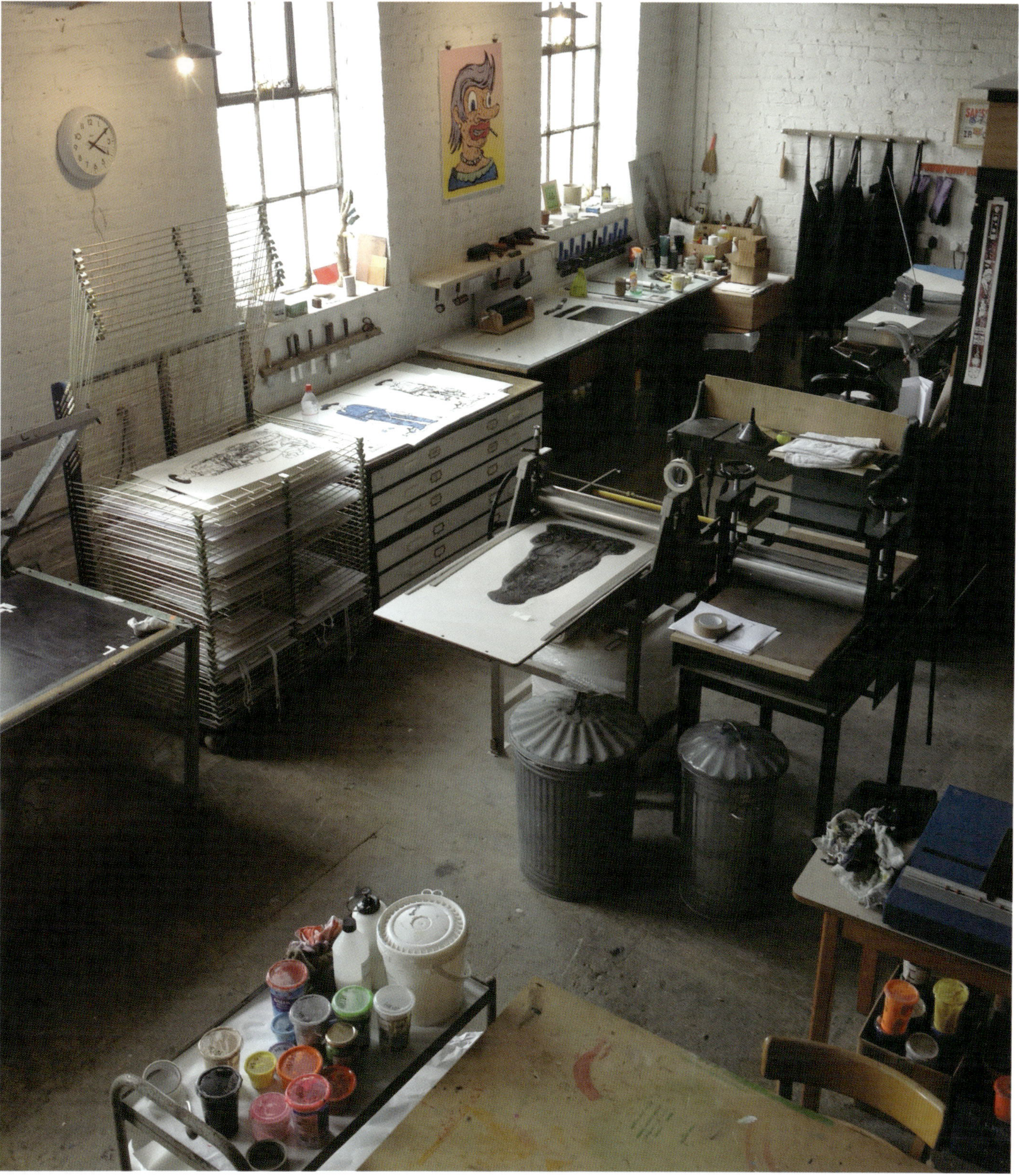

Hello Print Studio in Margate has facilities for etching, letterpress and screenprinting as well as relief printing. It is used by members of Resort Studios as well as members of the public, who can attend workshops and hire the space on Wednesdays. The equipment is laid out to allow for several people to work at the same time with everything easily accessible.

General principles

The main functions you need to consider are: drawing and idea development, carving, paper preparation, inking, printing, drying and storage. Try to keep separate clean and inky areas. In addition you need to think about heating, lighting, access, electricity supply and water. Whether you are building your own workbenches or using an old table it is worth making a floor plan to get the positioning right. Measure up the room and draw the outline to scale on a piece of paper. Be as accurate as you can. Next do the same with each thing that will go in the space, cutting them out individually so you can move them around and try different layouts. Imagine yourself working in the space: carving, printing, walking around. Make sure you leave room to open doors and drawers and try to maximize the use of natural light for carving and inking.

When you are printing you want your inking area near your printing area and your printing area near your drying area. If you are making a hundred prints you don't want to walk right across the room a hundred times. For optimum ease of use these three areas should form a triangle.

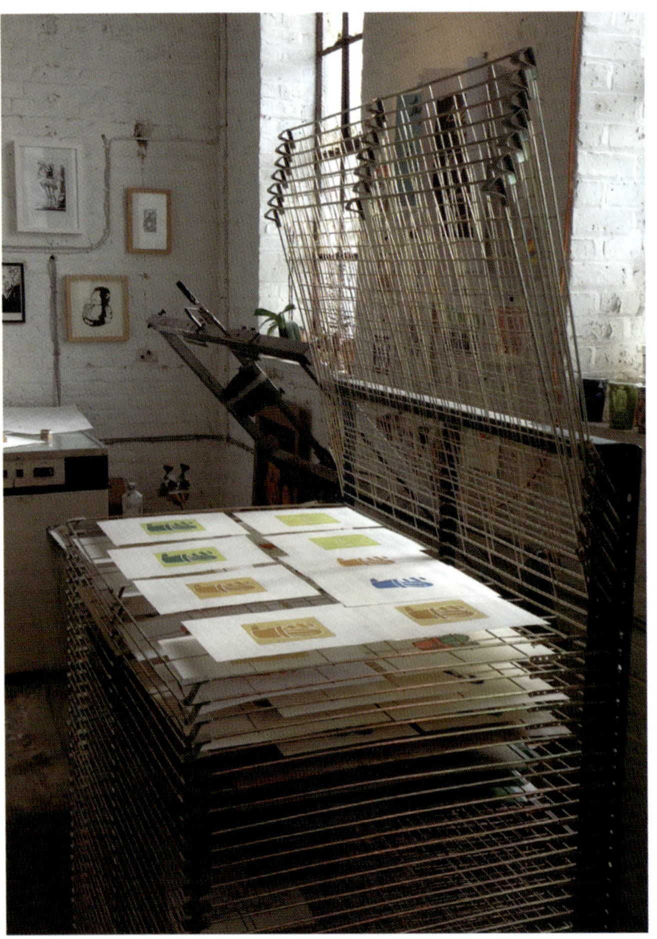

A print drying rack is ideal for larger prints and can be moved around the studio as needed.

Key functions to consider

Drawing and carving

A smooth, flat table or drawing board is useful and should be set up at the correct working height for you. If your furniture needs to be multi-functional, you can get an adjustable height table which you can use for both sitting and standing.

Computer desk

A computer, scanner and printer are a feature of many studios. Keep them away from water, lino shavings and ink, covering with a sheet if necessary.

Paper preparation

If you have room, set aside a clean area for paper tearing and cutting. The top of a plan chest is ideal and can be covered with thick card or a cutting mat. If you don't have this luxury, keep a large piece of clean card or a cutting mat that you can lay down on a work surface when you need it. Keep a long steel ruler and a craft knife handy.

Inking

Inking a block is best done standing up so, if you can, set up a higher surface for this. It should be at around the same level as your hips and have an overhang so you have room for your feet. The inking surface should ideally be white, so you can judge the ink colour as you roll it out. For a permanent set-up, paint the surface white or tape down some white paper and lay a large sheet of glass on top. Toughened glass with bevelled edges is safest but can be expensive. An old glass shower screen makes an excellent surface as does the glass taken from a coffee table. Avoid glass that is too thick as it can appear green, making it harder to judge colours. Store your ink rollers and inks nearby so you can grab them when needed, as well as ink knives, newspaper and rags for cleaning up.

Printing

Whether you are printing by hand or with a press your printing area should be clean. If you have your press on a table or other surface it needs to be sturdy enough to take both the weight of the press and any force you exert on it during printing. If you have an etching press make sure you allow enough room for it to fully extend.

Drying

Prints can take anything from a few hours to several days to dry. If you only need to dry a small number, your prints can be laid flat on a table, as long as they are out of the way and not in danger of being damaged. Do not stack the prints; you need air to circulate around them. If you are going to do lots of printing on a regular basis set up a dedicated drying space, otherwise you will quickly cover every available surface. There are two solutions: hanging and shelving. A hanging system could be a simple string with pegs on or a ball rack designed for the job. These can be set up above head height to maximize the use of space. You can even set up a pulley system to raise the drying prints out of the way. Drill holes in the top of the pegs so you can thread the line through them and the prints will hang closer together. For larger and heavier prints you may need two parallel lines. Ensure they are secure and won't sag or fall down – a line of large prints is surprisingly heavy.

If you are making large prints, you should consider getting a specialist print drying rack. These stand on the floor and have spring-loaded wire shelves that can be raised and lowered. They usually have wheels so can be moved around as needed. Smaller table-top versions are sold for use in schools. Second hand drying racks can be found on eBay. If you buy one make sure it is rust free and still has all its springs.

Do not stack your prints until they are perfectly dry. If you are not sure, the way to tell if a print is dry is by touching it gently. If the ink is still tacky there is a danger of it sticking to another surface and pulling the ink off. Note that different colours dry at different speeds and thick layers of ink will dry more slowly.

Storage

No matter what size space you have, it is important to keep it clean and tidy and organized. Anything you don't use on a regular basis can be stored away. Make the most of the space you have by using dead space for storage: under tables, in corners and on high shelves above work surfaces.

Paper and prints should be kept flat, away from moisture, light and extremes of temperature. This could be in a box, chest of drawers or plan chest. Inks can be stored in a box or on a shelf. Keep them away from heat. Tools are easy to lose, especially the small ones. Keep them together in a toolbox. A wall-mounted knife rack is useful for keeping spatulas, ink knives and scissors handy. Rollers can be kept on a shelf or hung on hooks. Don't just throw them in a box with other things as the surfaces will get damaged. Clean rags can be kept in a bag or box. Dirty rags, especially oily or solvent-soaked ones, should be kept in a sealed metal bin as they are a fire hazard and solvents will evaporate into the air you breathe.

Lighting

An anglepoise lamp is repositionable and can be moved around for different tasks. Ambient light from windows or strip lights will eliminate strong shadows, reducing strain on the eyes. Daylight bulbs help with judging colours when printing.

Heating

Keep the temperature as constant as possible. Swift changes in temperature affect the moisture content of paper so should be avoided. Heaters should be placed so air can circulate. Avoid placing paper, inks, etc. too close to sources of heat.

Water

It is useful but not essential to have running water in the studio. A sink with a draining board is handy for washing brushes, rollers and ink knives.

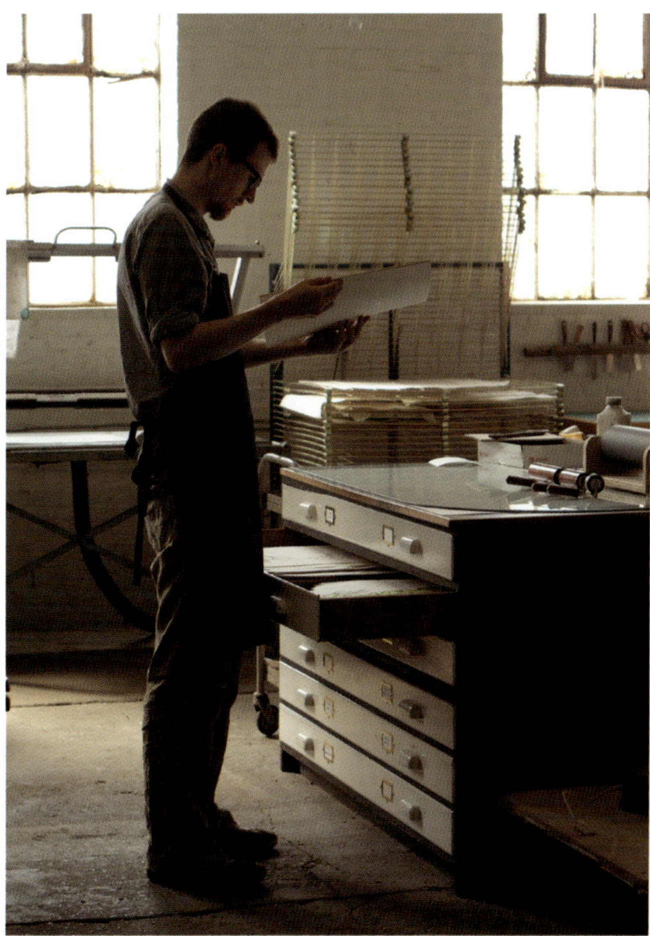

A plan chest is perfect for storing prints, paper and lino blocks. The top can be used as a work surface.

Carving

Embarking on any new creative project is exciting and it's very tempting to get stuck in and carve an image straight away. Before you do, however, it's a good idea to try out your different carving tools on a test block. This will give you a chance to experiment freely with making a variety of marks, without worrying about the end result. Once you have seen what effects can be achieved you will be able to apply them to making an image or other design. Practising mark-making will also help you to get a feel for the tools, giving you more confidence and control.

Preparation

Cutting the lino to size

Both traditional linoleum and other modern alternatives can be cut to size easily by hand. You will find this easiest with a strong craft knife. The blade should be sharp and will need replacing frequently as it will become blunt quickly. Cut onto a cutting mat or a thick piece of card on a non-slip surface. Ideally you should use a heavy steel ruler or straight edge for cutting straight lines; plastic and wooden rulers are easily damaged. Do not press too hard on the knife as you risk snapping the blade and are more likely to slip. Instead, make several lighter cuts along the same line.

To cut a straight line in traditional lino, simply score the top surface several times then bend it along the scored line and it will snap. The two pieces will be held together by the hessian backing so carefully cut through this to separate them. This will not work on vinyl, which requires repeated cutting until you go right through it. Curved lines and right angles should be done this way too. Keep any off-cuts for practising on.

Good practice

Working height

When carving you should make sure that you are working at a comfortable height, whether you are standing or sitting. Do not hunch over the block as this will cause back and neck problems. You should be able to see what you are doing clearly and carve with a relaxed arm. For very fine detail you may find a magnifying glass useful. Free-standing versions are available, often with a light attached, which leave both hands free.

Lighting

Make sure you have sufficient light to see what you are doing. It will reduce strain on your eyes and the risk of mistakes. Daylight is ideal, otherwise position a lamp nearby. Too strong a light can be equally unhelpful, as it casts dark shadows along one side. You can bounce the light off a wall or the ceiling to diffuse it.

Taking breaks

It is easy to become engrossed in carving a lino block. Take a break every half hour or so to relax your eyes and your hand. Get up and walk around, shake your hands and arms to loosen them, make a cup of tea, stare at the clouds, whatever takes your fancy. The point is to avoid being in one position for so long that you start getting muscle fatigue or cramps. Take a longer break every few hours (don't forget to eat and drink) and get some fresh air if you can or do something completely different.

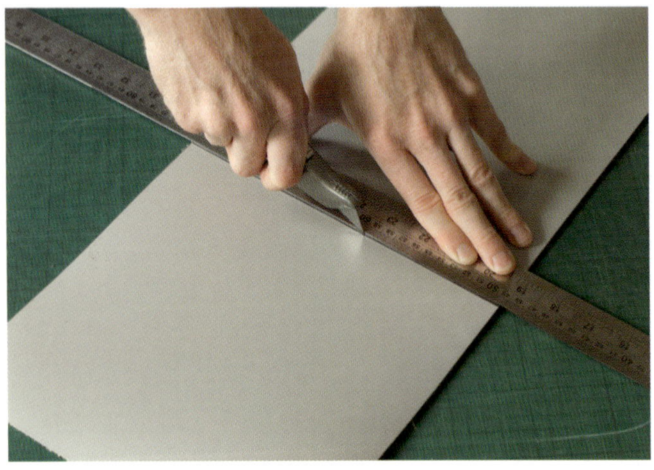

Cutting the lino with a sturdy knife and a steel ruler.

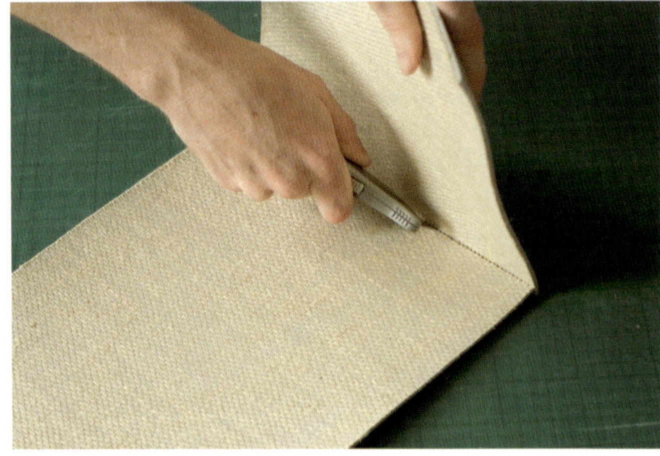

After scoring, bend the lino and cut through the hessian.

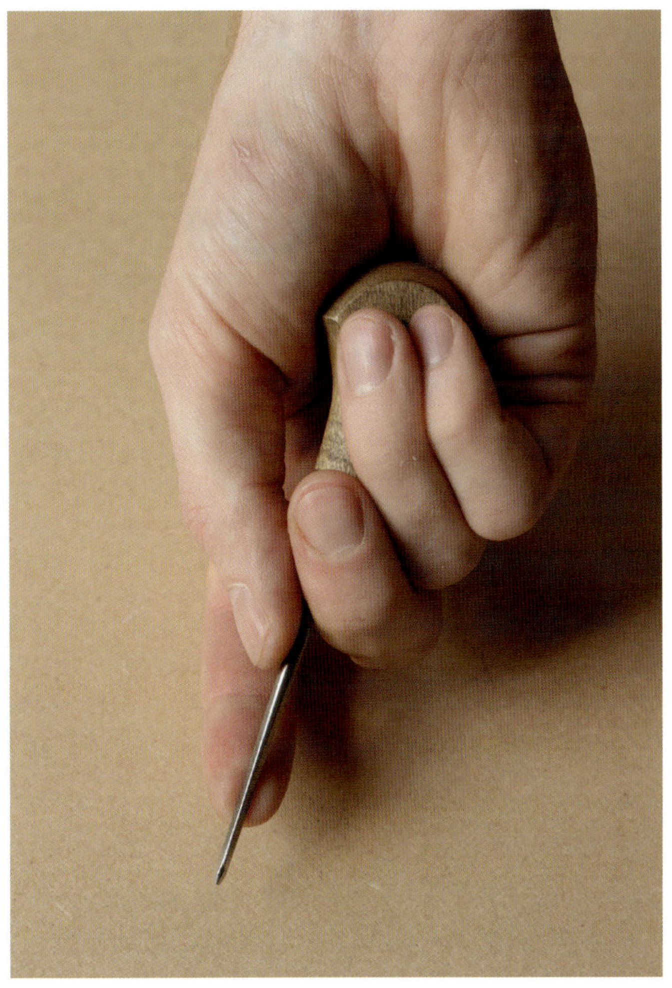

Holding the mushroom-shaped tool.

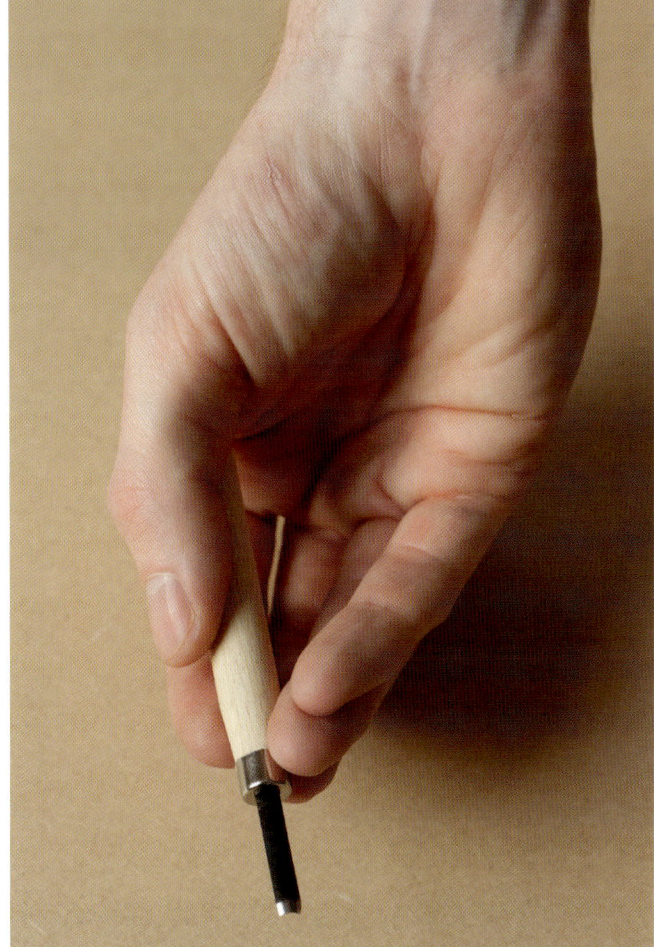

Holding the pencil-shaped tool.

How to hold the tools

Make sure the tools are comfortable in your hand. Don't grip too hard; your hand and arm should be fairly relaxed. If you have to push very hard this will be difficult, so make sure your tools are sharp and your lino is fresh and soft.

The way you control the depth – and therefore the width – of a gouged line is by the angle at which you hold the tool. A steep angle will force the cutting tip downwards into the lino; a shallow angle will make the cutting tip rise. With practice you should be able to find an angle somewhere in between which allows you to carve a continuous line, maintaining a consistent depth of cut. With a bit more practice you should be able to raise and lower the angle of the tool as you move it forward, resulting in a line that gets thicker and thinner.

Note: If you carve too deeply the cutting tip will become submerged beneath the surface of the lino. It may become stuck completely or you may persevere and end up ripping the lino. This is not good for the tool and will result in fuzzy prints and a sore arm. If you find this keeps happening, simply lower the angle of the tool as you carve. On the other hand, if the tool keeps slipping, hold it at a slightly steeper angle.

Try to keep the cutting tip upright and avoid rolling your wrist to one side as you carve as this will make your line lopsided and over time the blade will become misshapen as it blunts faster on one side than the other.

Health and safety

You should ALWAYS CARVE AWAY FROM YOUR HAND. Hold the lino behind the cutting tip of the tool. If you find it hard to keep a grip on it this way, place the block on a non-slip surface. Materials like rubber, felt and suede work well.

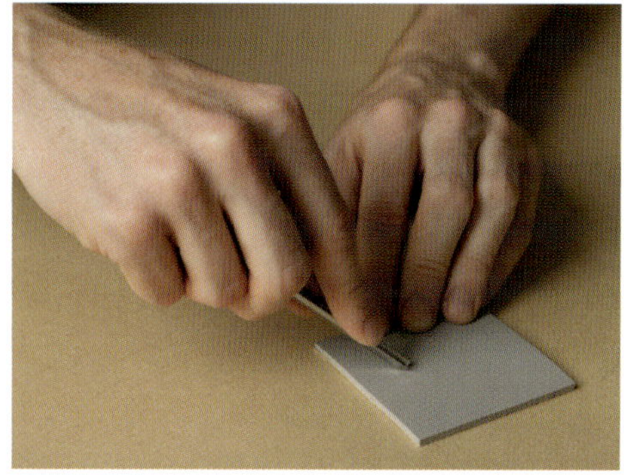

Too steep an angle:
the cutting tip will sink into the lino.

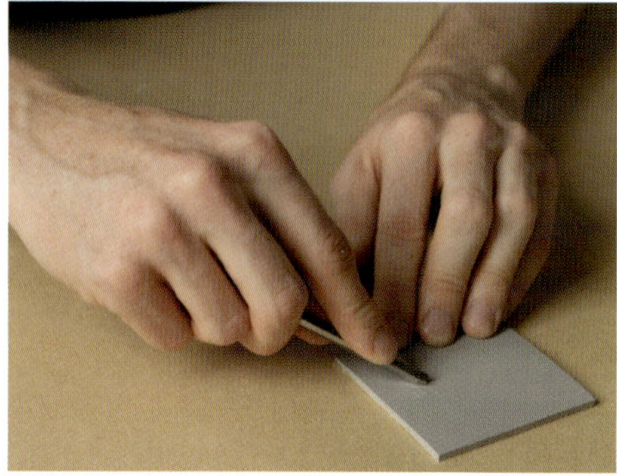

Correct angle:
the tool will carve easily through the lino.

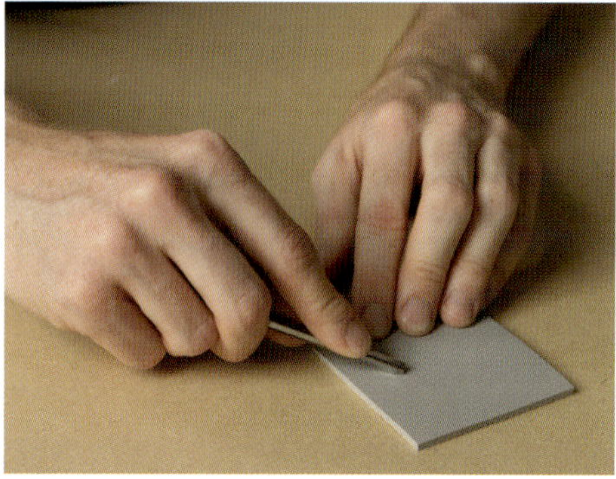

Too shallow an angle: the cutting tip will slip.

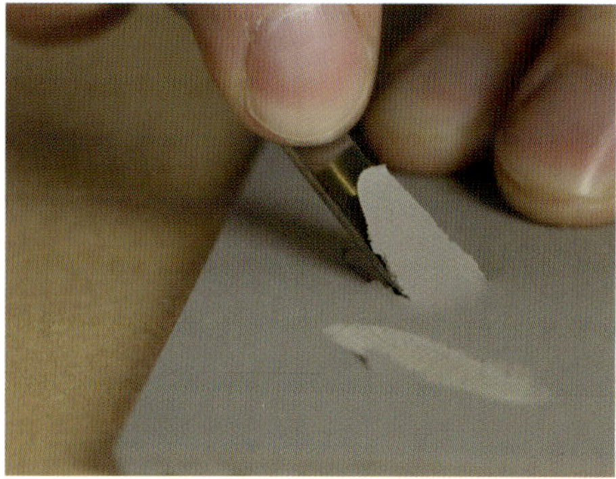

If the tool goes too deep the lino will tear.

The beginner's wiggle

One common mistake made by beginners is to rock the tool from side to side as they carve. This is usually down to either blunt tools or lack of confidence and will result in a line with jagged edges. Of course, this could be the look you are going for, but if you want an even, steady line, try to push the tool forward in a smooth motion. Carve with confidence and don't be afraid to make mistakes.

How deep to cut

You don't have to carve a very deep line to make a mark that will print. If you can feel the line with your fingernail it should come out on the print. Any shallower than that and there is a risk it will fill in with ink. On the other hand, you don't need to go too deep either. If you carve right down to the hessian backing (or the table) you have gone too deep. This is a waste of energy and could make the block floppy and weak. Generally speaking, you should be carving away up to half the thickness of the lino. The exception to this is if you want a large open area, without any ink. Sometimes in this case, you need to go a bit deeper. If in doubt, take a print of the block. You can always remove more, but it is nearly impossible to put back.

Pencil rubbing – taking a quick impression

If you want a rough idea how your block is going to print without going to the bother of printing it, you can place a piece of paper over the carved areas and rub the paper with a pencil or piece of charcoal. You will not get a perfect impression, but it will show you the light and dark areas. Remember, however, that when you come to print the block it will be a mirror image.

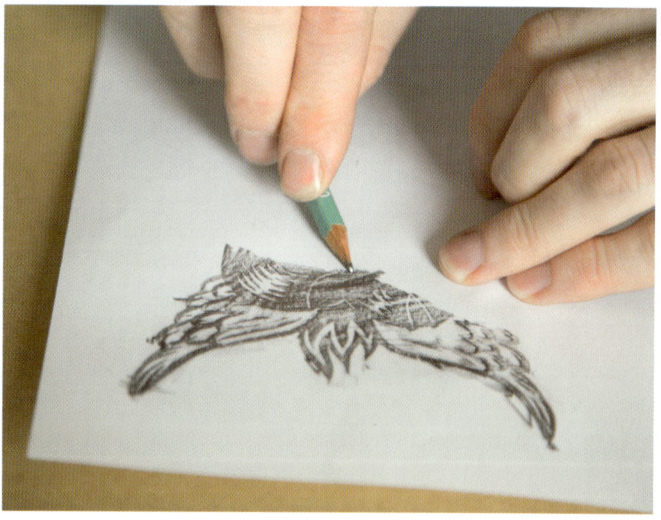

Take a quick pencil rubbing of your block to test progress.

Project: test print

Carving and printing a test block with different marks will help you to develop a mark-making language and will give you more confidence when you come to make your first proper print. This can be done with any colour of ink but black is the best as it will help you see the marks more clearly. The idea here is not to make any kind of recognizable image, but to experiment as much as possible to achieve a wide range of different marks and to get a feel for the different tools.

You will need:

A piece of lino roughly 6in or 15cm square, black permanent marker pen, ruler, range of carving tools, non-slip mat, sheet of glass or perspex, black relief printing ink, ink knife or spatula, ink roller, newspaper, thin paper for printing (printer/photocopy paper is ideal), wooden spoon or other printing tool, rags, vegetable oil or soap and water for cleaning.

Paper for hand printing

Printing blocks by hand works best on a thin, smooth paper. Certain Japanese papers are ideal for this, being designed for the job. They are very strong, being made up of long threads of fibre from plants like the mulberry bush. The threads hold the paper together and stop it falling apart, so you can print many layers of colour. Try a range of different papers to see how it changes the look of the print.

Carving your test block

Divide your lino into a grid of nine equal sections using the marker pen. Making sure you use all the tools at your disposal, fill each section of lino with a different kind of mark: straight lines, wavy lines, zigzags, cross-hatching, dashes, big dots, small dots, parallel lines, converging lines, tapered lines, circles and S-shapes. Remember to carve away from your hand and place the block on a non-slip mat to make holding it easier.

Straight lines

It sounds easy but carving a perfectly even, straight line takes some practice. Try to keep the tool at the same angle as you carve and maintain a steady speed. It is easier if you do it in one go but if you stop, try not to remove the tool from the lino. Use the V-gouge to make some very fine lines.

Hatching and cross-hatching

Hatching is lots of parallel lines close together. Practise getting them as even as possible. Cross-hatching is two or more sets of hatched lines crossing each other at different angles. As you carve away more and more the remaining lino will form dots and other shapes.

Curves and circles

When carving a curved line try rotating the block as you carve. If you only move the tool you will quickly find that you are cutting at an awkward angle. In this way with a bit of practice you can cut a circle without taking the tool off the lino. Cut one section of the circle at a time, leaving the carving tool in place as you rotate the block ready for the next bit. If you are using a piece of lino that is too big to rotate you will have to move your body round as you cut. This is easier if you are standing up.

Tapered lines

This is a little more advanced. Using a large V-tool, carve a line that starts as a point and gets wider by pointing the tip of the tool downwards slightly into the lino. Carve a series of lines next to each other to create an illusion of going from light to dark.

Dots, dashes

By flicking away tiny bits of lino with the tip of the gouge you can create dots. Try making various sizes with the same tool. By holding a U-gouge at an angle of 45 degrees and rotating the block around it you can create a round dot. Try making a series of dashes. Vary the size, shape and direction to suggest movement.

Clearing large areas

When clearing a large area of the block you should use the biggest tool at your disposal. When inking the block, there is a tendency for the roller to go into these areas and deposit ink. As a rule of thumb, the larger the area you are clearing the deeper you will need to cut. If a very large area needs to be cleared completely it can be cut out with a knife or scissors. Carve a channel in the lino where you want to cut, using a gouge. This will make it easier to cut through in one go. Keep any offcuts for smaller projects or for practising on.

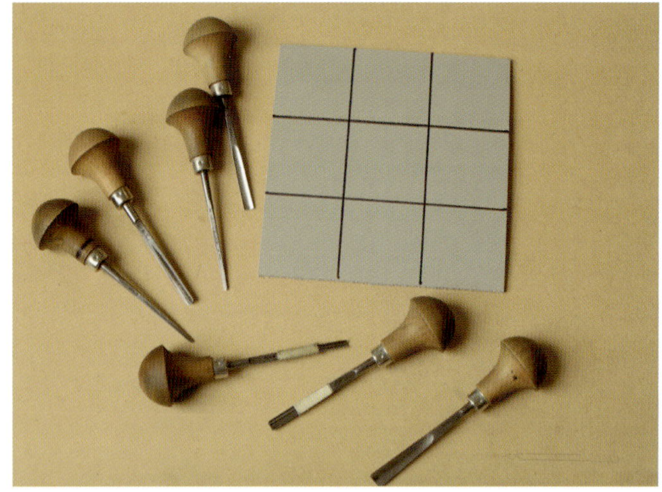

Draw a grid onto your lino block.

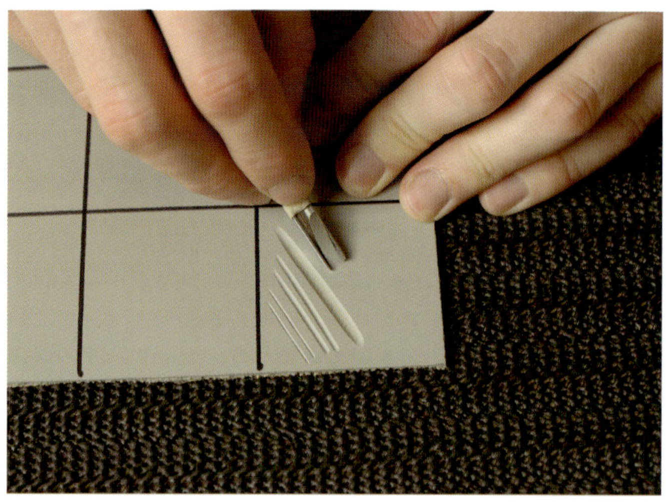

Start by carving straight lines of various widths.

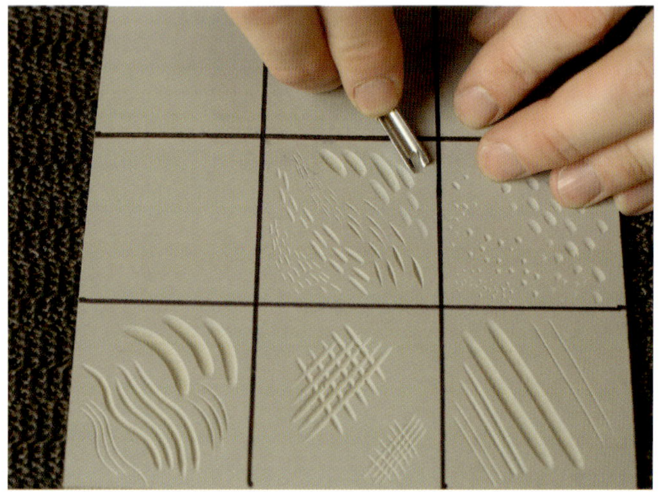

Continue with hatching, curved lines, dots and dashes.

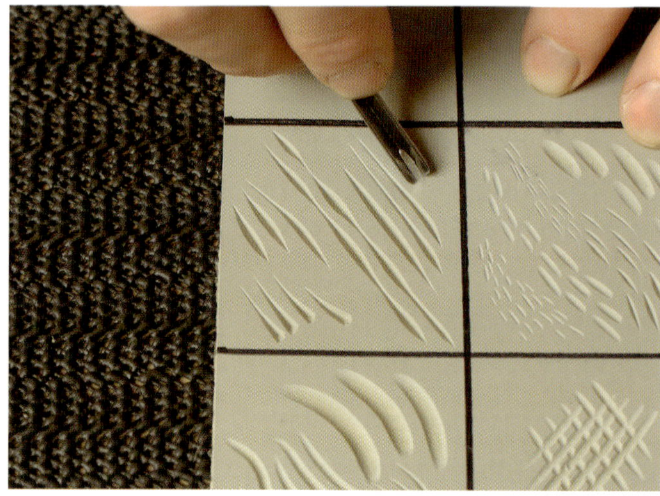

Use the V-gouge to carve lines which get thicker and thinner.

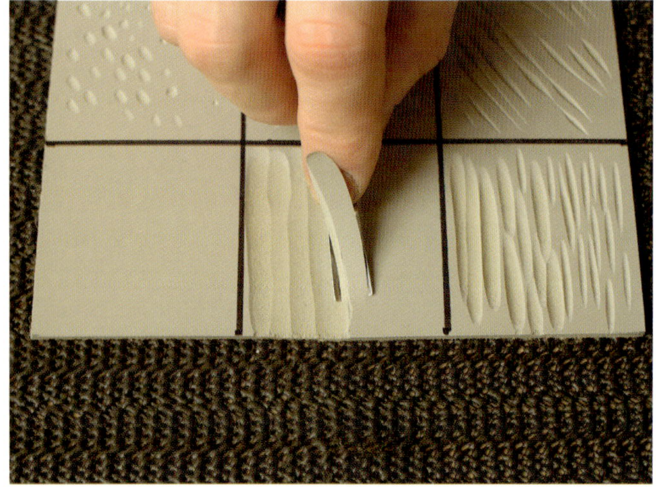

A large flat scoop tool clears areas quickly.

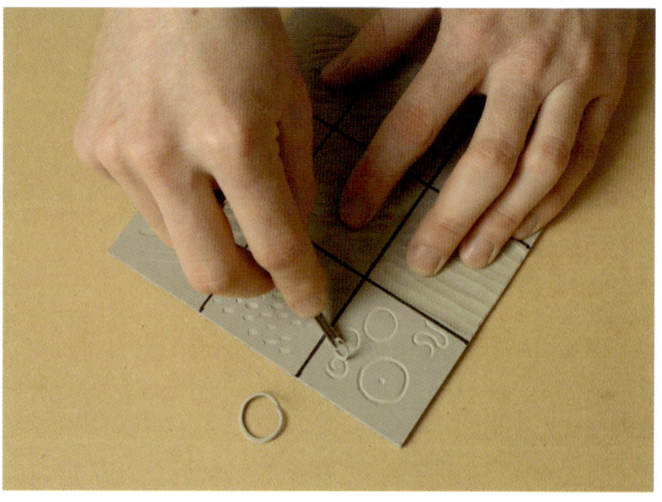

Carve circles and dots by rotating the lino.

Printing your test block

Preparing paper

Before you get your hands inky it is a good idea to prepare your paper for printing. You should wash your hands first, even if they look clean, as oils and sweat can be absorbed by the paper and cause long-term damage. This is worth doing, even if you are just doing a test print, as it will help you form good habits.

Cut or tear your paper to size before you start printing. The paper should be a little bigger than your block. This makes it easier to handle without getting inky fingers and gives a nice border to your print.

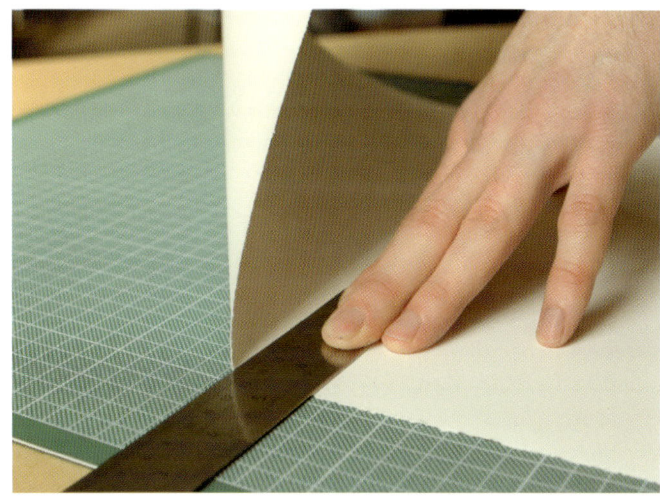

Paper is torn to mimic the deckle edge. Pull the paper across and towards you.

Preparing your inking and printing areas

Before you print your block, you need to set out your inking and printing areas. If necessary, protect the work surface with newspaper or a plastic table cloth. Your ink slab should be at a comfortable height for working – around the level of your hips. The slab is where you will roll out the ink before transferring it to the block. Try to keep things organized and put each tool in its place when you are not using it. This will help to stop the ink spreading and getting on your hands, clothes and paper. Whether you are a messy person or not it's a good idea to wear an apron or some old clothes.

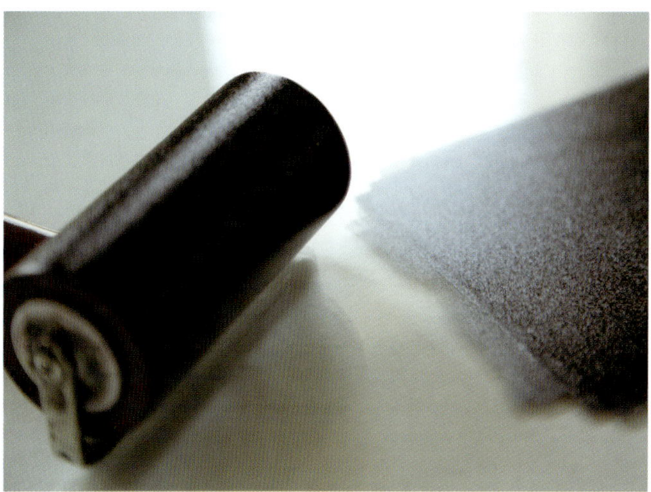

Correct amount of ink on the roller.

Rolling out the ink

Place a small amount of ink (about half a teaspoonful) on the ink slab, near the top. Spread the ink out evenly to form a line the same width as your roller using a palette knife. This is your ink reservoir. Dip the roller in the ink once and start rolling it out below your ink reservoir. You are aiming to get an even, smooth layer of ink on the roller. You will probably need less ink than you think, so make sure you keep the rolled-out area of ink separate from the reservoir and only dip into the reservoir when your rolled-out ink needs topping up. As you spread the ink, roll forwards on the glass and then lift the roller back to the start. In this way you will spread the ink on the roller much more quickly. If you just roll forwards and backwards without lifting the roller you are picking up and depositing the ink in the same place. You should also turn the roller sideways and roll across the inking area. This will ensure you get an even spread of ink in all directions. You should end up with a flat even square of ink on the ink slab and an even coating on the roller.

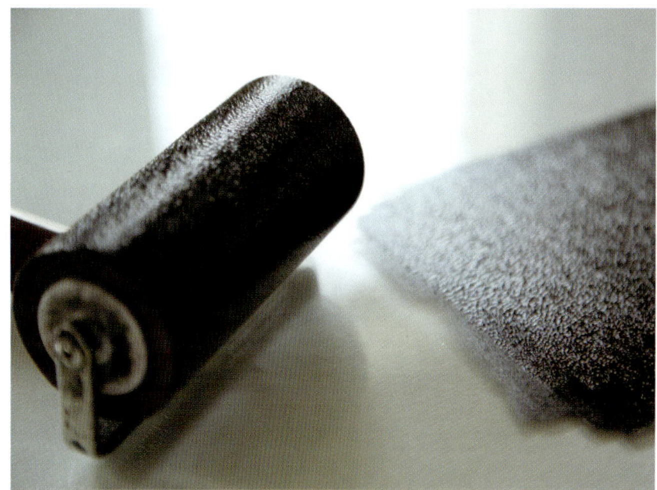

Too much ink on the roller.
Note the 'orange peel' texture.

Controlling the amount of ink on the roller

To get good results, you need to be able to judge what is the right amount of ink on the roller and to be able to control this. You can use three of your senses to judge the amount of ink when you are rolling out: sight, sound and feel. The ink should look even and have the texture of fine sandpaper. If the surface resembles orange peel there is too much ink. The correct amount of ink will also make a quiet hissing noise as you roll it. If this becomes a loud crackle, again, there is too much ink. Finally, you should be able to feel by the resistance of the roller: more ink means more resistance as it will slow the roller down.

You can adjust the amount of ink on the roller in two ways. If you don't have enough ink on the roller, simply dip it in the reservoir and roll out again. Repeat this until you are happy. If the reservoir runs out, replenish it with more ink. If you have too much ink on the roller scrape up some ink from the ink slab, returning it to the reservoir, and roll out again on the same spot. Repeat if necessary. Never scrape the ink off the roller itself as you can damage it.

Inking up the block

Once the roller is evenly coated in ink, roll it onto your block. Roll once onto the block then re-ink the roller. Continue until all the raised parts of the block are covered in a layer of ink. You do not need to apply a lot of pressure to the roller. If using a large roller the weight of the roller itself should be enough; with a small roller use the weight of your arm. It is a good idea to roll in different directions to make sure all areas of the block are covered. To make this easier you can turn the block; hold it by the edges and try not to touch any ink. When the block is covered in an even layer, put the roller down by your ink, being careful to keep the handle clean.

Roller speed

The transfer of ink to and from the roller can be controlled to some degree by the speed you roll. Rolling fast will pick ink up onto the roller and rolling slow will lay it down. So when rolling on the ink slab, move the roller faster and when rolling on the block move it slower. Excess ink on the block can be removed with one or two quick rolls. Bear in mind also that ink will always want to move from a surface with more ink to a surface with less ink.

Hand printing

Printing with a wooden spoon

Keep the block ink-side up and carefully move it to your printing area. At this point, clean your hands if they are inky. Next, place the printing paper on top of the block. There is a knack to this. Hold the paper with one hand and use the other to guide it. You need to avoid the paper touching the block while you do this. Use your thumb and forefinger to hold the edge and when it is lined up release the paper with your other hand. Once the paper is laid down, try not to move it as this will cause the ink to smudge. Press down on the paper gently with the flat of your palm. The tackiness of the ink will help the paper stick to the block while you are printing.

Hold the paper down with one hand and use the back of the wooden spoon to rub. Burnish the whole printing area, using quite a lot of pressure. As you do this you will start to see the image through the paper. Continue until you have burnished the whole print evenly.

Tip: if the ink comes right through the paper or the paper is starting to rub off, place a sheet of tracing or greaseproof paper on top and burnish through that.

Once you think you have finished, hold the paper down firmly and lift one edge to check the print. If it needs more pressure, or if you have missed a bit, lower it again and continue rubbing with the spoon. As long as you hold the paper down each time, so it doesn't move, you can keep doing this until you are happy. When you are confident you have done enough rubbing, lift the paper off the block by peeling it back from the corner.

Printing with a baren

The baren has the advantage of a flat surface, so you can print a larger area in one go. Because the force you exert on it is spread over a larger area you have to press a bit harder than with a spoon. Hold the baren with your fingers wrapped loosely around the handle and use your bodyweight to push down, keeping your arm straight and resting your weight on the heel of your palm. As with the wooden spoon, move the baren around over the back of the paper.

You can vary the printing pressure, making some areas darker than others by pressing harder. Use the edge of the baren to concentrate the pressure over a smaller area.

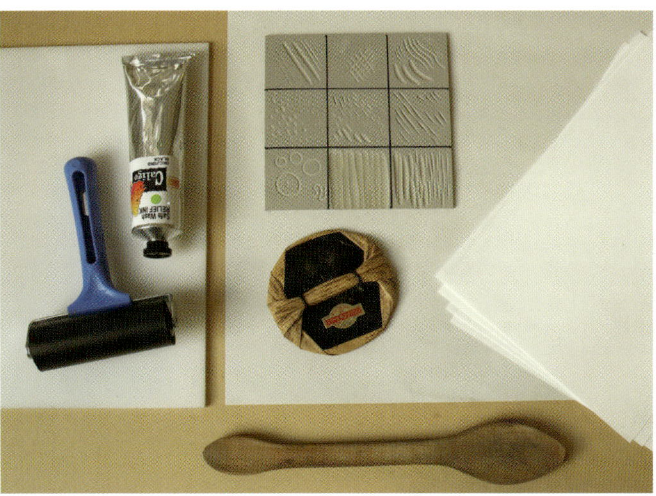

Try to keep your inking and print areas separate.

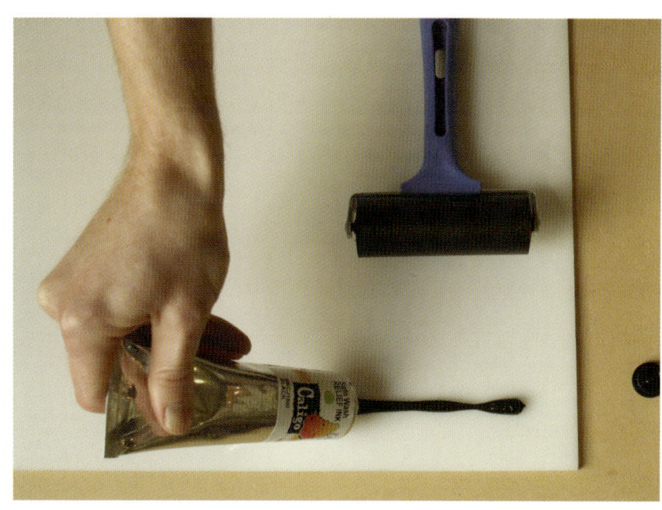

Squeeze some ink out onto your ink slab the same width as the roller.

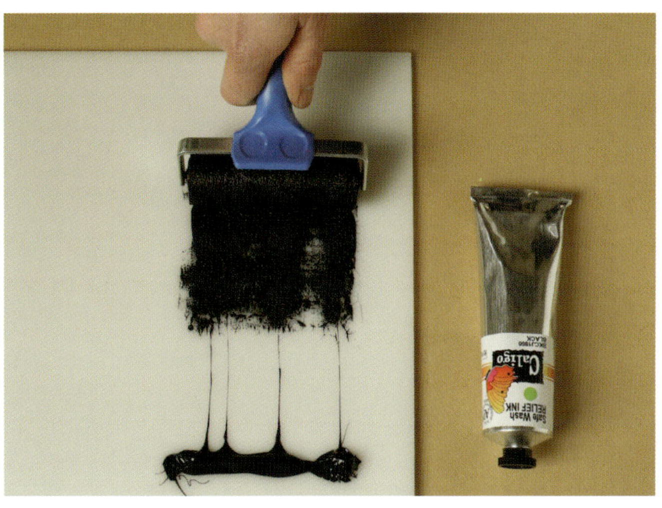

Dip the roller in the ink and roll out a neat square below.

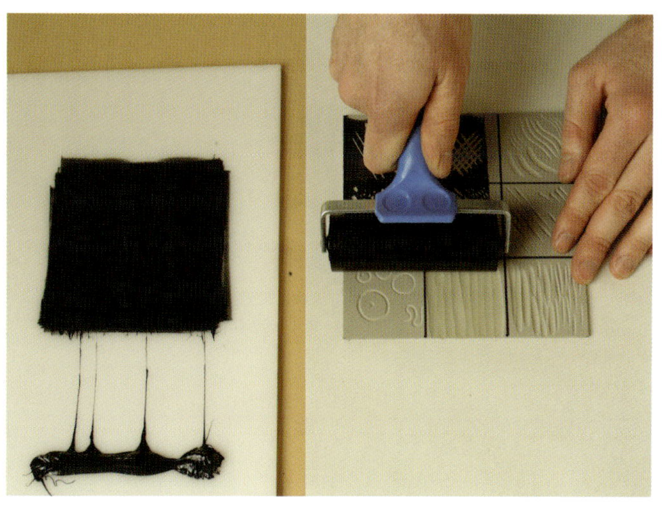

Roll onto the block slowly.

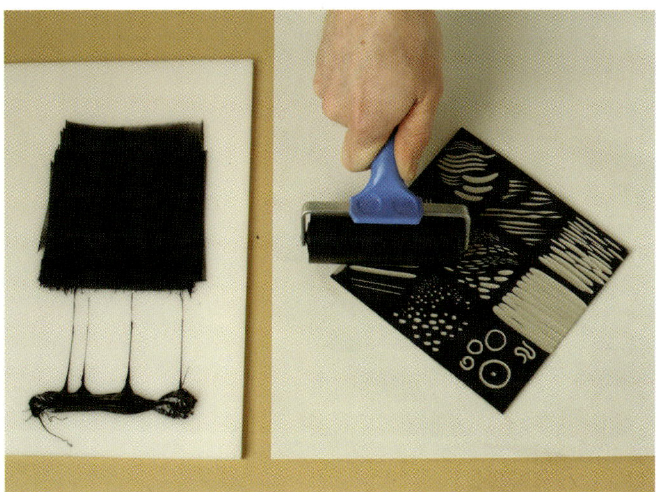

To get the corners, roll at a diagonal.

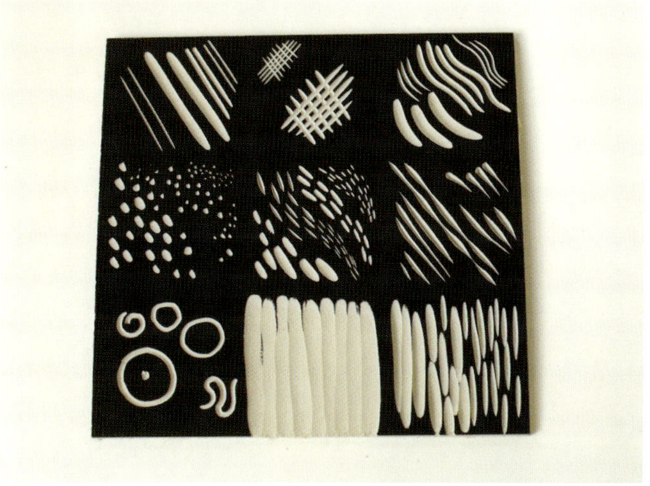

Your inked up block should be solid black with the carved out areas clean.

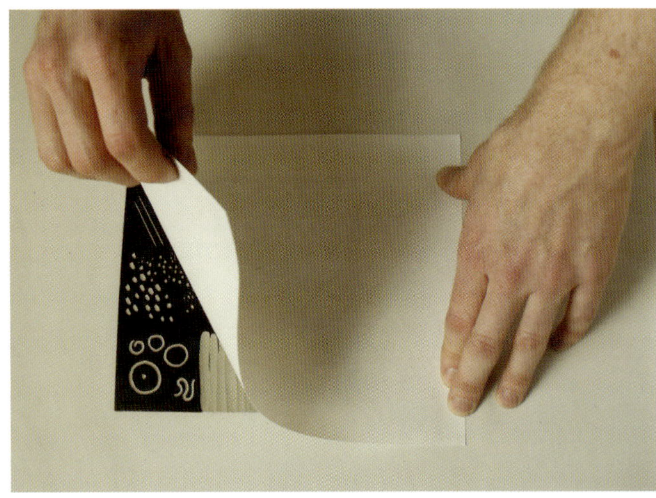

Lay your paper down by holding it with forefinger and thumb.

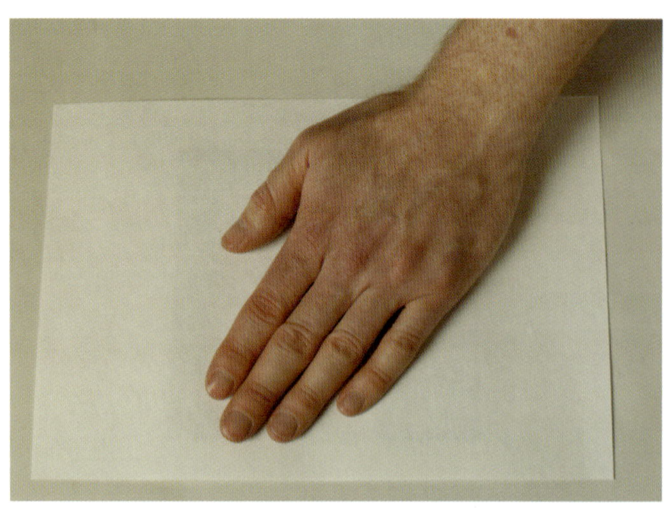

Gently press the paper down to help it stick to the block.

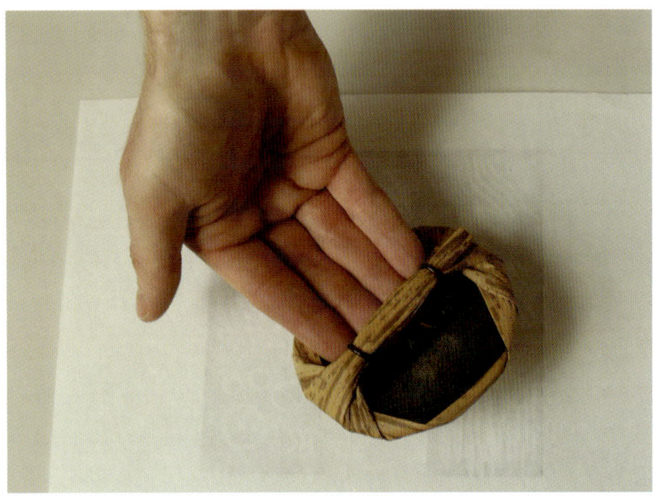

Hold the baren by inserting your fingers into the handle.

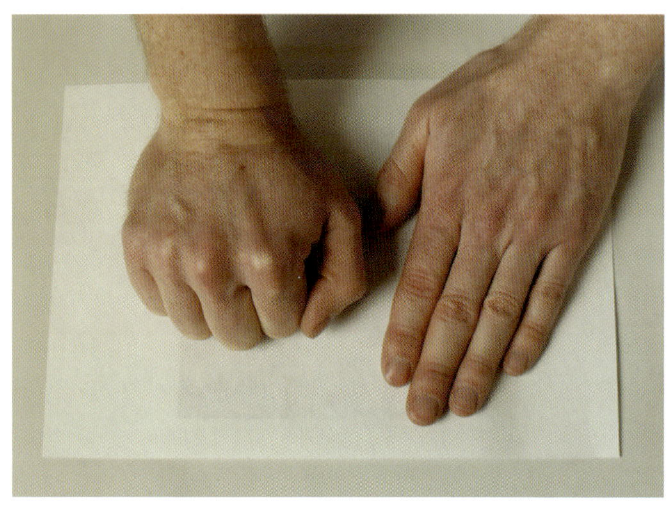

Push down on the baren as you rub, using your body weight.

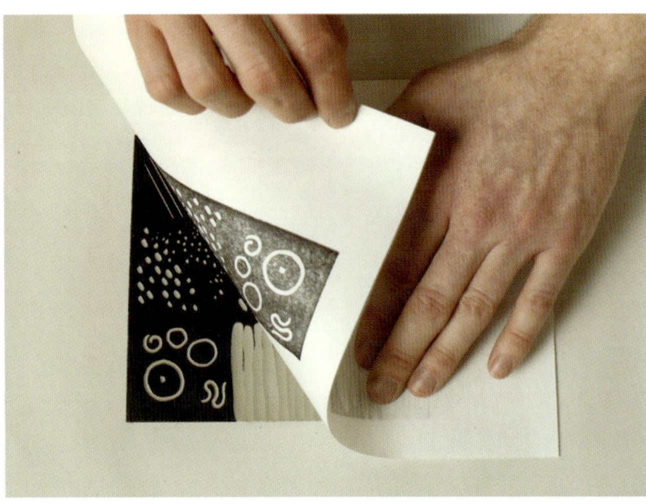

Check your progress by holding the paper firmly and lifting.

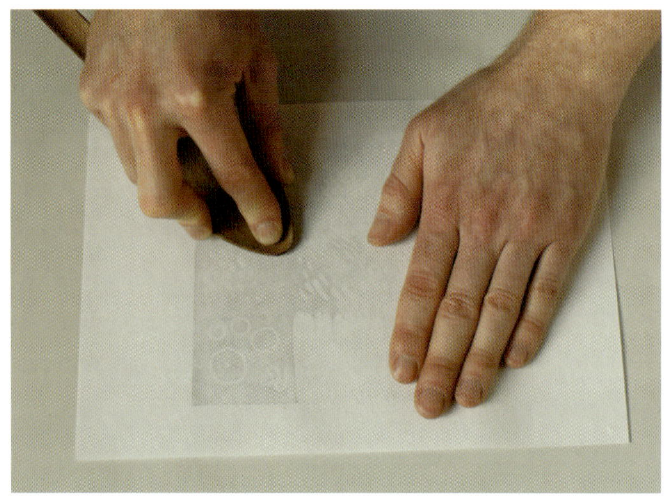

Burnish with a wooden spoon to get a strong black print.

Analysing your print

With luck, your first print will come out well. In this case, give yourself a pat on the back and enjoy the moment. If it didn't come out perfectly, don't worry, you will be able to work out why and remedy it. Either way, it is important to remember that there are a lot of things that can go wrong in printmaking and you will always get the odd dud print.

Take a good look at your test print and see which marks were successful. Some may have printed the way you expected; others will surprise you. If you want you can write on the print which tools made which marks and keep it for reference.

Common printing problems

There are many variables when printing, including the type of ink and paper you use, the amount of ink on the block and the amount of pressure you apply when printing. All of these will give different results. If you are not sure what has caused a certain problem or effect, keep everything the same except for one variable and change that. If that doesn't work try another variable. This way you will quickly learn a lot about the subtleties of the printing process. With experience you will be able to look at a print and know exactly what went wrong and how to fix it. You will also get a feel for the process, knowing instinctively when you are doing it right.

The most common issues for beginners tend to be getting the right amount of ink on the block and accidentally moving the paper when printing. With care and attention these problems are easily avoided. Too much ink will result in the finer details filling in on the print, and fuzzy edges generally. Too little ink will result in a speckled texture in some areas, or a print which is lighter than it should be. A double-printed image is the result of the paper moving during printing. Try using slightly more ink, as this helps the paper to stick to the block, and make sure you are holding the paper down firmly while you are printing.

Making a second print

If you want to make more prints from the test block, simply apply more ink and print again. There is no need to clean the lino between prints. You will find the first print needs slightly more ink than the rest as you are starting from an ink-free block. You may also find that as the ink works itself into the surface of the lino your prints get progressively stronger. If you want to print the block in a new colour, you need to clean and dry the block first and use a clean roller.

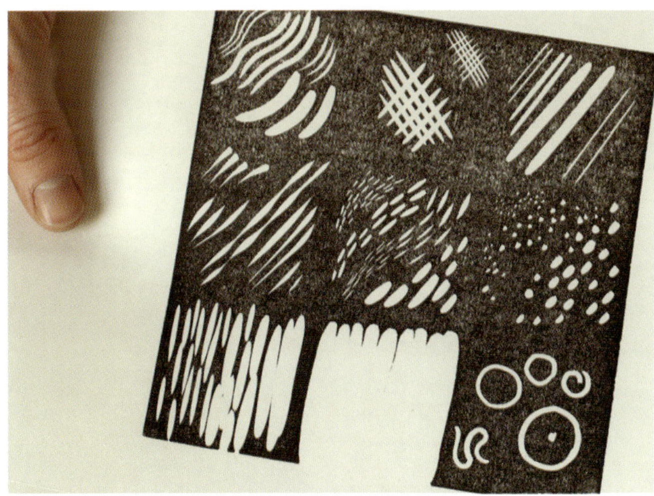

The test print with the baren has a lot of texture.

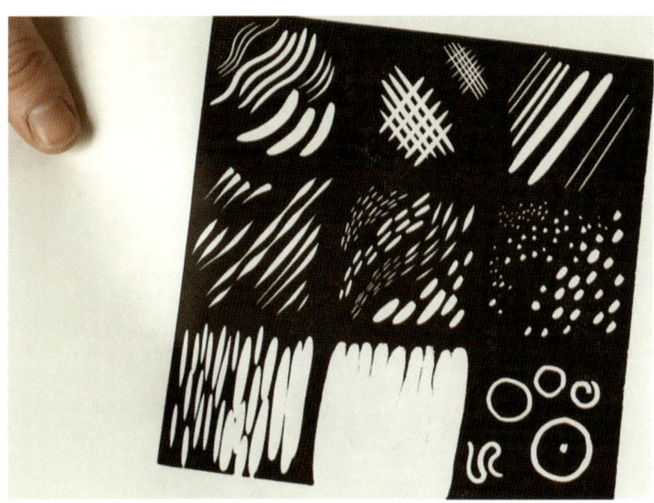

The test print with the spoon is more solidly printed.

Drying prints

Hang your print to dry with a clothes peg or place it flat somewhere where it will not get disturbed. Inks take different times to dry, from half an hour to a few days. Drying times will also be dependent on atmospheric conditions like temperature and humidity.

Never throw a print away

Keep all your prints, at least to start with, as they can be very useful. If something went wrong, you can write on the print what you think it was and use it as a reference in the future. Sometimes you won't like a print at first but it may grow on you. You might want to print over the top of it when it is dry, use it as scrap paper or even cover a book with it. If you're that way inclined you can even cut it up and use it in a collage or make origami.

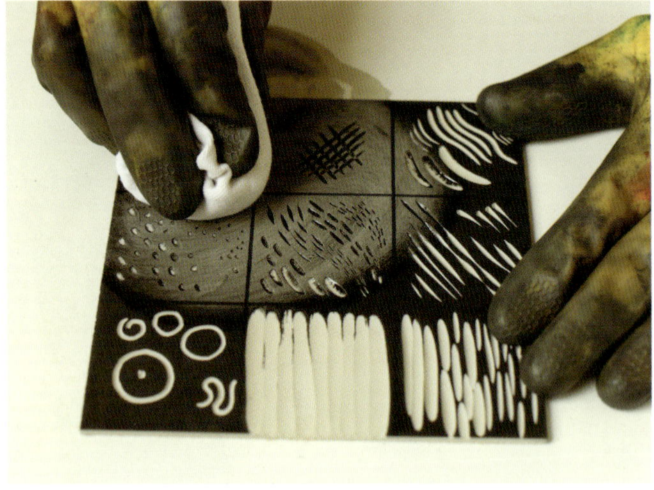

Clean the block with vegetable oil and a rag.

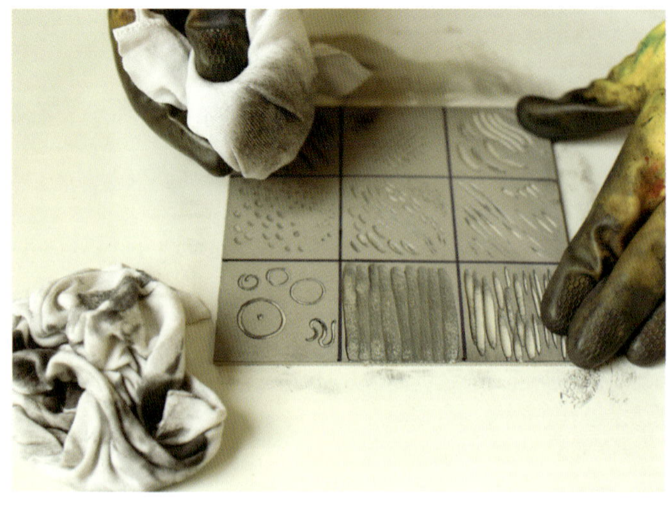

If necessary, finish the block with a drop of Zest-It.

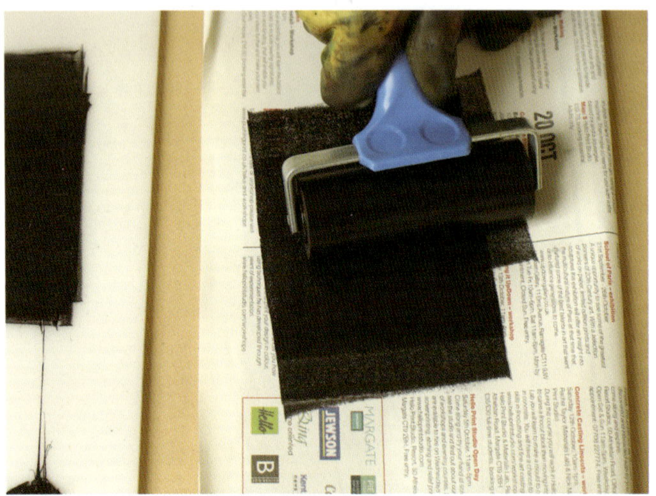

Remove most of the ink by rolling on newspaper.

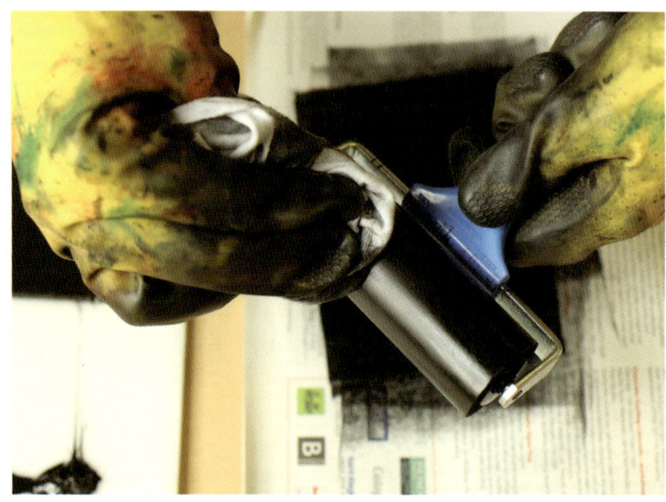

Wipe the roller clean with oil or Zest-It.

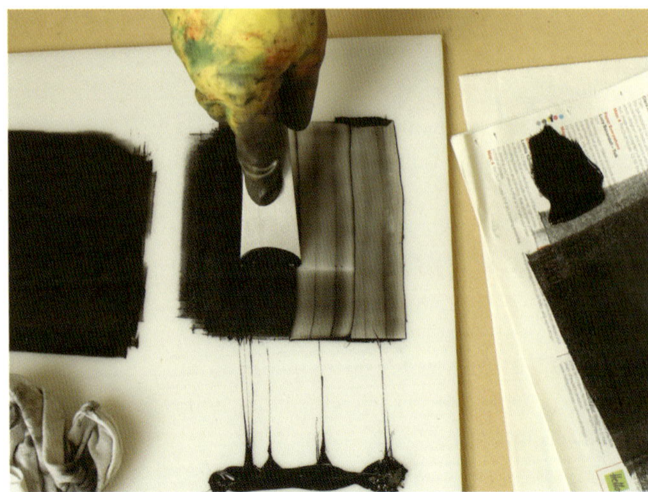

Scrape up unused ink with an ink knife.

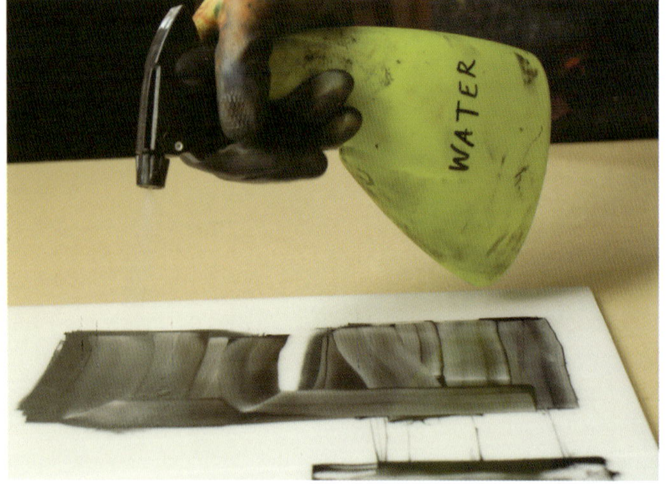

Clean the perspex or glass with water or oil.

Cleaning up

This part is boring but important. Make sure you leave yourself time to clean up thoroughly at the end of a session. Get in the habit of cleaning up straight away. You will need to use the appropriate cleaning agent for the ink you have used. Oil-based inks can be cleaned with vegetable oil, a citrus-based cleaner like Zest-It or a solvent like white spirit. Water-based inks and water-washable inks can be washed up with soap and water. Whatever you use, wear rubber gloves, especially if using solvents.

Old T-shirts and other cotton fabrics can be cut up into rags for cleaning. Keep inky rags in a sealed metal bin and re-use them. When you are cleaning up, use these first, and finish off with a clean rag.

When cleaning, do your rollers and blocks first and then your work surfaces. NEVER leave ink to dry on a roller as it can be impossible to remove, ruining the roller surface. Take special care to clean your roller thoroughly. As well as risking damaging it, any colour left could contaminate your ink the next time you use it. Don't forget to clean the edges of the roller too. To test if a roller is clean, use a light coloured rag to wipe it; if any colour comes off, it is not clean.

Clean the block gently with a rag. Do not scrub at it as you will wear it down and risk breaking bits off. If you are using traditional lino you will find it stains, especially in the carved-out areas. This is OK. The main thing is to get the printing surface as clean as you can. If you use vegetable oil make sure you give it a final wipe with a dry rag, as any remaining oil could affect future prints. If you let the ink dry on your block you may still be able to clean it. If not, you can still print with it although if it was heavily inked you may lose some of the details.

Note: If you are cleaning traditional lino with water, be careful not to get the hessian backing wet, as it will curl up.

To clean your ink slab, scrape up as much ink as you can with an ink knife, then clean it with water or vegetable oil and a piece of scrunched up newspaper. Finally, give it a drop of water and a final polish with newspaper to remove any residue.

Handling and storing prints

How to handle prints

There is nothing more frustrating than carving and printing a perfect impression and then smudging it, creasing it or getting an inky fingerprint on it. Of course accidents will always happen, but if you are careful you can reduce them to a minimum.

Clean hands

Keep your hands clean. There is generally no reason for them to be covered in ink if you are careful. If you are a naturally messy person, wear a pair of latex or plastic gloves for inking and take them off for printing. Check your hands for ink before you handle any paper. Tiny smudges can be wiped off on an apron; otherwise wash and dry your hands thoroughly. Wet hands can also damage prints.

Picking up the print

Pick your print up being careful to avoid the ink. Most linocuts have a border which makes this easier. Avoid twisting or kinking the paper as you do this. Big prints should be picked up by two corners. You can either carry the print by supporting the back or by two opposite corners. Allowing it to sag as you carry it will help to avoid kinking. Moving around too fast with a print in your hands can create a draught which can whisk it out of your hands, so take your time.

Storing prints

Once your prints are thoroughly dry they should be stored safely in a box or drawer. If your prints are special interleave them with sheets of acid-free tissue paper.

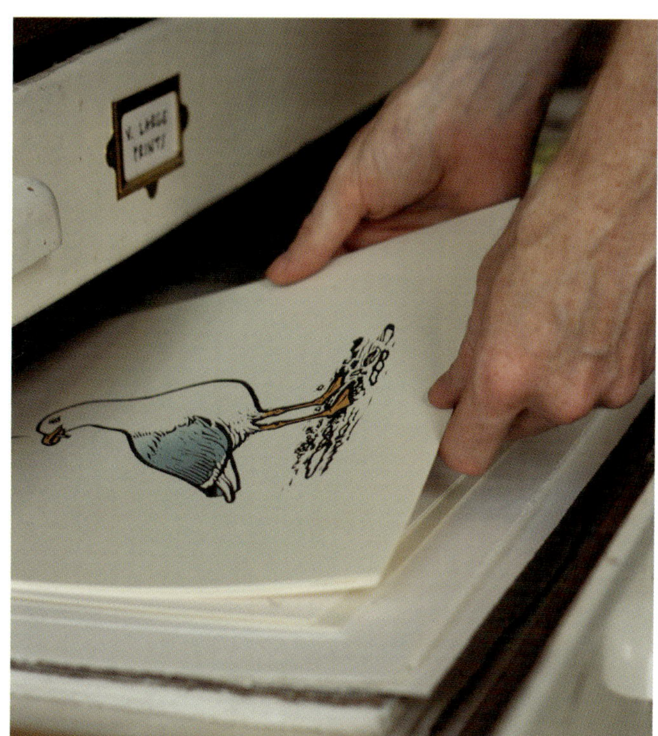

Store prints safely in a drawer when they have thoroughly dried.

Deborah Klein (Australia)

www.deborahklein.net

Deborah Klein is a visual artist who makes paintings, drawings, prints, zines and artists' books. She divides her time between Melbourne and Ballarat, in south-western Australia. Since 1988 she has held regular solo exhibitions and participated in group exhibitions in Australia and internationally. Her work is represented in public and university museum collections throughout Australia.

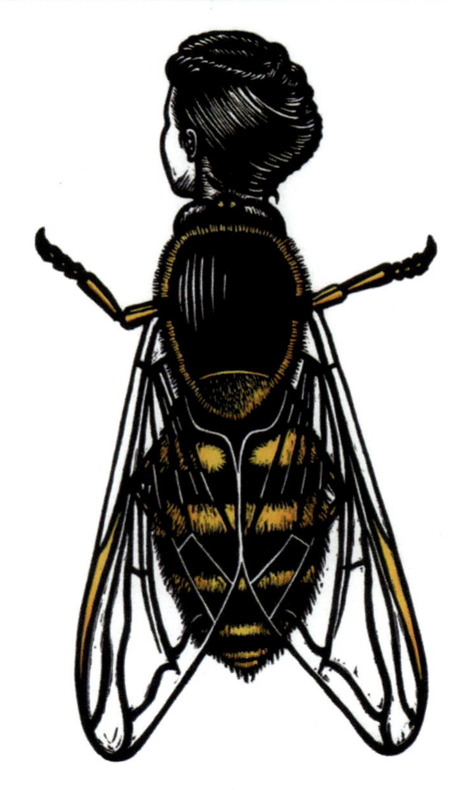

Hover Fly Winged Woman, Deborah Klein, 29.5 × 21cm, hand coloured linocut.

As an undergraduate in the early 1980s I was initially attracted to etching and lithography. Along with screen-printing, these were the mediums that were most encouraged. Although I majored in printmaking at art school, as a linocut artist, I'm largely self-taught. Even though I wasn't discouraged from making linocuts at art school, I wasn't exactly encouraged either. The head of printmaking believed it to be entirely simplistic, if not downright primitive.

I like linocut's directness. I also very much admire its extraordinary versatility. I can't imagine any other medium that would have led my work in the various directions it has taken over the years, both technically and conceptually.

I developed my mark-making skills by studying examples of relief prints. The linocuts of Australian Modernist artists Margaret Preston and Thea Proctor were among my early influences. I still believe that many of the relief prints produced in Australia during the 1920s and 30s are as fine as any produced elsewhere in the world. In my initial ignorance, however, I wasn't aware of the difference between woodcuts and wood engravings. I was particularly drawn to the latter, especially those by Australia's Lionel Lindsay. Unaware that the small reproductions of wood engravings were probably close to actual scale, I began to adapt similar mark-making to my own very much larger scale linocuts.

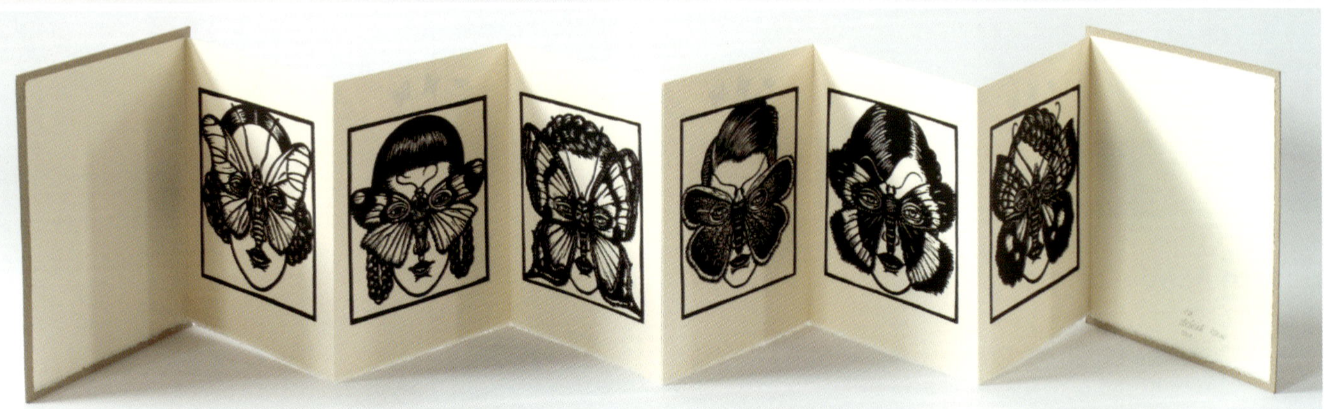

Women with Wings, Deborah Klein, 24 × 20.5 × 3cm, concertina artist book with linocuts.

All of my images begin their lives as thoroughly researched sketches, which are generally transferred freehand to the lino. In the past I used felt pens, but now I prefer India ink, which is more subtle and fluid. I use white acrylic or poster paint to make alterations. Although I allow certain room for the design to develop during the cutting process, overall I still have a fair indication of how the finished work will look.

I carve the lino using a variety of tools, depending on the type of mark-making required. I have a fine set of wooden-handled German tools that I've owned for many years. I use a Speedball number one V-shaped cutter for really fine details. I use an Australian brand of lino called Silk Cut which is easy to cut.

I use an etching press to print my linocuts. I place a sheet of cardboard on top of the paper to stop the block moving, which can cause blurring of the image. For a number of years I've worked with water-based inks, most frequently the American brand Graphic Chemical.

> *Be wary of cutting too much of the lino away. It's virtually impossible to replace what you've removed and it can result in a rather sterile image.*

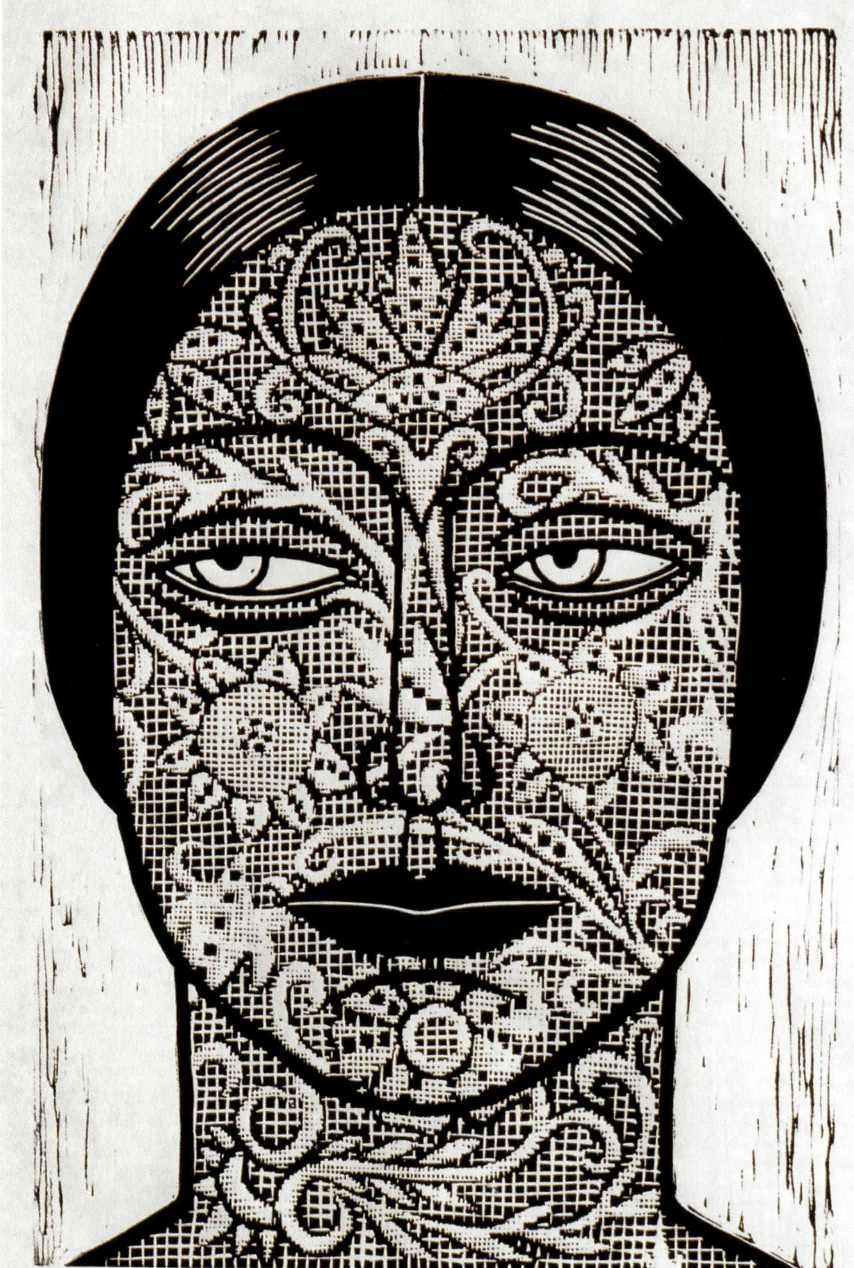

Lace Face, Deborah Klein, 46 × 31cm, linocut.

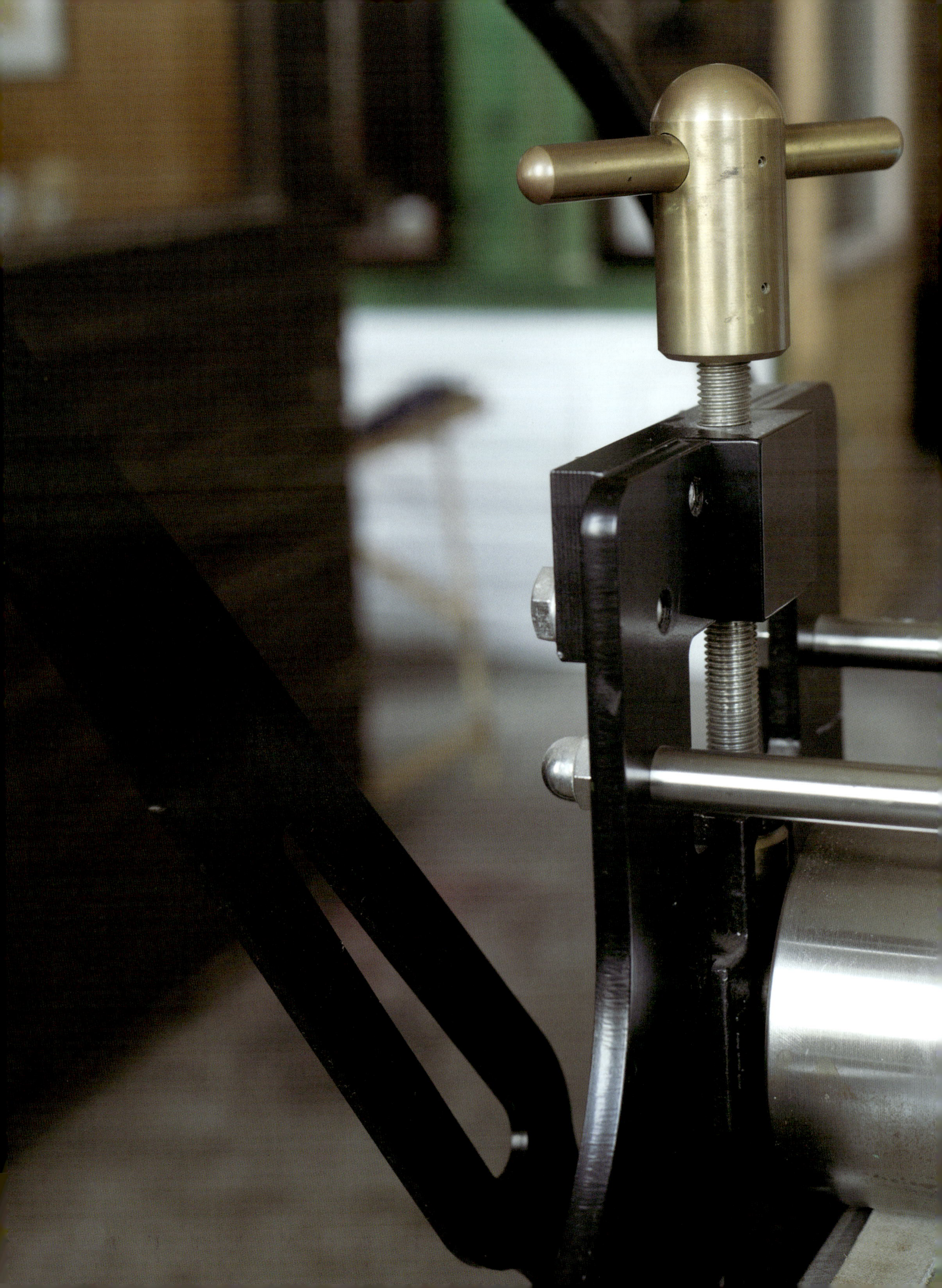

CHAPTER 3

PRINTING ON A PRESS

While hand printing is easy and cheap, printing linocuts on a press opens up new possibilities. It allows you to print faster, more consistently and with greater pressure. This is particularly useful if you are making large prints or prints with large flat areas of colour. There are many kinds of printing press that can be used for relief printing. They vary in size, cost, age and beauty. Choosing the right press can be a daunting prospect. This chapter contains information about what kinds of presses are available, how they work and their pros and cons. It also guides you through printing linocuts on four common types of press: the book press, etching press, iron hand press and Adana 8-5 letterpress machine.

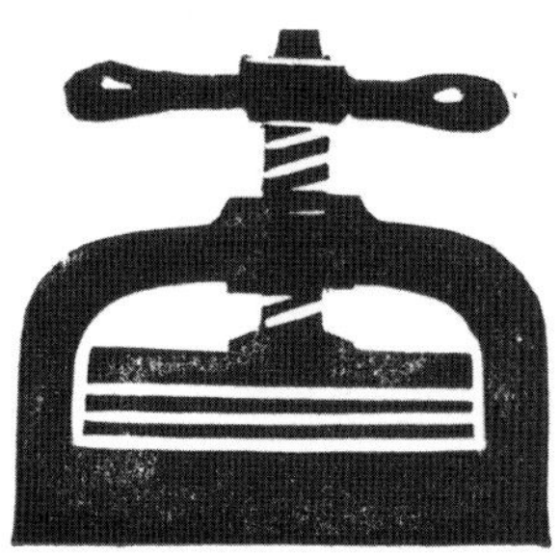

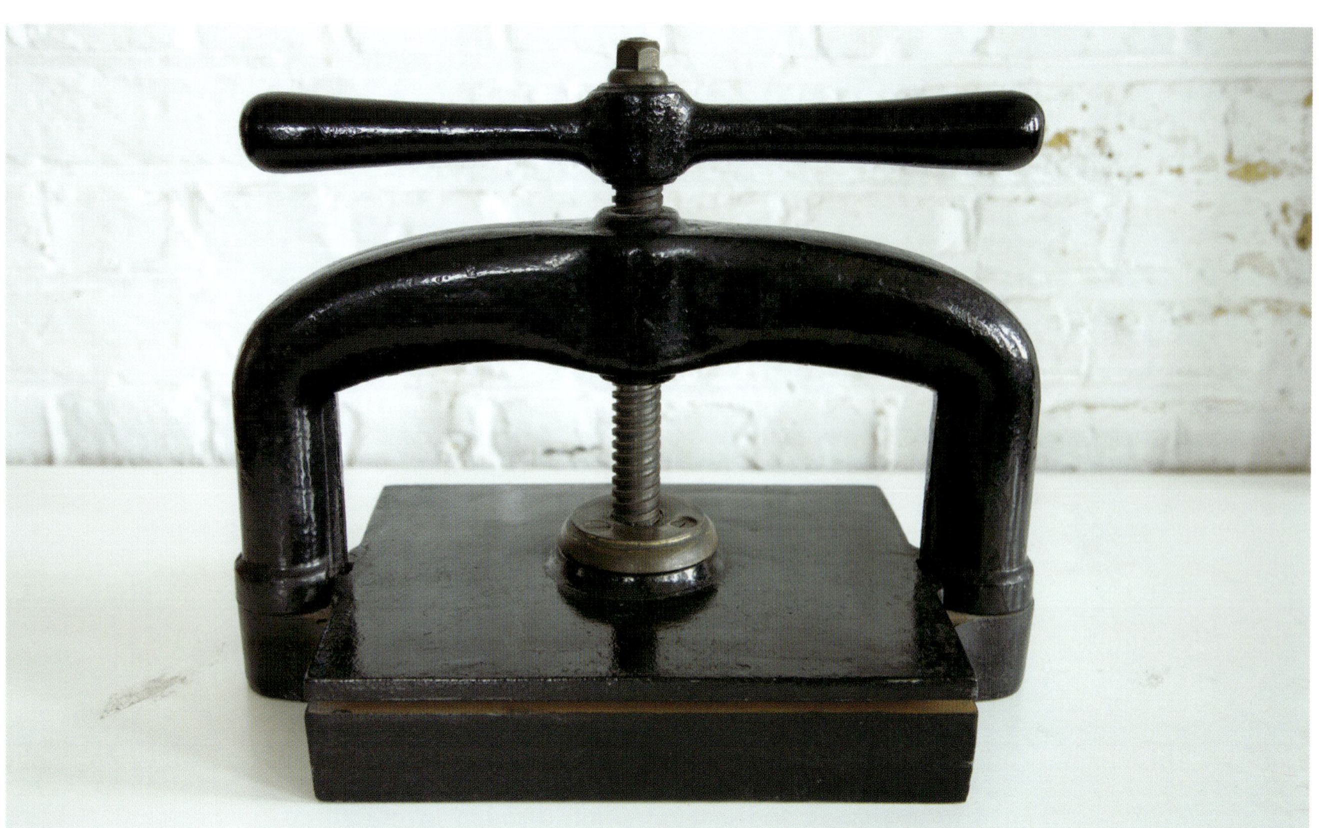

Book press.

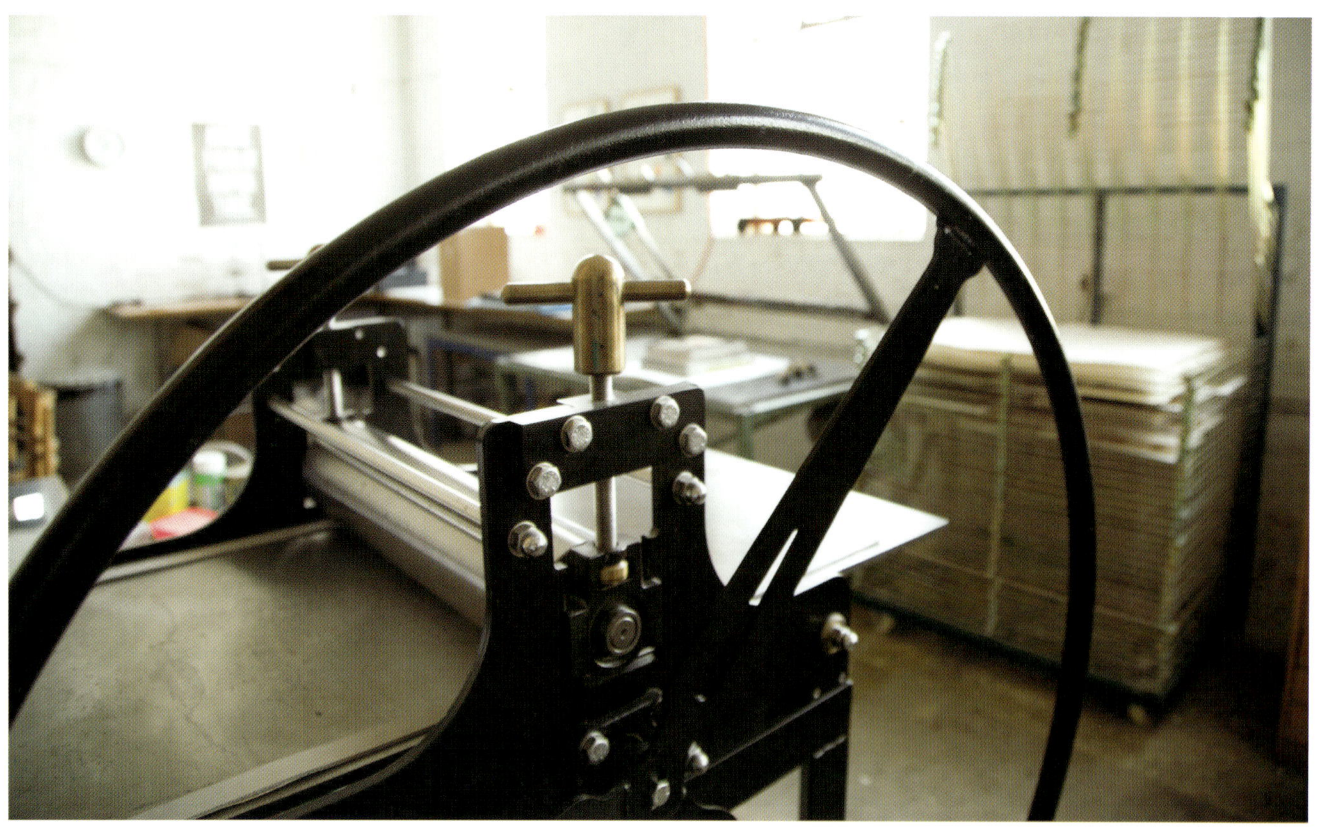

Etching press.

Types of printing press

There is a dizzying array of printing presses available, both new and old. They can be referred to according to their function (etching press, relief press), the way they are built (roller press, platen press), their model (Albion, Columbian) or their maker (American French Tool Co., Rochat). Many different kinds of press can be used for printing linocuts, but some work better than others.

Small presses for beginners

There are three kinds of press commonly bought by beginners: book press, lever press and tabletop etching press. In addition, you may also want to consider an Adana press, especially if you also want to print letterpress. All of these presses are small and light enough for one, or at the most two, people to move easily so have the advantage that they can be stored out of the way when not in use. They are the most affordable too.

Book press

Also known as nipping presses, book presses are relatively cheap and can be picked up on eBay fairly easily. They are usually made of cast iron and are operated by turning a screw handle. Although they give good results they require some exertion and are slightly slower to use as the block and paper have to be carefully slid in and out for each print.

Lever press

These modern presses are made for the hobby and beginner market and are simple and easy to use. They will not exert as much pressure as other presses.

Tabletop etching press

A great all-round press as it can also be used for printing drypoints, etchings and collagraphs.

Adana press

The Adana press was designed for hobbyists who wanted to make letterpress prints at home. They are still popular a century after they came onto the market and are great for printing very small prints quickly as the block is inked automatically after each impression.

Etching press

The etching press has a bed or plank which passes back and forth through a pair of metal rollers. One of the rollers is driven by turning a handle or wheel and this pulls the bed through the press. As the plate or block passes through pressure is exerted by the top roller. Most etching presses can be used for printing lino, as long as the top roller can be raised sufficiently high to fit the block underneath.

Because the pressure is concentrated on a smaller area it is possible to take a strong impression. This is particularly useful when printing a large block or one with a larger area of ink. If too much pressure is used the block and paper can be stretched as they pass through the roller, leading to difficulties in registration (alignment of the layers in a print). In a studio where different printmaking processes are used, an etching press is a useful all-rounder. Large etching presses are sometimes driven by a motor.

Platen press

These are designed for relief printing, often including letterpress printing. The platen is a solid, flat surface which exerts an even pressure over the whole printing area at the same time. The advantages of a platen press are that there is no lateral movement and no risk of stretching the paper, making it easy to achieve consistent prints and accurate registration.

Screw press

The same as a book press but made specifically for relief printing. This is the simplest kind of press and could be built fairly easily and cheaply by someone with the right skills and tools. There are one or two manufacturers in the UK who make screw presses aimed at artists.

Cylinder press

The cylinder press was designed for printing letterpress and has a flat bed with a cylinder, or roller which moves back and forth over it. The cylinder is set at type high (in the UK and USA this is 0.918in or 23.3mm, but slightly more in other parts of Europe), so any adjustment to pressure needs to be done by packing a combination of pieces of wood, card and paper under the block to bring it up to the correct height. Cylinder presses come in both manual and motorized versions. Small manual cylinder presses are known as proofing presses because they were used for checking test prints before committing to a large print run on a mechanical press.

Letterpress machines

Pretty much any press for printing wooden or metal type will print linocuts. Letterpress machines are set up for printing blocks which are type high, so when printing linocut or woodcut the blocks need to be brought up to the correct height by mounting them on pieces of wood.

Some letterpresses are designed for printing by hand, one print at a time; others have complex mechanisms that allow for automatic or semi-automatic printing. The fastest automated machines are capable of thousands of impressions per hour.

Iron hand presses

This category includes the Stanhope, Albion, Columbian and Imperial presses.

Before the invention of modern production methods, ephemera like newspapers, chapbooks, broadsides, posters and pamphlets were often printed on these beautiful cast iron machines. They are much sought after today by printmakers, perhaps as much for their impressive looks as for their function. They will only print as big as their platen, which is usually small relative to the size of the whole press.

Iron hand presses are operated by pulling a lever horizontally, as if rowing standing up. This exerts a downwards pressure onto the block via the platen.

Vandercook press

Vandercook began making proofing presses in Chicago in 1909 for the commercial printing market. Their designs vary but often consist of a cylinder which travels along a fixed bed by means of a geared system. Some have built-in ink rollers which automatically ink the block with each pass. These are fast to use but take a while to clean up.

Clamshell platen presses

These small to medium sized presses were designed for printing smaller items like business cards and stationery and are so-called because they open and close like a clam. They are powered by electricity or by a foot pedal which turns a flywheel. This in turn operates the opening/closing action via a clever system of moving parts. The clamshell press can be operated continuously by hand-feeding: replacing the printed sheet with a new piece of paper each time.

Galley press or proof press

When typesetters were preparing text for printing they would do it on a flat metal tray called a galley. The type was then transferred to the printing press. A galley press or proof press was designed to make it quick and easy to take a proof while the type was still on the galley. Any mistakes could then be rectified before printing, saving time and bother. The extra thickness of the galley would raise the printing surface above type high, so on galley presses the distance between the bed and cylinder is slightly increased.

Home-made presses

Jack press

Several enterprising people have constructed platen presses out of wood, using a car jack to exert pressure. If you attempt this, your press will need to be solidly built to withstand the forces involved. At least in theory this is a sound idea as a jack requires relatively little effort from the user to crank up the pressure. If you have the urge to try this, do some research online. You may be able to find someone willing to share their plans with you.

Converted mangle

A clothes mangle works in a very similar way to an etching press, with two rollers which rotate by turning a handle. They can be picked up cheaply on ebay or from a junk yard if you are lucky. The rollers are often made of wood so watch out for worn, warped or rotten areas. You will need a flat plank to place between the rollers on which to put the block, ideally supported on either side by runners. Again, if you want to try this, do some research and try to talk to someone who has done this successfully first.

Alternatives – car, steamroller, lawn roller

In theory, anything that exerts enough pressure can be used for printing. For small prints, standing on a board laid on top of your block and paper will be enough. For larger prints the wheel of a car can be slowly rolled onto the block. Care must be taken to keep well clear while this happens. For an even more impressive trick, perfect impressions can be made of large blocks using a steamroller. Many print studios hold steamroller printing events which attract crowds of onlookers. Again, utmost care should be taken to avoid any risk of injury.

Investing in your own press

If you are lucky enough to be able to buy your own press you will find it a worthwhile investment. Many printmakers develop a relationship with their press and certainly some of the antique presses have a lot of character, maybe even personality. Whether you see your press as simply a machine or something more personal, it is something to be looked after; if it is well cared for it will give you years of faithful service.

A well built press has very little wear and tear and second-hand presses shouldn't devalue much over time. Having said that, it is easy to damage one through misuse and care should be taken to use it only as it is designed for. Foreign object such as keys, coins, scissors and rulers should not be placed on the press as they will cause permanent and costly damage if accidentally squashed in it.

What size press to get

The maximum size of press you can get will depend on affordability and practicality. If you are printing on your kitchen table a small, portable press will allow you to put it away when not in use. At the other end of the spectrum if you have a dedicated studio and are dependent on artistic output for your livelihood you will probably want the largest press you can afford to allow you to make prints in a range of sizes. Bear in mind that the biggest presses are extremely heavy and will require specialist help to move and install. Not only will you need a very solid floor for it to sit on, but you will have to get it into the space to start with. There is a good reason that many studios are on the ground floor in industrial buildings rather than on the third floor of a townhouse.

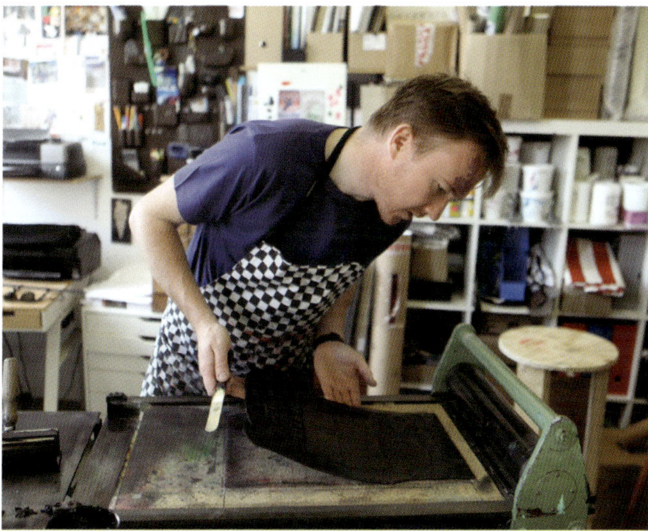

James Brown with his proofing press, which gives his prints a distinctive texture.

Printing with a press

In order to get the best out of a press, you need to know how to set it up, how to use it and how to make adjustments as you go along. There is not scope enough in this book to do this thoroughly for every kind of press but following is a guide to using some of the most common types.

Health and safety

There are risks involved in using a press, particularly the larger, heavier type. Keep any press out of the reach of children and do not allow others to use it without knowing how it works. A floor-standing press should ideally be fixed in place to avoid movement. The heaviest presses are made of cast iron and will need to be situated on a solidly built floor. Specialist moving companies can advise you on this.

When using a press, beware of moving parts. By their nature, presses exert large forces so can easily crush a finger. Moving parts can catch loose clothing or hair, so keep them well out of the way.

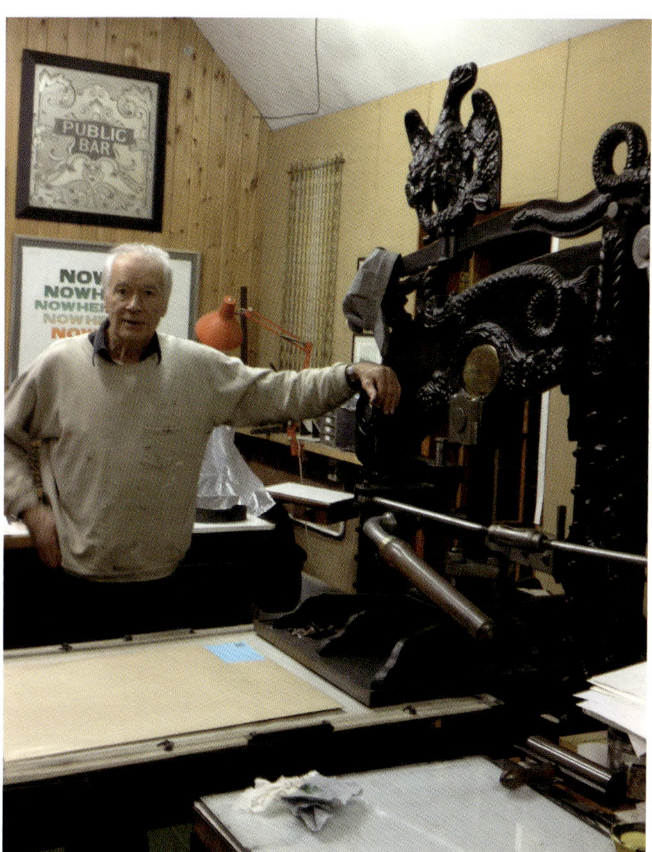

Letterpress printer Tony Smith with his Columbian press. The eagle on top acts as a counterweight.

Printing on a book press

Set up your press on a sturdy surface. In order to exert enough pressure you will need to tighten the press as hard as you can. This is especially true for larger blocks and blocks with large printing areas on them. If you can, secure the press to the surface it sits on. This can be done by screwing it down, or with batons. If this is not possible, make a snug frame out of pieces of wood for it to sit in, or rout out a hole the exact shape and size of the base of the press to sit in. If you cannot do this, at least you should sit the press on a piece of non-slip matting.

Cut two pieces of MDF to the size of the platen of the press. These will be used to sandwich the block and printing paper to make it easier to insert them into the press. It is important that these are smooth and flat. You can use another material, like plywood, but MDF is best as it is perfectly flat and even and doesn't warp.

Ink up your block as usual and place it in the dead centre of one of the pieces of MDF. Lay your printing paper on top followed by the other piece of MDF. Being careful not to move the paper, insert the boards into the press. Make sure they are centred and then tighten the press down by turning the screw. Loosen it off again and remove the boards.

The most common problem with printing on a screw press is uneven pressure, resulting in some parts of the print being darker than others. This can be fixed by making sure the block is in the centre of the press. Using a piece of felt on top of the paper may also help to even out the pressure.

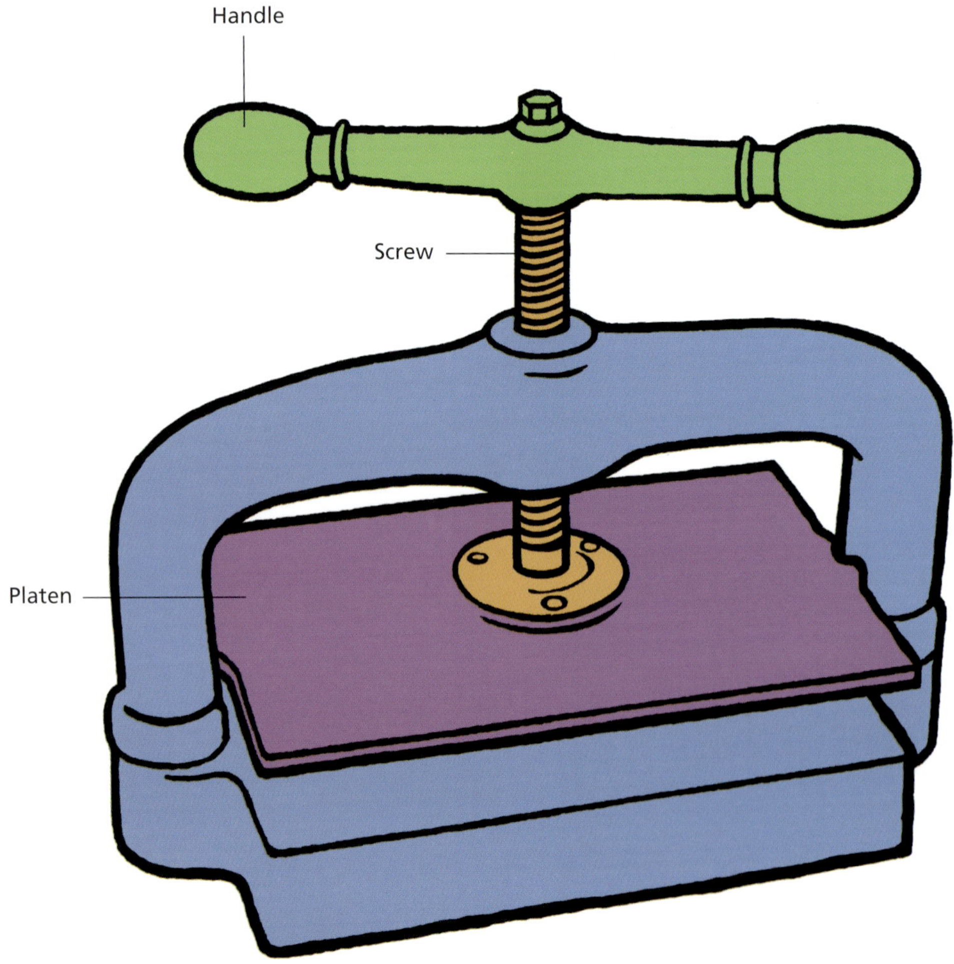

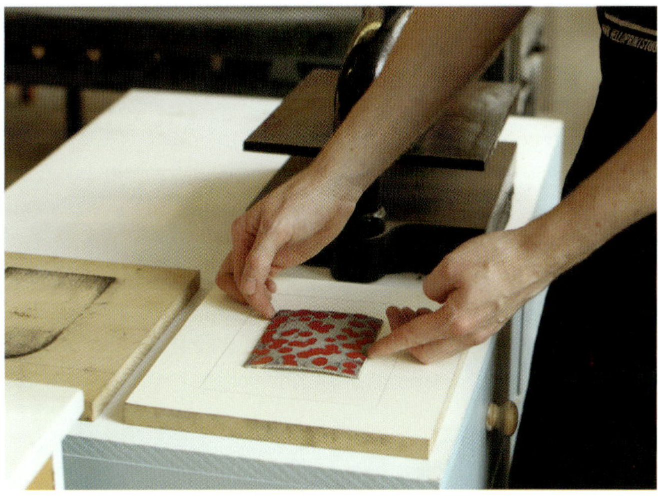

Place your lino block in the centre of one of the wood blocks.

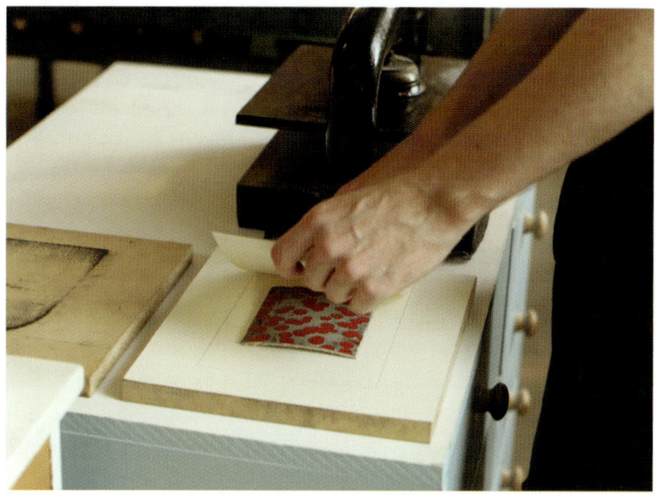

Lower the printing paper onto the block.

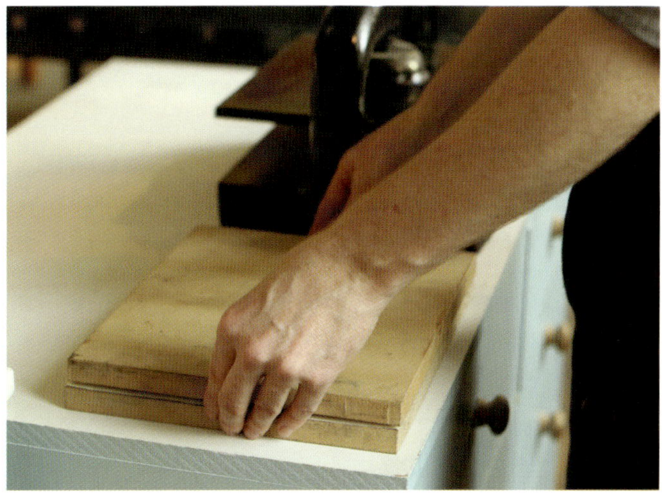

Carefully place the second block on top to make a sandwich.

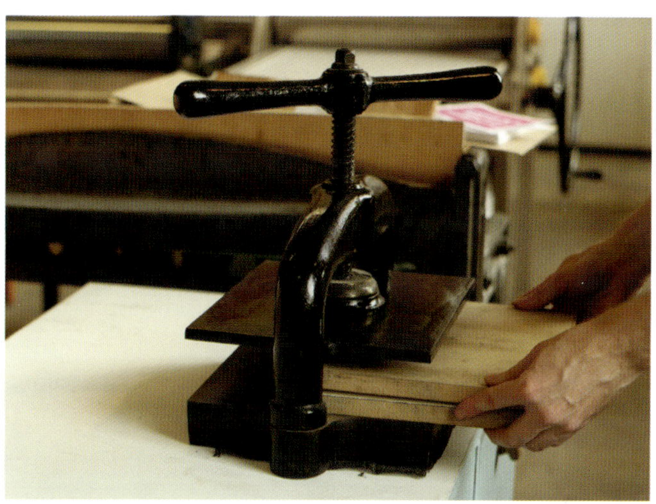

Insert the sandwich into the press.

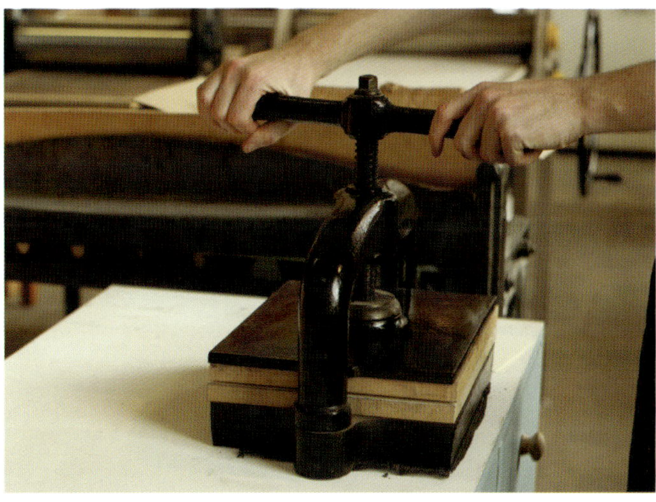

Turn the handle to screw down the platen.

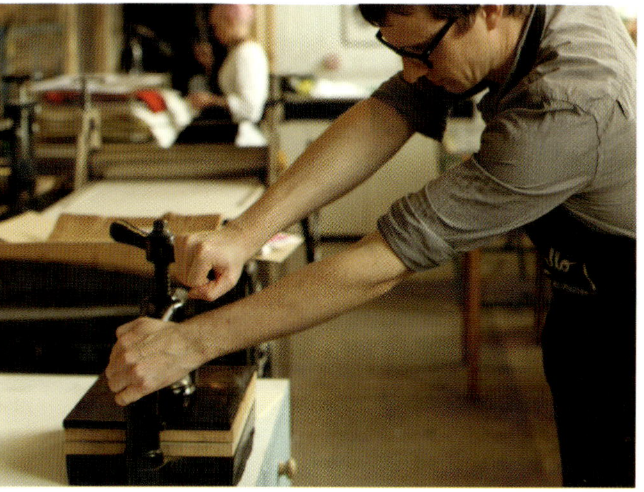

To exert more pressure, push and pull at the same time.

Printing on an etching press

Of all the presses, the etching press exerts the most pressure so it is particularly good at printing large areas of flat colour. The main problem with printing on an etching press is that both the paper and lino can get bumped and stretched on the way through. This leads to problems, particularly when trying to register larger blocks. There is also a danger of squashing delicate areas of the lino if too much pressure is used. Both these issues can be helped by using runners. These are long, narrow strips of lino laid along either side of the bed of the press. The top roller rests on them, ensuring it is held up from the bed at the correct height. The runners also connect the top and bottom roller and ensure the bed moves as the rollers turn.

To insert the runners, centre the bed of the press and raise the top roller by turning the screws on either side. It is important to turn these at the same rate to avoid uneven pressure. Insert the runners along the edges of the bed. If you find they move during printing, you can use double-sided tape to stick them down. Lower the top roller onto them, being careful not to over-tighten and squash them.

Skidding

A common problem with using an etching press is that the paper moves in relation to the block, resulting in inky skid marks. These will appear as scumbled smudges along the edge of the carved out marks. One way to eliminate these is to keep the paper from touching the block until the very last second.

Before you start, make a registration template (*See* Chapter 4). Place your paper on the registration template, making sure the template is free of ink. Use masking tape to secure the paper to the template in two places on the edge nearest the roller. Lift the paper up and rest it against the roller of the press. Place your inked up block in position on the registration template. Wind the paper and block through the press, holding the paper up until the last second.

Important note: Keep your fingers well clear of the roller as it is turning.

For very large prints you may need to lift the print as it comes out of the other side. This is easier with a helper.

Blankets

Etching plates are printed with woollen blankets on top of the plate, so many etching presses come with blankets. They are quite expensive to buy so if you want to try blankets but you are on a budget you may find a thin, dense rubber or foam blanket does the job for printing linocuts.

Whether you choose to print with blankets on the press depends on what look you're after. Blankets form a cushion between the top roller of the press and the paper. This cushioning effect pushes the paper into the carved out areas of the block, resulting in an embossed surface. This has the secondary effect of picking up any ink that may have been deposited in these areas. If you are looking for lots of texture in the carved out areas, then you should use blankets. For a cleaner print, go without.

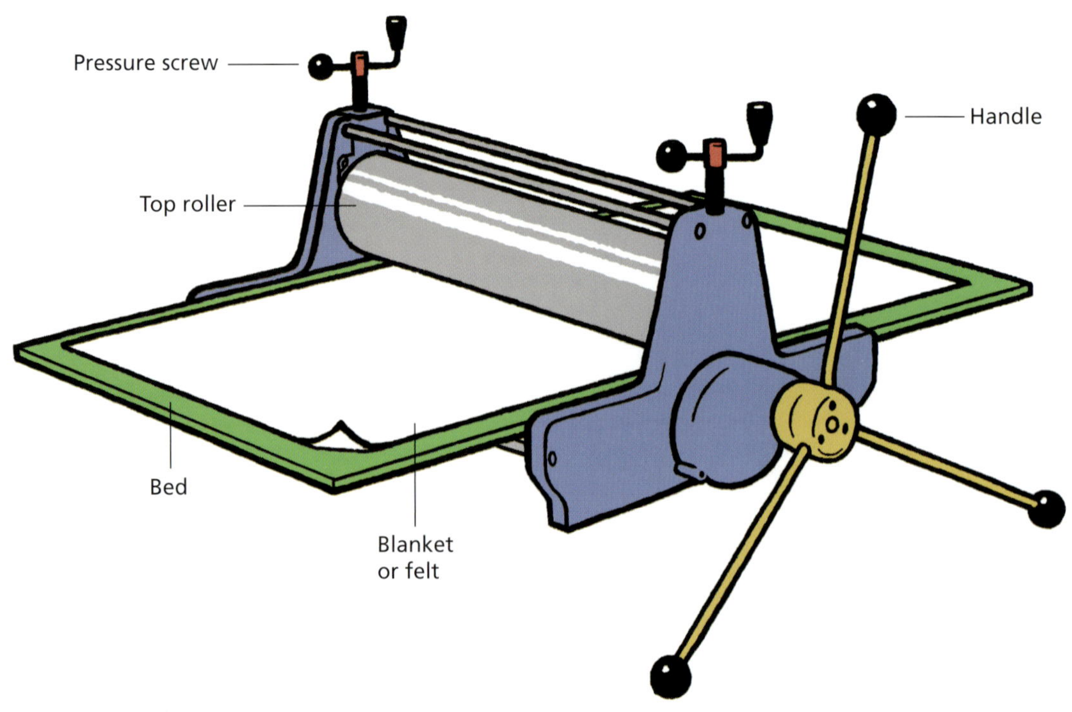

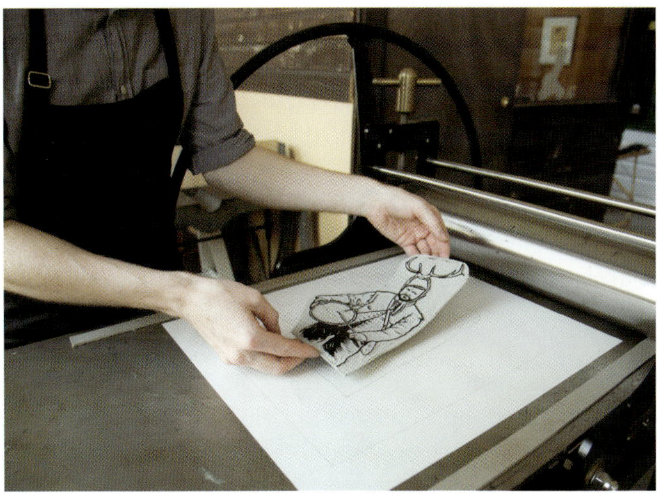

Place your block on the bed of the press. Note the runners on either side.

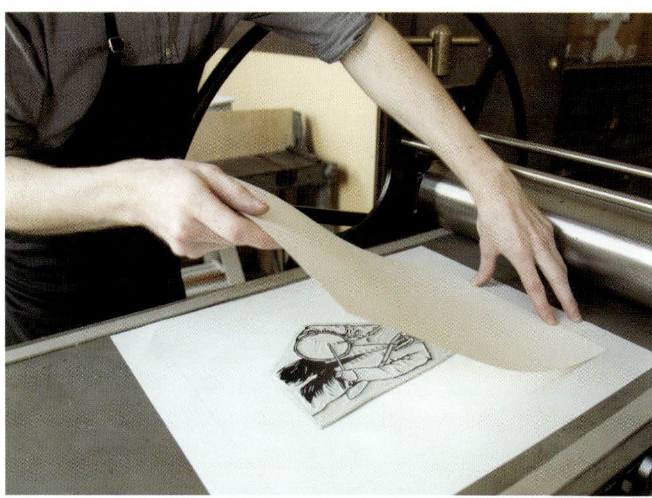

Lower your paper onto the block.

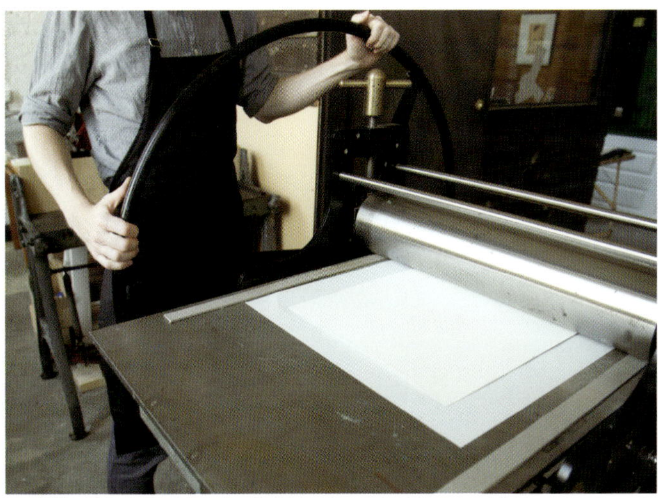

Turn the wheel of the press to move the bed.

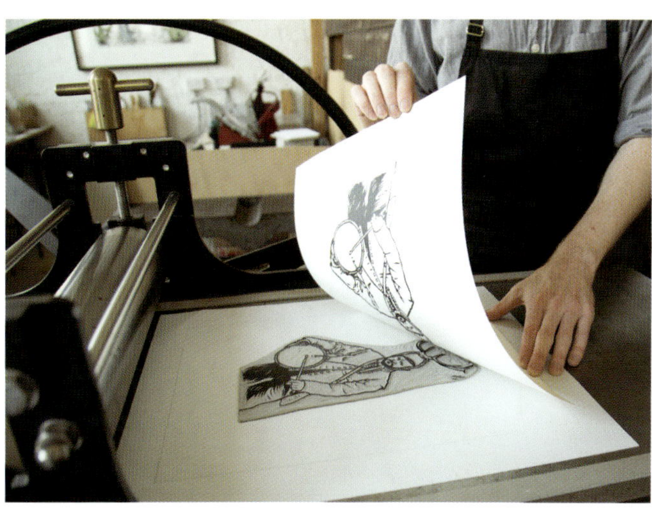

Lift the print from one end while holding down.

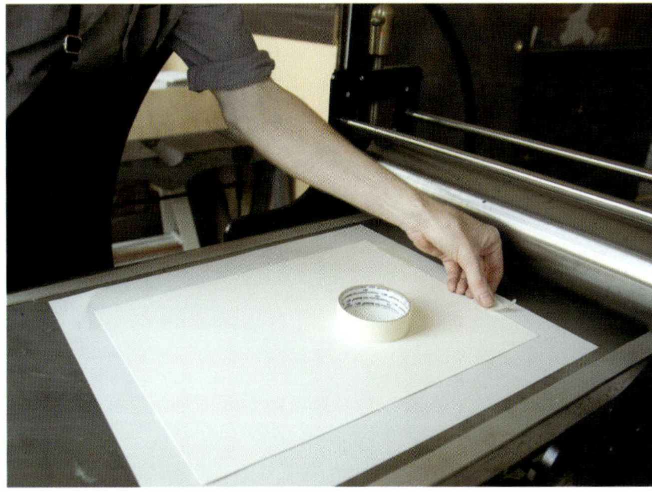

To avoid skidding, tape the paper down on the leading edge.

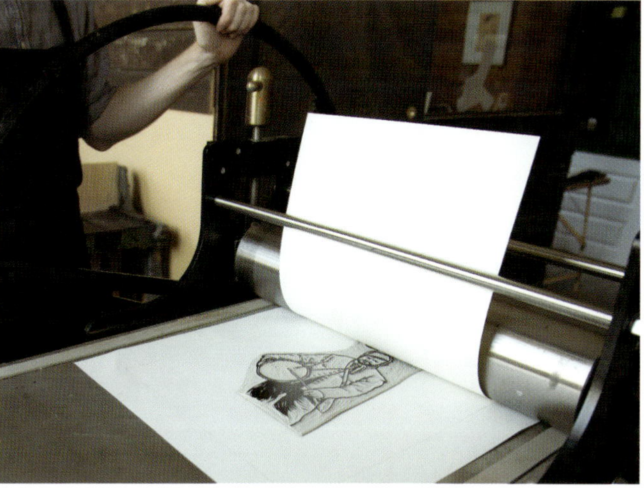

Hold the paper off the block with your hand or crossbar.

Printing on an Adana Eight-Five

Adana started making letterpress printing machines for the hobbyist market in England in 1922. Although production has now stopped, the little red machines are still widely traded on the second hand market and reconditioned machines and spare parts are available from a UK company called Caslon. Adana produced a number of models, but the most sought after, and useful, is the Adana 8-5, being named after the size of the printing area, which is 8 × 5 inches.

The Adana 8-5 is a clever machine which inks the block, re-inks the rollers and prints in one action. It is brilliant for printing small prints and greetings cards in large numbers. If set up correctly, with a bit of practice you can become a small production line. You will not achieve the precision of printing linocuts that you get with other types of press due to the way the block is inked and printed, but this is offset by the amount of fun you will have using it. You also have the option of printing small linocut blocks alongside text, using the metal type for which the Adana was designed.

There are instruction manuals for Adanas, digital versions of which are easy to find online. Here is a brief summary.

Mount the lino on a piece of wood to bring it up to type high. You can use PVA glue for a permanent mount or double-sided tape (carpet tape is ideal) for temporary adhesion.

Secure the piece of wood into the chase, making sure the lino is in the centre. Mount the ink rollers in their carriage on the machine. This is easiest to do with the handle half depressed. Place a few blobs of ink on the ink disc and press the handle down and up a few times until the disc is covered with a thin, even layer of ink. With the rollers in the lowest position, secure the chase into the machine.

Check the position of the lay gauge, gripper arm and gripper fingers (if present) to ensure they are correctly positioned and do not touch the printing area. Place a piece of paper in position on the laygauge and press the handle down as far as it will go. If the pressure is correct there should be a little resistance at the bottom, followed by a satisfying clunk.

Check the print and adjust the pressure accordingly using the four impression screws or by adding a sheet or two of paper behind the printing paper. You will need to add more ink every now and then, depending on how much ink each print uses up.

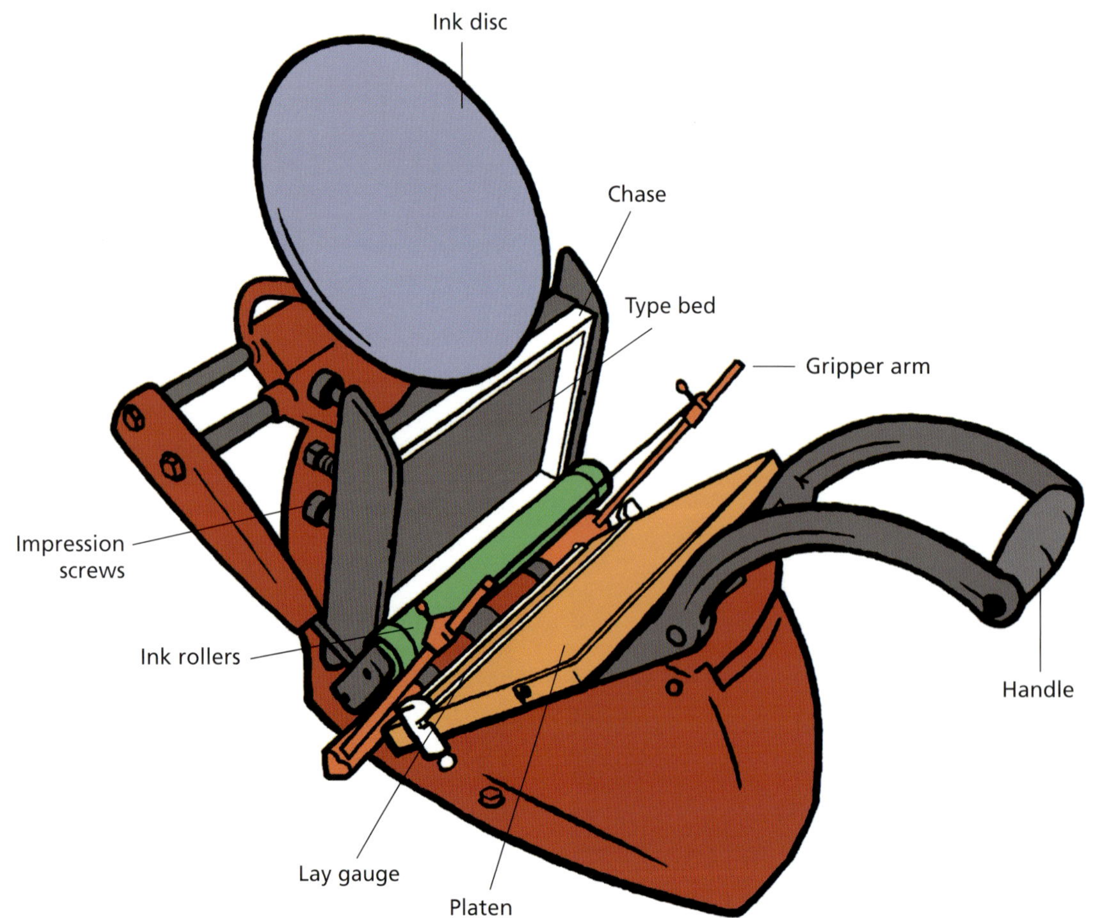

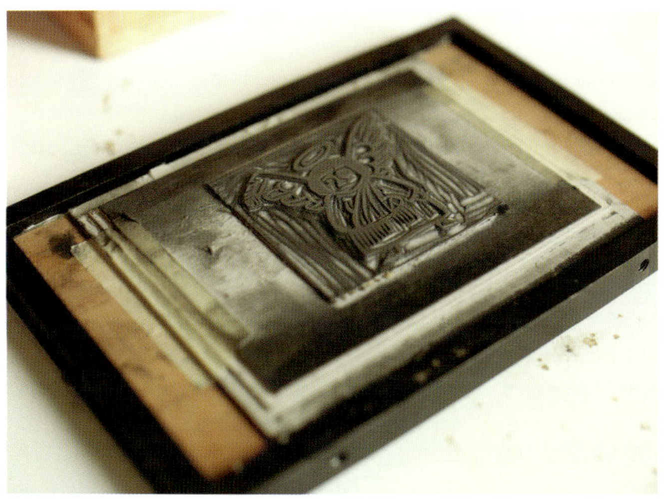

The lino block is mounted on a piece of wood which is held in the chase.

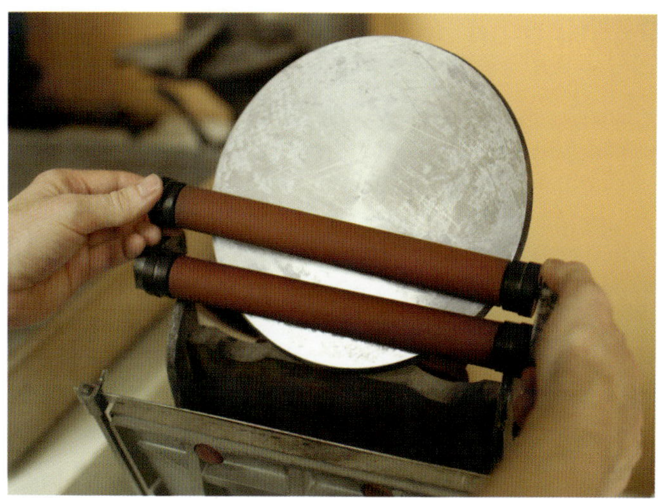

Depress the handle half way and mount the two ink rollers in their carriage.

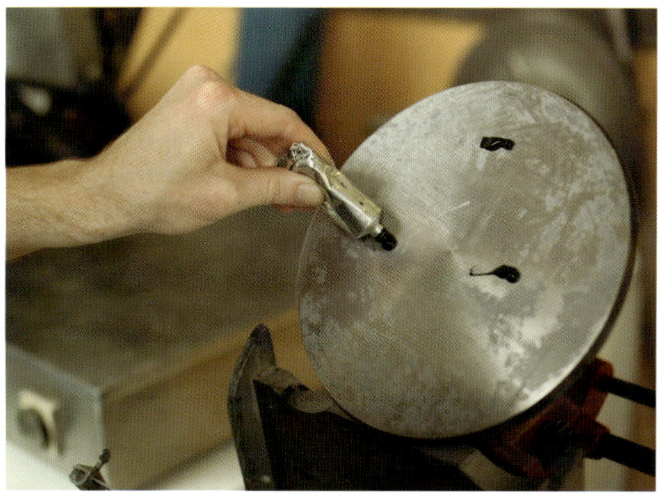

Place some ink on the ink disc and pump the handle until it is covered in an even layer.

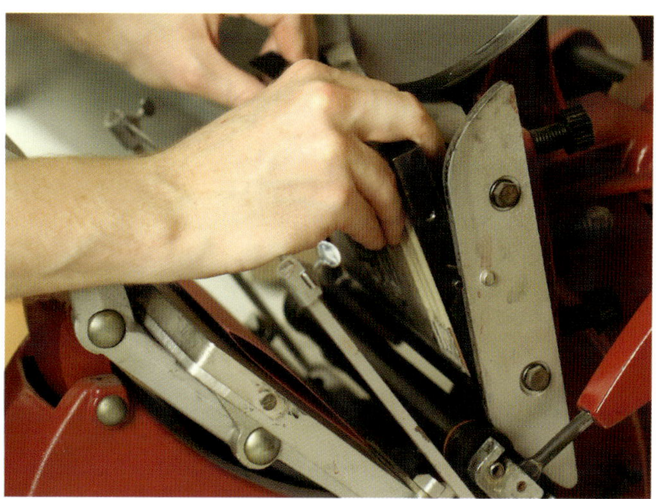

With the rollers at the bottom, mount the chase in position.

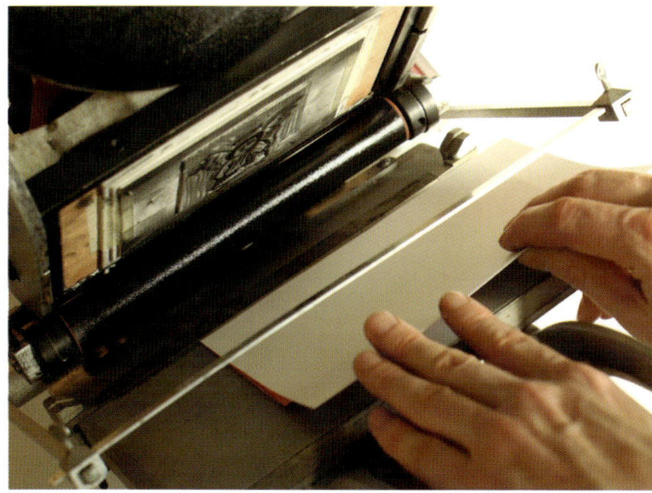

Place a piece of paper on the lay gauge, ready for printing.

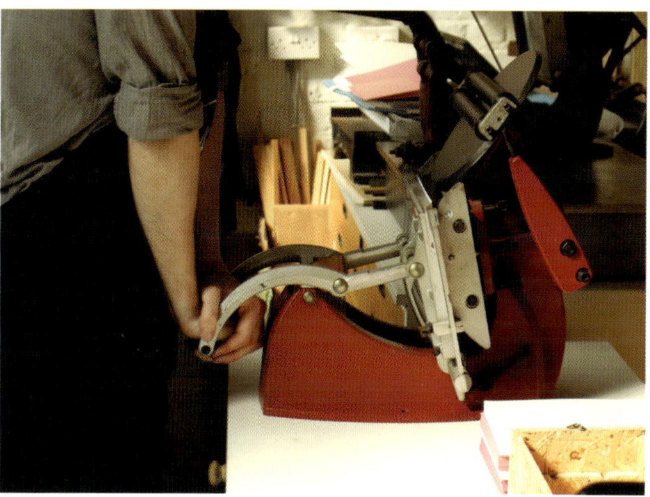

Fully depress the handle. You should feel some resistance followed by a satifying clunk.

Printing on an Albion

Printing on one of these big, heavy cast iron presses is a joy. When printing large blocks you do have to exert a fair bit of pull on the bar and winding the bed in and out each time is akin to a workout at the gym. Making sure all the parts are well oiled will make it easier.

The bed of the press is designed for printing type so is too deep for unmounted linocut. You will need to rest the lino on a sheet of wood to bring it up to height. Use extra sheets of heavy card or plywood to bring it to exactly the right height. Mounted lino may be the right height or may need a sheet or two of card underneath.

The printing pressure is adjusted by means of sheets of thin paper known as packing. These can be newspaper, newsprint or thin cartridge paper. The packing is traditionally inserted into the tympan where it is held in place between two sheets. It can also be placed on top of the printing paper before the tympan is lowered.

Place your inked block in the centre of the bed and the printing paper on top, followed by any packing. Lower the tympan and wind the bed into the press until it rests centrally under the platen.

With your feet firmly on the ground, pull the bar towards you in a rowing motion. When the pressure is set correctly you will feel some resistance when pulling the bar across. You should be able to pull it all the way until you feel the stopper. If not, you have too much packing. Release the handle gently.

Wind the bed out all the way and lift the tympan up. Place the inked block face up in the centre of the bed, followed by the printing paper and packing. Lower the tympan and wind the bed back under the platen. The platen should sit squarely over the tympan. Make sure it's centred and not sitting over the metal edge. Pull the bar all the way towards you with two arms and hold it for a second before gently releasing. Do not let go as you release it or you risk damaging the press. Wind the bed out again and lift the tympan followed by the packing and then the printing paper.

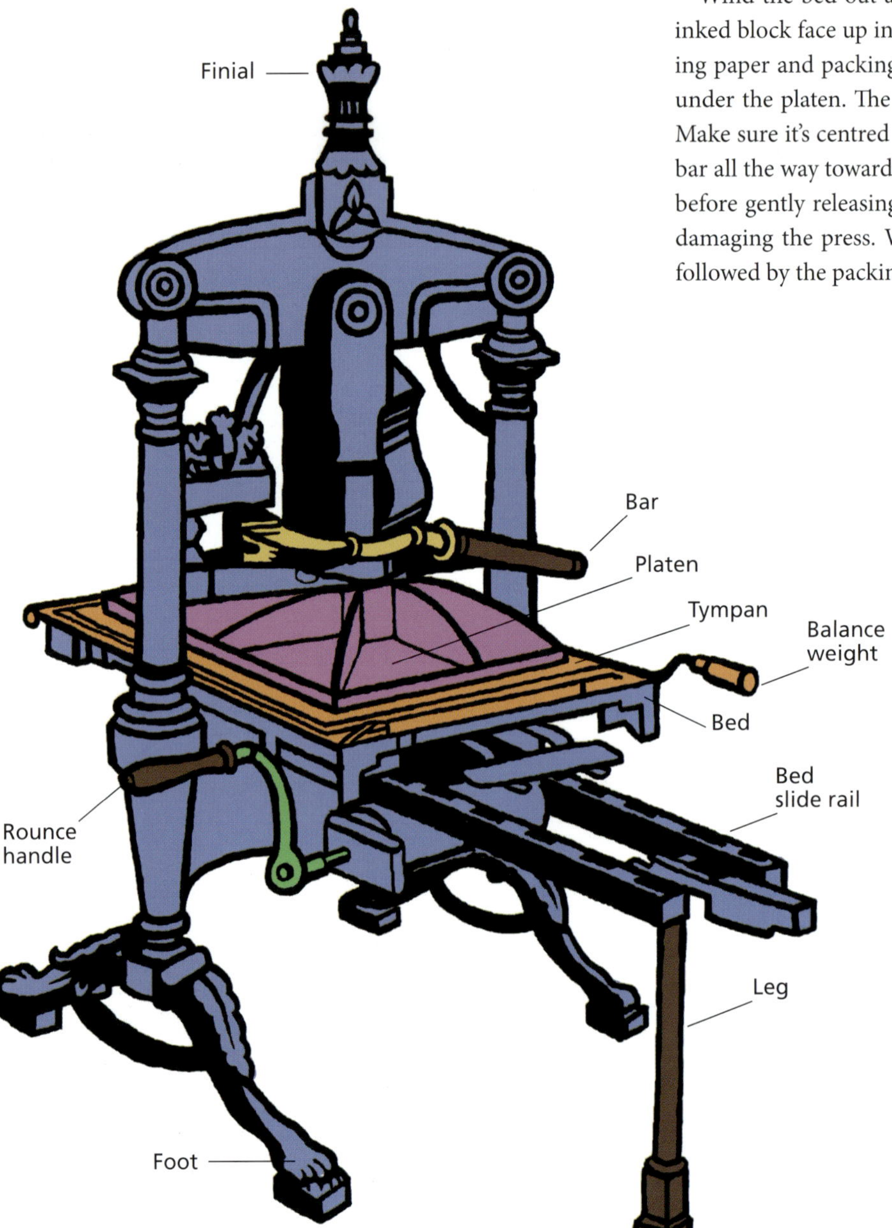

The Albion press on the right is the only one in production today and is made by Harry F. Rochat in London. The design is based on an 1854 Ulmer & Sons press but is cast from a stronger metal alloy rather than cast iron.

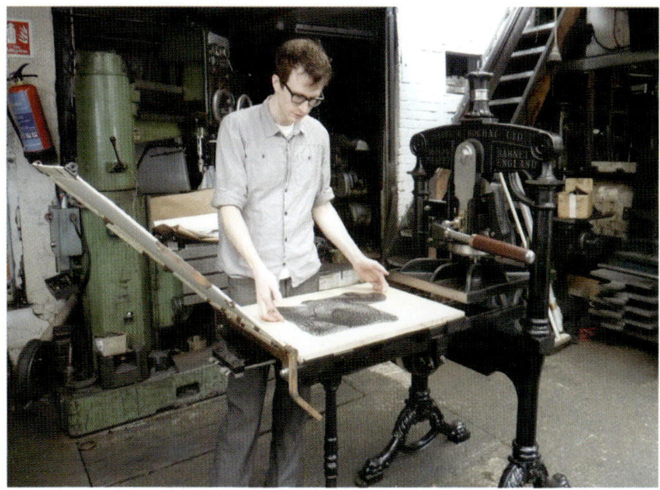

Place the lino face up on the bed of the press.

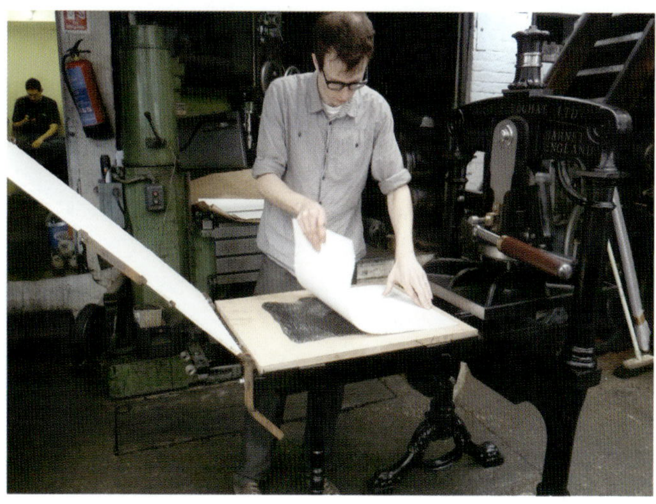

Place the paper face down and lower the tympan.

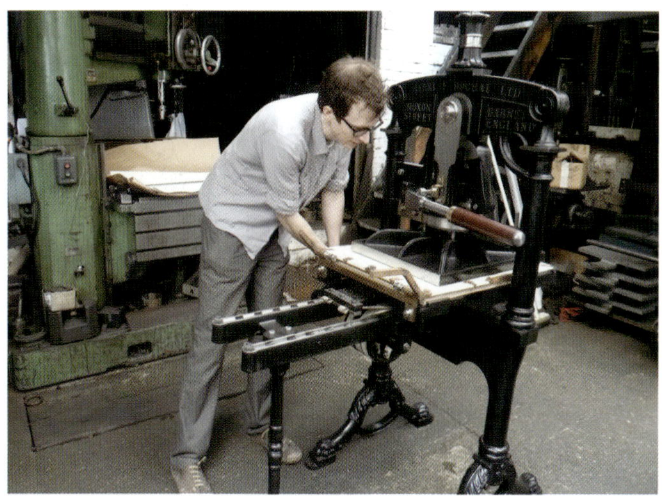

Wind the bed in, to sit under the platen.

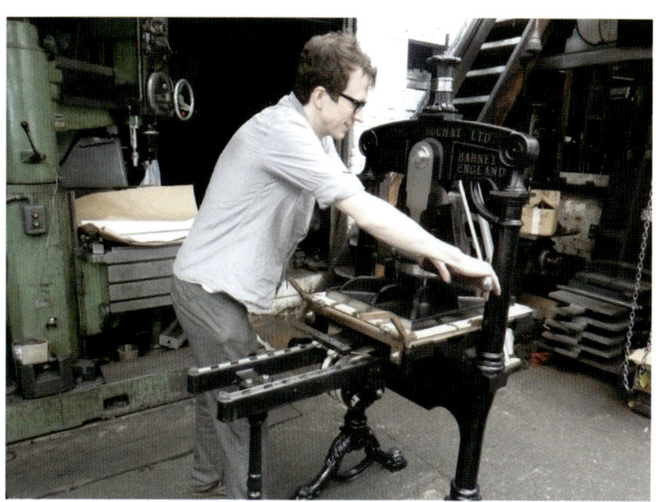

Pull the bar towards you.

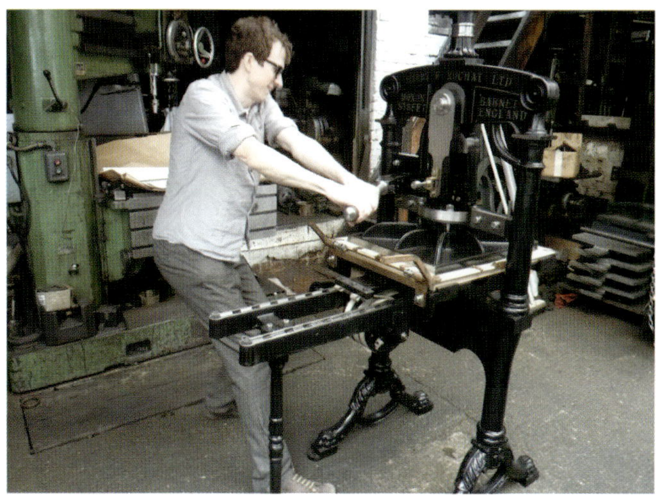

Hold the bar for a second and release gently.

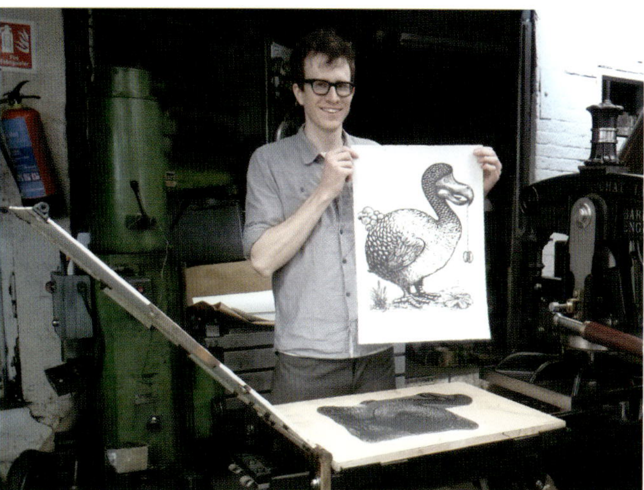

Wind the bed out all the way and lift the tympan.

Sonia Romero (USA)

www.soniaromero.net

Sonia Romero is a fine artist and public artist based in Los Angeles. She shows her work in galleries and museums and produces large scale permanent public artworks in Los Angeles and beyond.

I have always been a painter, but in college at Rhode Island School of Design, I deviated from that path and decided to major in printmaking. In college I was a fan of lithography, but I found that linocut was a much more manageable and versatile medium. I like the graphic quality of linocut and I can pair it with a variety of other processes.

Although I tried linocut in school, I did not understand its potential until I did an internship with Artemio Rodriguez at Self-Help Graphics in Los Angeles. While I was working with him I created *The Challenging Work of Alphabetical Transportation*, a pictorial linocut artist book which took me a year to complete. I started with letter A, and by the time I got to Z, I had mastered the medium.

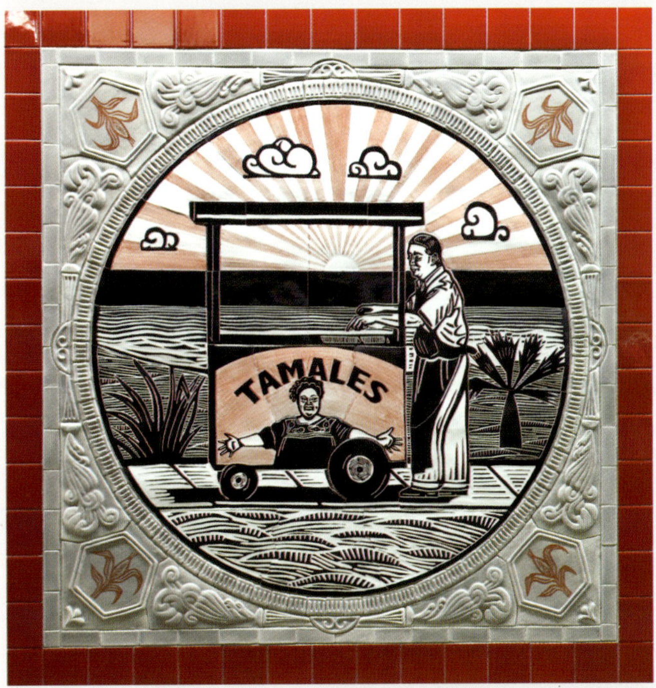

Macarthur Park, Urban Oasis, Sonia Romero
4 x 4 ft, porcelain tile mural (detail)
MacArthur Park Metro Station, Los Angeles.

I am also a fan of painting, mono printing, collographs, paper cut, and most recently I have delved into tile making. I produce large scale public art projects in a variety of materials, such as ceramic, steel, and powder coated aluminum. I also frequently incorporate linoleum prints into my paintings, printing on Japanese washi and applying with a collage technique.

In 2006, I designed a 13 vignette mural for the Los Angeles Metro using the linocut technique. My prints were translated into hand-carved porcelain tiles, which exactly mimicked the linocut feel. Each vignette is 4 × 4ft and the entire piece was installed in 2010. I have also participated in the San Francisco Center for the Book steamroller fundraiser. They invite artists to carve 4 × 4ft pieces of linoleum, which are then publicly printed on the street by a steamroller.

I work in a warehouse/studio space, where I have a medium-sized etching press. For seven years I had a space at the Avenue 50 Studio, which is an art complex with a gallery and two other artist spaces. Recently, however, I moved into a new, larger, space that I am sharing with my father and a ceramic artist, where I intend to expand my public art business.

I buy linoleum in bulk from a flooring company. It comes in a 6ft roll, and is like the battleship linoleum they sell at the art store. I also use the speedy cut material from Speedball quite often to make stamps. For carving I use Speedball linocut tools, numbers 1, 2, 3 and 5.

I draw directly on linoleum with pencil. Occasionally I use photo reference, depending on the project. I develop the bulk of the design during the drawing phase; however, I allow the creation of the lines to evolve as I carve. The act of carving is where the artwork takes place.

I use a Takach etching press, although I was trained on a letterpress proof press. I am a fan of ghost printing, or double printing an image to achieve a half inked tone, and then combining the ghost print with a fully inked image. I've used Daniel Smith oil-based relief ink for years, but they recently discontinued the line. I've been experimenting with Akua Intaglio lately, which is water-based.

> *My best work happens when I turn off all electronic media and am completely focused on the task at hand.*

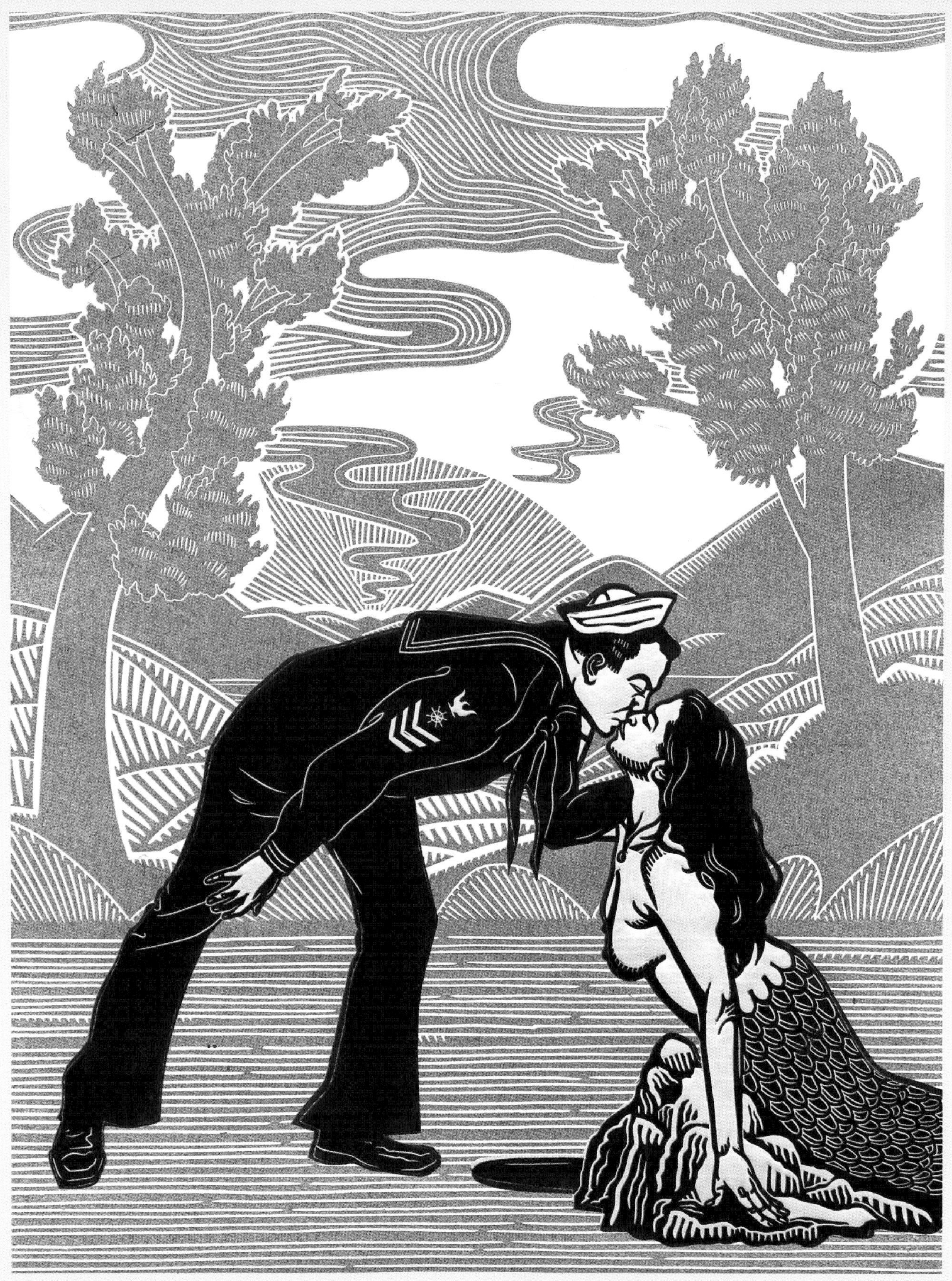

Sailor and Mermaid, Sonia Romero, 13.5 x 17.5 in, Linocut on paper.

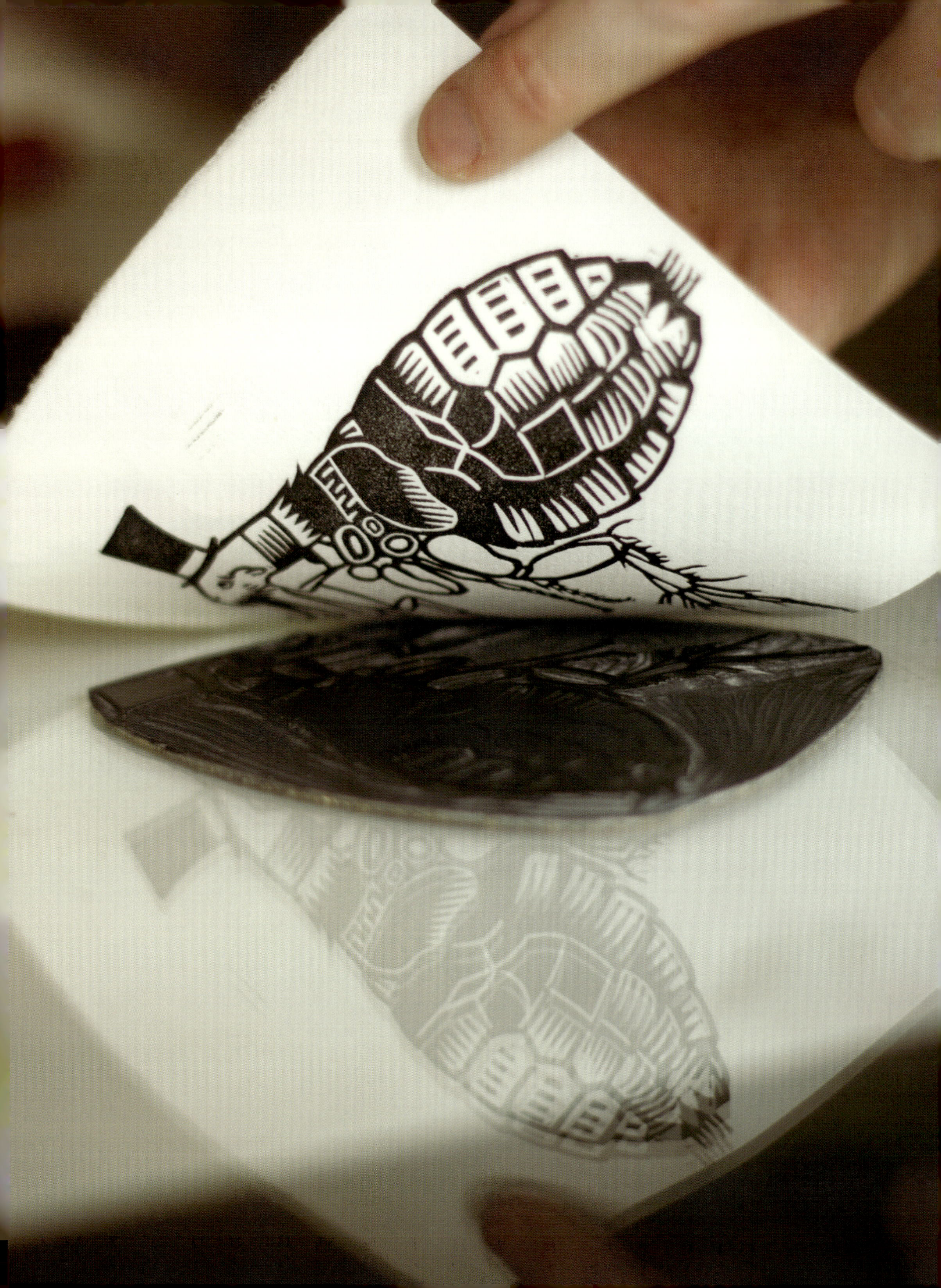

CHAPTER 4

BLACK AND WHITE

By now you should have an understanding of how to carve and print a simple linocut, by hand and on a press. This chapter will take you onto the next step, showing you how to design, print and carve an image of your choosing. You will also learn about transferring an image to the block, and registration, the technique for lining up print and paper accurately. The last sections explore carving and printing in more depth, helping you to expand your repertoire of marks and gain a greater control over the end result through controlling ink and pressure. You will find your own way of working, of course, but much can be learned from looking at the prints of other artists and a selection is reproduced alongside the text for you to take inspiration from.

Seeing in black and white

The world does not exist in black and white, so when you represent it through a monochrome linocut a lot of design decisions have to be made. This involves simplifying visual information: turning complex three-dimensional objects into simple two dimensional shapes and subtle shades of colour into black and white lines and dots. There are a hundred and one ways to interpret a view and over time you will develop your own visual language to do this. If you are new to linocut there are some simple projects to help you get started.

Drawing

There is nothing better than drawing for training the eye to look in a particular way. Line drawing, using a pen or pencil, is great for outlines of shapes and fine detail but translating a purely linear design into linocut is fiddly and time-consuming and doesn't exploit the medium to its full potential. Using drawing materials like charcoal and indian ink will allow you to quickly fill in large areas of tone. These can then be worked into using an eraser or white paint. By working from dark to light as well as light to dark you will train your eyes and brain to better understand tone which will help when you come to design an image for linocut. Try making a white on black drawing. Use white ink, paint or a correction pen on black paper. Go over any mistakes in black ink.

Tonal drawing

Make an observational drawing using blocks of light and shade. Try to eliminate all unnecessary details and concentrate just on shapes. Areas of midtone should become either black or white. Half close your eyes to help you. Don't try to draw identifiable things; try to forget what you are looking at and just draw the tones.

Jarvis Cocker, Nick Morley. This design has a balance of lines and solid shapes.

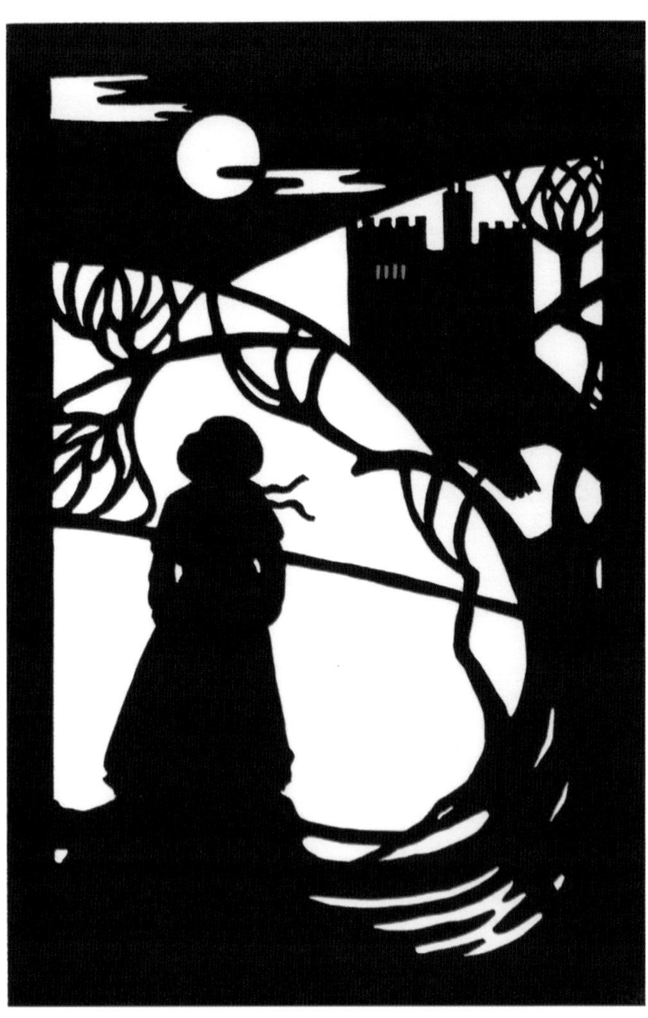

Jane Eyre, Nick Morley. This was a design for a book cover which was rejected. The brief was to produce a linocut which looked like a paper cut-out. The orange colour was added digitally.

Photography

Most digital cameras will allow you to take photos in black and white. Colour photographs can also be converted to black and white using Photoshop or similar software. There are also a number of effects which can be applied to adjust tones of an image, including brightness/contrast and levels.

Paper cut-outs

Cut a design out of a sheet of black paper or card with a craft knife. This will help you to think in a similar way to carving lino as you are removing the white areas. If you like you can trace your finished design onto a block and make a linocut.

Silhouette

Draw a silhouette of the profile of a familiar face. Notice how the line moves as you draw. Once you are happy with the outline, fill it in with black ink. This exercise is great for focusing your attention on just one line and demonstrates how much can be conveyed without extraneous information.

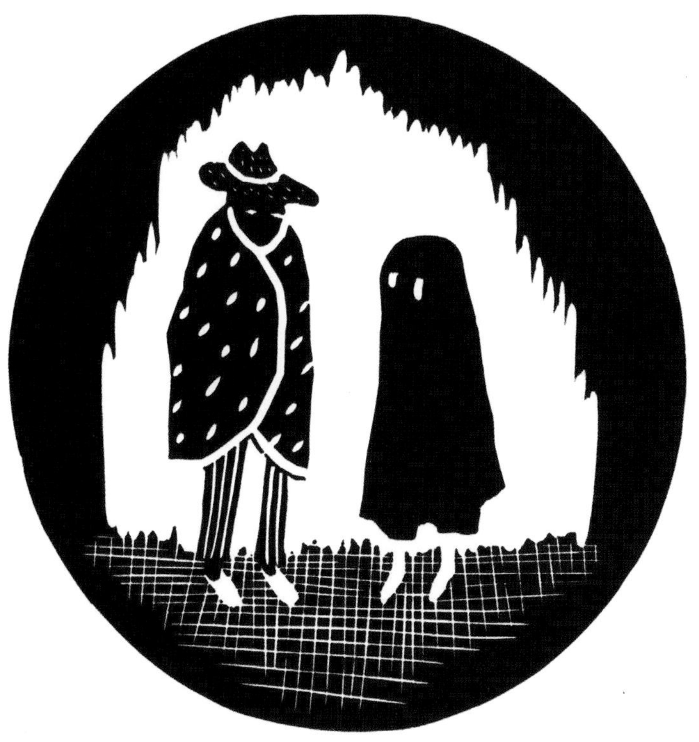

Dos Amigos, Heidi Plant. This has a very direct, innocent quality to it due to the simplicity of marks used. This belies a sophistication of design.

Making a black and white design

It is tempting, when attacking your first proper linocut, to forget about mark-making and revert to working as if drawing with a pen. It is also easy to get uptight about making something look right, or even just look like anything at all. Try not to control everything too closely, but continue to experiment with mark-making and using a variety of tools. This will give your prints more richness and variety. Just as a good musician varies the tone, volume and length of notes, a good linocutter should vary the size, shape and direction of the cut mark.

Planning your first black and white design

Your test print will have given you some ideas about what marks the tools can make but you now need to find a way to translate this into a meaningful image. It is possible to carve directly into a block without any planning. This will give a spontaneous look to your print and will allow you to work freely and respond to the feel of the tools as you carve. However, if you want more control over the end result you need to plan your design before you start carving. Your design can be drawn by hand, created on a computer or taken from a photograph. You may choose to create a fully finished design before you start carving. To start with it is better to allow the design to develop as you carve. Leaving areas of the design unfinished until you carve them will allow for some spontaneity.

Drawing directly onto the block

Your design can be drawn directly onto the block using a pencil, pen or brush and ink. Bear in mind that the image will be reversed when you print it. If you want the design to remain visible on the block after printing and cleaning it should be drawn with permanent ink. Beware that some permanent markers will transfer onto the print. Pigment-based permanent ink is best. Drawing with pencil has the benefit of being erasable so you might want to get the design right in pencil first, before going over it with ink. A brush and ink, or a brushpen, will allow you to make a variety of marks, including tapered lines. It also gives you the option of blacking in entire areas of the block. This is especially useful if you find you are becoming confused about which areas to carve away. Simply colour in black all the areas you want to print and remove the rest.

Registration

Registration is the process of positioning the block in relation to the paper. In most cases you will want the block to sit square and central to the paper so that it prints with an even border. When you start making multi-block prints (see chapter 5) you will discover that accurate registration is crucial to getting good results as it dictates whether the layers line up properly. It is worth being as careful and accurate as you can when setting up your registration system, whether you are printing one or several blocks.

Note: be consistent when laying down your printing paper. Always line it up using the same corner on your template.

Paper template

Probably the simplest method of registration is to make a template drawn onto paper or acetate. The relative positions of the block and the printing paper are drawn onto the template and you use these to place each before printing.

Method

The paper for your template should be bigger than your printing paper. Take a piece of the paper you are going to print onto, draw around it neatly onto the template sheet, and remove it. Next, take your uninked lino block and place it, face up, in the centre of the shape you have just drawn (or place it off-centre if you want it to print off-centre). Use a ruler to measure if you want to be really accurate. Draw round the block to mark its position in relation to the printing paper, and remove it. You should now have two shapes, one inside the other. Each time you print, the block is placed inside the outline you have drawn for it and the printing paper is lined up with its outline. Mark the top of your template so that you can put the block and paper down the right way each time.

Foamboard template

A registration template can be made in a similar way out of foamboard. Instead of drawing around the block, cut a hole in the foamboard for the block to fit into. This technique works better for prints with a small border.

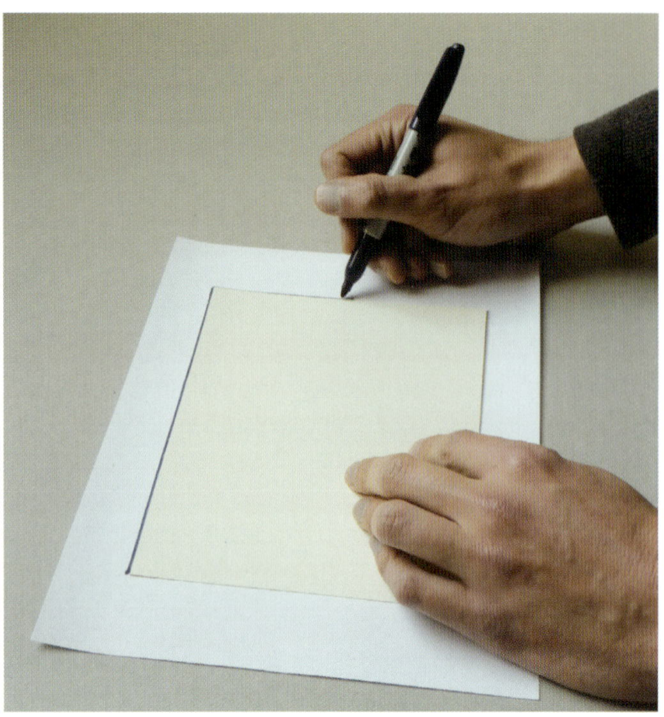

Draw round your printing paper onto the template.

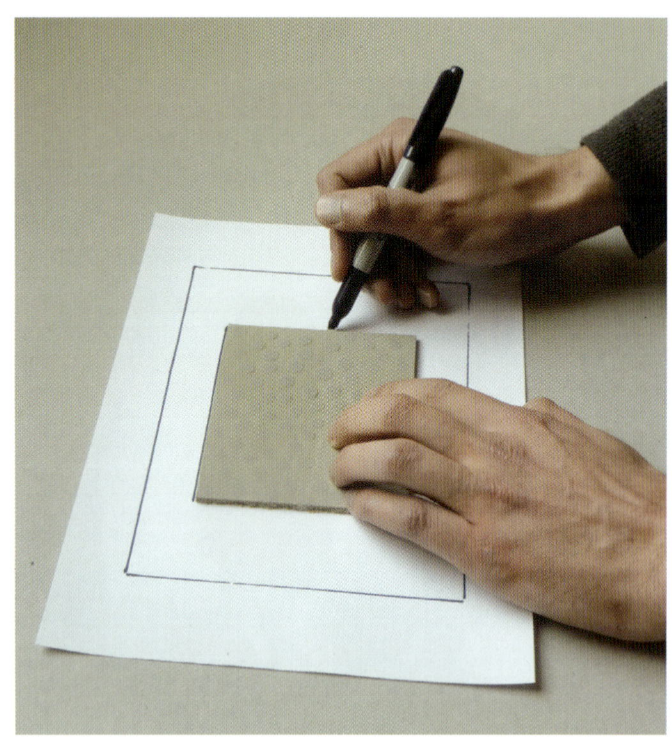

Position your block face up, then draw round it.

Project: simple black and white design

You will need: a piece of lino, pencil, marker pen, carving tools, non-slip mat, black ink, roller, ink slab, paper, wooden spoon or other tool for printing, cleaning materials.

Draw your design onto a piece of lino with pencil first. This way you can erase and adjust the design until you are happy. Next, go over the design with a permanent marker pen. This will help you avoid having any lines which are too thin and you can colour in any areas which are going to be black. Carve away the areas of lino which don't have any marker pen on them, using a non-slip mat. Ink up and print your block in the same way as you did with the test print in Chapter 2.

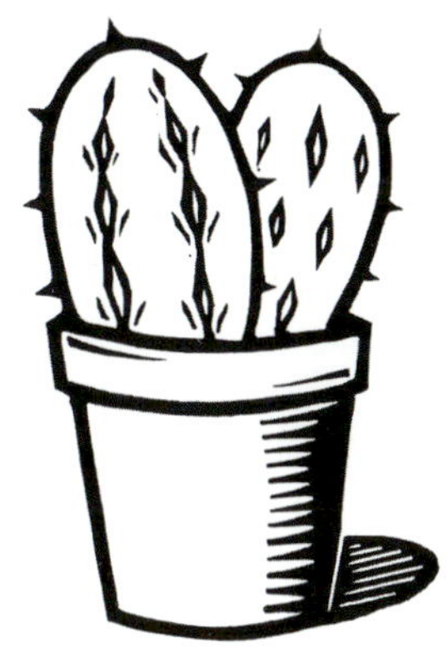

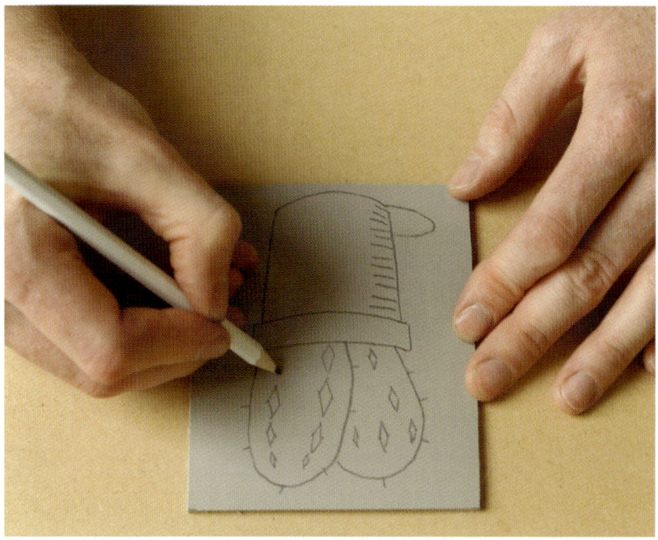

Draw your design onto the block in pencil.

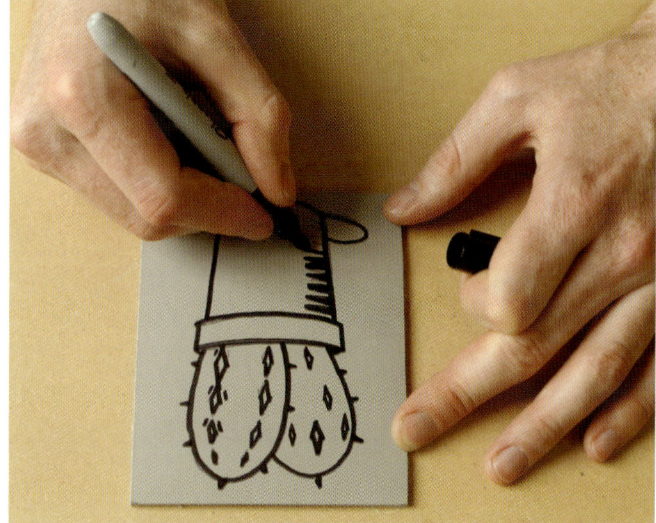

Go over the pencil with marker pen.

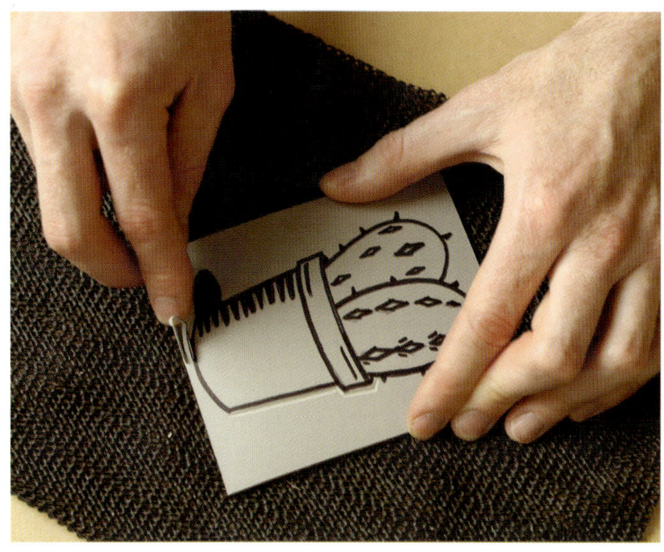

Carve away the areas which haven't been drawn on.

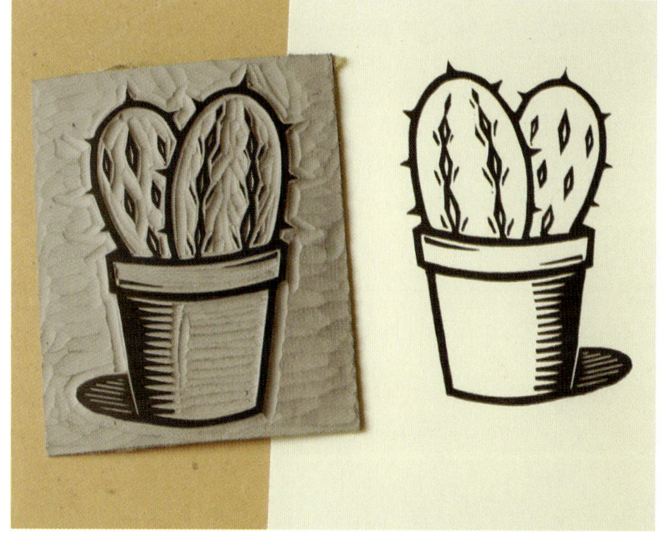

The finished block and print. Note the image is reversed.

Project: white lines

A simple design of a carved white line on a solid background of colour can be very effective. If you use one tool and carve a continuous line you can create a striking image in a very short time. This is also a great way to practise controlling the tool; any variations in the width of the line will be very noticeable. Try to carve in a smooth, continuous motion without taking the tool off the lino. As you change direction, rotate the lino rather than your body. If you need to you can pause and start again where you left off.

You will need: lino, pencil or marker pen, small U-gouge, ink, roller, ink slab, paper, wooden spoon or other tool for printing, cleaning materials.

Take a piece of lino. Draw your design directly onto the lino using one continuous line. Try to be fluid and draw freely. Your drawing can be figurative or abstract. Even a scribble will look good. Starting at one end of your line, start carving with the tool and continue until you reach the other end. Ink up and print your block as before. Try printing onto different coloured papers with black ink. The colour will really stand out.

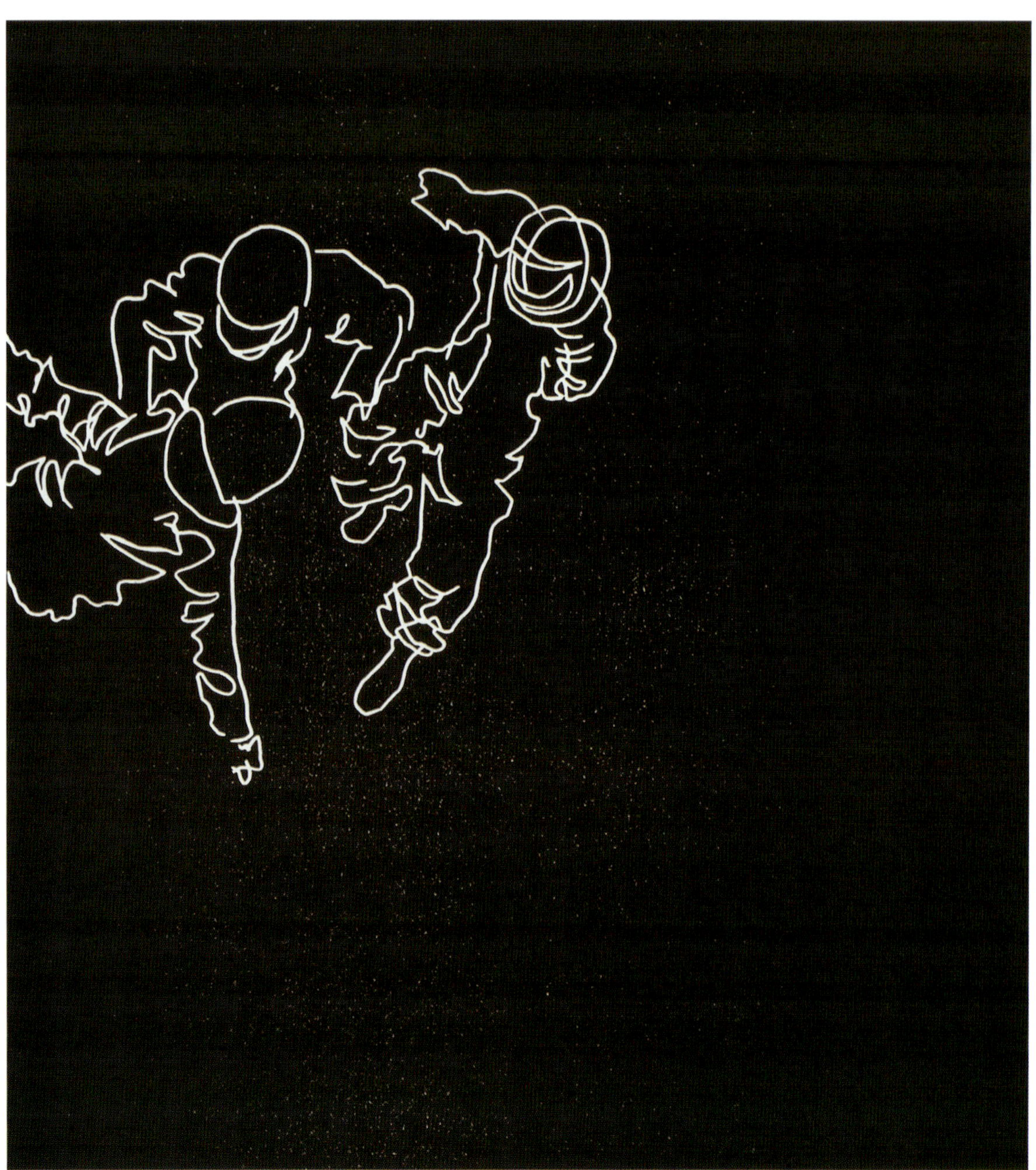

Cosmonauts, Nick Morley. A continuous line drawing was made directly onto the block. This was then carved away with a small U-gouge, leaving the background. The block was printed on an etching press with slightly less pressure than normal to give the speckled background.

Transferring an image to the block

Most of the time you want your image to come out the right way round. This is especially true if you are using text or making an image of a recognizable face or building. In this case, you can prepare your design on paper or on the screen and then flip it when you are ready to transfer it to the block. There are several ways of doing this.

Tracing

If your image isn't too complex you can trace it onto tracing paper with a soft pencil. This can then be placed drawing-side down on the block and transferred by burnishing the back of the paper with a pencil, ball-point pen or bone folder. This process reverses the drawn image onto the block.

Flipping an image in Photoshop

There are several pieces of software which allow you to reverse your image left-to-right. In Photoshop the command is called 'Flip horizontal'. You may also want to resize your image at this point. Once you are happy, print it onto paper, making sure it is printed at 100% size. You can now transfer this image to the block, safe in the knowledge that it will end up the right way round in the final print.

Carbon paper

You can use carbon paper to trace down an image onto your block. Carbon paper is coated on one side with a coloured, waxy substance. It commonly comes in blue, black and red and can be re-used several times. It is available from very old-fashioned stationers and some art suppliers. There is a red variety from Japan which is excellent and can be re-used many times. Carbon paper should be handled with care and stored in an envelope or plastic sleeve to avoid marking other surfaces.

To make a transfer, place the carbon paper on the block, carbon side down, with the paper with your design on top. It is a good idea to tape the design to the block to stop it moving. Use a hard, almost-sharp pencil or a ball-point pen to draw over the image. Check you haven't missed any areas before removing the tape. The lines you make on the block can transfer when printing so it is a good idea to remove them with an eraser before inking.

Solvent transfer method

Photocopies and laser prints can be transferred directly onto the lino using a solvent such as acetone or xylene. A blender pen, which is a pen containing solvent for blending marker pen drawings, is ideal as the solvent is more contained and easy to control. Place the print, image side down, on the lino and tape it in position. Then apply the solvent to the back of the paper. Use a pencil or bone folder to burnish the back of the paper. As you do this, the image will be transferred onto the lino. You can also run the lino through a printing press, being careful to prevent any damage to the press by placing several sheets of newsprint on top of the solvent-soaked sheet. You will need to work quickly to transfer the image before the solvent evaporates.

Health and safety

Always use solvents in a well ventilated area or outside and away from naked flames and sources of ignition. If necessary, wear a suitable mask. You should also wear plastic or rubber gloves.

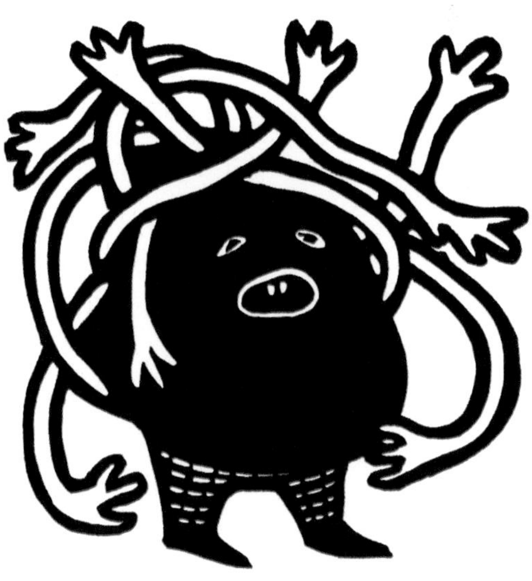

Transferring a design by tracing

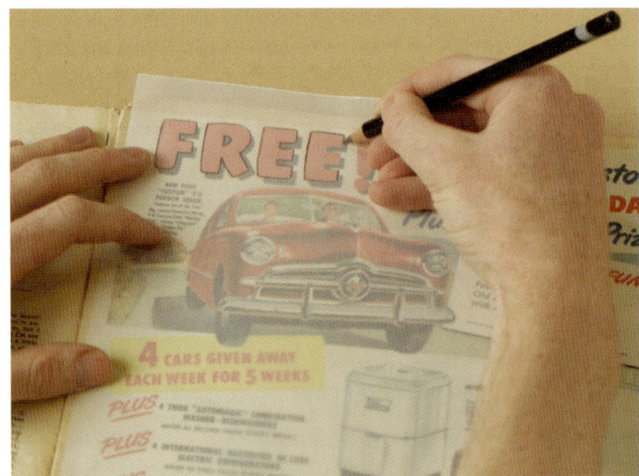

Trace around the image with a soft pencil (2B or softer).

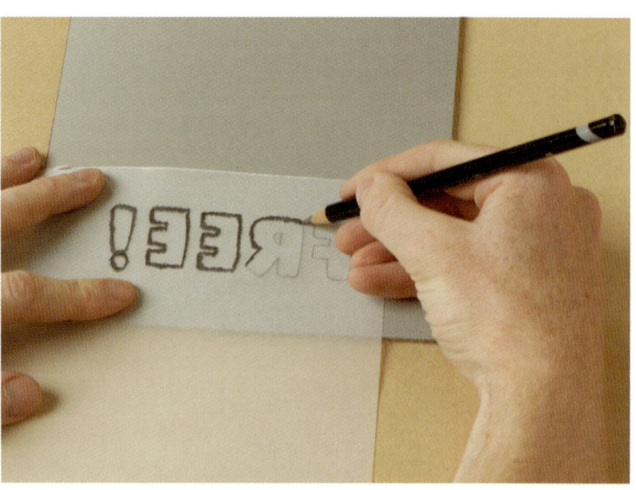

With the tracing face down on the block, scribble on the back.

Your design will now be in reverse on the block.

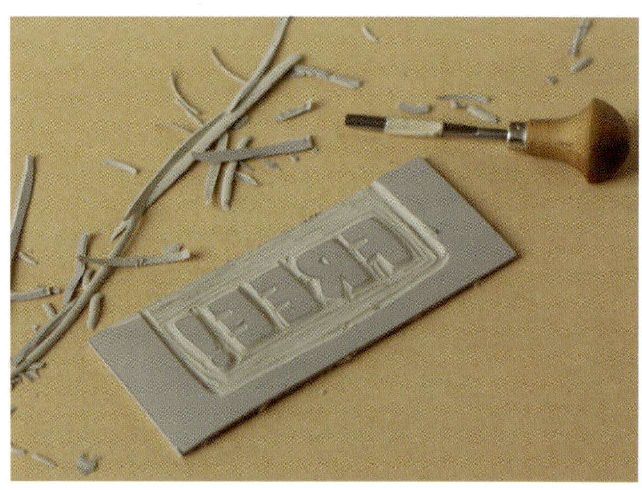

Carve around the design, leaving the area to be printed.

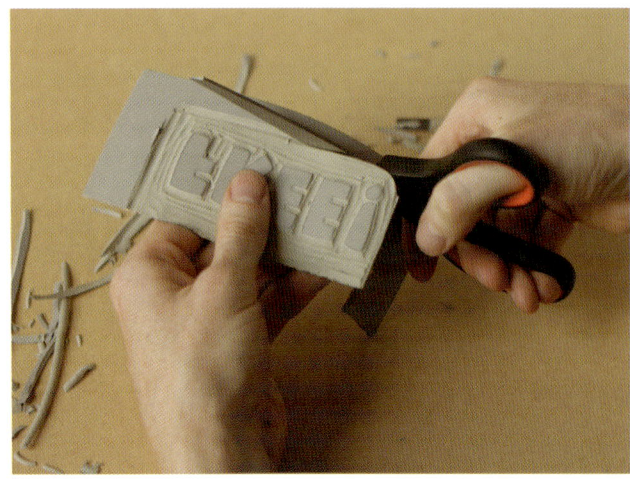

Trim any excess lino away with scissors.

When you print your block the image will be the right way round.

Transferring a design with carbon paper

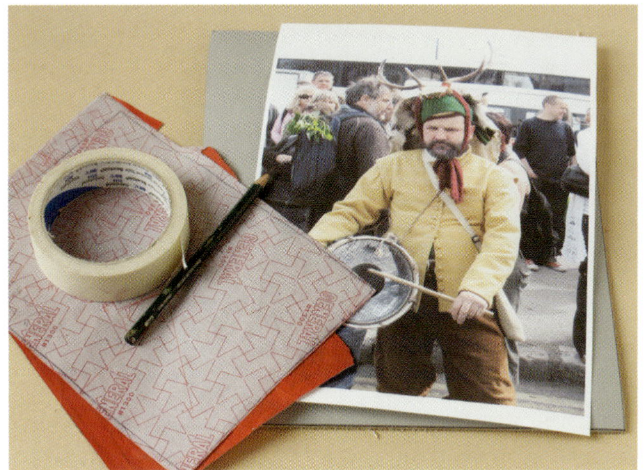

You will need carbon paper, tape, pencil, lino and your design.

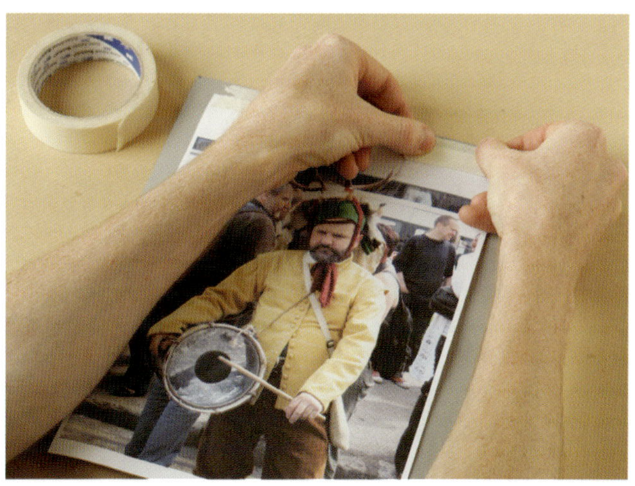

Tape the design to the block on one edge so you can lift it.

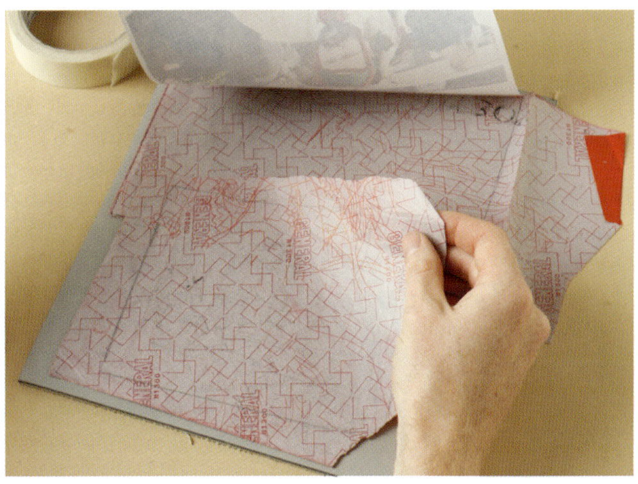

Place the carbon paper face down between the design and block.

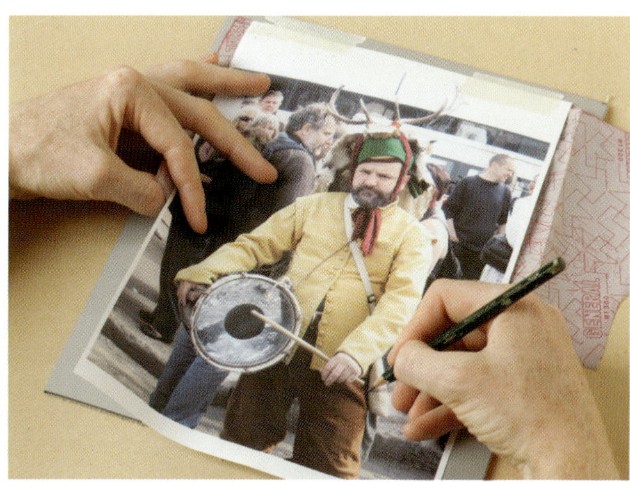

With a hard pencil or ballpoint pen trace the design onto the block.

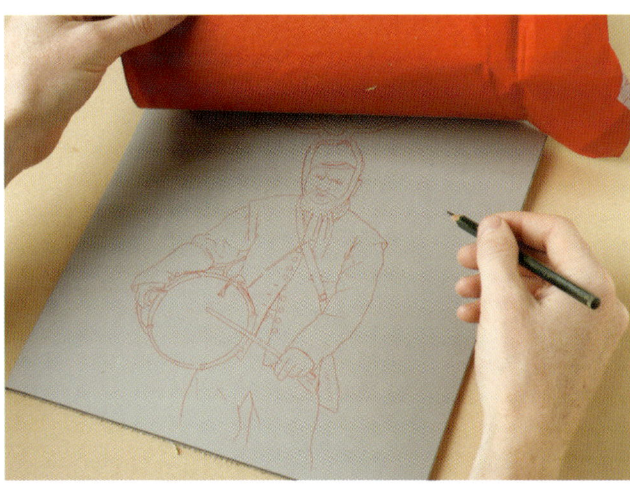

Check to make sure you haven't missed anything.

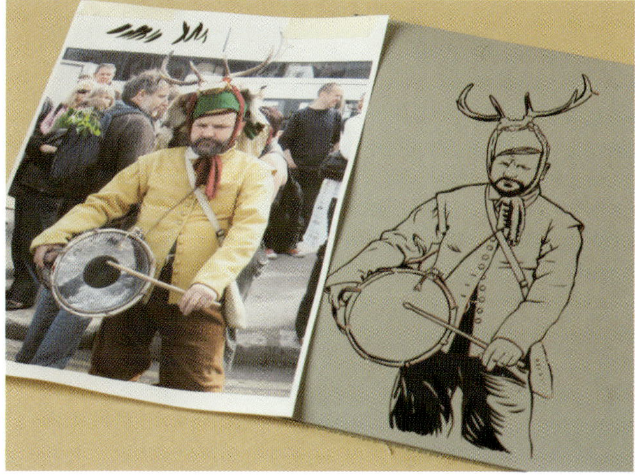

Go over the carbon tracing in pen to make it permanent.

Design considerations

Keep it simple

This can be a useful mantra, whatever you are doing, but applies especially in this case. When you are making your first linocut (hopefully of many) it is easy to underestimate the time it takes to carve a block. The simpler the design, the easier it will be to carve. As you develop your carving technique, so your designs will become more complex.

Don't feel like you have to fill the whole block with detailed information. Sometimes it is more effective to leave a large area uncarved, or carved away completely. These blank areas give the eye a rest and by contrast can impart extra energy into the 'busy' areas. A good target for the beginner to aim for is a design made up of 50% black and 50% white overall.

Black lines

With a pen it is very easy to create a black line drawing. When this becomes a linocut, however, you will quickly discover this is the most laborious kind of design to carve. You must carve carefully either side of the line and then clear away all the white areas, which may be most of the block. For this reason, most linocuts are not composed simply of black lines.

Defining edges without outlines

One of the skills of the linocutter is to stop thinking purely in terms of outlines and start using solid blocks, shapes, textures and patterns to create an image. An 'outline' or line defining where one area ends and the next begins can be simply where a block of black meets a block of white.

Direction of cut

Always consider the direction you are cutting. This applies even when clearing a large area as any ridges left behind can pick up ink and print. These marks can be removed by further carving or by wiping with a dry cloth before printing, resulting in a clean area of white. However, often these unpredictable marks can add something of value to a print and you may decide to keep all or some of them. At this point, the direction of the marks you carved will become important.

The hand of the artist

Each time you carve a line you leave your signature behind. The little wobbles and changes in direction when you are carving are a natural part of making something by hand. Over time you will gain a greater control over the marks you make but they will still contain tiny imperfections. This is what linocut is all about. Along with the slight variations in the application of ink and the printing process, the hand-carved mark is something to embrace. As you spend more time carving you will gain a feel for the action of each tool you use, and you will become familiar with how it responds to your movements and the resulting marks it makes.

Practise carving straight lines, curves and tiny dots. Try to control the speed of the cut, the depth and the direction. You will be surprised how much fine detail you can carve with a larger tool, so try making an entire image with just a large V- or a large U-gouge. As you become more confident you will worry less about slipping and making mistakes and will find it easier to make positive, decisive cuts that will come across as such when you take a print.

Mistakes

You will make mistakes. Try to embrace them. In order to progress you need to take risks. Learn from your mistakes and do not let them put you off. Very often a mistake that is glaringly obvious at the time will be unnoticeable when a print is finished.

If you make a major slip and carve away a part you didn't mean to, it is possible to use wood filler (some swear by a relatively new product called Sugru) to repair the hole, although it won't be perfect. If you have the piece which was carved out you can glue it back in with PVA glue.

Mistakes are most often made when you are tired, so make sure you take frequent breaks. You can also reduce the risk of carving away the wrong bit by carving away from the part you want to keep.

Learning from others

A great deal can be learnt from studying and copying the technique of others. Just as great musicians borrow from and are influenced by others, so artists can do the same. Luckily for printmakers there is a wealth of reproductions available, online and in books, of both contemporary and historical works. As well as studying linocuts it is worth looking at woodcuts, wood engravings and other techniques.

While looking at reproductions is useful, nothing can compare to looking at original prints. Most galleries and museums exhibit prints regularly. Some major museums also hold print collections and allow members of the public to study works by appointment. You will need to be organized and know what you are looking for as it is unlikely you will be allowed unfettered access. Ask to see specific artists or simply to see some linocuts. The staff are usually helpful and knowledgeable and don't mind being asked questions. Viewing works unframed gives you the opportunity to really get up close and view them from different angles. This will allow you to appreciate the subtleties of the print, from the thickness of the ink to the texture of the paper.

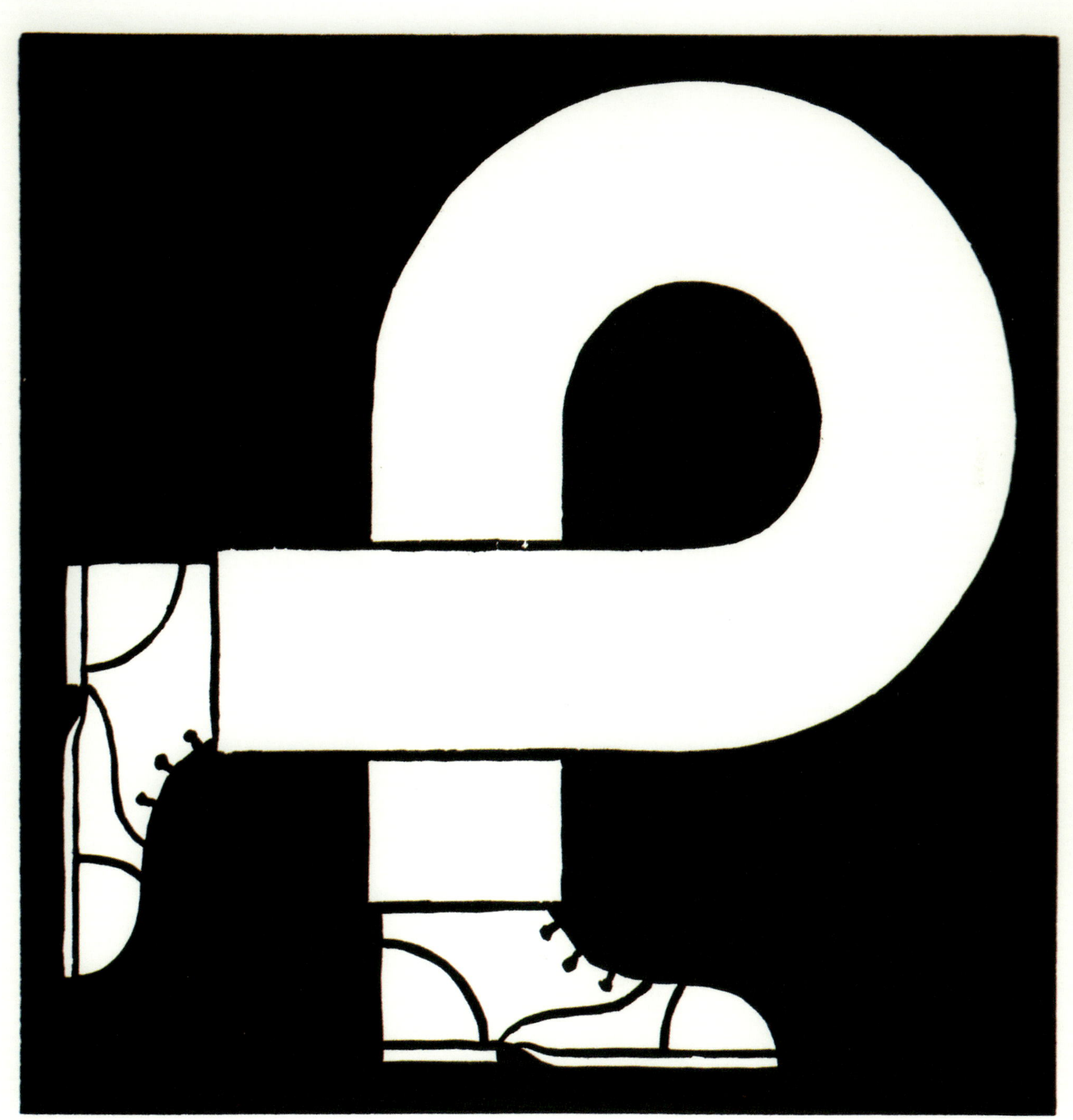

Legs, The Project Twins. A bold, simple design.
The neat perfection of the composition is saved from being too clinical by the soft carved edge.

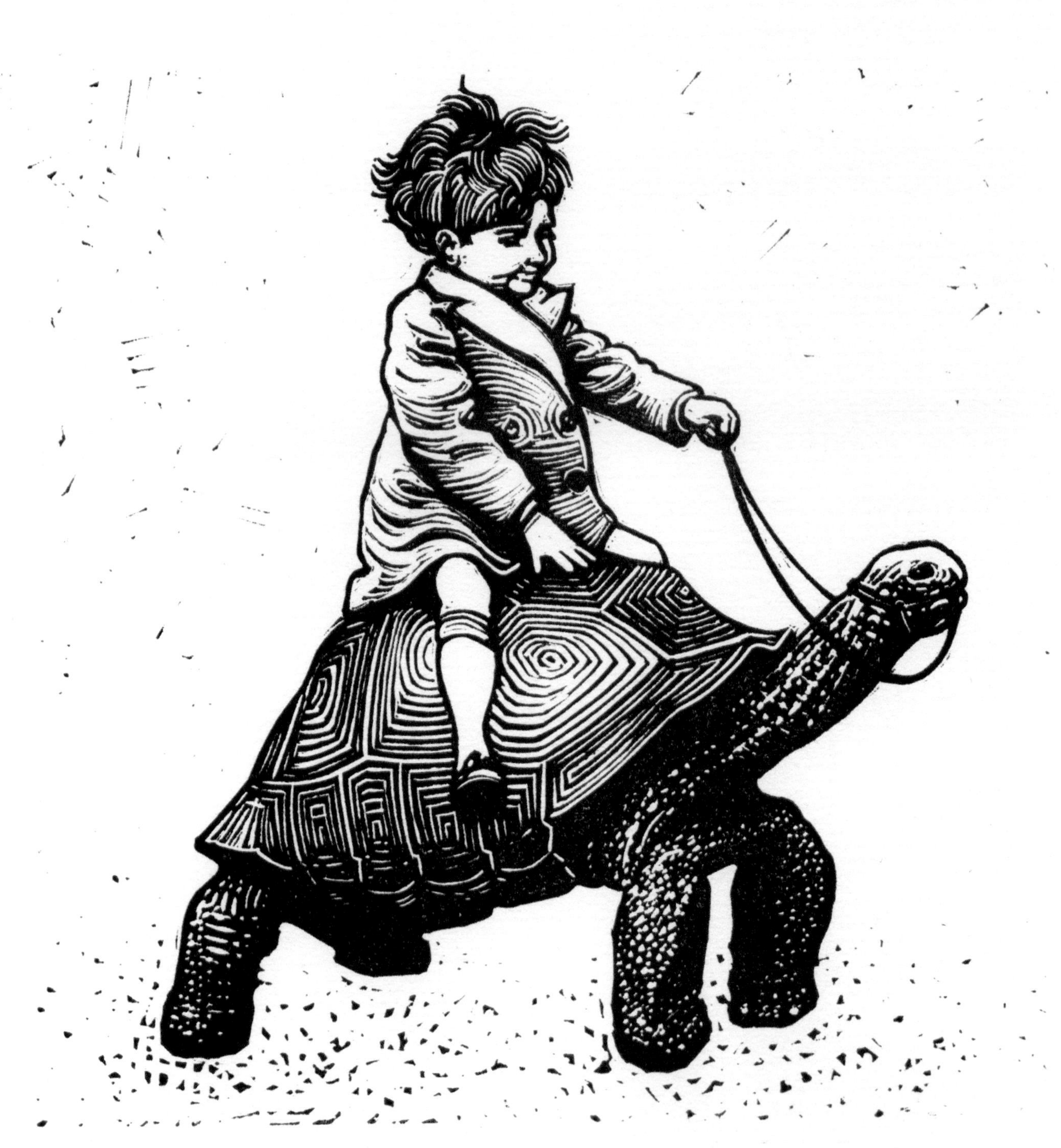

Tortoise Boy, Nick Morley.
This print was an exercise in creating different textures.
The background was carved in every direction to give the printed marks a random look.
The similar marks in the boy's hair and coat and the tortoise's shell
pull the design together.

Advanced carving techniques

Once you have mastered the basics there are some ways you can develop your carving technique. Using a variety of line, pattern, texture, blank areas and solid shapes will add interest to your linocuts. Here are a few suggestions.

Cutting around a shape

Often you will want to cut around a shape accurately. The easiest tool to use for this is a small U-gouge. Once you have traced the outline of a shape you can then switch to a larger U-gouge to clear away the section next to it, and so on. With practice you will be able to trace edges with a larger tool, which will save you time.

Cutting out corners

Again, a small U-gouge is best for this. Start in the corner and carve away from the bit you want to keep. That way, if you slip you will not remove any lino by accident. For more control, use the forefinger of your non-cutting hand to guide the tip of the tool as you carve.

Weight of line

When you draw a black line with a marker pen you will get a fairly even width of line. If you draw a line with a brush and ink you can vary the width of the line. The brush line will have much more life to it, as it gets thicker and thinner. This is called the weight of the line and it is something to consider carefully when carving a linear linocut. As you create each line by carving in two motions – once along each side – you have great control over the weight of line. Use this to your advantage as you carve by considering how strong you want the line to be. The same goes for a white line on a black background.

How to create tone through carving

Tones are the shades of a colour from light to dark. In a black and white print they are the shades of grey. You can create variations in tone through carving by using small dots, lines and other patterns of black and white marks. When viewed from a distance these will look like grey. Because each little mark is carved individually this can take a long time but it also gives you an opportunity to give certain characteristics to them: direction, size, shape, variation and spread. By harnessing these characteristics you can portray texture, pattern, smoothness, movement and even give a sense of depth and 3D.

Tapered lines

Before the arrival of photomechanical printing processes, most mass-produced images were either lithographs or engravings. Engravers were highly skilled at rendering realistic, three-dimensional looking images through lines and dots. You can get an idea of this if you look closely at a face on a banknote. Notice how the lines follow the form of the face to give it depth and how they vary in weight to create tonal variation. This is something you can try with linocut. It takes a steady hand and strong nerves as any slip will be immediately obvious. Using just a large V-gouge you should be able to control the width of line by going deeper and shallower. Remember this is done by adjusting the angle of the tool: a steeper angle will give a wider cut and a shallower angle will give a narrower cut.

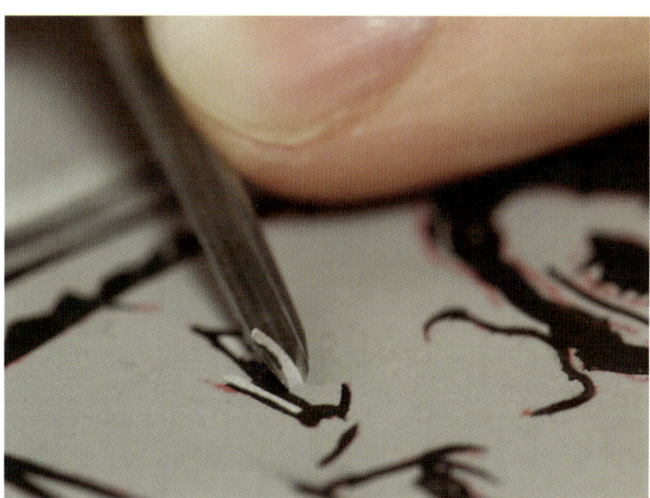

Use a small U-gouge to carve around a shape accurately.

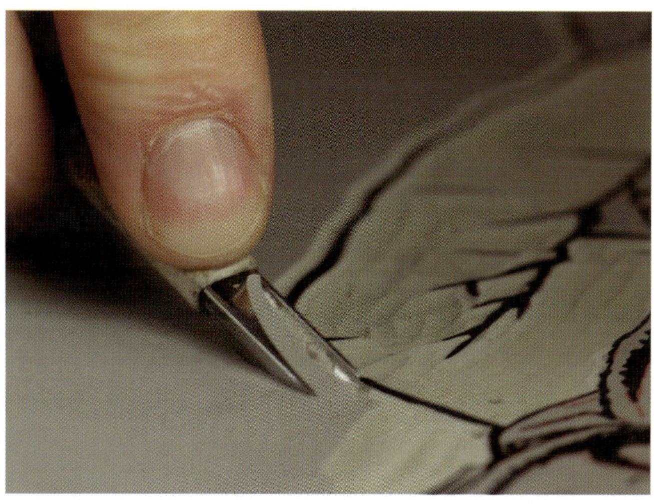

Use a larger U-gouge to clear away the adjacent area.

Project: light to dark

The illusion of a tone which goes from light to dark can be created by varying the size and spread of the marks. Try making a test print using different patterns of lines, dots and other shapes to go from black to white.

Different ways to create the illusion of a transition from light to dark using a variety of tools.

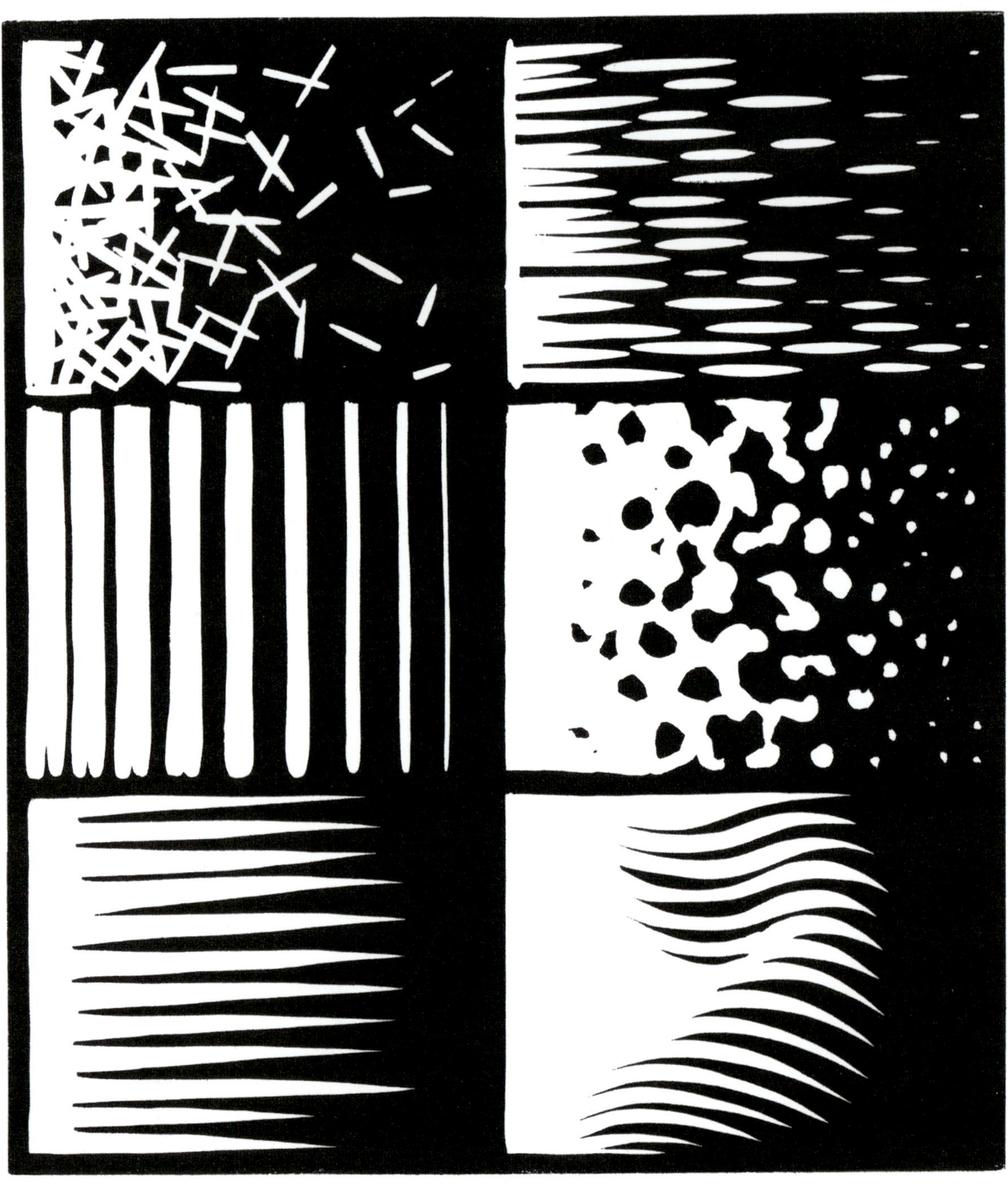

Advanced printing techniques

Adjusting ink and pressure

By printing with black ink and reducing either the printing pressure or the amount of ink on the block you can create lighter tones. If you are printing by hand more pressure can be applied to one area to darken it. If printing on a press this isn't possible but by using less ink you can achieve a similar effect. As well as lightening the tones, there will be some texture apparent in the printed areas.

Ghost printing

If you print a block a second time without re-inking it you will get a considerably lighter print, known as a ghost print. You may be able to get two or three of these per inking. This can be a useful way of printing a lighter tone in a controlled way as long as you use the same amount of pressure to remove a consistent amount of ink in the first printing. You will obviously get through more ink and paper this way.

The images over the following two pages were printed from the same block, with varying amounts of ink and pressure.

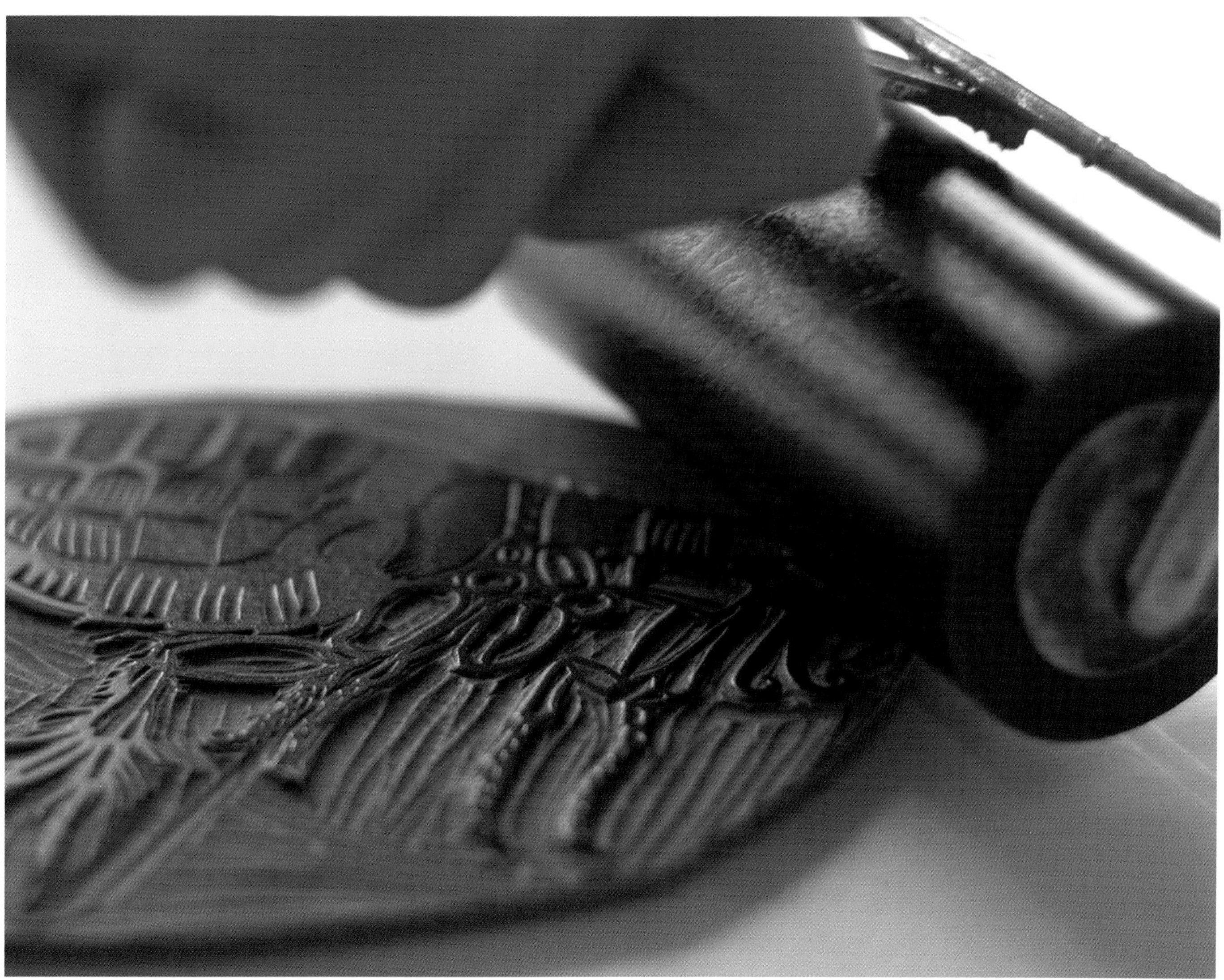

The amount of ink on the block will determine how it looks when printed.

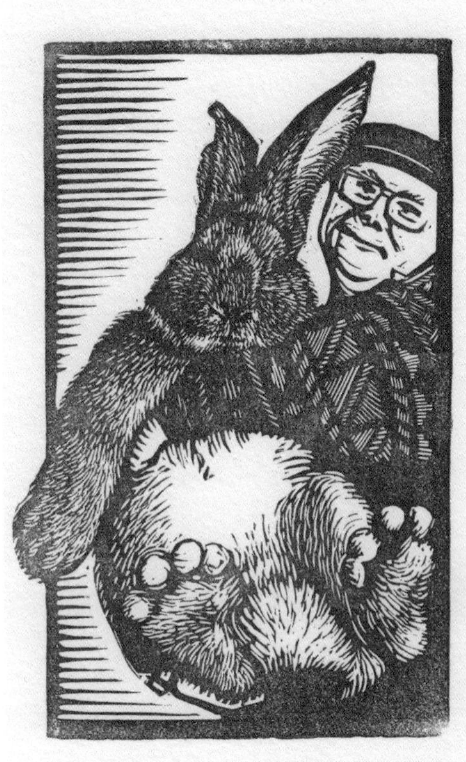

Not enough ink results in a light, patchy print.

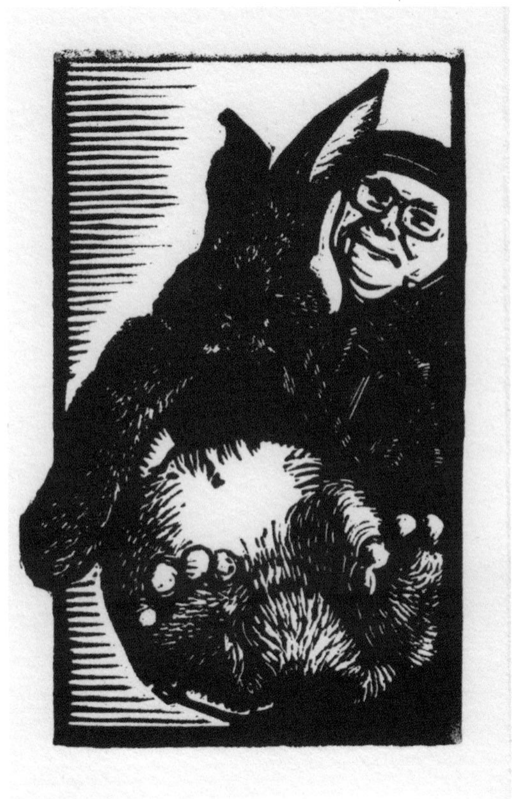

Too much ink results in loss of detail.

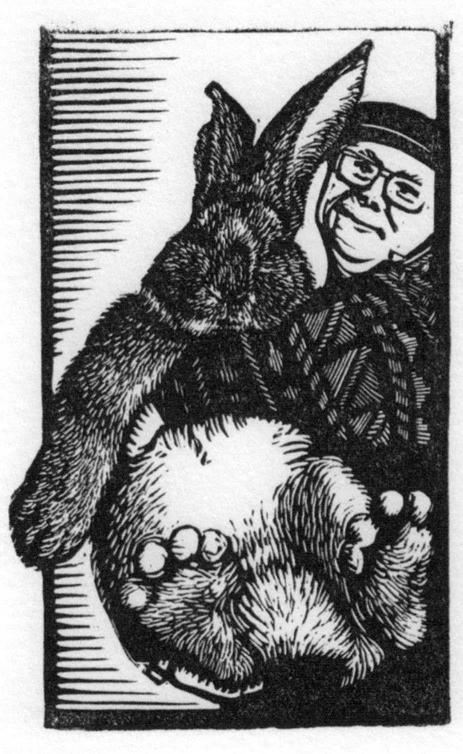

Not enough pressure results in lighter or missing areas.

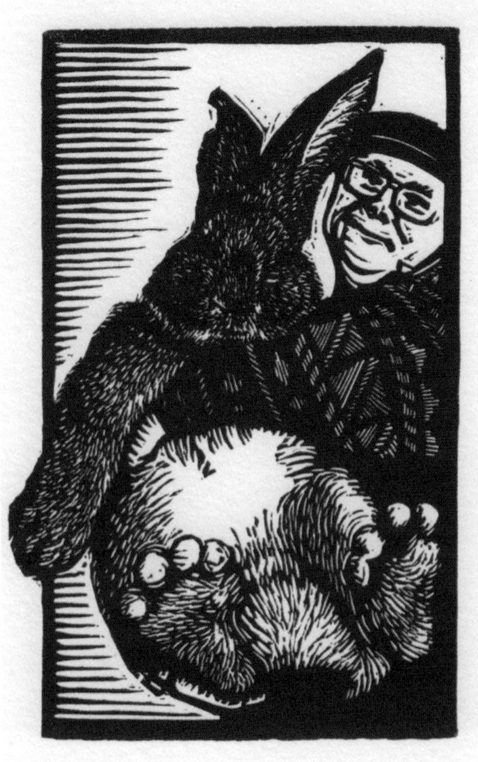

Too much pressure brings out unwanted marks and can damage the block.

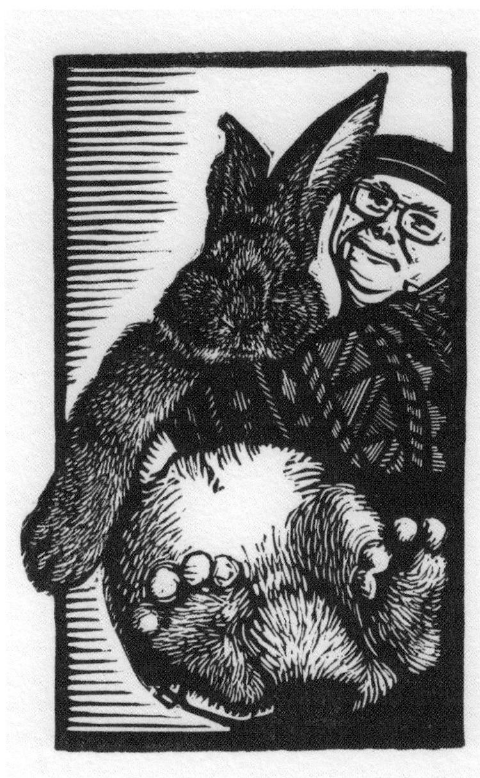

Correct ink and pressure.

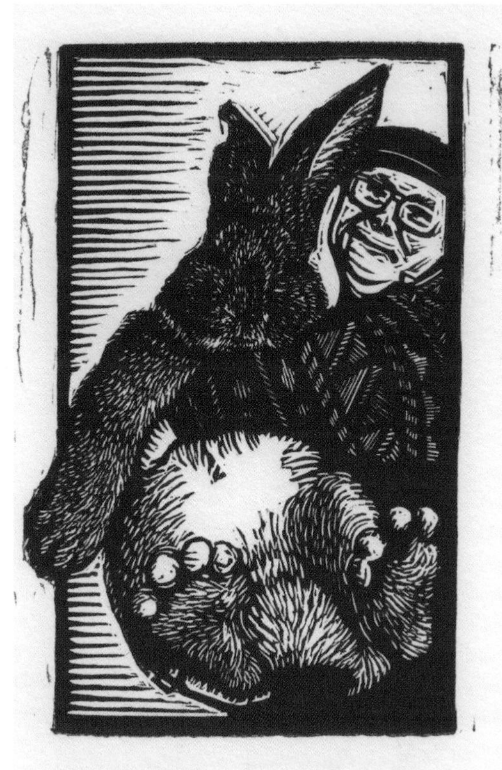

Printing with blankets results in extraneous details.

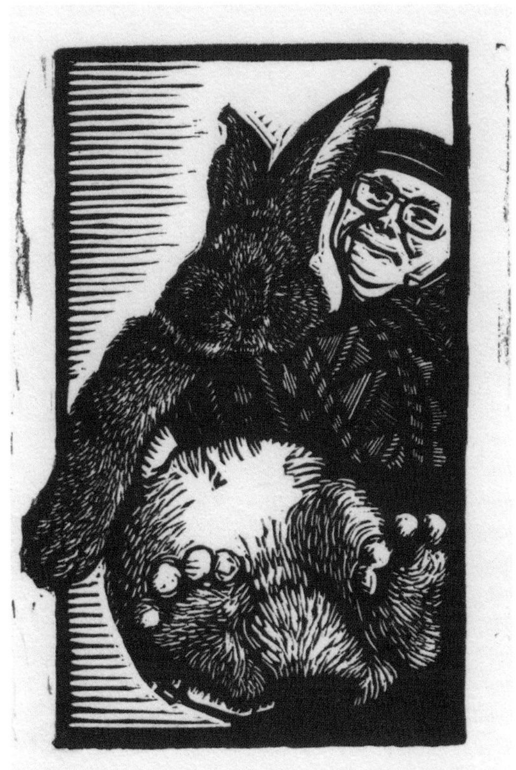

Hand printing can pick up unwanted marks.

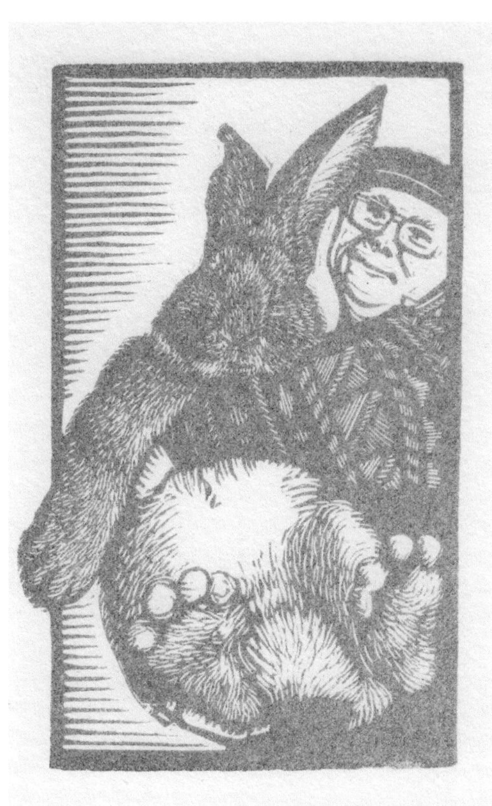

Ghost print.

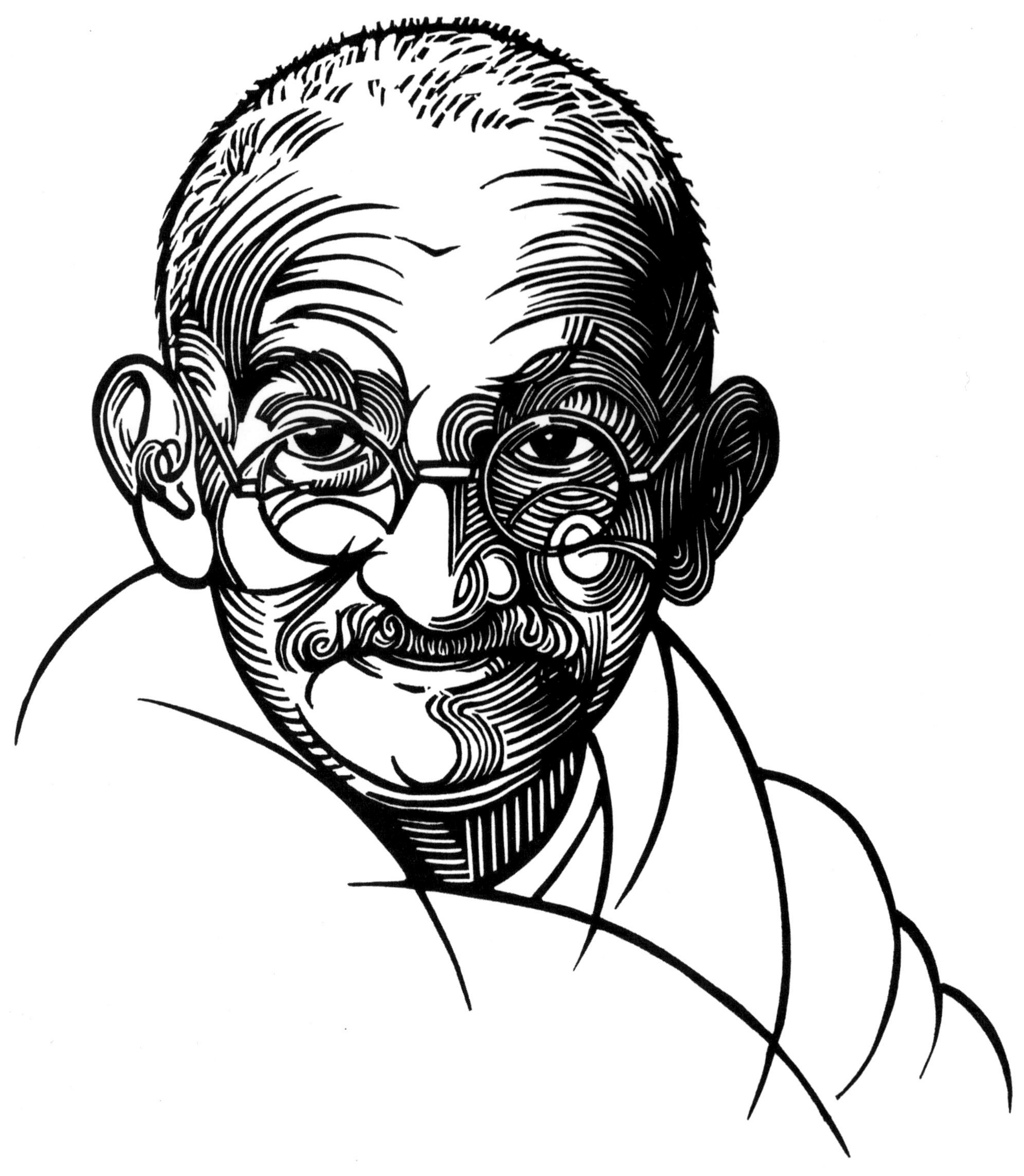

Gandhi, Nick Morley.
The idea for this design was to use the circle from Gandhi's iconic glasses as a repeated shape. Most of the lines in the print are made from the arcs of a circle. Carving an image like this takes great care as any mistake is immediately obvious.

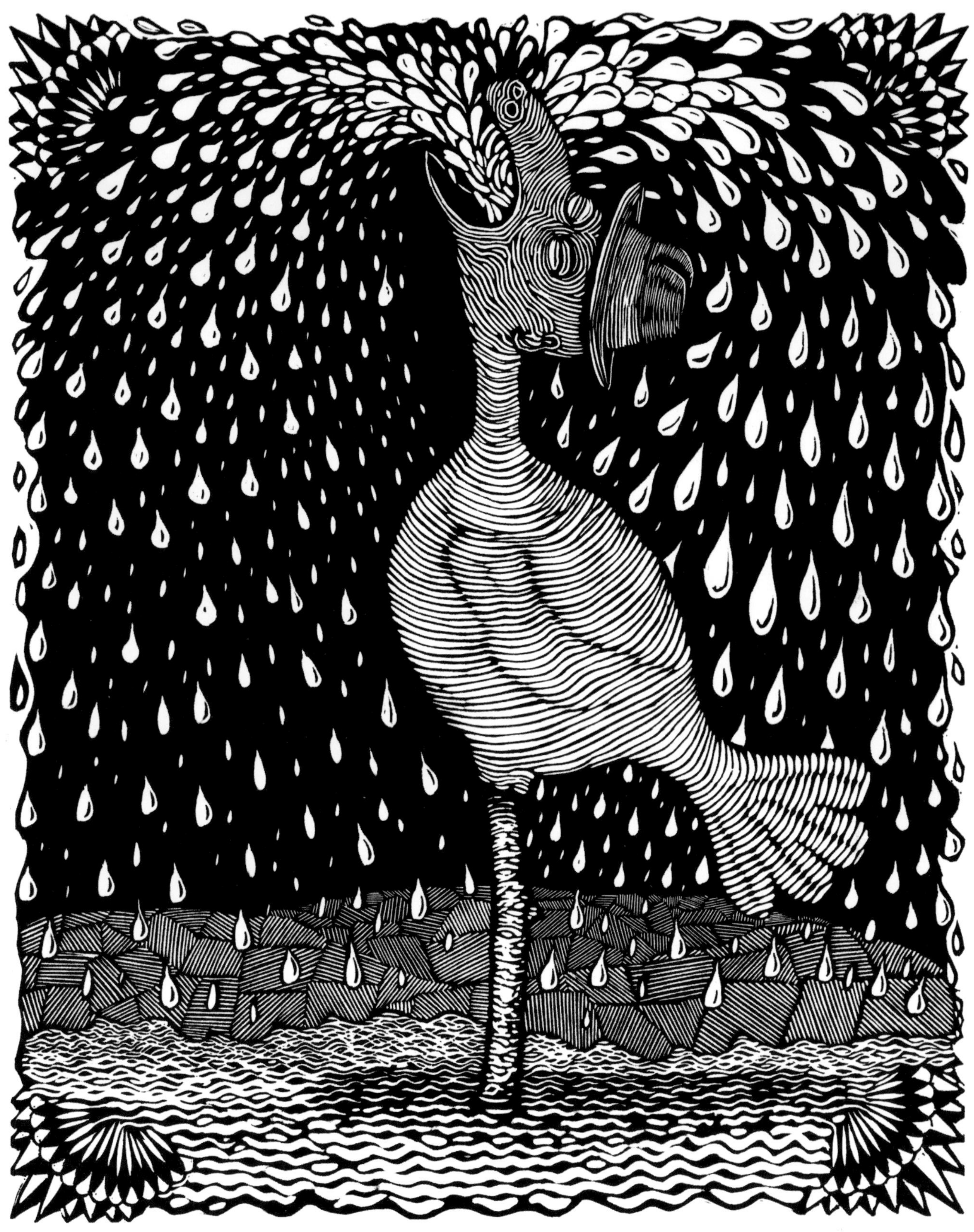

The Rain Bird, Peter Rapp.
This print is from a series of linocuts inspired by *The Book of Imaginary Beings* by Jorge Luis Borges.
Note how the tapered lines on the bird's torso skilfully describe three dimensions.

Bill Fick (USA)

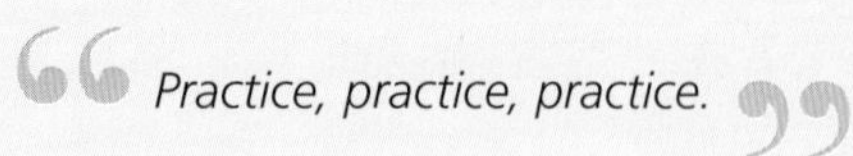

www.billfick.com

Bill Fick is an artist/printmaker based in Durham, North Carolina. He runs Supergraphic, a creative art studio dedicated to the production of fine art prints and print media. Bill is a member of the group of artists known as Outlaw Printmakers.

I started using linocut in college in the mid-1980s as part of a printmaking class. I loved it and have been making linocuts ever since. I developed my linocut technique on my own as it became my primary form of art making. I like linocut's ability to make graphic images. I keep it simple and I only use black ink. I like to make bold images that have visual impact. I'm influenced by pop culture imagery, comics, signage and all types of narrative art.

I work in a printmaking studio called Supergraphic where I'm the director and co-owner. It's a terrific space with excellent equipment and work surfaces.

I use battleship grey linoleum because it's easy to find, I can buy it in large sizes and it cuts perfectly. I use homemade cheap plastic gouges. The blades are Speedball disposable blades.

Most of my images are drawn directly on the lino. I use pencil, markers and brush and ink to develop the image. The image is completely drawn before I start to carve. I cover the lino with a thin coat of white gesso before I make the drawing as this adds a bit of tooth to the surface of the lino and creates a lighter toned drawing surface.

I work very directly. I draw directly on the lino and finish it before I start to carve; I don't proof the image as I go. I'm totally committed to the drawing. If it doesn't work as a drawing then it won't work as a print.

I use oil-based inks. I'm currently using Hanco litho ink and Speedball ink. Speedball is developing a professional grade ink that is very good.

The block is printed using an etching press. I use a stiff board and one blanket on top of the block. This provides both rigidity and cushioning as it passes through the press.

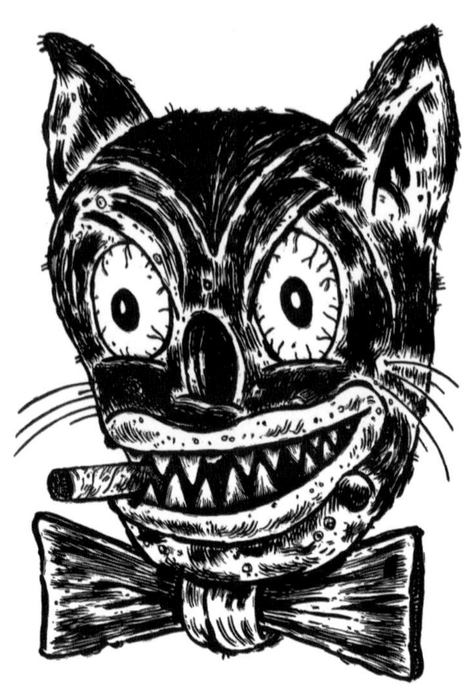

Big Boss Cat, Bill Fick, 23.5 × 16.5in, linocut.

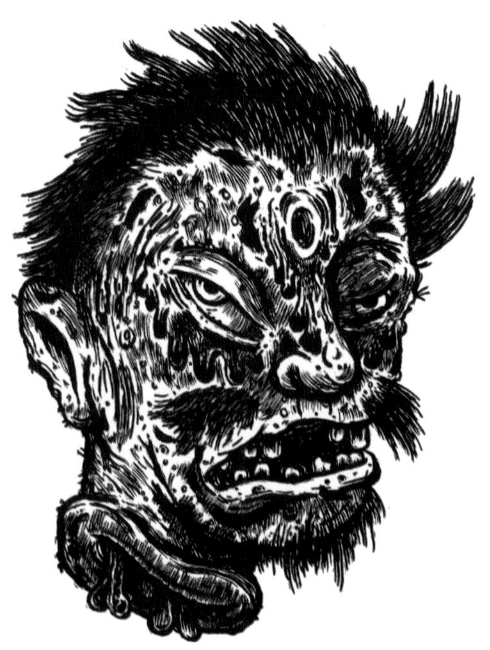

Homage to Posada, Bill Fick, 24 × 19in, linocut.

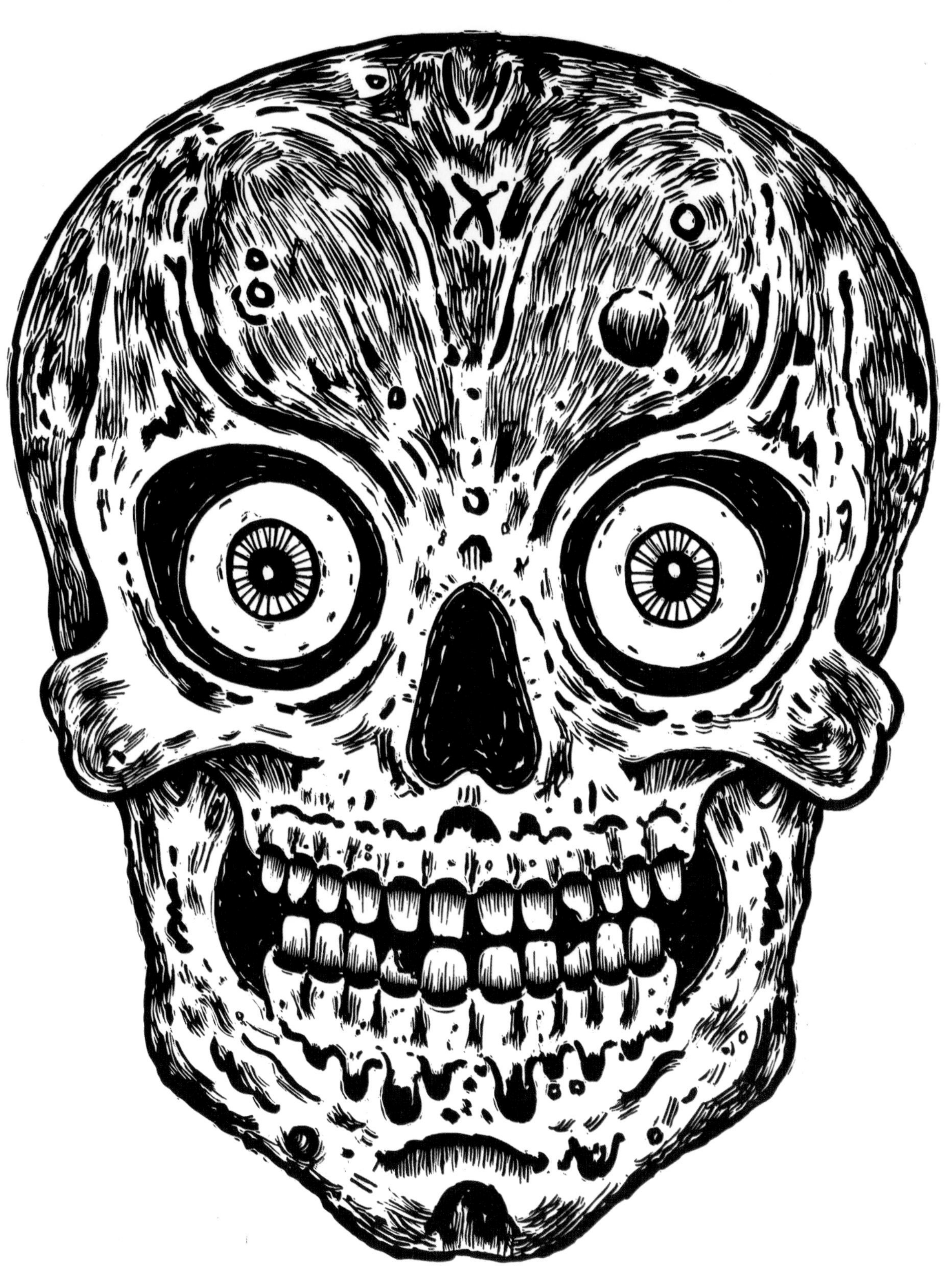

Hypnotic Skull, Bill Fick, 24 × 19in, linocut.

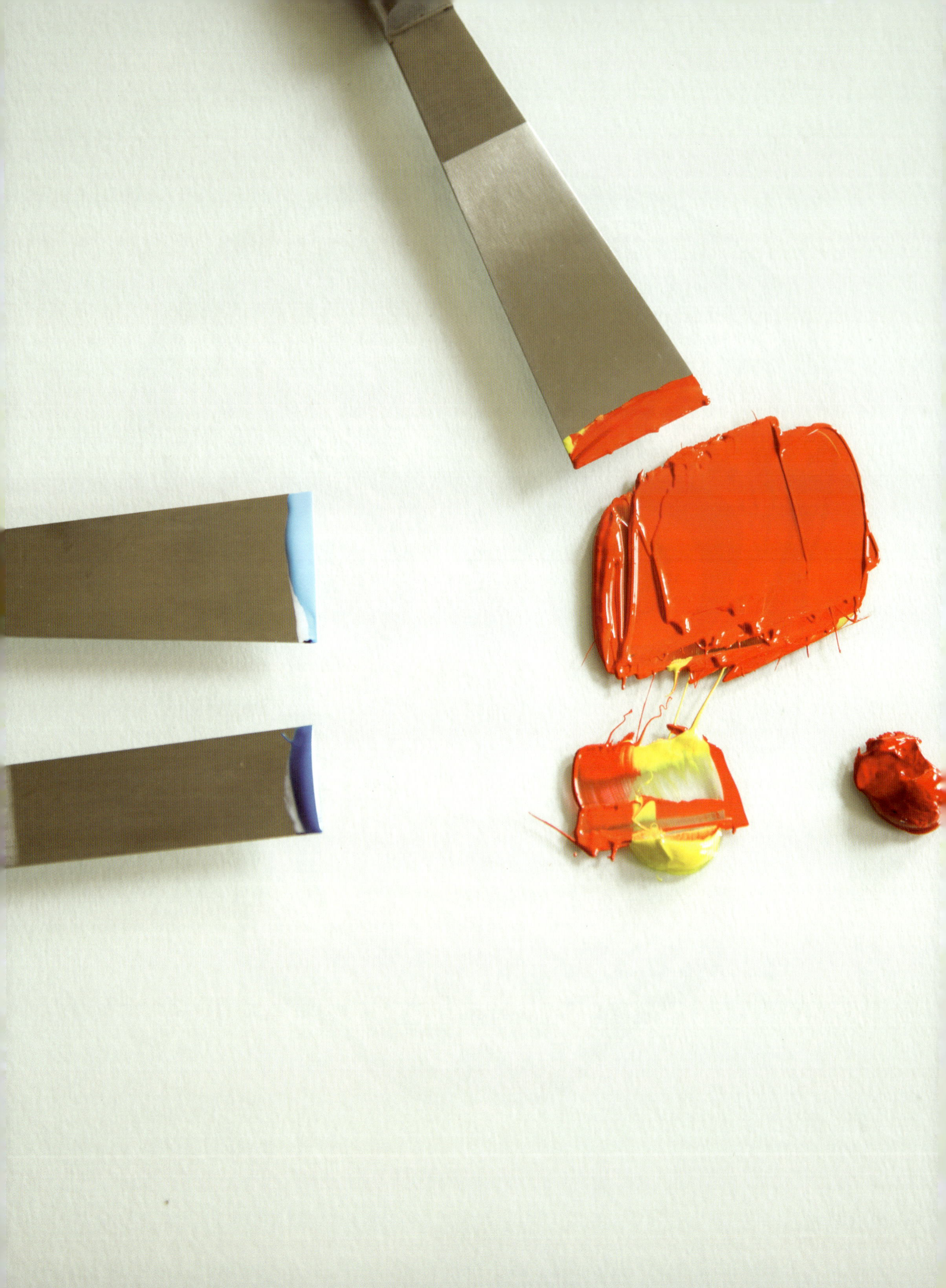

CHAPTER 5

COLOUR

Many artists spend a lifetime making black and white prints, while others want to dive straight into printing in colour. Some use colour in a naturalistic way; others see it as an opportunity for expression and experimentation. What you do with colour is up to you, but some basic knowledge of how inks are made, colour theory and mixing colour will give you a good grounding to explore further. In this chapter you will learn how to control colour, how to lighten and darken it, and what happens when you print layers of colour over one another. This is an expansive and exciting topic and can only really be touched upon here. In order to fully master and understand colour you need to experience it. Make colour tests, practise mixing colours, play around and have fun.

Inks

Inks, paints and dyes

These are all ways of applying colour to paper and fabric. There is some cross-over between the different terms and this can be confusing. Inks and paints generally sit on the surface once applied, whereas dyes are absorbed into the fibres. The difference between inks and paints is mainly in their usage. If printed or applied with a pen, we usually say ink; if applied with a brush we usually say paint. For the purposes of this book, ink means printing ink. Printmakers also use 'ink' as a verb, as in inking a block, or inking up, meaning to apply ink to a surface ready for printing.

How printing ink is made

At its most basic level, printing ink is made up of pigment, which provides the colour, and a vehicle, which carries the pigment and binds it together. In oil-based inks the vehicle is linseed oil and in acrylic inks it is an acrylic polymer.

Ink can contain a single pigment or a mixture of different pigments. Historically these came from nature: rocks, minerals, plants and even animals. Today they are usually man-made in a factory. This allows them to be produced to a consistent colour. The pigments in ink are ground into tiny solid particles. They do not dissolve, but remain as particles in suspension, reflecting and absorbing the light in different ways to produce the colours we see. How much the pigment in ink is ground varies according to its use. Relief printing ink contains very finely ground pigment.

Where coloured pigments were once commodities of rare value, today manufactured colour is part of everyday life. For artists and designers using linocut there is a wide spectrum of coloured inks with such enticing names as Carbazole Violet, Emerald Green and Azure Blue. Some are named after their chemical content: Naphthol Red and Cobalt Blue. Others like Warm Red describe their particular hue. Making the right choice of colours and finding the right kind of ink is crucial to getting good results.

Permanence

If you've ever walked past a shop window with an ancient poster for hair gel or toothpaste in it you may have noticed that the colours have turned blue with age. This is because the red and yellow inks have faded in the sunlight. They are less stable in ultraviolet light than blue ink. The industry measure for how stable colours are in UV light is lightfastness. Most paints and inks aimed at artists are labelled according to a scale of lightfastness, or colour permanence. There are different systems in use, so make sure you ask about this when you buy your ink. Simply, the more lightfast the ink, the longer the print will retain its colour.

Lightfastness is not always an issue. If you are printing greetings cards or other ephemera likely to be thrown away after a short life the colours won't have time to fade. However, if you are making prints on paper or fabric which will be around for a long time it is worth investing in lightfast inks. The cheaper brands of ink tend to use lower quality pigments which fade faster.

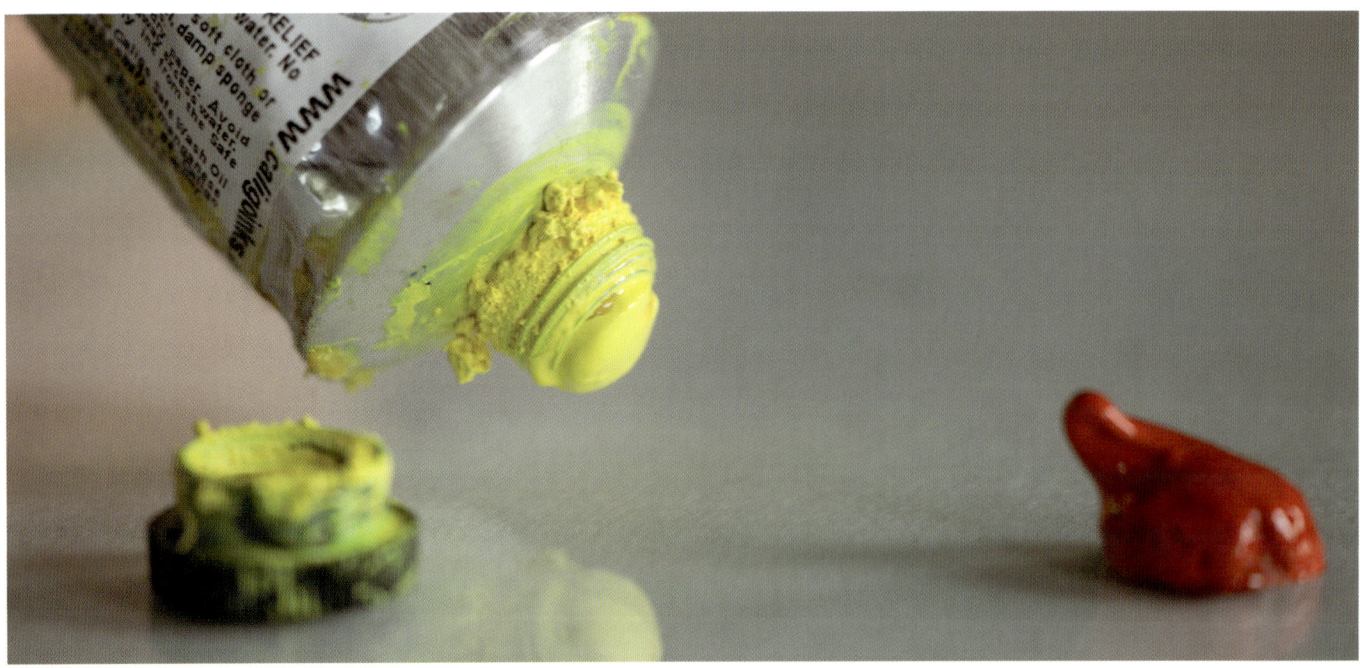

Ink brands

Different brands of ink use different recipes and pigments, which means the colours can vary considerably. For instance, an ink with the name Ultramarine can be a very intense, vibrant blue or quite washed-out looking. As long as they are the same kind of ink (i.e. water-based or oil-based) you should be able to mix and match colours from different brands. If in doubt, ask before you buy.

Prices also vary wildly between different brands. Generally speaking, you get what you pay for as the more expensive inks tend to have better quality pigments. They also have a higher pigment content, whereas the cheap inks contain fillers to bulk them out. Inks with a higher concentration of pigment go a lot further so you need less ink to give you a strong colour. For this reason it is worth getting the best inks you can afford.

When buying colours, try to look at a genuine sample. You may be able to buy a colour chart made from swatches printed with the actual ink. These are worth getting, even if you have to pay for them, as they accurately show the colour you are buying. At other times you will have to make do with a computer-printed chart, which will only give an approximation of the colour. If you are viewing colours on a website, remember that they can vary significantly depending on the screen you are looking at and are unlikely to be accurate.

What colours to buy

It is very easy to become a kid in a candy shop when buying inks. Try not to get carried away and remember some colours (usually the most beautiful ones!) are more expensive than others. It is a good idea to start with a basic palette and build on it when you need to or can afford to. Start off with one of each of the primary colours: red, yellow and blue. With these you will be able to mix up a wide range of colours. Next most useful to get is white, maybe followed by a few earth colours, then more blues, reds, and so on.

Here are some of the most useful colours. Remember, different brands use different naming systems.

Black and White
Naphthol Red, Crimson, Process Magenta
Prussian Blue, Ultramarine, Phthalo Blue, Process Blue
Lemon Yellow, Cadmium Yellow, Process Yellow
Raw and Burnt Umber, Yellow Ochre, Raw and Burnt Sienna, Sepia

Extender

Extender is a must. It is a liquid which is added to the printing ink and mixed thoroughly before rolling up. It has the effect of making the ink more transparent. This is especially useful if you want to print one layer of colour on top of another to make a third colour. It also has the effect of lightening a colour when printed on white paper. Make sure you buy the correct extender for the type of inks you are using. Extender appears yellowish white but is more or less transparent in a thin layer. When printed over a dark colour an extended ink will usually make it appear even darker. The addition of extender to an ink can slow its drying time, so bear that in mind if you are in a rush.

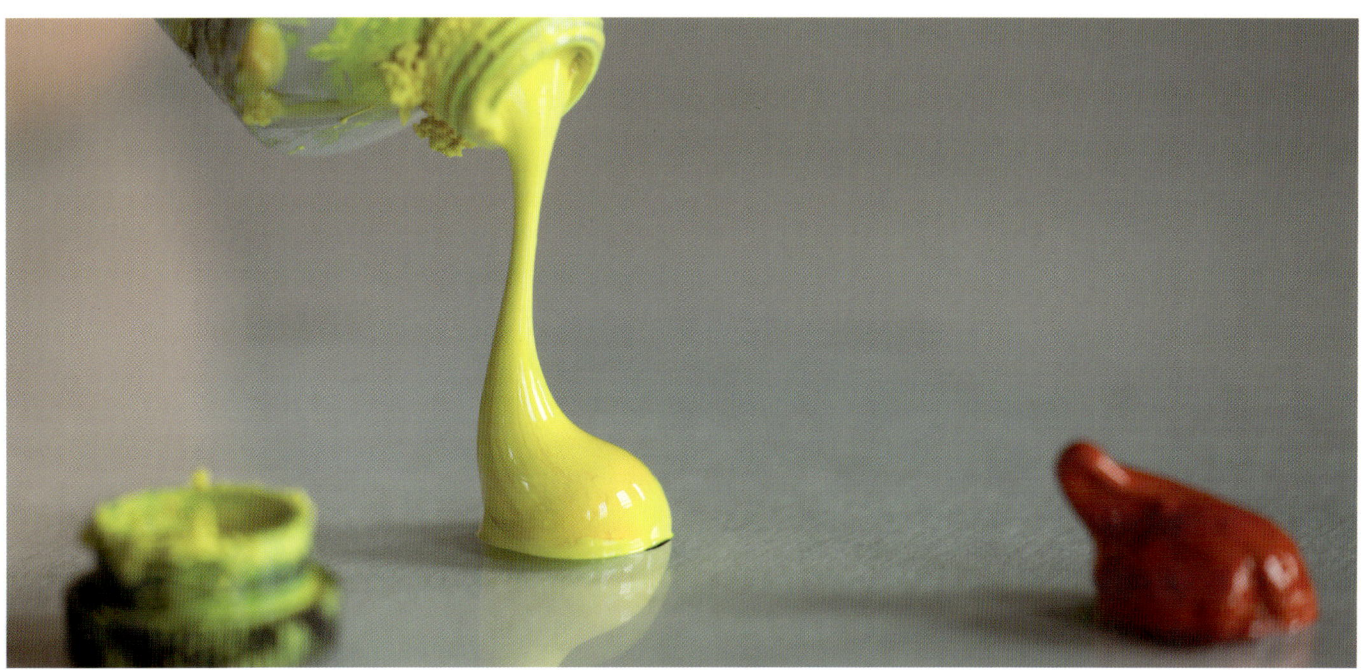

Mixing colours

Your inks should be mixed on an ink slab made of a non-porous surface. Glass, ceramic, marble and plastic all work well. Squeeze out each colour you are going to use separately and make sure you reseal the ink container immediately to stop the ink drying. To mix the ink you need an ink knife or something similar like a palette knife or even an old credit card. You will need a separate ink knife for each colour.

Always start by mixing a small volume of ink until you know the correct proportions for your desired colour. You can then increase the amounts until you have enough. This avoids the problem of wasted ink when things don't go to plan. As a rule of thumb, start with the lightest constituent colour and add the darker colour a little at a time. For instance, if you are mixing green, start with yellow and add a tiny bit of blue at a time. You will soon learn that some colours are more potent than others and have a dramatic effect, even in small quantities.

It's important to mix colours thoroughly. Do this by using the flat edge of the knife to pull the ink out into a thin layer, working it on the glass a few times, then scraping it all up and repeating until you are happy that it is the same colour and consistency throughout.

Testing the colour

The only way to get a completely accurate idea of the colour you have mixed is to print it. However, you can get a rough idea by dragging a thin layer of ink onto a piece of paper with an ink knife. Rolling the ink out onto a piece of paper (or a piece of glass with white paper underneath) will also give you a good idea of the printed colour.

Making colours lighter

There are two ways to lighten the colour of an ink. The first is to add extender. To make a very light colour, add only a little ink at a time to the extender. Even the tiniest amount of some inks will give quite strong colour.

The second way to lighten an ink is to add white to it. This gives what is known as a tint. The colour you get by mixing a tint can be very different from that of an extended ink; think pastel colours. Because white is a very opaque ink, any tints you mix will also be opaque. If you are printing over other colours the ink with white in it will cover up the colours underneath.

Making colours darker

If you want to make a colour darker you can add a darker ink to it, like Ultramarine or Burnt Umber. If you want to maintain the vibrancy of the colour you will need to add a similar colour. For example, adding violet to blue will give a deeper blue. If you want to deaden a colour, add its complementary colour. For example, adding orange to blue. You can also add black but this can sometimes do strange things. Adding black to yellow makes it look green and adding black to red makes it brown.

Mixing black

If you do not have black ink it can be mixed from a dark blue and an earth colour like Burnt Umber. In fact this gives a very beautiful black, full of character, and some artists will always mix their black this way. You can also add a touch of blue, red or brown to black ink to give it more interest.

Colours that cannot be mixed

As well as the primary colours, you cannot mix up certain other colours, such as white, violet, viridian green, cyan and magenta. If you want these colours, you will have to buy them.

Process colours (CMYK)

Commercial printers commonly use a process called CMYK. This name comes from the four colours used: Cyan, Magenta, Yellow and Black (the 'Key' colour, hence K). Together these are known as the process colours and when printed over one another can be used to make up almost any colour.

Lino blocks can also be printed in CMYK. You will need to make the inks semi-transparent by adding extender. Try printing four random blocks in CMYK over each other. It will make some really eye-popping colour combinations.

It is possible to take a full-colour image such as a photograph and convert it into four layers, one for each process colour, using Photoshop or other photo-manipulation software. The layers can then be separated and each one transferred to a block to carve. The four blocks can then be printed, each in its corresponding CMYK colour to make up the full colour image.

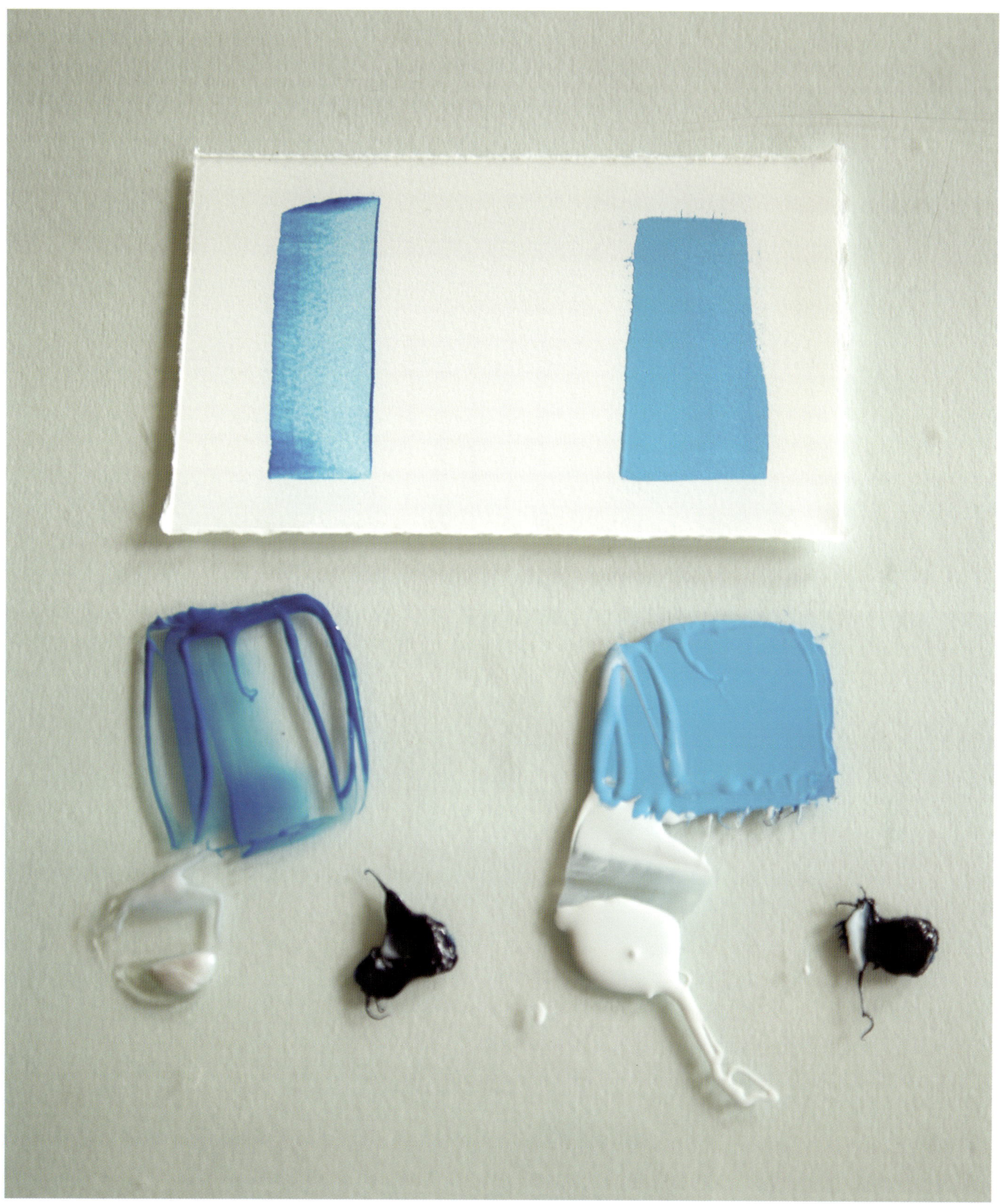

You can get a rough idea of how a colour will print by pulling it out on a piece of paper with a knife. Here you can see the difference between the extended colour (left) and the one mixed with white (right). The extended colour is much more transparent.

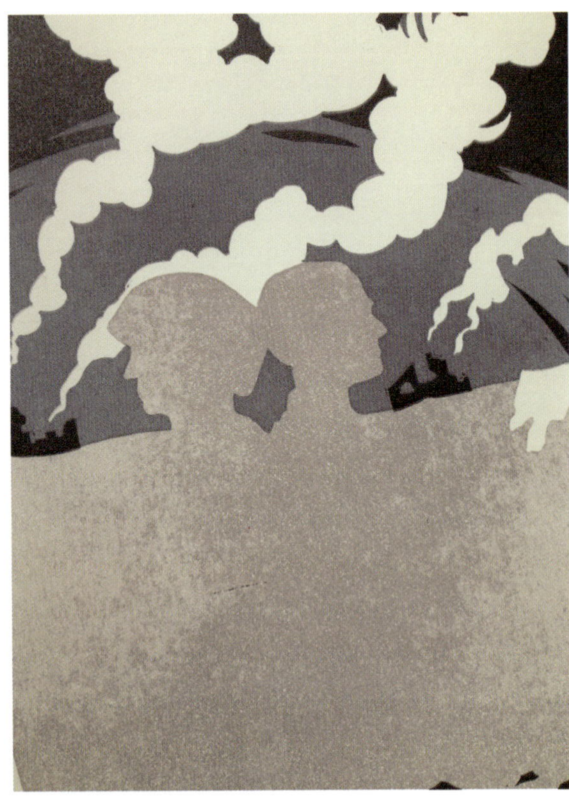

This illustration for *The Independent on Sunday* is made up only of different shades of grey, some warm and some cool. The texture was created by printing one of the layers on an old book press which printed with uneven pressure.

Left: The print with the first three layers of colour.

Below: The final image. The black silhouette of the figures was the last layer to be printed.

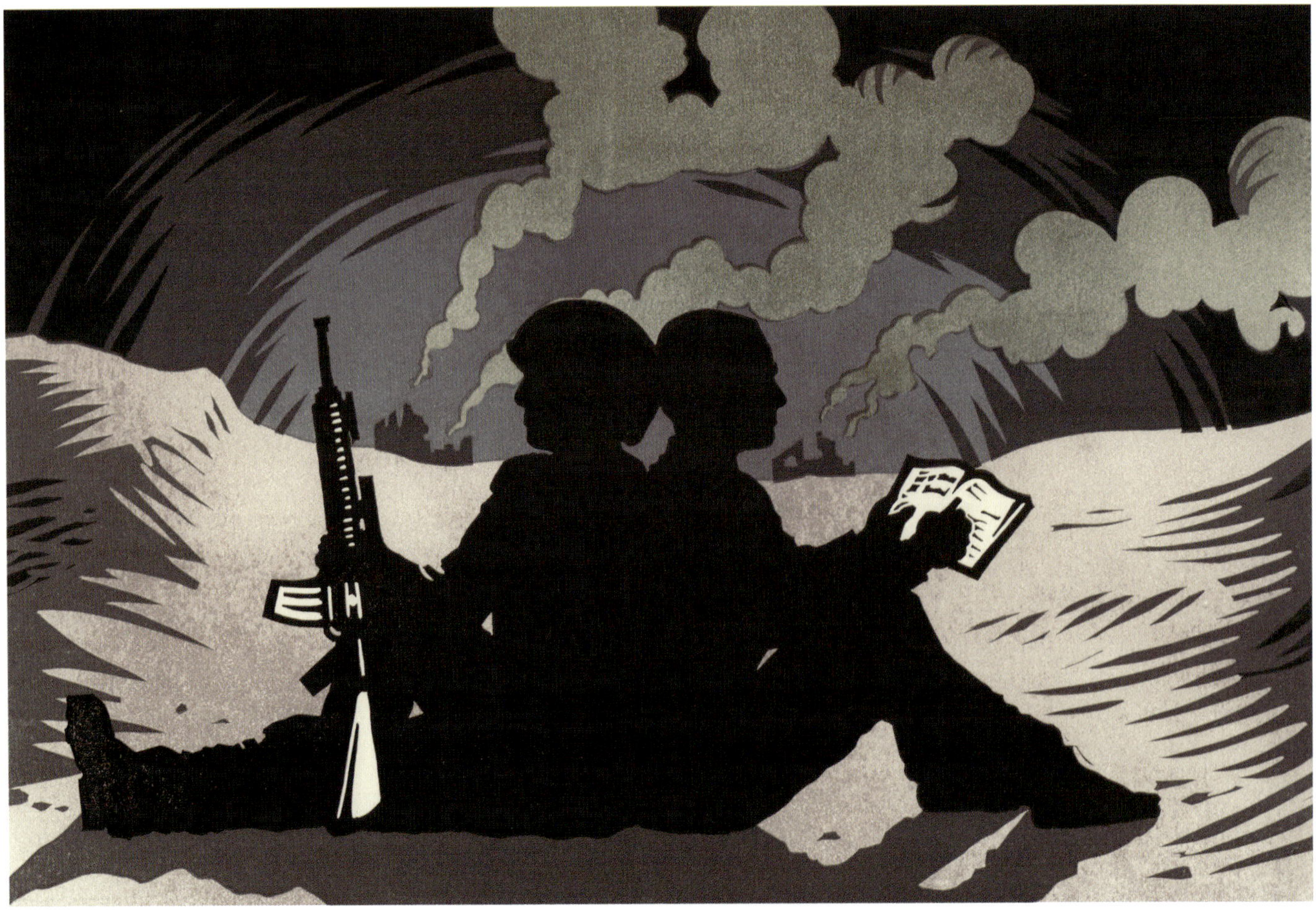

Printing in colour

Layering colours

Although it is possible to apply more than one colour of ink to a single lino block, to start with it is easiest to think about making prints with one colour per block. Each block is printed in turn and, depending on the transparency of the inks, where the two colours overlap a third colour will appear. The possible number of colours in a print increases exponentially in relation to the number of blocks. From two blocks you will get three colours. From three blocks you will potentially get seven colours, and so on. It is impossible to predict the exact shade of the overlap colours, so it is a case of experimenting until you get it right. With experience you will get a feel for it.

Controlling colour through inking

You can also control how light or dark a colour is by how thick a layer of ink you apply to the block. This is more true for some colours than others. The more transparent the colour the more this is the case too. With practice you will learn how to control the amount of ink on the roller and therefore the block. Remember: a fast roll will pick up ink from the block and a slow roll will lay it down. Ink will also transfer from a more inky surface to a less inky one, so you can remove ink from the block with a clean roller.

Wet-on-wet printing

Some inks will allow you to print wet-on-wet, in other words, printing the second layer before the first is dry. If you are using very thick layers of ink, however, you may have to wait for each layer to dry before adding the next. If you don't do this the inks can smudge or even repel one another, giving unsatisfactory results. The first layer of ink does not necessarily need to be completely dry; if it is tacky it should be OK. If printing wet-on-wet watch out for colour transferring from the print back onto the block. Depending on the colours you may need to clean the block between prints.

Note: As you build up multiple layers of ink, each layer will take longer to dry. This is because the moisture from the first layer of ink can escape in two directions: into the air and into the paper. Once there is a layer of ink on the paper, however, this will form a barrier and the moisture from subsequent layers can only escape into the air.

Chemical driers

Chemical driers can be used to speed up the drying time of ink. There are two kinds: Cobalt driers, which dry from the surface down, and Manganese driers, a body drier which dries the ink at the same speed throughout. You need only add one or two drops of driers to your ink with a pipette and then mix it thoroughly with a palette knife before rolling out. Although they are dark in colour they shouldn't affect the colour you are mixing them with, although they can make the ink slightly less tacky. Driers are harmful chemicals and should be handled with care using gloves.

Other considerations

Juxtaposition of colour

One of the most fascinating, and potentially frustrating, things about colour is that it changes depending on its surroundings. A mid-blue next to orange will look bright blue, but next to a stronger blue it might look grey. The human eye and brain make adjustments depending on what they are seeing. When mixing colours for a print, you need to take this phenomenon into account and make test prints to check how the colours look next to each other.

Lighting conditions

As any photographer will tell you, natural light is a very different colour to artificial light. When making colour prints, try to work in daylight or a mixture of daylight and artificial light. Failing this, check your prints in daylight at intervals. Make sure you have enough light too; colours lose their intensity in low light. What might have looked like neutral tones during a late night printing session could turn out to be quite garish in the morning.

Paper colour

The colour of paper you print on will affect your ink colours, so make a test print before you mix up a whole batch of ink. Even papers described as white will vary considerably. It can be difficult to see this until you hold two different shades of white next to each other, when the difference will be easier to see. If you want bright, vibrant colour, make sure you are using a bright white paper.

Wet and dry colour

Some inks will dry lighter or darker than they looked when wet. This is more true of the cheaper, acrylic-based inks. If colour accuracy is important make sure you do a test print and let it dry to check this.

Project: layering colours

This project will give you an idea of what can be achieved by layering colours, without having to worry about carving a design or lining things up. This works best with cyan, magenta and yellow ink but you can use any shade of blue, red and yellow. Ideally, you should have a different roller for each colour of ink. If you only have one roller you can still do this exercise, but you will have to clean it between using each colour.

You will need:

Lino, carving tools, craft knife and cutting mat (or scissors), three different ink colours, extender, ink rollers, ink knives, ink slab, paper, printing tool or press.

Preparation

Cut out three blocks of lino into whatever shapes you want (circles work well). If you have some off-cuts lying around you can use those. Use a strong craft knife to cut the lino on a cutting mat or thick piece of card. If you find it easier you can cut a groove in the lino with a gouge and then cut it with scissors.

Cut a few pieces of paper the same size. The paper needs to be big enough to fit the three blocks.

Before you ink up the blocks, make a registration template. Take a piece of paper slightly larger than your printing paper. Draw round the printing paper onto the template paper. Then do the same with your three blocks. Draw them one by one, face up, positioning them so their outlines overlap like a venn diagram. All three shapes should overlap in the centre. If the blocks are the same shape you can number them on the back and write the numbers inside the shapes you have drawn to identify which goes where. Mark which edge of the template is for the top of the paper.

Printing

When you print multiple blocks you need to be more organized than you were with one colour. Each colour will need a separate roller and area to roll out on. Be careful not to let the colours touch as even a small amount of one colour can contaminate another. As well as space to roll the colours out you will need somewhere to place your blocks while you ink them. Try to be systematic and give yourself extra time to set up and clean up.

Ink up the first block in yellow and place it, ink side up, within the corresponding outline on the template. Take a piece of paper for printing and place it over the first block, aligning it with the template. Print the first block, and repeat the process for the other two in the other colours.

Before re-inking a block to make further prints check to see whether the other colours have transferred (off-set) from the print onto the block. If the colour is contaminated you should be able to clean it sufficiently by simply wiping with a dry cloth.

Try printing the blocks in a different order and with varying amounts of ink. You may find some of the colours repel each other, depending on their consistency. It is worth noting when this happens so you can avoid it in future printing sessions.

You can also repeat this exercise using inks with varying amounts of extender added. You will find the increased transparency of extended ink allows the colours underneath to show through more. Make a note of the optimum level of transparency for layering colours. This will depend on the inks you are using.

Mixing black from primary colours

If you have any ink left over from this exercise, try mixing a black from the primary colours. Mix a small amount at a time and keep adding colour to try to make the ink as neutral as possible; if the ink looks green add red, if it looks purple add yellow and if it looks orange add blue. Once you have a colour which is as close as you can get to black, ink up a block and print it. Add some extender to the ink and print it again to get a grey. Try printing the extended ink over the black ink and see what happens. Now add white to the ink and try this again.

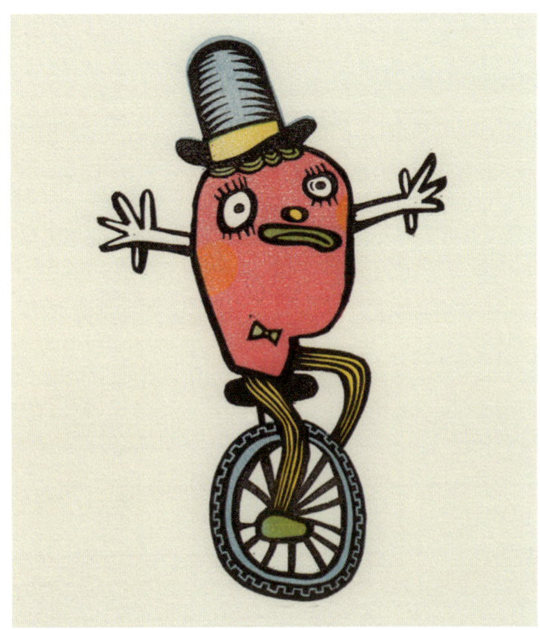

Unicyclist, Nick Morley. This was printed from four blocks, in cyan, magenta, yellow and black ink. Green is created where the yellow and blue overlap.

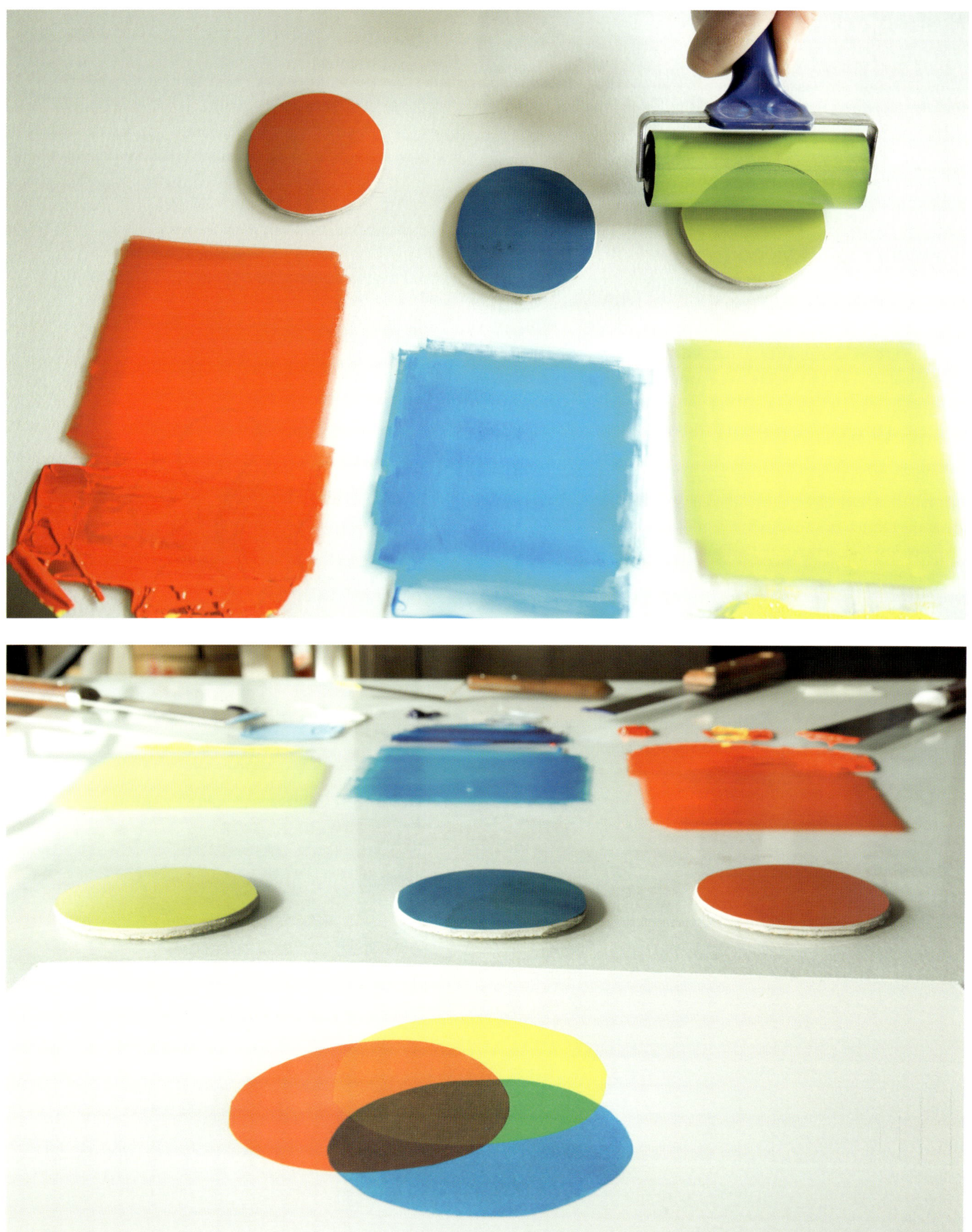

Multi-block printing

As we have seen, layering colours quickly opens up new possibilities. In order to harness the potential of this technique you need to be able to control exactly where each colour goes. This requires careful planning. The more care you take at each stage the more likely you are to get good results.

Planning a multi-block image

When planning a multi-block print it is worth spending some time thinking about how everything is going to fit together. You will find it helpful to draw things out on paper or use a computer to create an image made up of layers. There are several ways to do this.

Tracing paper

Tracing paper is a very useful tool when thinking about layers as you can draw each layer onto a different sheet and overlay them to see if they match up. You can trace from one layer onto the next. You can even look at the image back-to-front to see how it will look when printed.

Photoshop

Photoshop and other image manipulation software take some time to learn but, once mastered, will enable you to try things out much more quickly and easily. You can create an image file made up of layers which can be individually edited, re-sized, re-ordered, rotated and reversed. You can adjust the hue, lightness and saturation of colours to mimic what will happen in printing. By adjusting the transparency of layers you can even see what happens when two colours overlap.

You can scan a photograph or drawing, create an image from scratch or download one from the Internet. When you have finished planning everything you can print the layers out onto separate pieces of paper to transfer to the blocks.

The key block system

The key block system is a good place to start when learning about registration as it is easy to visualize and any mistakes become apparent very quickly. The key block is the last block to be printed and usually contains a black outline and all the fine detail. The coloured blocks are printed first and when the key block is printed on top all the edges should be neatly covered by the key block. The thicker the outline, the more room for error there is as any blocks which are slightly off-register will be covered by the black ink. Traditionally these kinds of images often had a black border.

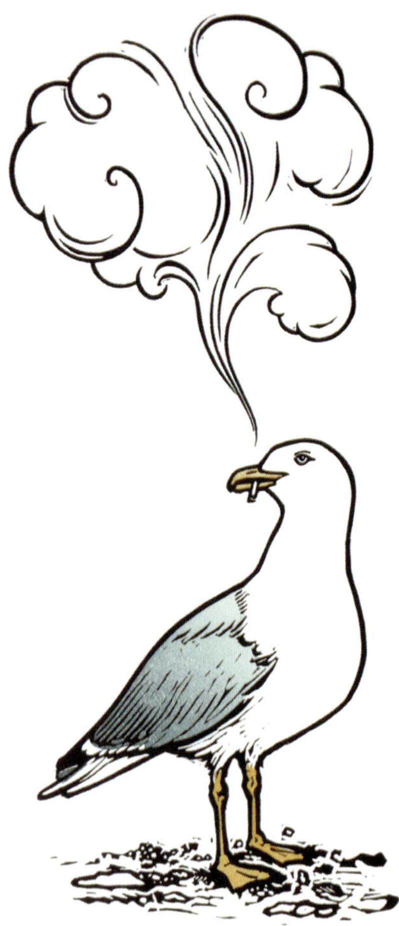

Smoking Seagull, Nick Morley.
The black key block was carved and printed.
This was then used as a guide for making the colour blocks which were carved from three small pieces of lino.

Project: three colour key block print

You will need:

Three pieces of lino the same size, soft pencil, coloured marker pens or felt tips, drawing paper, tracing paper, carving tools, black ink plus two colours, ink rollers, ink knives, ink slab, printing paper, printing tool or press.

For this project you will need three pieces of lino the same size. Try to cut them as accurately as you can as this will make it easier to get accurate registration. You are going to draw the design for each layer on paper first, before transferring to the lino blocks. If you want your print to come out a certain way, remember to reverse the design right at the start. The use of tracing paper and coloured marker pens will help you to see how the three layers are going to print before you start carving.

Planning your design

Start by drawing the outline of one of your blocks onto a piece of paper. Next draw out the design for your key block – think of it as an outline drawing – within this outline. Start in pencil, and when you are happy with the design go over it in pen. Make the lines nice and chunky.

Take a sheet of tracing paper and lay it over the drawing you have made, making sure it is bigger than the outline of the block. Mark the four corners of the block outline accurately on the tracing paper. You are now going to draw the design for the second block, which will be in colour. To help you visualize how the block will look printed, pick a marker pen in a matching colour. Colour in all the areas you want to be that colour in your design, including where it will overlap with the black outline and the colour of the third block.

Take a second sheet of tracing paper and repeat this with the colour you are going to use for the third block. At this point you should start to see what happens when the colours overlap. You can go back and change the designs for the other layers if you feel the need.

Carving

When you are happy with the designs, transfer them onto the three blocks, making sure the corners are aligned accurately. To do this you can use a pencil transfer or carbon paper. Make sure the design on all three blocks are the same orientation. Carve each block, colouring in the areas you want to leave behind first if it helps. The key block will take you the longest to carve because you have to trace round each line and clear a larger area.

Preparing to print

Before you put any ink out and risk getting your hands dirty, prepare your printing paper and registration. Cut or tear up enough printing paper to the right size before you start. It helps if you make all the paper exactly the same size and leave room for a generous border on the print. Prepare a registration template as before by drawing round the printing paper, followed by one of the blocks. Remember to mark the top of the template to make sure you put the block and paper the right way up each time.

Drying times and layers

Depending on which ink you are using and how thickly you apply it, you may or may not be able to print all your colours in one session. The more layers you build up in succession the more this will be an issue. The other problem that can occur is ink that is already on the paper transferring onto the block. This then gets onto the roller and can contaminate the colours. If you are experiencing either of these problems you can print the first layer and let it dry before printing the next one.

Order of printing

The rule of thumb is to print from light to dark, but feel free to experiment with printing the blocks in different orders. Once you have carved and inked up the blocks the printing is relatively quick so take advantage of this to try things out. Nine times out of ten you will want to print the black key block last.

Inking up

Once you are printing, try to get into a rhythm and do things in the same order. You may prefer to ink up all the blocks first or you may want to ink one and print it before inking up the next. After the first print it is sometimes hard to tell at a glance if a block has been re-inked as it retains a lot of colour after printing. If you are not concentrating it is easy to print a block that hasn't been re-inked or even to ink one twice. Try to be consistent in your approach to avoid mistakes.

Using the registration sheet

Once the block is inked up, place it carefully face-up on your registration sheet. Make sure the top of the image is in the right place. Try to get the block in exactly the right place; the more care you take at this stage, the more likely you are to get accurate registration. Place the printing paper on top, using the registration sheet to line it up. Always line up the same edge of the printing paper when you put it down. Print and repeat with the other blocks.

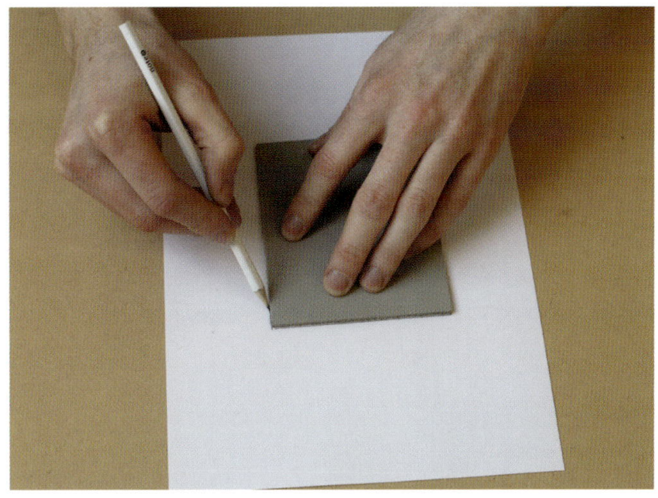

Draw round one of the blocks onto a piece of paper.

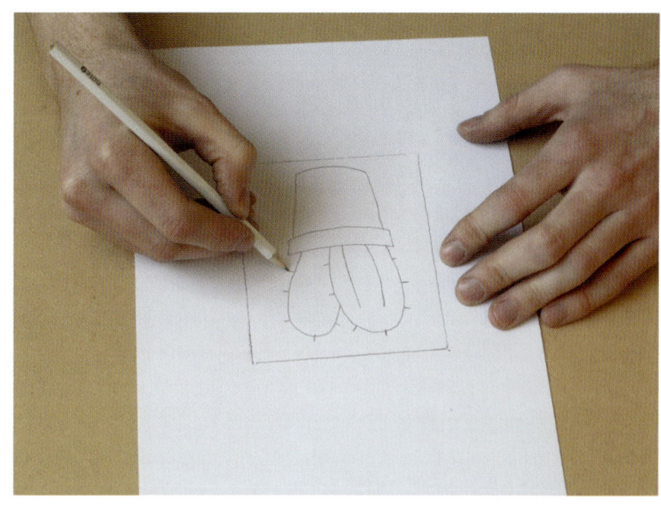

Draw your outline design in pencil within the outline.

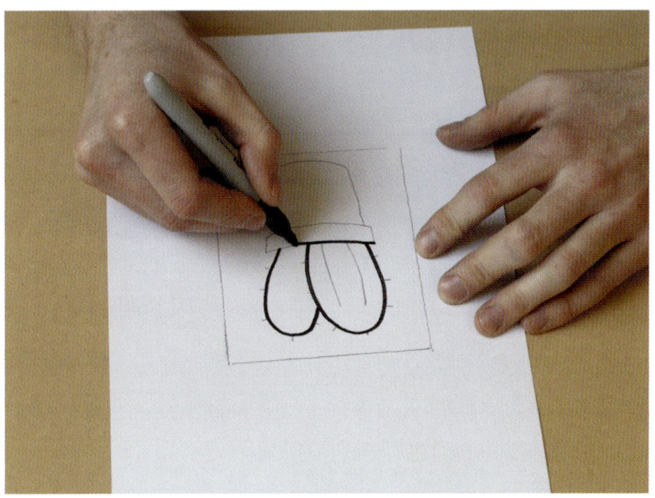

Go over your design in marker pen.

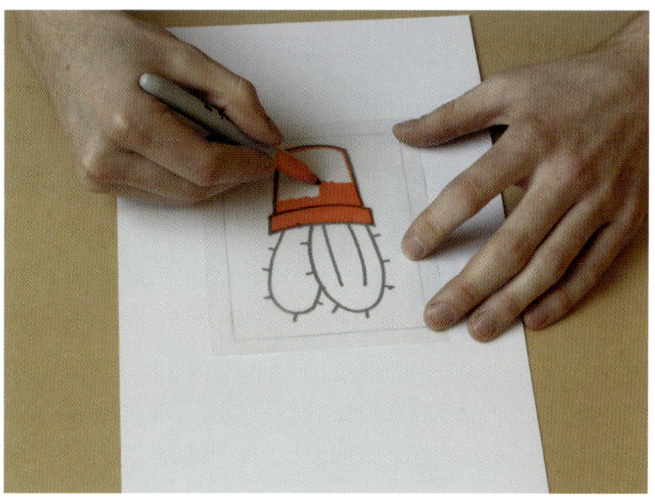

Draw the design for the second block on tracing paper.

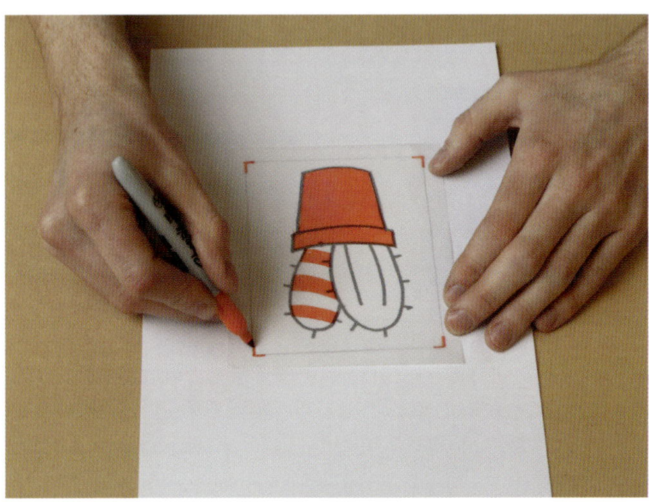

Mark the corners accurately.

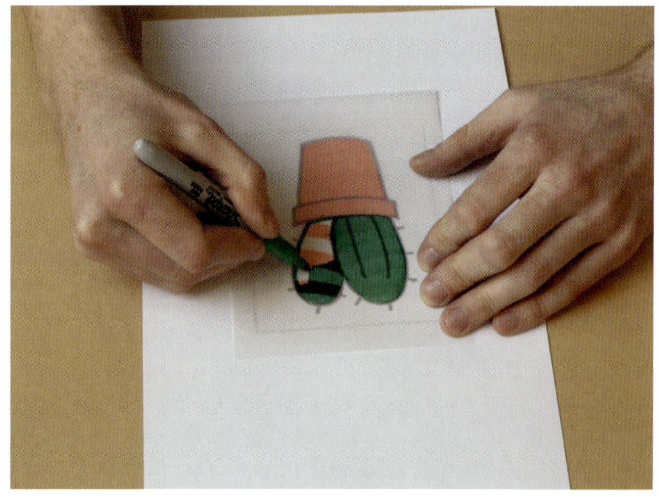

Draw the design for the third block on a new sheet.

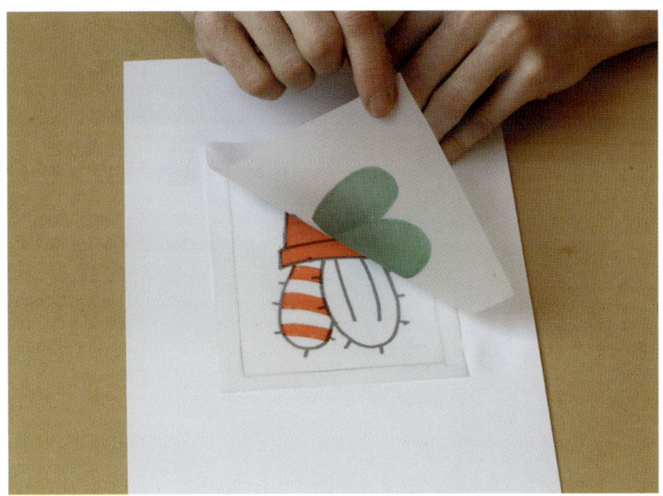

Adjust the designs as necessary.

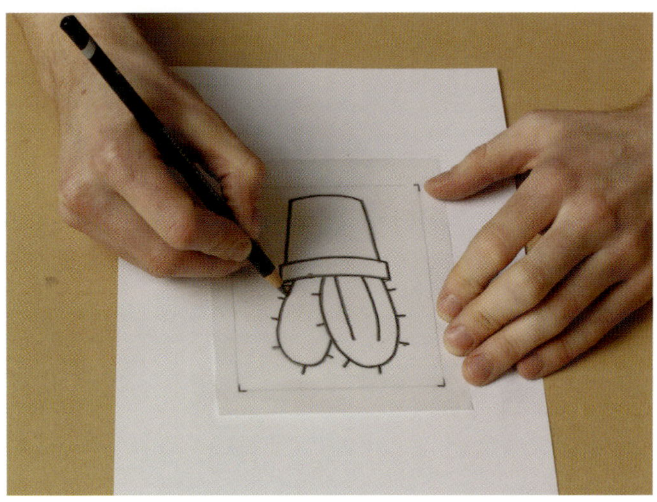

Trace the key block design in soft pencil.

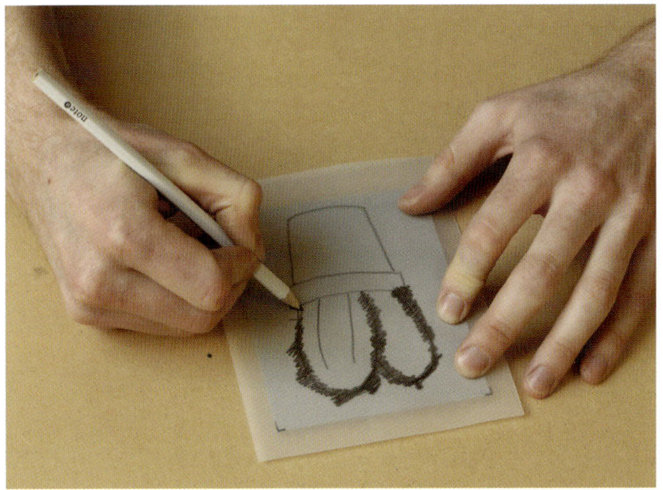

Place the tracing face down on the block and transfer.

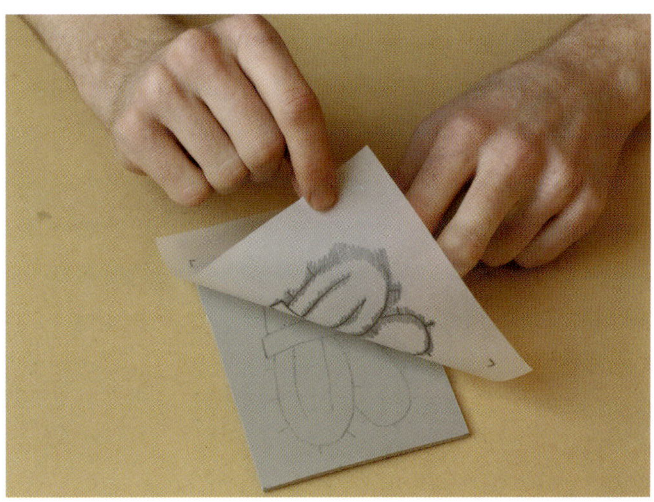

Check the transfer and repeat for the other two blocks.

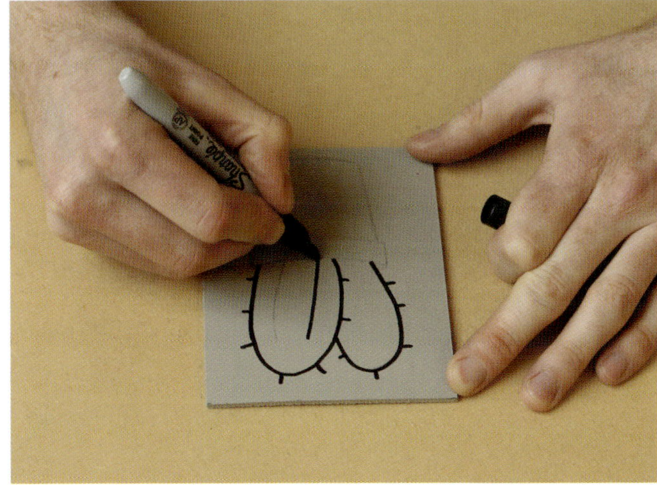

Go over the key block design in marker pen.

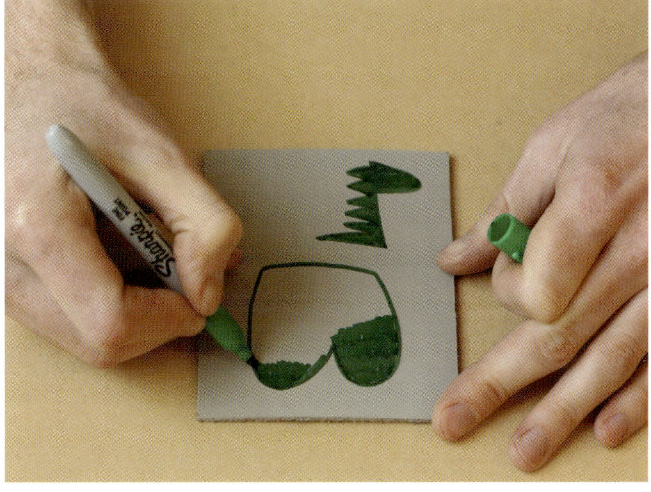

Colour in the designs on the other two blocks.

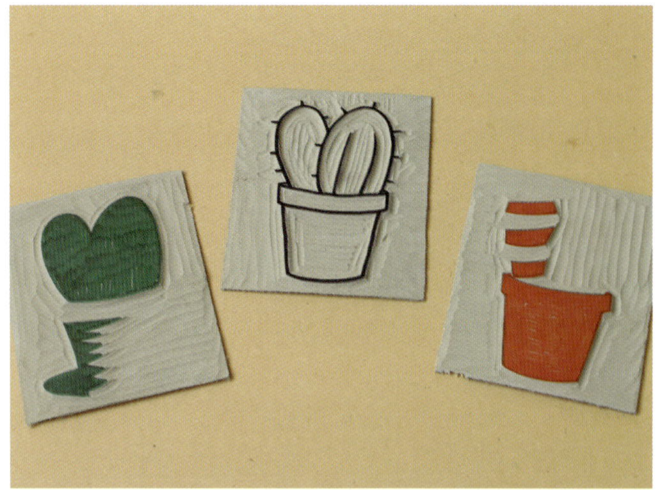

Carve the blocks, leaving the coloured in areas.

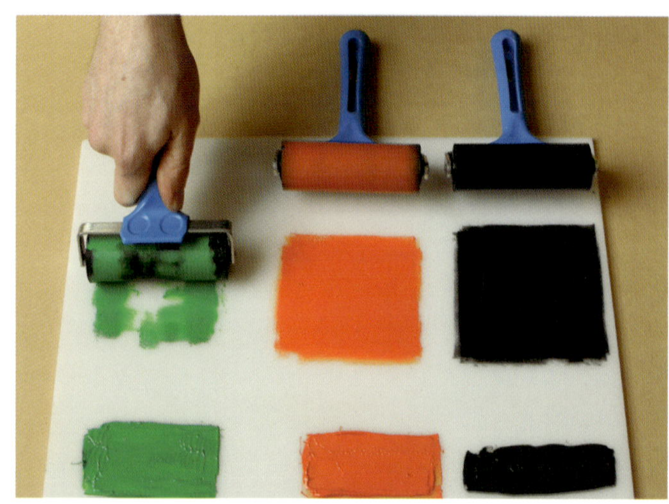

Roll out your inks, keeping them separate.

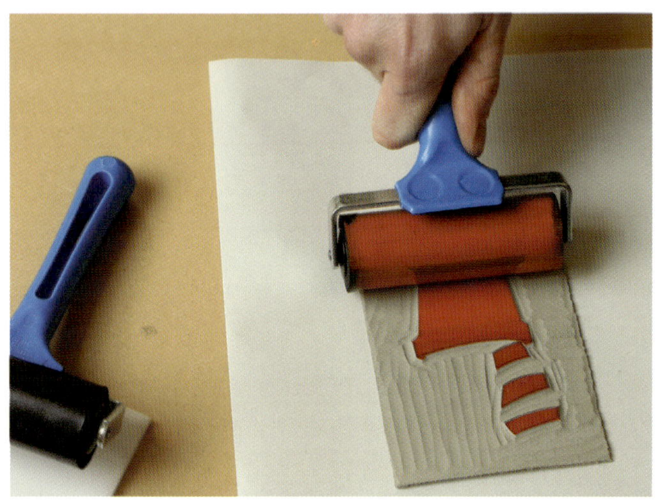

Ink up the first block.

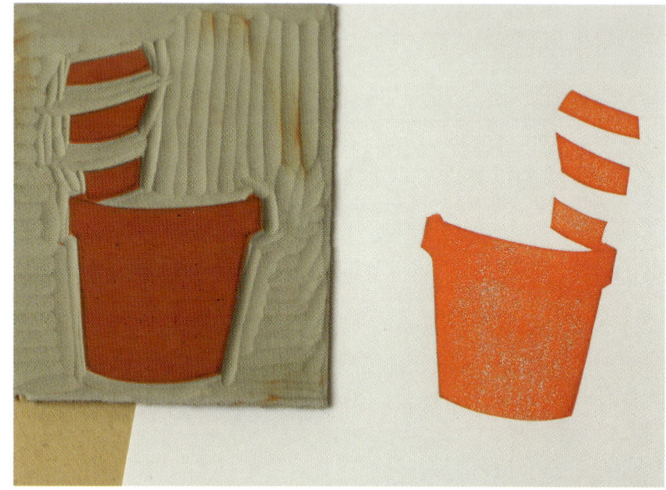

Print the first block in its matching colour.

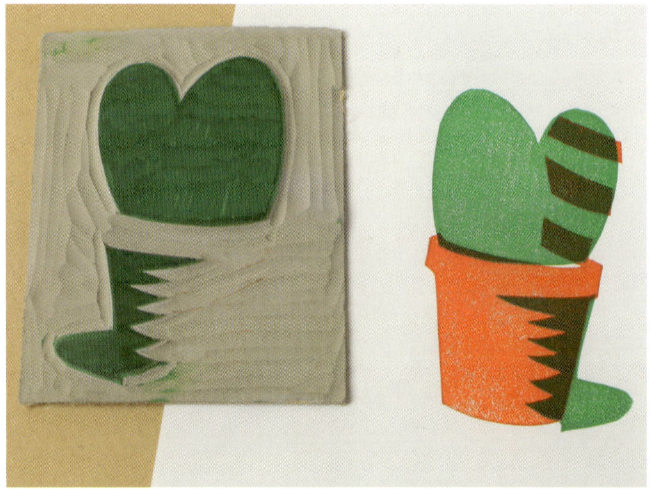

Ink up and print the second block on top.

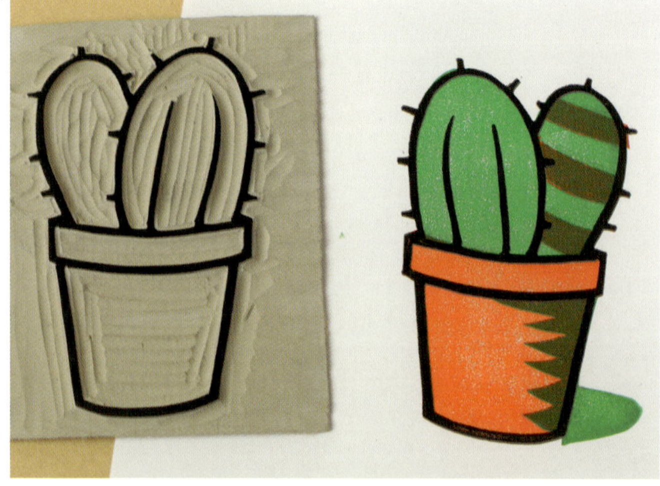

Finally, print the key block in black.

Reduction linocut

The reduction technique is a way of making a multi-layered linocut from a single block. The block is carved and then printed in the first colour. It is then cleaned, carved again and printed in the second colour and so on. At each stage the size of the printing area is reduced, hence the name.

There is no going back with this technique, so the whole design has to be carefully planned. If multiple prints are required they must be printed right from the start; you cannot print more at the end as you will have destroyed the block. For this reason you should always start off printing more than you need to allow for mistakes along the way. Any imperfect prints can be useful for testing out colours. As a guide, aim to print twice the number you need. As you get better at registration and colour mixing you can reduce the number.

Although it can be a bit of a brainteaser to plan, the reduction technique has two advantages: you only need one block of lino and it is easier to register as the block is always the same size.

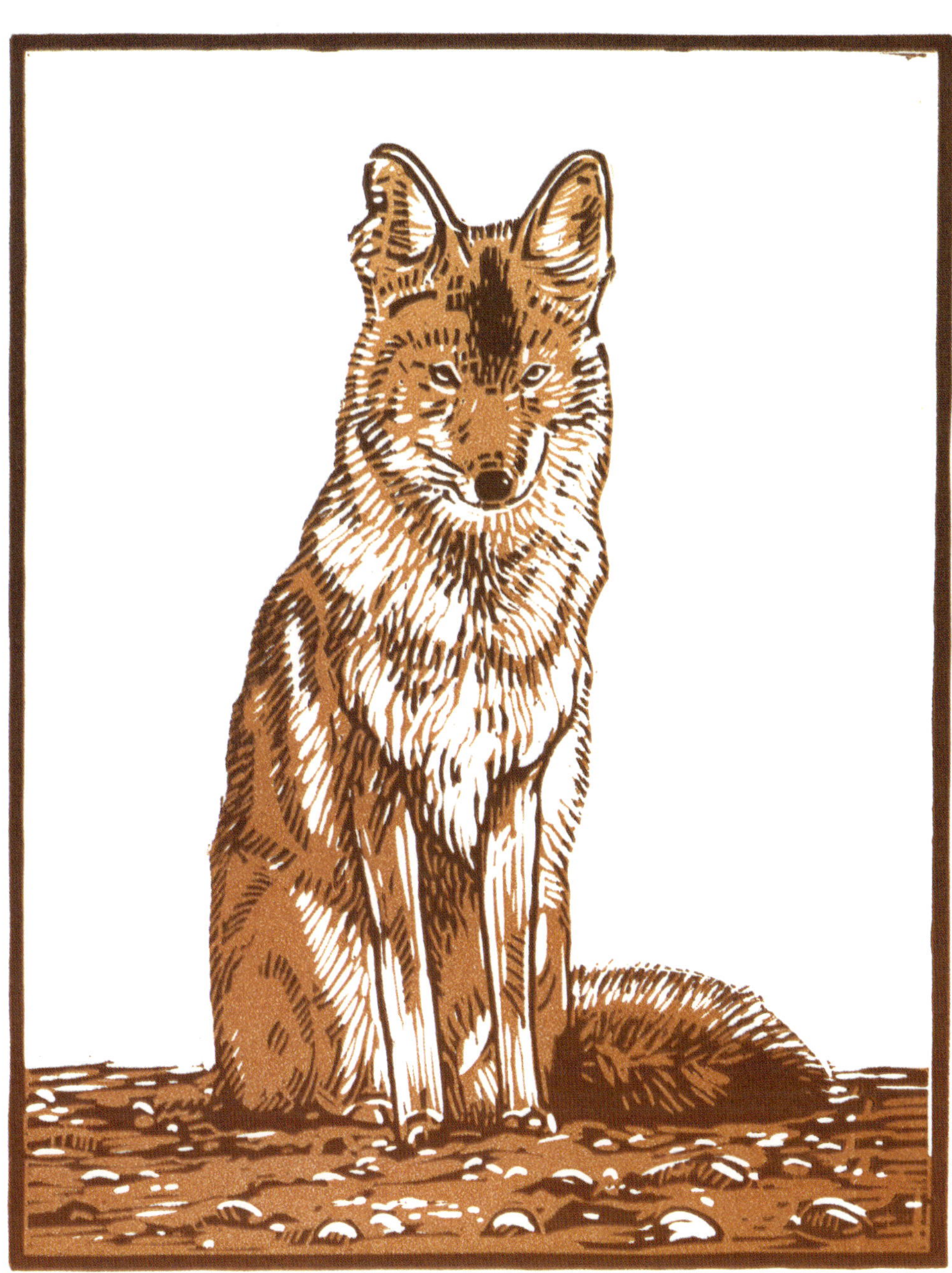

Coyote, Nick Morley. This is a reduction printed in two layers. Both layers have a slight colour blend from light to dark, in opposite directions. The white areas were carved away at the beginning to pick out the highlights. The background was also carved away at this point.

Project: tonal reduction print

You will need:

One piece of lino, coloured marker pens or felt tips, drawing paper, tracing paper or carbon paper, 2B pencil, carving tools, one or two colours of ink, extender, printing apparatus, cleaning materials.

Before you attempt a multi-colour reduction print, try making one using a range of tones of just one colour. This will help you understand the process of carving and printing without worrying too much about how one colour will look printed on top of another. You are going to print the block three times, carving it in between each layer. The first layer will be the lightest colour, the second will be a mid-tone and the third will be the darkest areas. You also have the option to have white in your image (for the purposes of this tutorial it is assumed the paper is white). This will give you a total of three tones, plus white, in your final print.

You may be able to complete this project in one session, depending on which inks you are using and how thickly you apply them. If necessary, you may need to wait for each layer to dry before progressing.

Planning the design

You can plan your design out fully from the start or make it up as you go along. If you are planning it you can use paint, pens or colouring pencils on paper, or you can use a computer. Your design should be made up of three tones plus white. Keep the colours distinct; do not blend them. You need to be able to see where one colour ends and the next one starts. It makes it easier if you reduce the design down to simple shapes.

Transfer your design to the block by tracing the edge of each colour. This can be done with the pencil rubbing method but is easier with carbon paper. Once you have transferred it, go over the lines on your block with a permanent pen. It is important that the lines do not come off during the printing and cleaning process as you will need them as guides when you are cutting the progressive stages.

Carving and printing

Keeping your design handy for reference, carve away any white areas of your design first. Next, set up your printing area, paper and registration template. Mix up the lightest shade of your colour. You can do this by mixing it with white or adding extender. Ink up and print the block a few times using your registration template. Be as accurate as you can with the registration. This is layer one.

At this point you need to clean the block thoroughly, being careful not to clean off the pen lines.

Now you are going to carve the block again for layer two. This time you are removing the areas which will be the lightest tone (the colour of layer one) in the finished print. This applies to each consecutive layer. Each time you carve, keep in mind the colour you have just printed. You are removing the areas that will be that colour in the final print.

Mix up the mid-tone colour and print stage two over the top of layer one. Again, be as accurate as you can with registration. The second layer of colour will sit on top of the first, but where you have carved this time the first colour will show through. At this point the printed image may start to look more like something recognizable.

Clean the block, carve and print the third layer in your darkest colour. By this stage there may not be very much at all left on the block. When you have printed this layer it should look like your initial design.

Do not worry if some of your prints aren't perfectly registered. This is common and is the reason you print extra at the start. If you get one or two perfect prints on your first go you are doing well. You will get better at registering the layers with practice.

Printing opaque colours

If you are printing progressive layers from light to dark and you suddenly decide you want a lighter area on your print you can mix up a colour with white in it. Because white ink is quite opaque, it will sit on top of the other colours and obscure them to a greater or lesser degree depending on the type of ink you are using. The same goes for primary colours; if you are using transparent ink you can only have one primary colour in a print (you couldn't have red and blue, for example). This is because when you layer the colours, they mix, producing a secondary colour (purple in this case). By mixing an opaque primary colour, by adding white, you should find you can get a red and a light blue, or a blue and a pink etc. The same goes for a primary colour and its complementary colour (blue and orange, red and green, yellow and purple).

Some oil-based inks are opaque enough to cover other colours completely. If you look at Picasso's reduction prints you can often see red and green together. This is because he used oil-based ink applied in very thick layers.

Layer one.

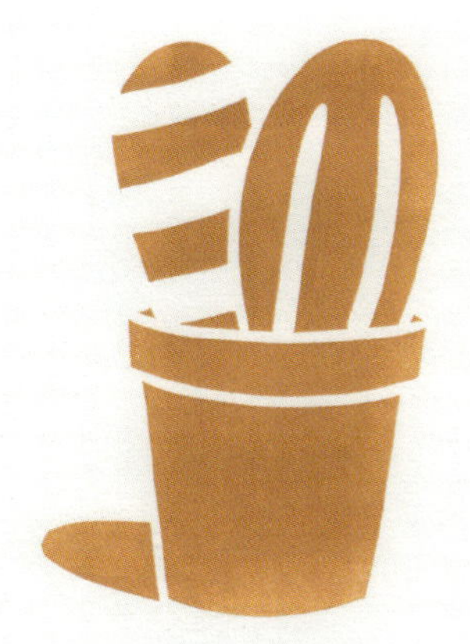

Layer two.

Layers one and two.

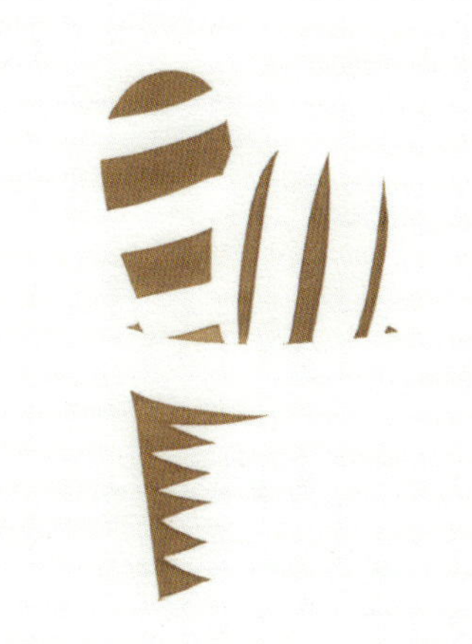

Layer three.

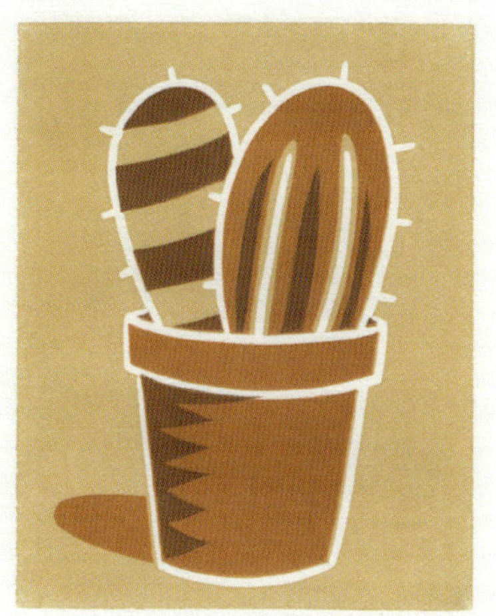

Layers one, two and three.

Project: three colour reduction print

Repeat the previous exercise, but this time using the three primary colours, printing in the order yellow, blue, red (or yellow, cyan, magenta). This time you will notice that when you print the second layer you get green. This is because the blue sits over the yellow. In fact, you shouldn't get any areas of blue in the image. When you add the third, red, layer, you will get a brown. The colours you get in the finished print depend on the order of the colours you print. So, if you were to print in the order yellow, red, blue, the finished print would contain yellow, orange and brown.

Layer one.

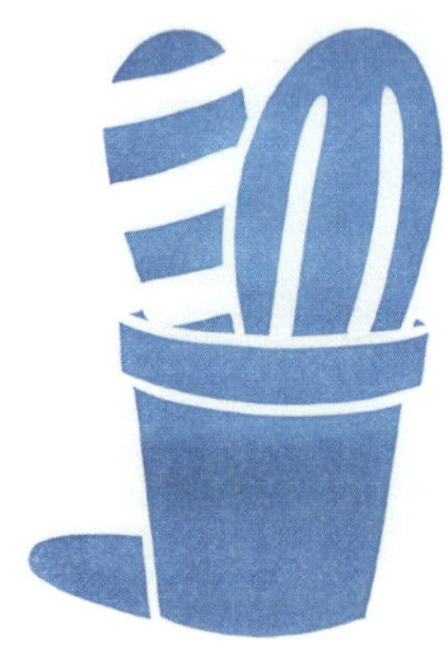

Layer two.

Layers one and two.

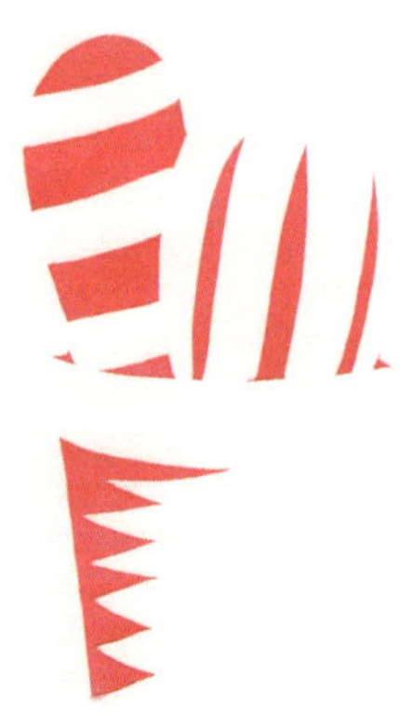

Layer three.

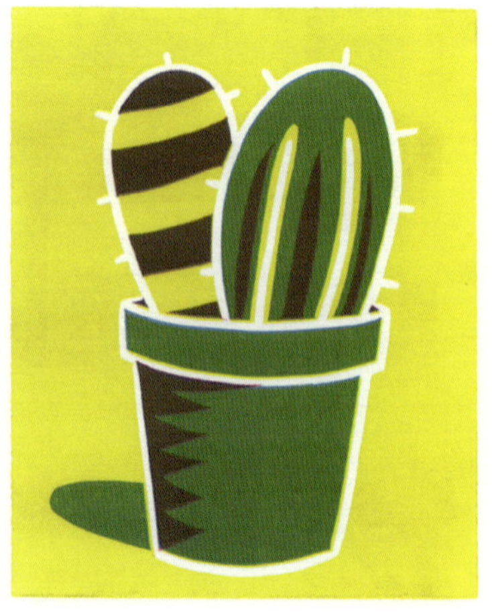

Layers one, two and three.

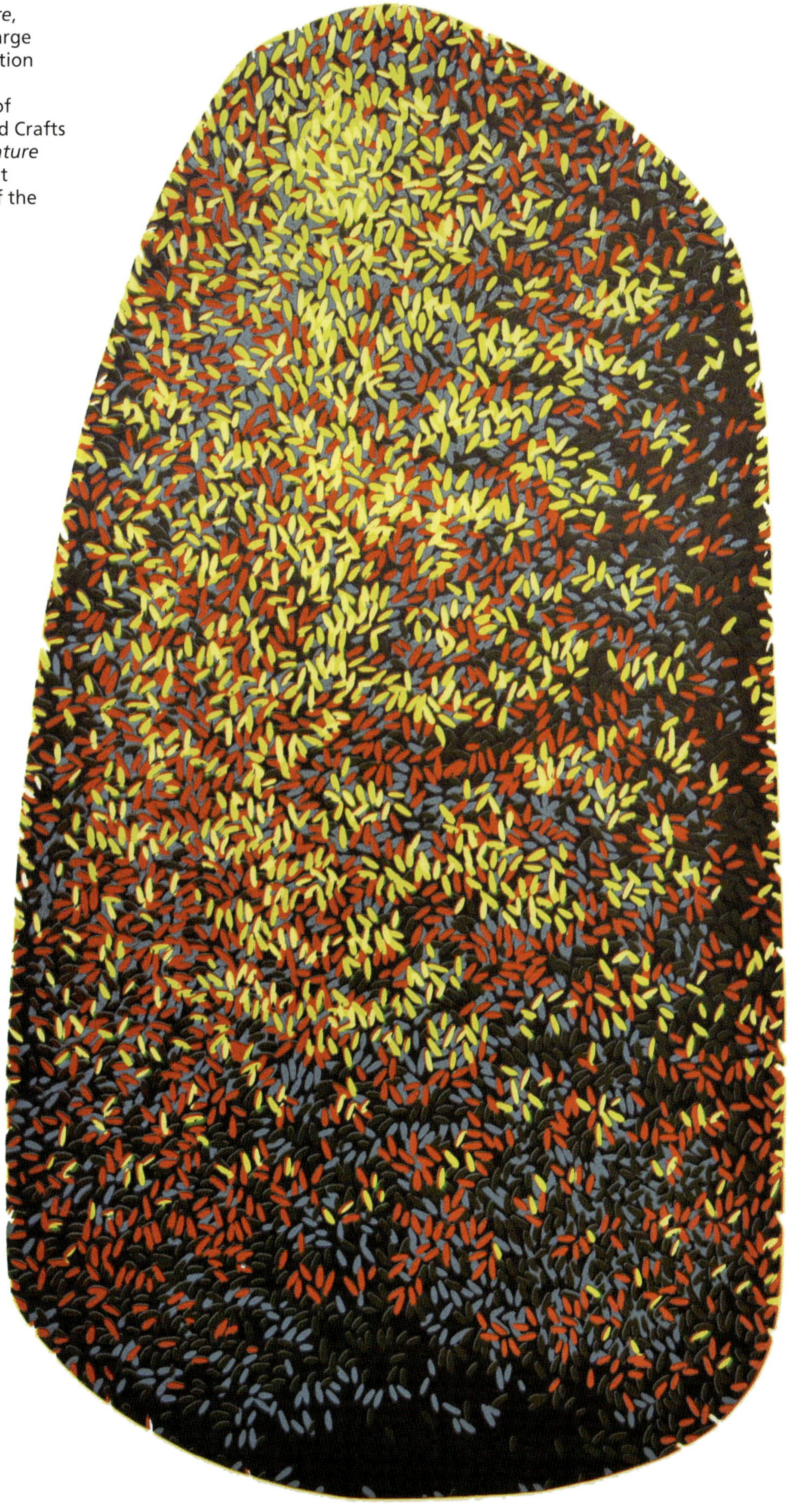

Twinkle, Training Nature, Victoria Browne. This large scale (60 × 92cm) reduction linocut is from a series inspired by the legacy of William Morris' Arts and Crafts Movement. *Training Nature* focuses on our incessant pruning and shaping of the natural environment.

Project: printing a colour blend

This is a technique which is very simple to learn but will have a dramatic effect on the look of your prints. It can give an illusion of space, shadow and movement and intensify colours. A colour blend, also called a colour graduation or rainbow roll, is a gradual blending of one colour to another across an area of the print. It is achieved by rolling out two or more colours of ink on the same roller.

You will need:

An ink roller wide enough to cover the entire area in one roll, two ink or palette knives, two colours of ink, a lino block, printing paper.

The idea is to place a blob of ink of each colour at the ends of the roller. Dip the roller in the ink and keep rolling it out on the same spot. It is very important always to roll in the same direction. If you lift the roller each time you roll it will spread the ink more quickly. As you roll the inks out they will slowly blend into each other until you get a smooth graduation of colour.

You can also blend a colour with extender, creating a graduation from dark to light. The pure extender may print with a slight yellowish hue. This is a great way of printing a blue sky, which gets lighter towards the horizon.

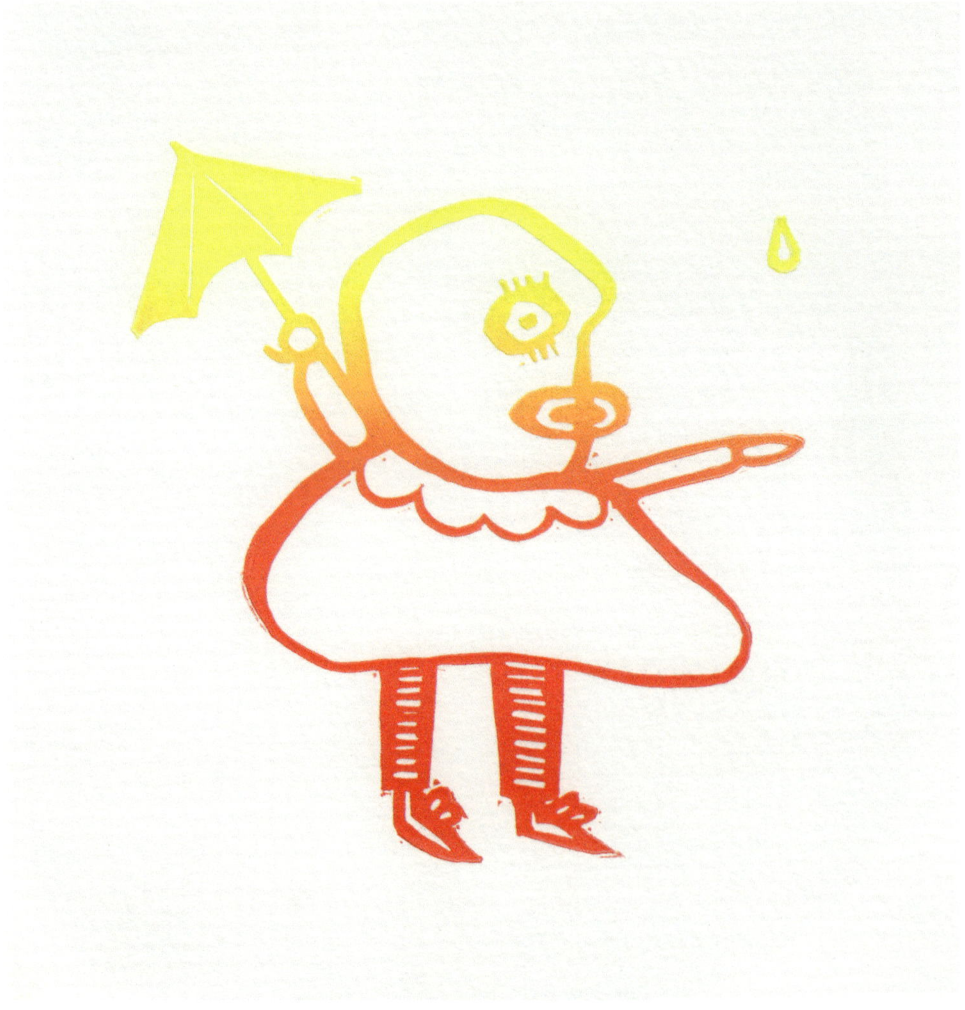

A colour blend or rainbow roll.

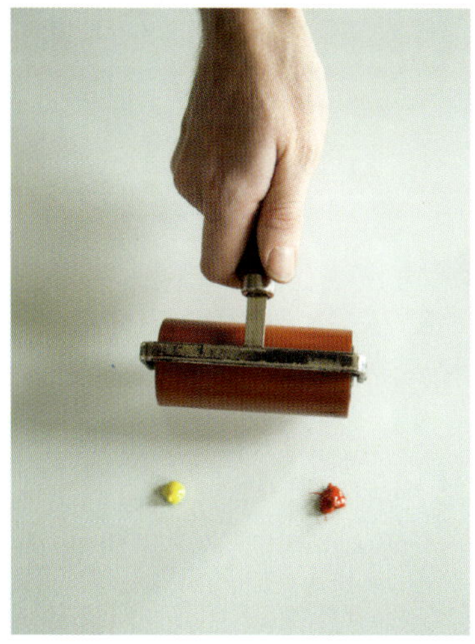

Place two blobs of ink the width of your roller apart.

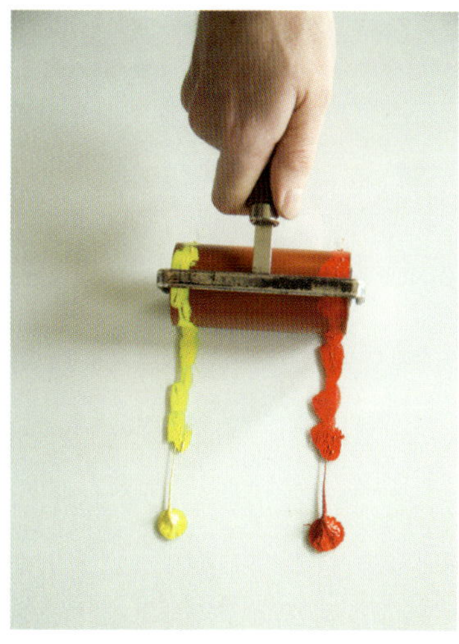

Dip the roller in the ink and start to roll out on the ink slab.

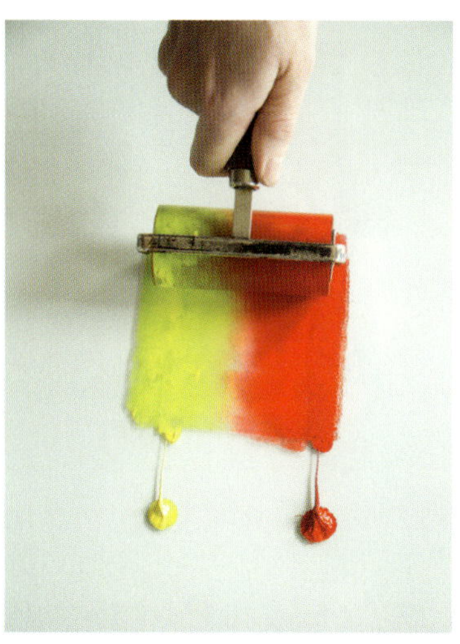

Continue to roll, moving the roller side to side very slightly.

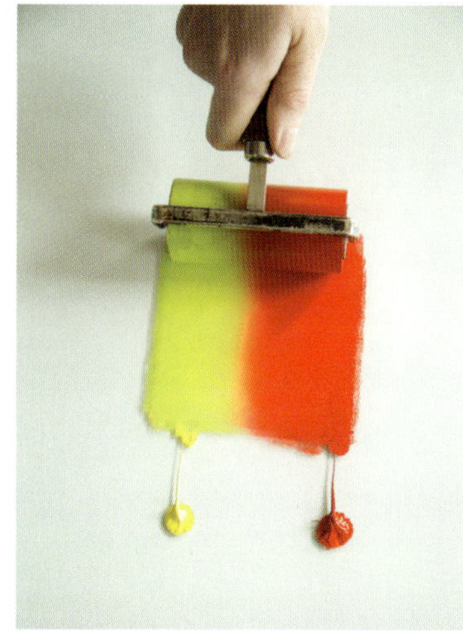

Continue rolling until the colours merge into a smooth blend.

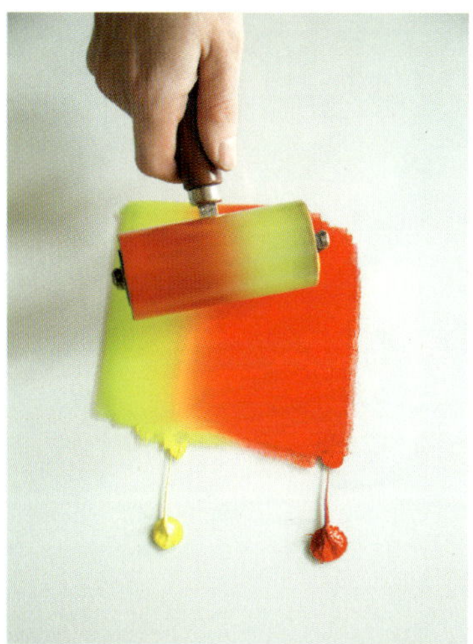

The roller should have a smooth, even coating of ink.

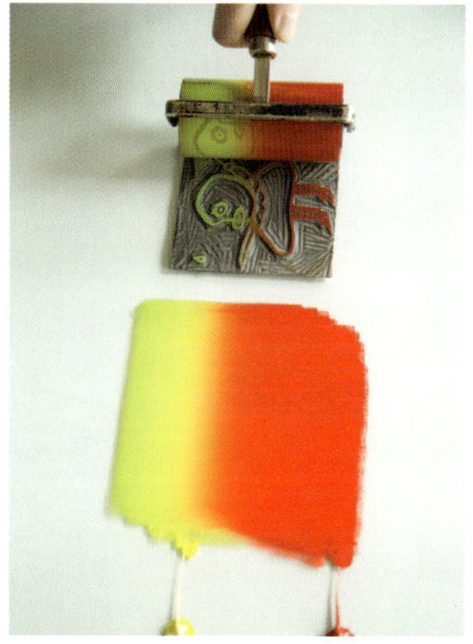

Roll onto your block in one direction only.

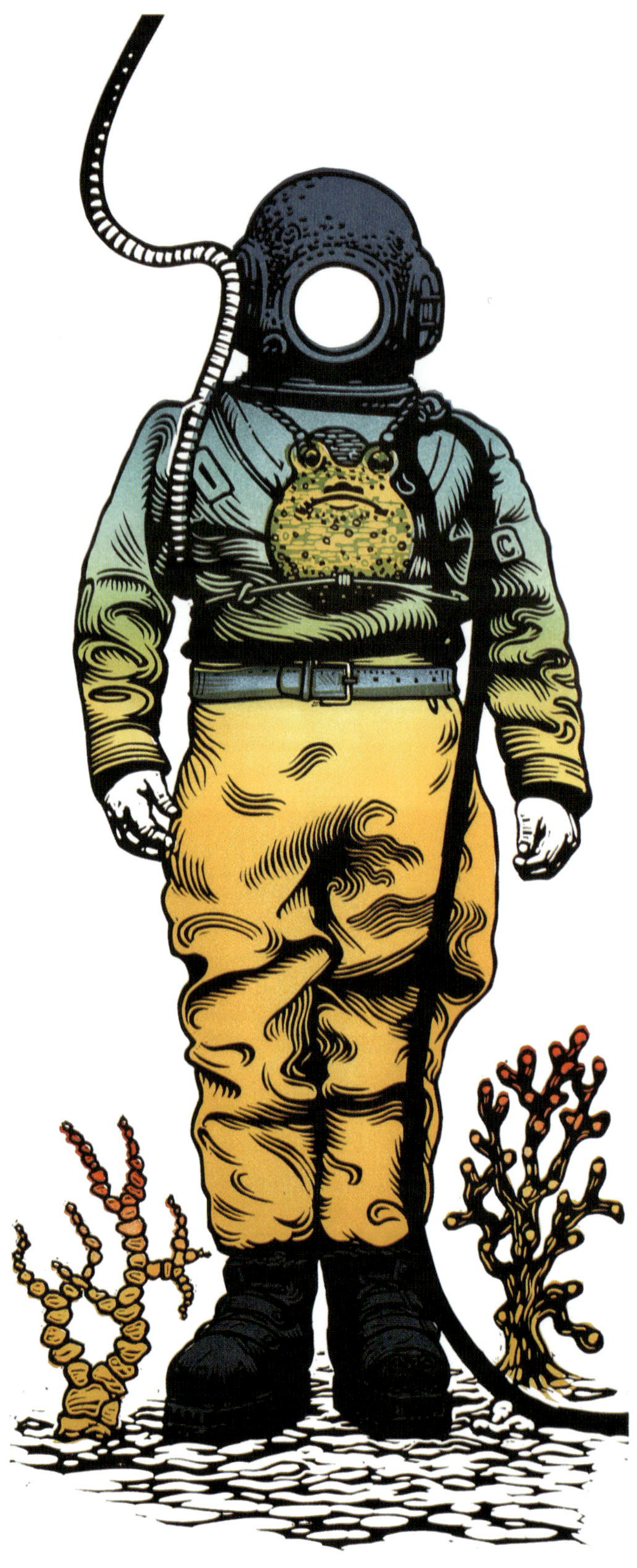

Deep Sea Diver, Nick Morley. This large scale linocut uses several colour blends and is printed from seven blocks: background colour blocks for the figure and seaweed, colour blocks for the diver's belt, weight and boots, and the key block in black, which is printed last.

Other ways to add colour

Multiple colours on one block

If there are areas of a carved block which are far enough apart you can ink them in separate colours. A small, one-inch (3cm) roller is useful for this.

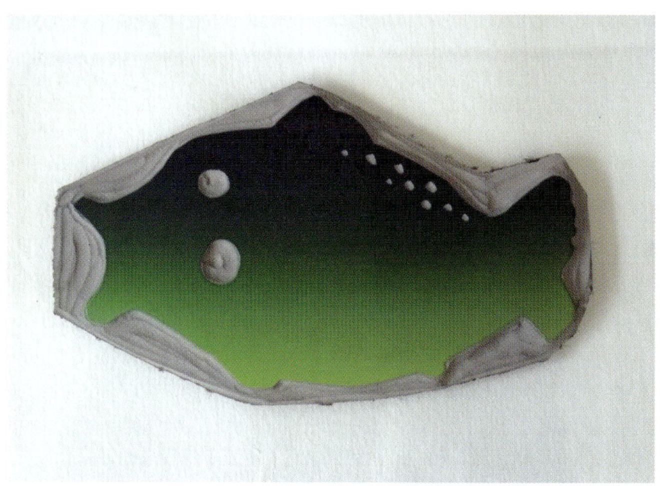

Hungry Fish was printed with two blocks. The background block was printed first with a colour blend.

Hand-colouring

Once a print is dry, if you wish, you can add colour by hand. Depending on your paper, coloured pencils and pens, drawing inks and paints can all be used. There is a long tradition of hand colouring prints using watercolour and it is very effective on a black and white print. Most printing inks will dry waterproof and will slightly repel water. This enables you to colour right up to the edges and to paint over printed areas without covering up the black ink. Thicker paints like gouache or acrylic will have more of a covering effect.

Try putting a wash of colour onto a sheet of white paper with watercolour paint. Allow it to dry thoroughly before printing over it.

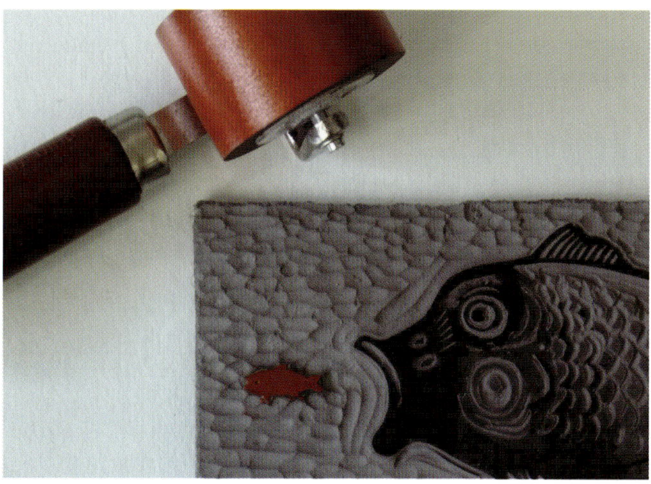

The second block. A small roller was used to ink up the red fish and the rest of the block was inked up in black.

Collage

Pieces of coloured tissue and other papers can be stuck to the printing paper in advance of printing. The glue should be dry before printing. Try adding patterned or textured papers but be aware that the ink will have a different appearance depending on the printing surface.

Inking through a stencil

If you want to ink up a small area of a block you can use a paper or plastic sheet with a hole cut in it to act as a stencil. This is also a useful technique if you are getting stray ink picking up from the roller on the carved-away areas.

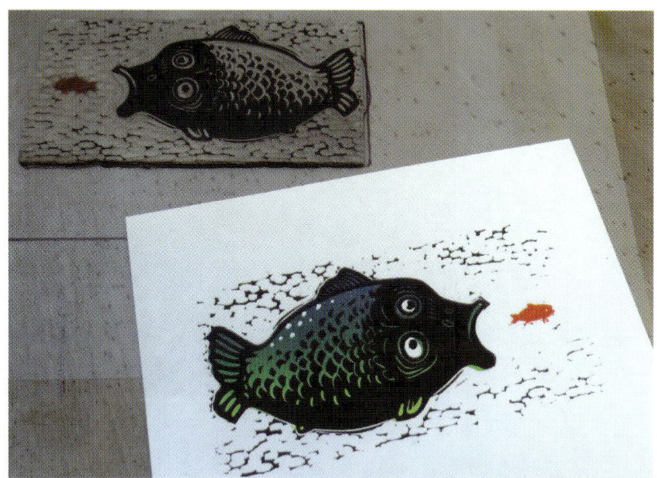

The finished print.

Jigsaw method

A single block can be cut into pieces to be inked in different colours before being reassembled and printed in one go.

AGUGN (Indonesia)

www.agugn.tumblr.com

Agung Prabowo is an Indonesian artist who goes by the name AGUGN. He started making woodcuts in 2006 as a student in the printmaking studio at Bandung Institute of Technology. He switched to linocut six years later, finding that linoleum was more stable in the high humidity of West Java. AGUGN's bright and playful prints often include multiple colour blends and are printed on paper that he makes himself. His artworks contain forms found in nature as well as human or anthropomorphic figures in various gestures.

The main reason for me to use linocut is to achieve a clean and sharp line in my works, visually. Lino is easy to cut, easy to clean the scraps, and easy to store. Lino is not very familiar in Indonesia, the only stuff called lino on the market was the black one, but I didn't really like it. I compared it to lino from Australia and Singapore, then I started to search everywhere. Then I found this brown lino I like. It's not called lino in the market (people here use it for making shoe soles) but it is suitable for my needs.

I use several other printmaking techniques like drypoint, photolithography, and carborundum print. Lately, I've also been fascinated with papermaking techniques and ceramics. I make my own paper to print on. It is thick but very porous and has the ability to absorb the inks, so the finished work seems very vivid and vibrant.

I sell my work in galleries, mainly in Indonesia (Jakarta, Jogjakarta, Bandung) and Singapore. Several times I've sold works from Instagram. People that followed me sometimes ask for an available list of works.

For now, my studio is just one small room in my home in Bandung City. Since I share it with my wife and young son, I must customize everything to become safe: handling the fumes, storing the papers, storing the finished works, etc. This setup is the best I can do for now, but I do need a bigger space, more proper storage, and a bigger press.

I make my linocut in a traditional way. I draw straight onto the lino then carve it. Sometimes I warm the lino in direct sunlight. I always try to improve or develop the design from my sketchbook to the lino, and then improve it again when carving it, and through the colour selections I make during the printing process.

Printmaking techniques are not very familiar in Indonesia, so the tools, equipment and inks are very limited, mainly imported stuff from the UK or Germany. I use standard carving tools from China that I got from my father-in-law as a gift. It's just a set of five carving tools (pen-shape with wood handle), and came with a little white stone for sharpening the knives, and a tiny baren. I use a local brand of oil-based printing ink called Cemani Toka, which I get from an offset printing supplier. I built my own presses; I have two. For small works, I use the little vertical press; for the bigger plates I use a flatbed press. Both are custom built, and the brayers too.

I make lots of plates to make my large prints, in a modular way, so I can play with different colours on different plates. I also like to print with reduction techniques. In the future I want to make three-dimensional large work with modular linocut prints.

> *Graphic art, for me, is a means of contemplation that helps me to find solace, a state of calm, a moment of freedom from the storm of fear.*

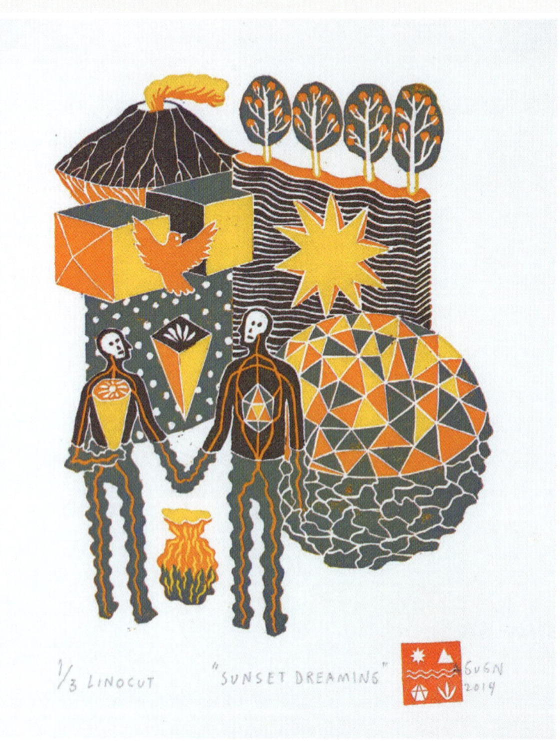

Sunset Dreaming, AGUGN, 20 × 25cm, reduction linocut print on handmade paper.

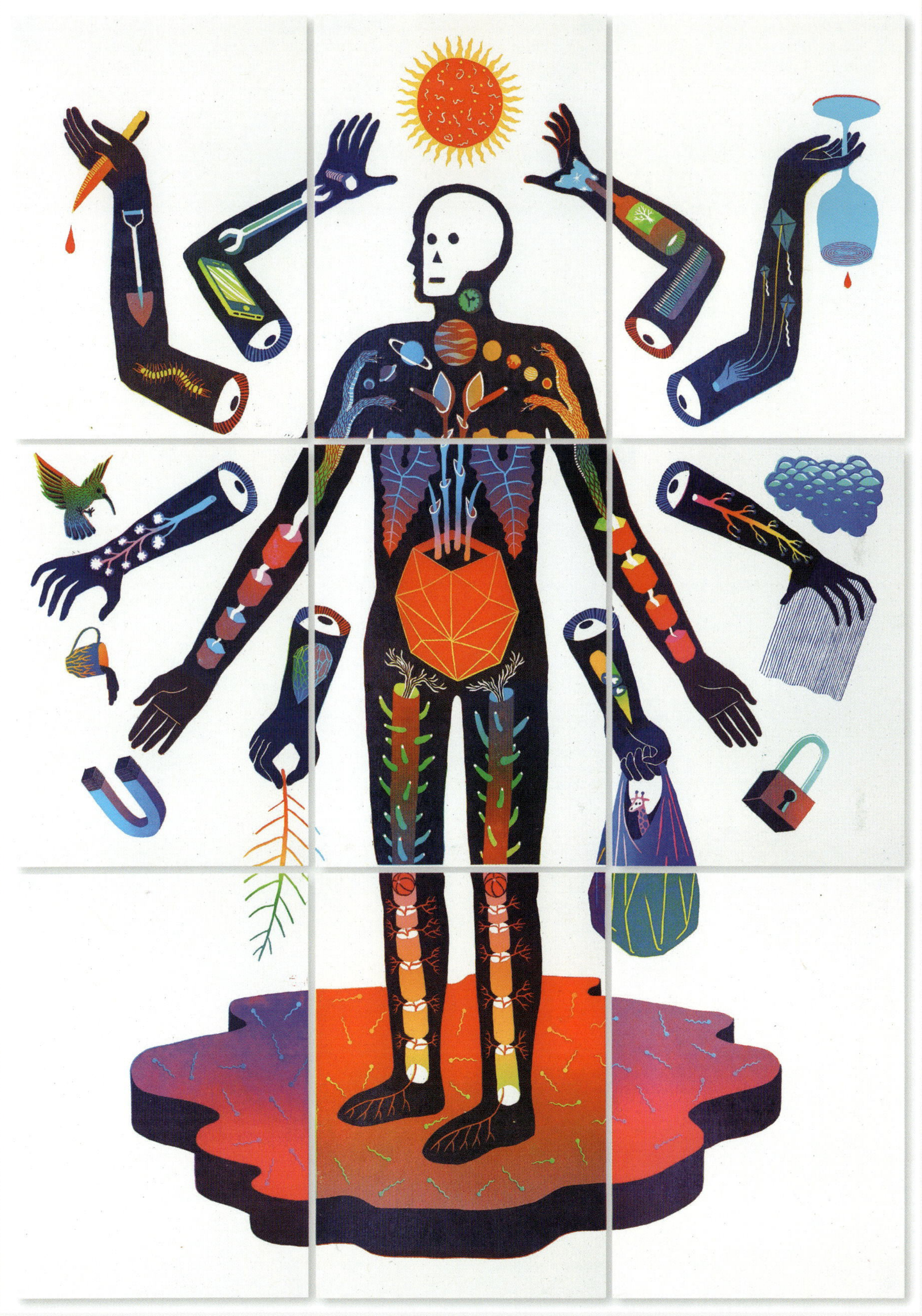

Raga Aruna, AGUGN, 145 × 107cm, reduction linocut print on handmade paper.

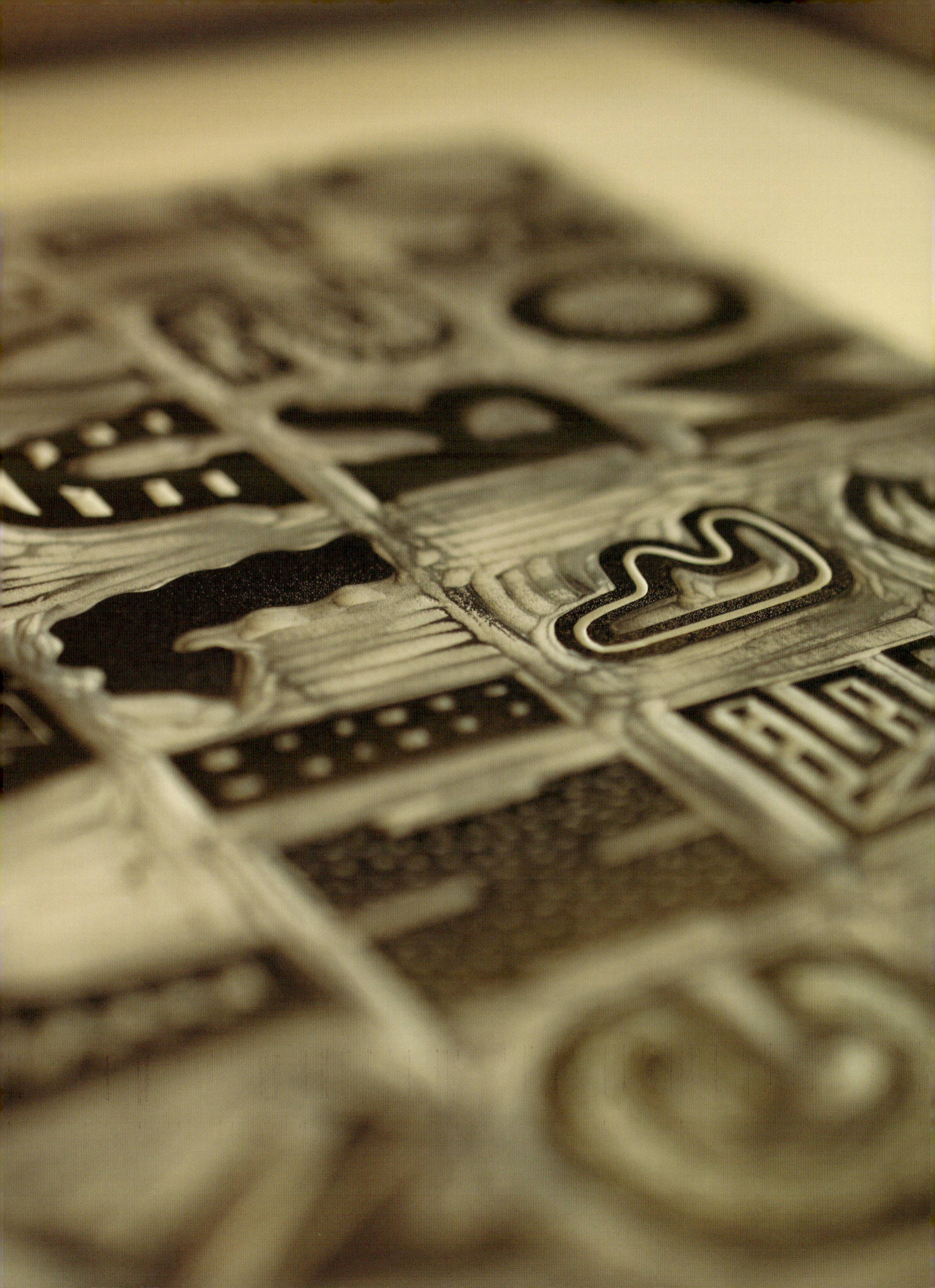

CHAPTER 6

FINE ART PRINTS, ILLUSTRATION AND GRAPHICS

Linocuts can stand as artworks in their own right, to be bought and sold, collected and exhibited in museums and galleries. They also have a long tradition in the world of illustration and graphic design, from the Constructivist posters of the Soviet era, to the London Underground posters of Edward Bawden in England. There are many illustrators working today who use linocut, either solely, or alongside other media, producing images for magazines and book covers, websites and gig posters. The bold look of linocut also appeals to graphic designers, who may be after a more honest, handmade quality. This chapter looks at making and selling prints as fine art, as well as the advantages of using linocut for illustration and graphic design.

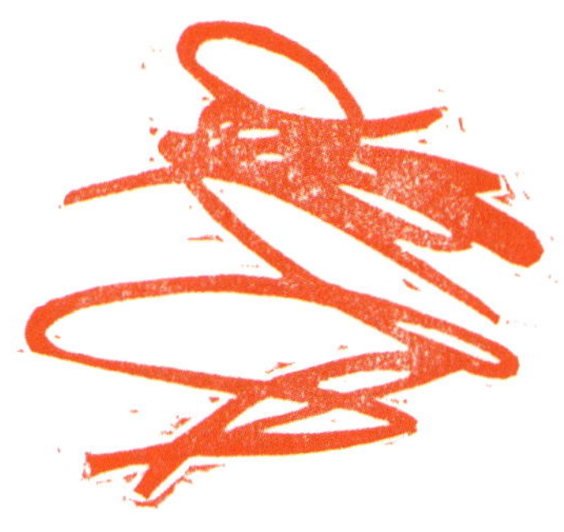

Exhibiting and selling prints

There is a large and rapidly growing market for affordable contemporary art and prints are perfectly suited to it. They are relatively quick and cheap to produce, take up little room to store and can be transported cheaply and easily. On top of the financial benefits, there is something very rewarding in selling your artwork. As well as being a stamp of approval for your efforts it is a great compliment when someone wants to own something you have made.

If you want to make prints for exhibitions you need a professional attitude which should be reflected in your work. Depending on where you are exhibiting there will be certain expectations and rules which you should follow, more or less, in order to be taken seriously. Not all galleries are the same. They can be large or small, exclusive or accessible, run as businesses or charities. Do some research into different galleries and decide where you think your work fits best. Be honest with yourself and try to look at your work with a critical eye. Once you have decided where your market is you can consider how best to approach it.

Presentation

You need to be sure that your work is seen at its best. Spend some time and money on presentation and you will be rewarded in the long term. A dog-eared print on cheap paper with a big inky fingerprint in the corner is unlikely to be taken seriously. Likewise there are certain conventions about where to sign prints, how to number them and so on. Whether you want to subscribe to these rules or not is up to you but certain standards will be expected, particularly from the more traditional galleries. Once a print has left your hands it becomes a product like any other in the marketplace. Put yourself in the place of the customer and think about what you would want in terms of quality and presentation.

Quality of materials

The materials you use should reflect the value you place on your work. If you are selling cheap prints off a market stall you might not want to use the most expensive inks and paper. But if you want to present the work in a gallery or pitch it at a higher price level you will gain more credence by making sure it looks good and will last. A heavyweight paper with a deckle edge and a watermark will impress more than cheap cartridge paper. Buy the best materials you can afford. As well as making the work look good it will make you feel more confident in its value. If you take your work seriously, so will others.

Pricing your work

Everyone finds this hard. Depending on who you ask you will get different advice about pricing prints. You must decide for yourself whether it is more important to sell a print quickly or sell it for a good price. When pricing your work, bear in mind how long it took you. Not just to print it, but to research, draw, carve, proof, print, present, market and sell. Balance that against what people will reasonably pay for it. A word of warning though: don't assume that by making a print cheaper it will automatically be more desirable. People expect art to cost a certain amount. Too low a price may raise questions as to a print's worth.

If you need help pricing your prints, ask someone impartial for their honest opinion. Then ask someone else and someone else. Treat it as market research and try to distance yourself emotionally from the work. The best way to find out what people will really pay is by starting to sell your prints. Once you have been doing this for a while you will get a feel for it. It may also be worth looking at what other artists are charging for their work. Artists who have an established reputation will command higher prices so pick someone at a similar level to you. You can always put your prices up when you become famous.

Commission on sales

If you are working with a commercial gallery or agent you should expect to give away up to 50 per cent of the sale price (sometimes more) in commission. In return the gallery can be expected to safely display, store and handle the work, market the work and the artist to the public in a positive way, process any sales, and cover any wrapping and delivery costs.

Try to keep your prices consistent, whether you are selling direct to the public, online or through a gallery. If you are selling the same print at different prices it will confuse people and if you undercut a gallery they won't be very happy.

Original prints

If you are making linocuts to sell as works of art it is important to understand the distinction between a reproduction and an original print. There is still some confusion among non-printmakers about this difference. A reproduction is a replica of an existing artwork, whereas an original print is not. One linocut is not a 'copy' of another, instead they both originate from the same printing block, therefore each print is original. This may seem like a subtle distinction, but when you are trying to explain to someone why they should pay more for one of your linocuts than they would for a cheap poster, it is useful to have your argument prepared.

Editioning prints

It is possible to make just one print from a lino block but once you have gone to the trouble of designing, carving, inking and printing one it is not much more effort to print a second. The process of producing multiple identical prints is called editioning and the resulting set of prints is the edition. It is a good idea to print the whole edition in one go if possible. This is more important if you are mixing up colours as these should be consistent throughout the edition. On the other hand, if you are printing an edition of black and white linocuts you may decide to just print a few at a time. Once you have run out of those you can print more.

The aim of editioning is to produce a set of identical prints. However, as this is a handmade process there will naturally be some minor variations. This is unavoidable and is part of the attraction for many people; linocuts are made by humans, not machines. Similarly the way you print will be different from anyone else. Your choice of ink and paper and your printing method will all have an effect on the look of the finished print.

Once you have finished an edition, tradition dictates that you should destroy the block so that no more prints can be made from it. This can be done by cutting the block in half or carving a large X through it.

Keeping records

Keep a notebook or database on your computer and keep it updated as you produce and sell your prints. It is also important to keep track of any works which are sent to exhibitions, galleries and shops. Ideally you should get a consignment note and each party should sign and keep a copy for future reference.

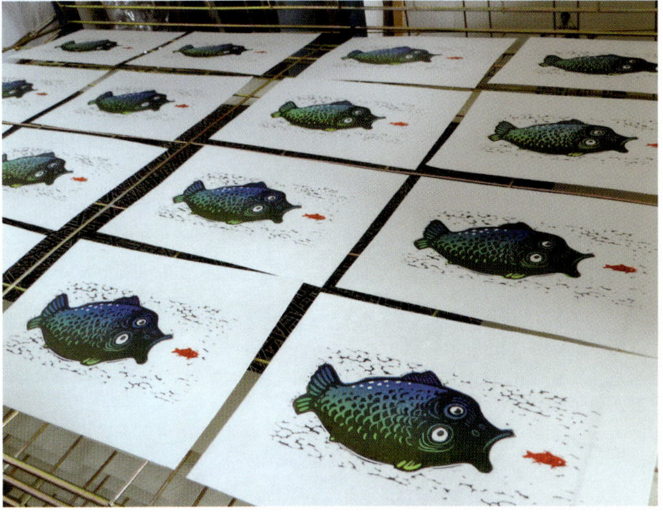

Editioned prints drying on the rack.

Terminology

Limited edition

Both reproduction prints and original prints can be produced in limited editions. The edition size could be anything from two up to thousands, so the term 'limited edition' in itself does not indicate exactly how rare or valuable a print is.

Edition size

As the artist, you get to decide the size of the edition you will make. To some extent this will be determined by how long each print takes to ink up, how many you think you can sell, and how much you can afford to spend on ink and paper. On top of this, you need to consider what effect the edition size will have on value. A print from an edition of five will be perceived to be rarer and therefore more valuable than one from an edition of two hundred.

Artist Proofs

In addition to the numbered prints in the edition, convention allows for a number of Artist Proofs to be made. These are identical to the numbered prints and are marked A/P or A.P. There should be no more than about ten artist proofs per edition. Traditionally the artist proofs were for the artist to sell, keep or give as gifts after the gallery or dealer sold the edition. These days they are seen more as an extension of the edition and many galleries will sell them once the edition runs out. Some collectors value artist proofs more highly than the editioned prints.

Trial Proofs and Colour Proofs

Proofs made in the development stages, when you are trying out ideas may be marked T/P or T.P. to indicate Trial Proof. Similarly if you are trying out a colour variation you can mark it C/P or C.P. for Colour Proof. Trial proofs and colour proofs are not usually sold but are useful to keep for reference.

Open edition

An unlimited, unnumbered edition. If you don't want to set a limit on the number of prints you will produce you can create an open edition. Beware that some collectors will only buy numbered prints and prints in an open edition are generally viewed as less valuable.

Project: making an edition

So, after much blood and sweat and possibly a few tears, you've produced a print which you are happy with. You decide you want to make a small edition of it to sell. How do you start?

Firstly, you need to get yourself organized. Make sure you have enough ink and paper to print the whole edition plus some extra. You will almost always lose some prints along the way to mistakes, so aim to make at least 20 per cent extra from the start. The more colours and layers there are in a print the more you will lose.

Try to organize your printing area in the most ergonomic way possible. Ideally your inking, printing and drying areas should form a triangle. Have everything you need to hand so you don't have to walk around too much. Prepare your paper while you have clean hands by tearing or cutting each piece to size. Stack your paper safely away from ink and other dangers.

If you are mixing colours, make sure you mix up enough ink for the whole batch. The last thing you want to do is run out half way through a print run and have to match the colour again. Try to be methodical in your approach. Ink your block the same way each time to give consistent results and use a registration system, even if you are printing in one colour, to ensure your block is printed in the same position each time. Keep your hands clean. If you are a messy worker, wear gloves while inking and take them off when printing.

When you have finished printing the edition and it is dry you should select the best prints from the ones you've got and sign and number them.

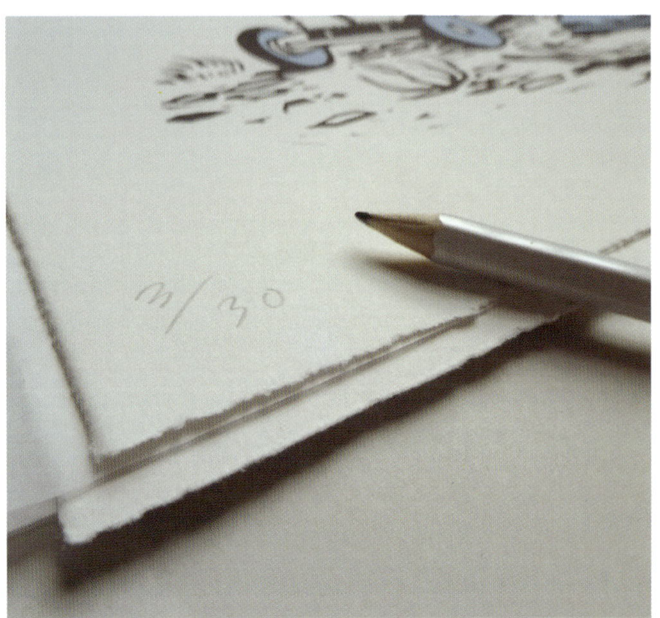

Sign and number prints with a pencil in the corner.

Signing and numbering prints

Convention dictates that prints should be signed a certain way. Unless you have some good reason to ignore this, it is best to follow the rules. Sign using a pencil rather than a pen. Pencil lead is stable and won't bleed or fade over time. Permanent pens are sometimes used but can distract from the print. Use an HB pencil as anything softer is liable to smudge. Make sure the point is not too sharp; if you have just sharpened it, scribble on a piece of scrap paper to blunt it slightly. This will reduce the risk of tearing the paper.

Prints are usually signed and numbered on the front, just below the image on the left or right. Some artists sign the back of their works, especially if they are very light coloured or subtle, but this can cause problems if the work is framed as the signature will be hidden. A print which goes right to the edge of the paper and has no border can still be signed; the pencil will show up silver when it reflects the light.

Numbering

Prints should be numbered from 1 upwards, using the format 1/20, 2/20 etc. The number usually goes on the left, below the image.

Signature

Your signature usually goes on the right. It is up to you whether you use your full name, initial and last name, or last name on its own. Very small prints may not leave enough room for a full signature so initials may be used. The signature you use on your prints may be different from your usual signature. You may choose to make it more legible than normal so that it is easier to identify.

Date

The year of the print's creation can be included, usually after the signature. This can be written in full or abbreviated.

Title

Writing the title of the print is optional. If included it should go in the centre. Adding the title can be useful for identification purposes, both for you and for others.

Selling unframed prints

Many galleries and shops sell unframed prints in print browsers or racks. Most will expect you to mount and wrap the prints yourself. If you run a market stall, take part in an art fair or organize your own exhibition this is a great way to sell prints. People love flicking through a stack of prints and picking out their favourites. Being able to handle something will make someone more likely to buy it.

Print browsers can be bought online or through larger art supply stores. They are wood or metal stands for holding unframed prints and can be folded up or dismantled for easy transport. Prices can vary wildly so hunt around. If you're handy you can make your own print browser, or find a nice box instead. Old wine crates work well for smaller prints and can be picked up from wine merchants for free if you're lucky.

Mounting and wrapping

Mounting your prints with board will protect the corners and stop them getting bent. Wrapping them in cellophane will protect them from fingerprints, dirt and moisture. Wrap the entire mounted print and seal it with tape on the back. Use Sellotape or, ideally, Scotch tape for this. Avoid masking tape as it quickly deteriorates and can eventually become brittle and fall off. Self-sealing cellophane bags are a neat way to wrap unframed prints, but only come in standard sizes, so may not fit odd-sized prints.

There are several kinds of board suitable for mounting. Mount board or matt board is purpose-made and comes in a range of colours. The cheaper stuff isn't acid-free and over time the core will turn yellow, then brown. This isn't a problem if it is only for short-term use but for more valuable prints you should use conservation or museum board, which are correspondingly more expensive. If you are on a budget you can use greyboard, or even corrugated card.

Cut your mount board larger than your print so if a corner gets a dent it won't affect the print itself. Use self-adhesive photo corners to hold the print in the centre of the board. For a fancier look you can use a window mount.

Window mounting

Window mounts can improve the look of many prints, but can look very traditional. If you don't have clean borders on your print a window mount can hide any fingerprints or other marks. If the print has a small border or no border at all a window mount can add visual space around it, giving the image more impact. Window mounts look best with a bevel, which can be achieved with a mount cutter. If you don't have one of these or find it difficult to do yourself, a framer should be able to cut them for a small fee.

Float mounting

Float mounted prints are attached to the backing board with mounting tape, which is hidden. The edges of the paper are visible. Use archival tape for this, available from framing suppliers and larger art stores. Use as little tape as you can whilst still making sure the print is securely attached. Two pieces at the top and bottom are usually enough, three for larger prints. Again, a framer can do this for you if you are not confident yourself.

Framing

Framing is one of the most expensive costs for artists but it can really enhance the look of a print, as well as protecting it. Choosing a frame is largely a matter of personal choice but the general consensus is that simpler is better. Your framer should be able to advise you and make suggestions while taking your thoughts into account. Black, white and plain wood are usually safe choices if you are unsure. Try different widths and depths of frame; your framer should have corner samples which you can hold up to the print. Check if the moulding you want is in stock; if you want a rush job this will make a difference although most framers can get deliveries the next day from their suppliers.

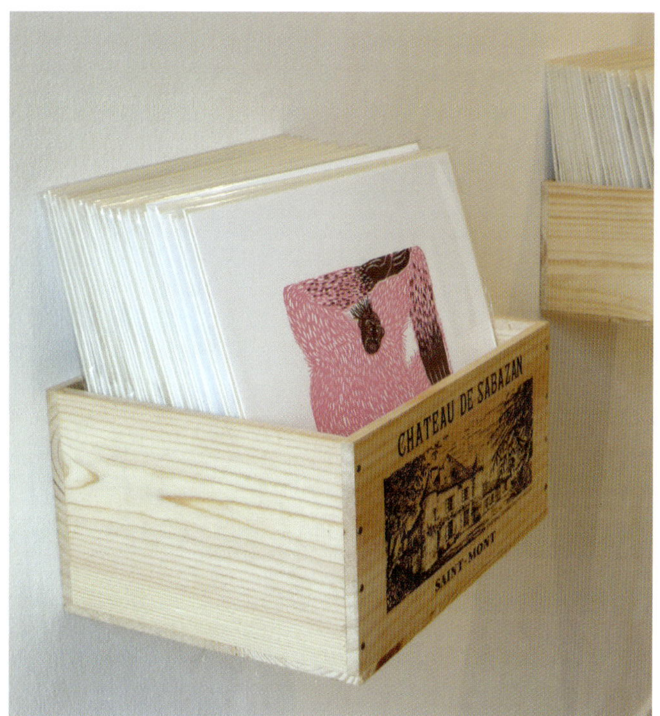

Old wine crates screwed directly into the wall to display small unframed prints.

Linocut and illustration

The look of linocut is attractive to many designers and art directors, especially in print applications like book and magazine publishing. Because most illustration and graphic design is now produced by computer and looks very slick, the handmade quality of linocut can be refreshing. In fact, what might be regarded as badly printed by you – patchy, off-register, unevenly inked – may even be more attractive to a client. Many linocuts are commissioned for historical or traditional material as they can look like woodcut, the oldest form of printed illustration.

The way multi-block linocuts are constructed in layers relates closely to the way many computer-generated images are put together. If necessary each block can be printed separately and scanned. The image can then be reconstructed and each layer adjusted individually: the colours and transparency adjusted, elements resized and untidy areas cleaned up.

The main problem with using linocut for illustration is how long it takes. For a tight deadline you will only have time to carve and print a very simple image. Something which might take only ten minutes in Adobe Illustrator could take an hour to carve, print and scan. Adjustments are harder to make too, so it's a good idea to get detailed roughs approved if possible before starting to carve the final artwork.

Many illustrators combine different techniques and linocut can be used in this way too. Printed elements can be scanned, manipulated, colour-adjusted, cut and pasted to form part of a larger image. An outline illustration can be quickly coloured in or a scanned texture added as a background. By building up a library of textures you have created you can ensure your work will look unique.

Project: thumbnail illustration

A thumbnail illustration is simply one around the size of a thumbnail. In practice nowadays they are usually slightly larger but the name has stuck. The trick with creating a successful illustration on such a small scale is to simplify it and remove any extraneous detail. There is quite a skill to this as you are being forced to convey a scene, a character or whatever with much less visual information. Using linocut effectively forces you to simplify things anyway as you are limited by the marks you can make. With practice you will develop your own shorthand of carved marks which will save you time and give your prints a directness and vitality. Working on a small scale will encourage you to refine your technique as mistakes will be more obvious.

Make a small, black and white linocut around two inches (5cm) across. Set yourself a time limit to force yourself to simplify the image.

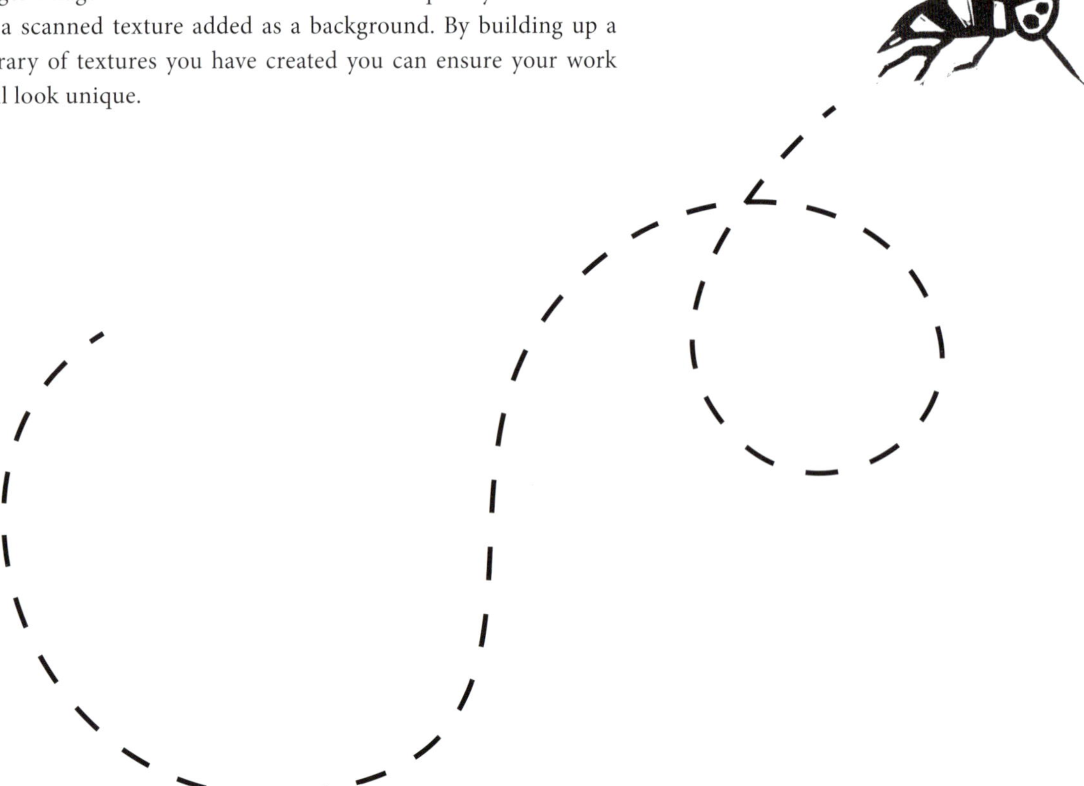

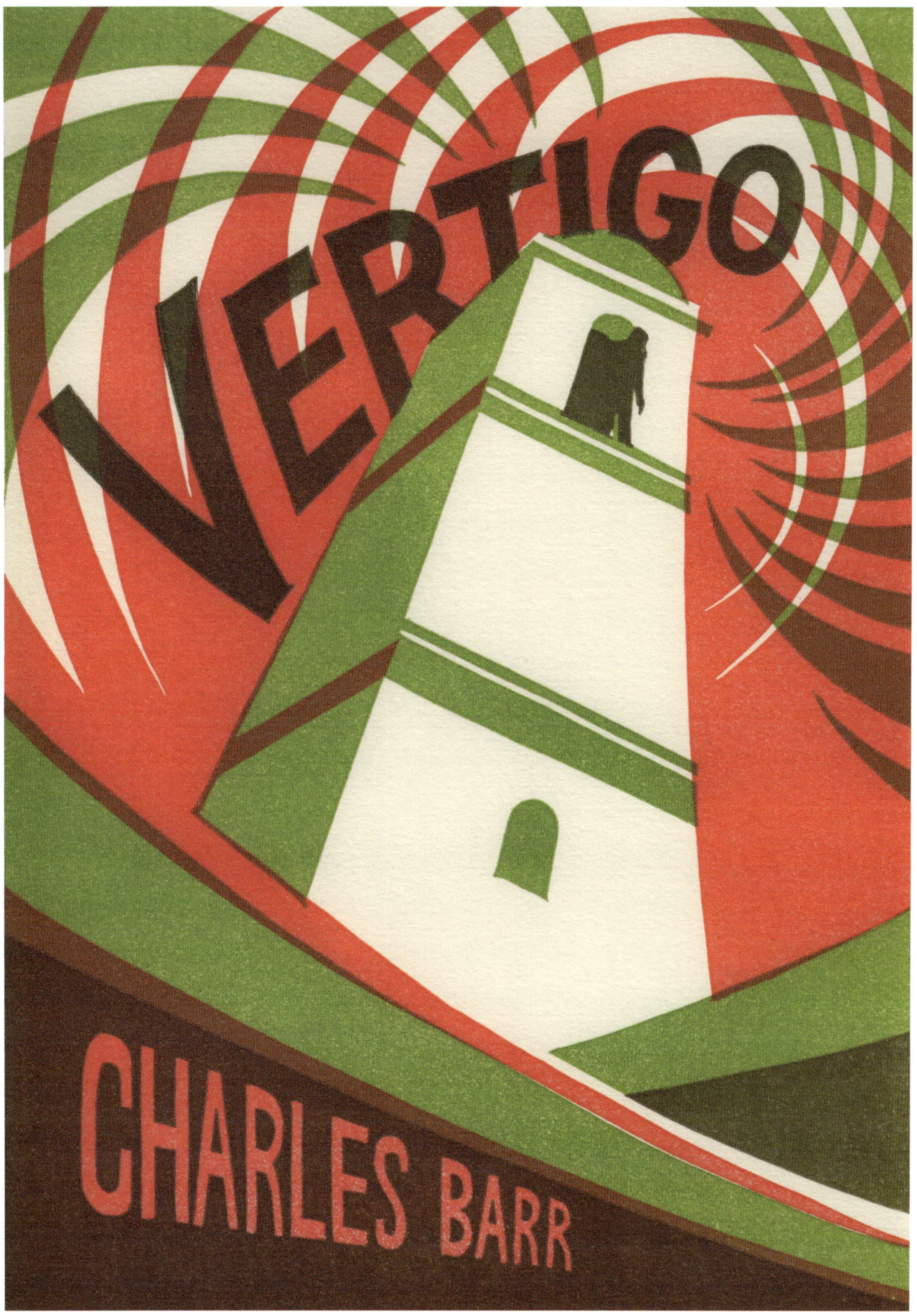

Vertigo, Nick Morley. This book cover design was printed from two blocks, the second block being a reduction printed in two stages. The text was carved from the same blocks as the image, giving it a more integrated look.

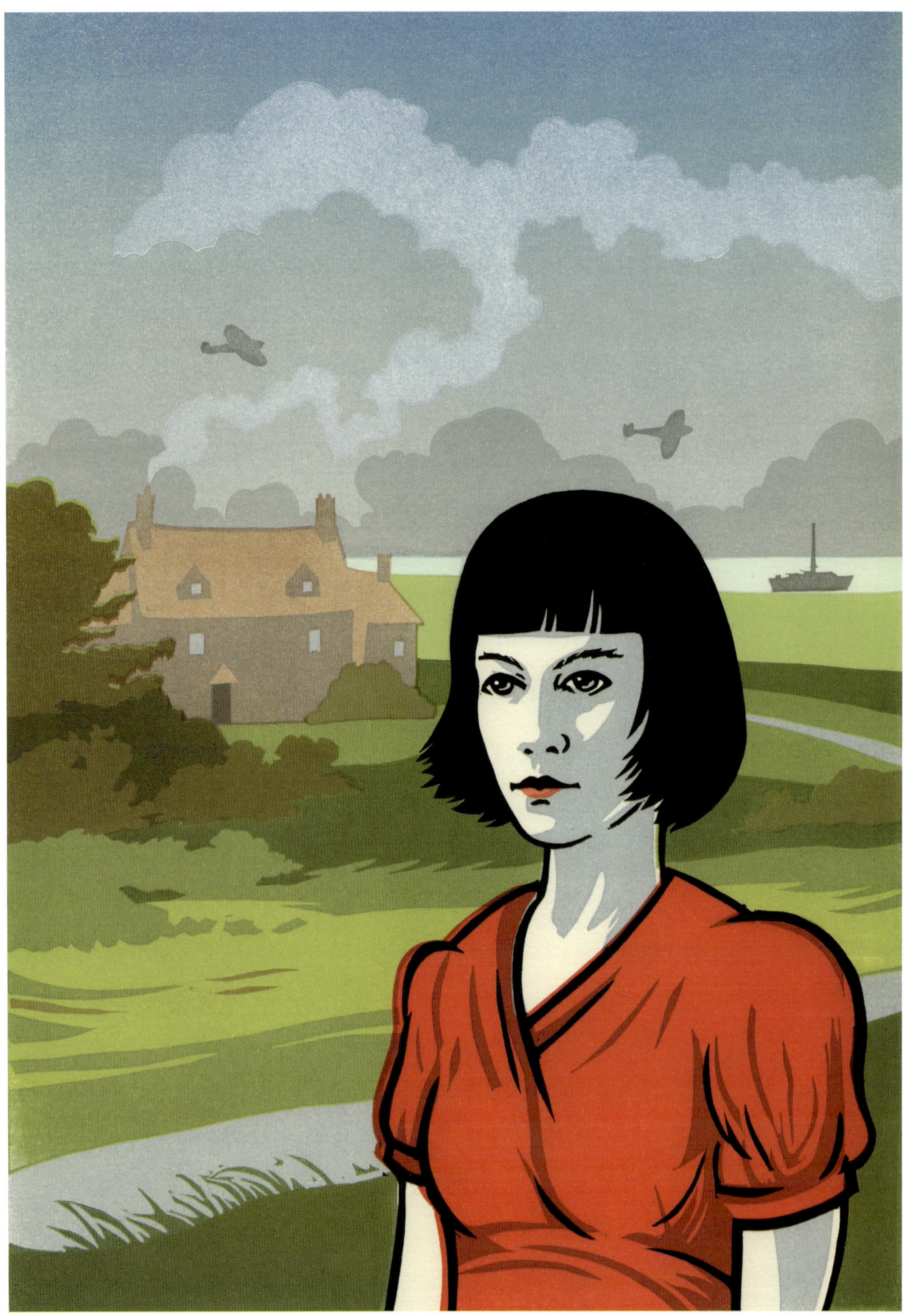

The Villa Rouge, Nick Morley.
This book cover design for MacLehose Press was printed on a yellowish paper to give it a vintage look.
It is a complex design printed with several blocks and utilizing layering of colours to create additional ones.

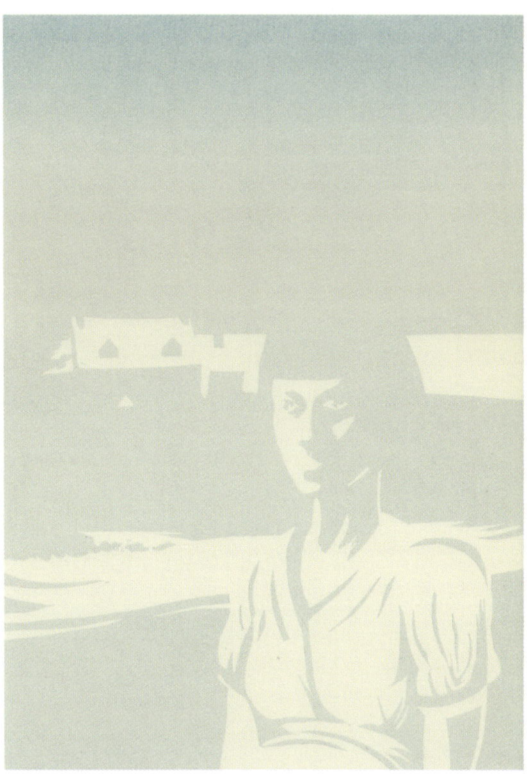

The first layer printed was a pale blue. This formed part of the sky, but also served to darken the following layers of colour for the shadows.

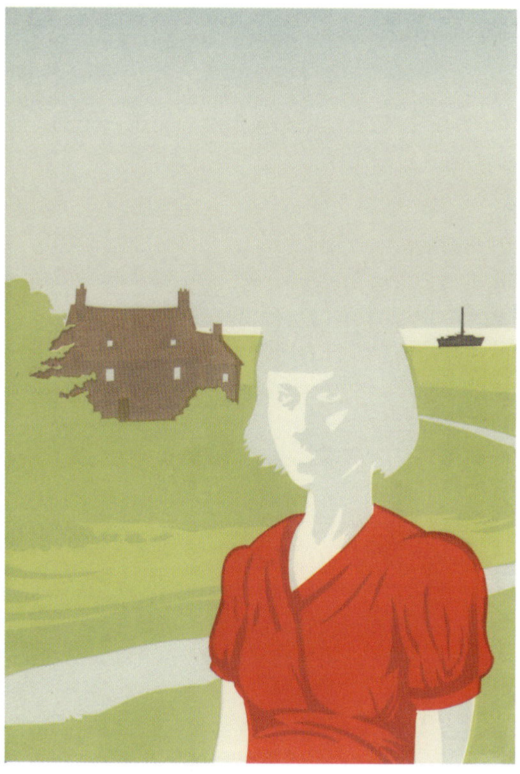

The second block printed in green. The third was inked up with three separate colours for the house, the woman's shirt and the boat.

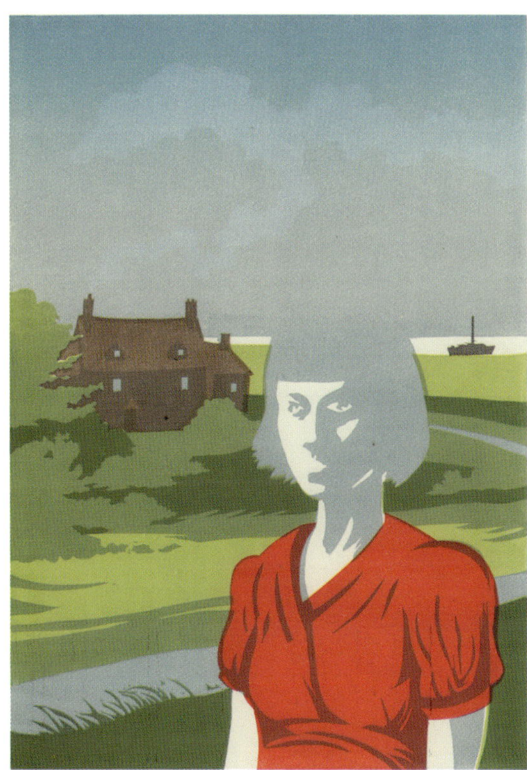

A darker green was added to the trees and grass, along with a pure white for the chimney smoke and clouds.

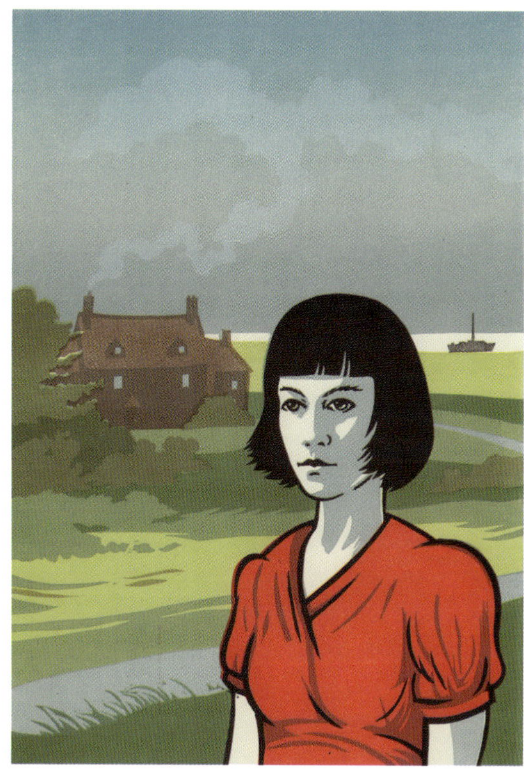

Finally, a third shade of green and the black outline of the figure. This image was then scanned and cleaned up and the spitfires added digitally.

Graphics

Linocuts lend themselves naturally to the use of text, either by itself or with an image. The earliest printed text was taken from carved wood in China: a form of relief printing closely related to linocut. Later, in the West, alphabets of moveable type were carved from wood or cast in metal for printing on the press. In commercial printing this has been superseded by a number of different technologies, most recently digital printing. Letterpress has enjoyed a resurgence in recent years among graphic designers, who are attracted by its retro feel, simplicity and imperfections. The same can be said for linocut and words or individual letters can be carved from blocks to mimic the letterpress look.

Typography and linocut

A great way to learn about typography is to copy it. Any letters that are big enough can be traced and transferred to the block for carving. Remember to reverse them first. Old newspapers and magazines are often full of beautiful typefaces, especially if they contain advertisements. You can also buy books containing full alphabets and there are lots of online resources where you can find free fonts, or ones you can buy.

Project: alphabet

If you want to feed your inner graphic designer you can create your own alphabet. Luckily for amateur typographers, converting your designs into linocut can make even the wonkiest letters look good, with the carving and printing process having a unifying effect. If you want to create only a word or two these can be carved from a single block. For more involved work with text you may want to carve individual letters. These can be mounted onto blocks and used as stamps to make up the words you want, or scanned and reassembled into words digitally.

Making an alphabet where each letter is different is a good way to demonstrate your design flair and carving virtuosity. Draw out each letter first, using a marker pen, brush and ink, or digital software like Photoshop. Try to use the full vocabulary of marks that you have developed so far, and add some new ones. Make each letter the same size to give uniformity to your typeface or vary the size and shape for a more eclectic look.

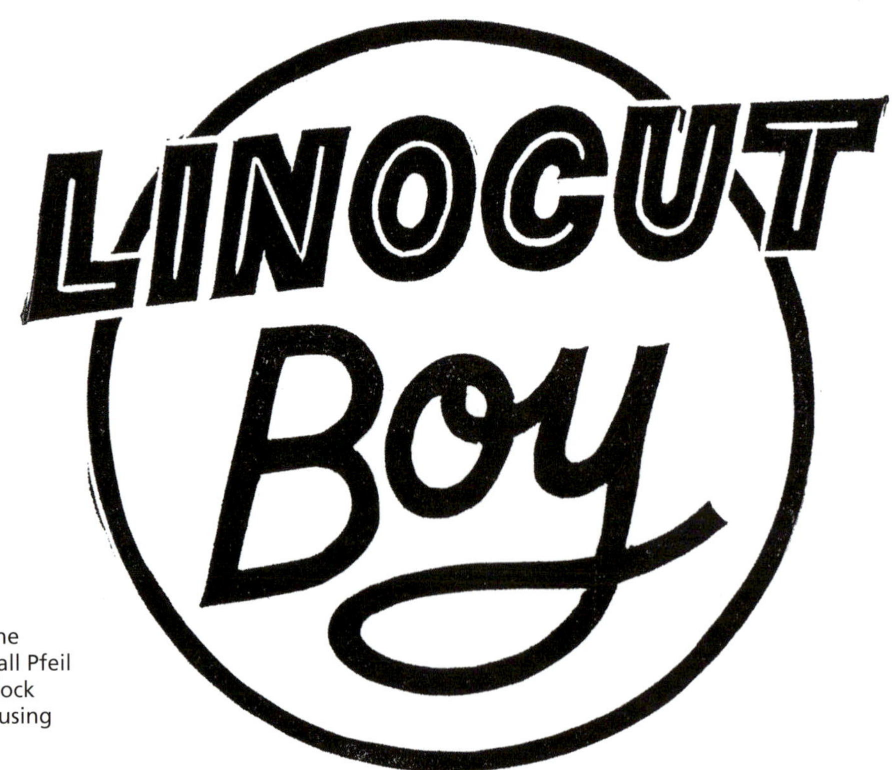

Linocutboy logo. The outline was carved first using a small Pfeil U gouge. The rest of the block was then carefully cleared using a larger U gouge.

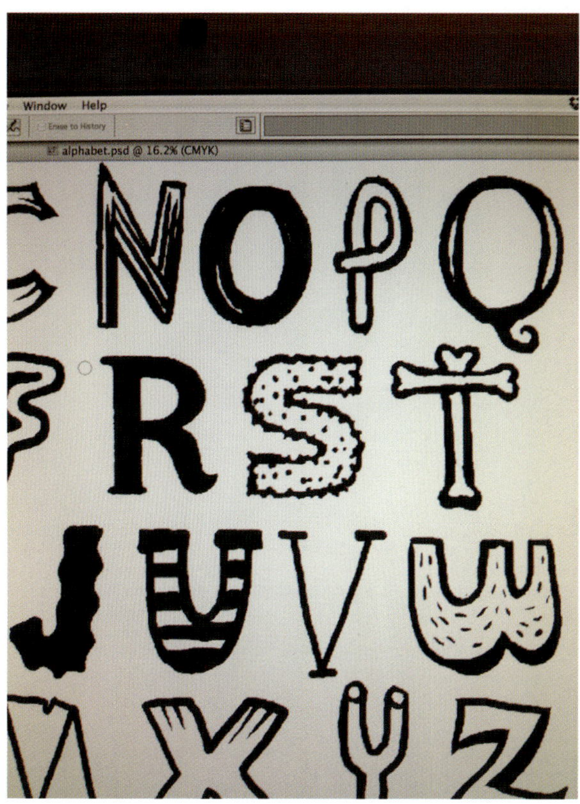

Creating an alphabet using Photoshop.

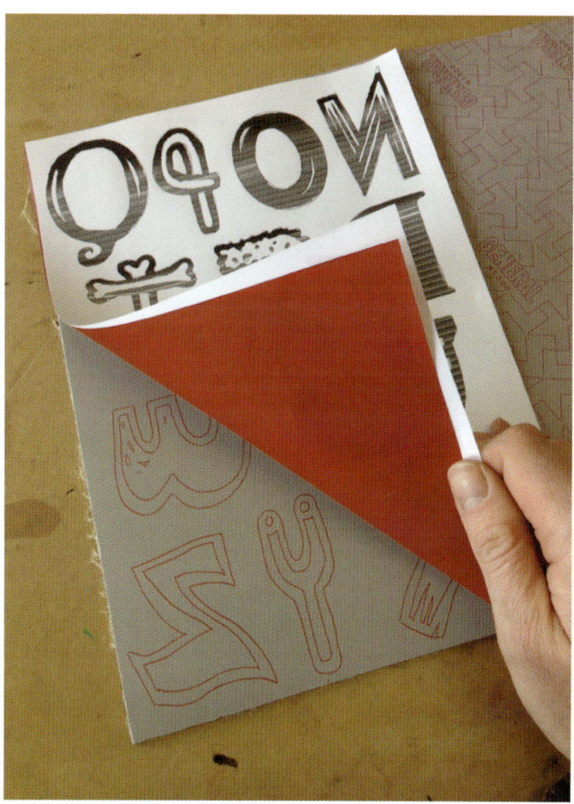

The image is printed in reverse and transferred.

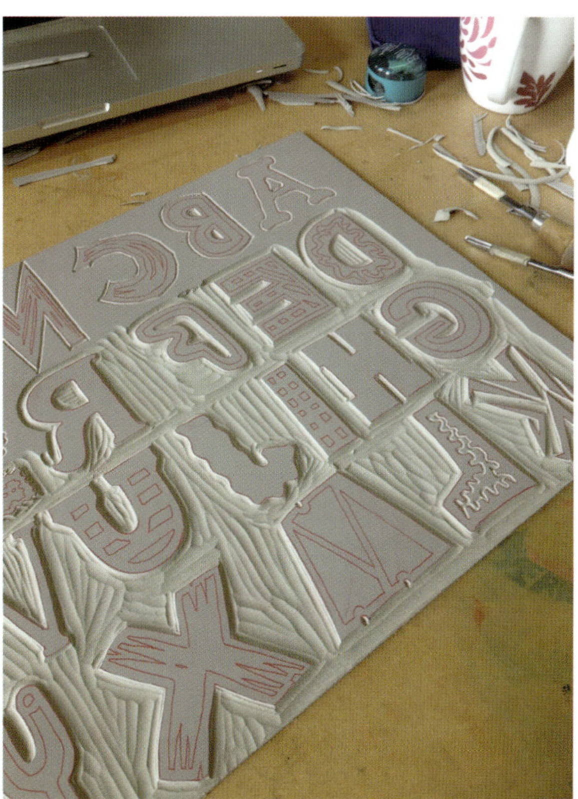

The block is carved, with details added at this stage.

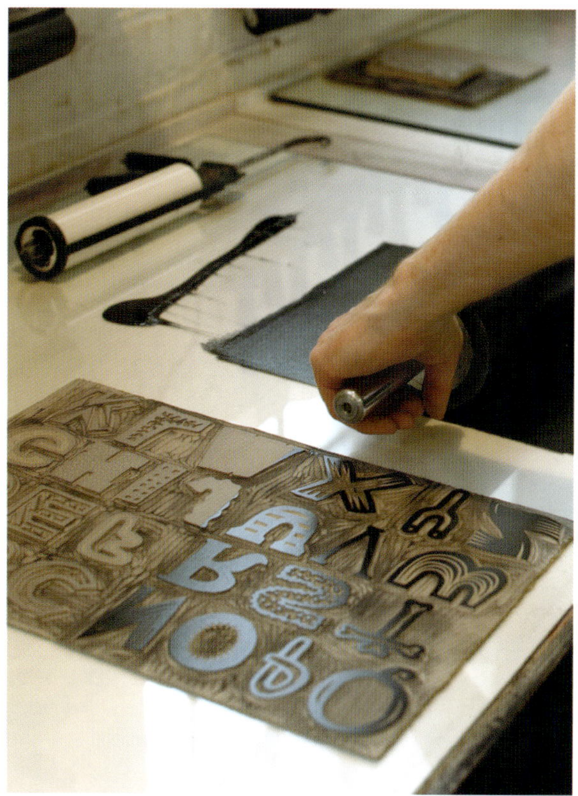

The block is inked up ready for printing.

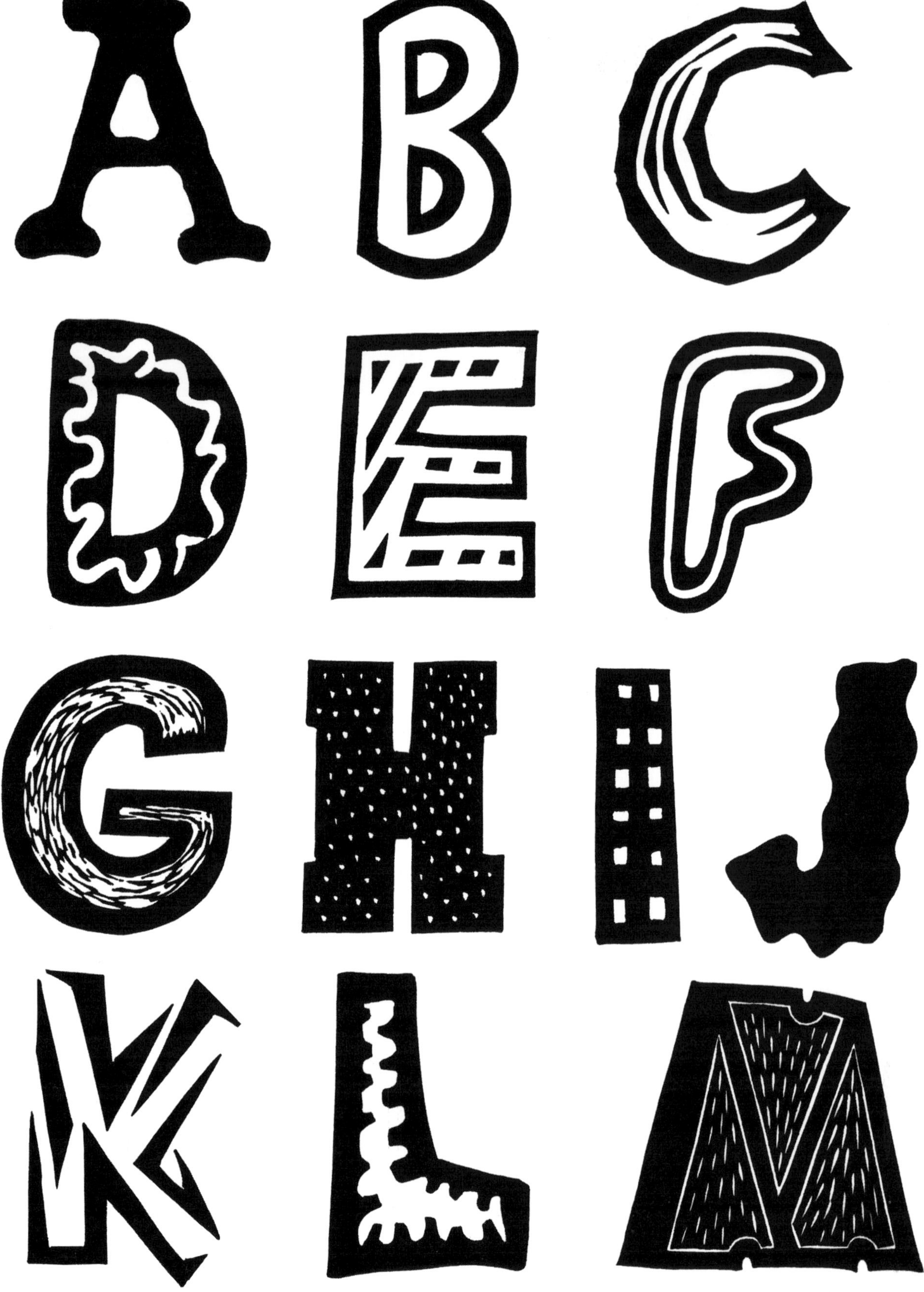

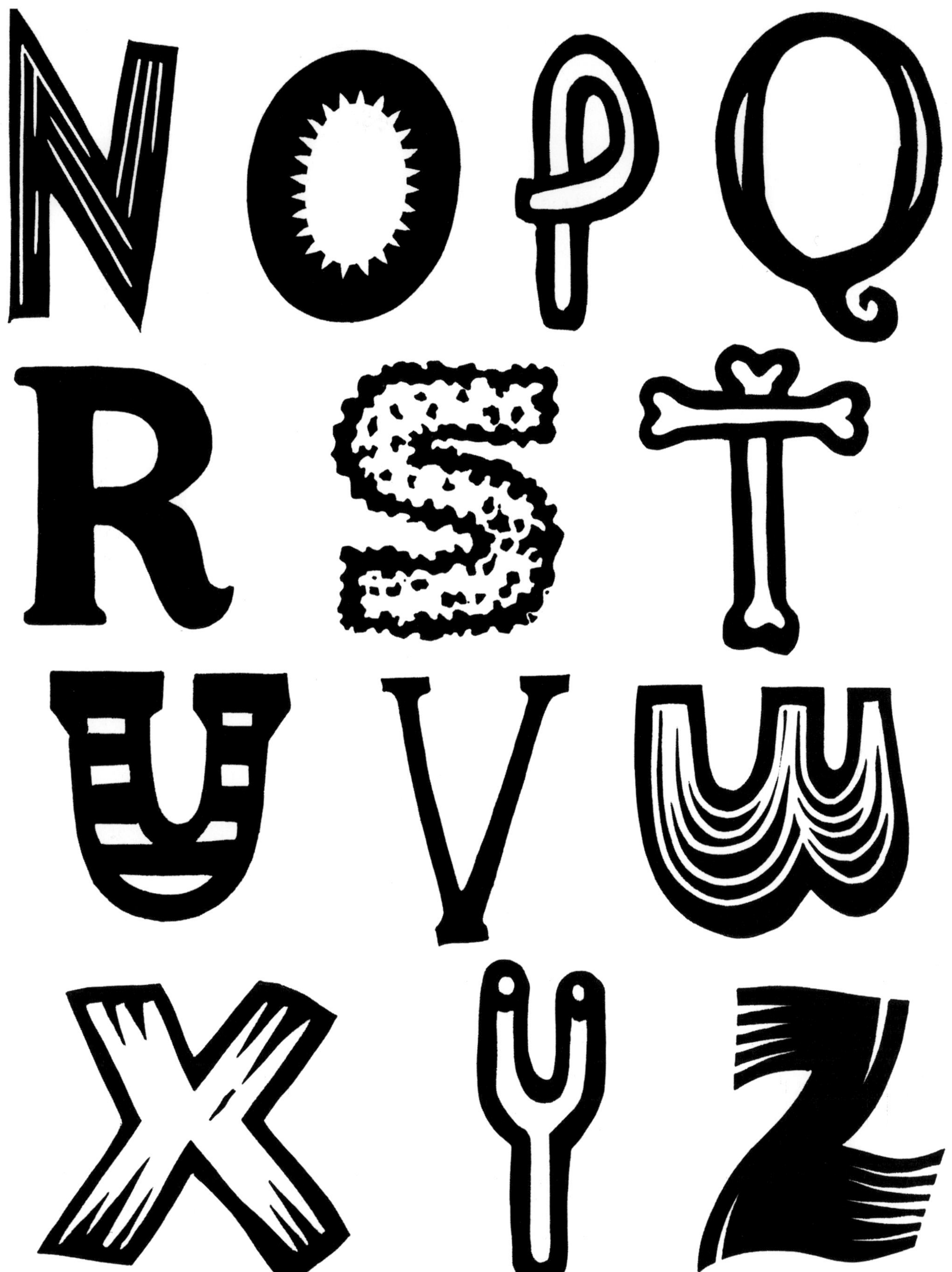
N O P Q
R S T
U V W
X Y Z

James Brown (UK)

www.jamesbrown.info

James Brown is a designer living in London. He trained as a printed textile designer and worked for over ten years in the clothing industry. He switched to illustration ten years ago and also makes linocuts and screenprints in his studio in Hackney Wick. He sells his work through independent shops and galleries and his illustration clients include The Guardian, The East End Trades Guild, Walker Books, and Cath Kidston.

I started making linocuts in about 2007, to give a print idea that I was working on a handmade quality. Up until that point I was making screenprints. I kind of do things my own way, I've worked out a method of making linocuts that suits me. I like the unpredictability and that there are so many variants in the process that cause each print to be unique.

After I became an illustrator I started to print for pleasure and a break from the screen. I began to show my prints on a very small, local level and then it snowballed from there. Printing has informed and directed the way I design. I approach it as if I were designing something that will be printed; the limitations of my processes inform my aesthetic.

I have a studio in Hackney Wick in East London. It's a great place to work with a great atmosphere and full of like-minded folk. I fear it will change very soon due to redevelopment so I am thinking of setting up a studio in my back garden; it will be less sociable but at least I won't be at the mercy of landlords and developers.

When I am planning a print I draw everything on the computer and then print it out in reverse and cut through the paper into the lino. I use the cheap tools for gouging out and clearing, for all other line and detail, I use a scalpel with size 10a blades. I pretty much know how it will look before I start to cut because I can mock up the final piece and try out colour combos on the computer. Obviously there are things that happen along the way that are unforeseen, those mistakes and imperfections can be rectified or not. The printing is when the magic happens.

I print all of my lino on a Stephenson Blake proofing press. I think my set-up is quite lo fi and bodged together, but it works for me and I wouldn't want it any other way. I think developing one's own ways of working means that you experiment, which leads to a greater understanding of the process. I use Graphic Chemical oil-based inks. I love the sheen that is achieved on the overprint.

For my alphabet series I wanted to make each letter differently, but printed in two colours. Each letter is created from a single block, which is printed in one colour, then rotated and printed in a second colour. For some of the letters, the shape is created by the way the two printed layers combine. Others are whole letters and the base colour becomes the background interest. I limited myself to one block per design to reduce the amount of lino I had to cut. I love tesselation and I would rather spend the time in the design process than in the cutting of the lino.

> *I didn't have a plan to be doing what I do now, it just happened organically, so I am in the very fortunate position to be doing something that I love.*

Alphabet series, James Brown, each 30 × 30cm, linocut.

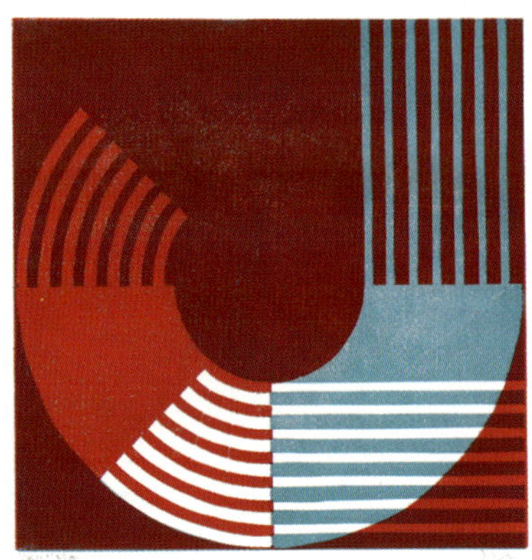

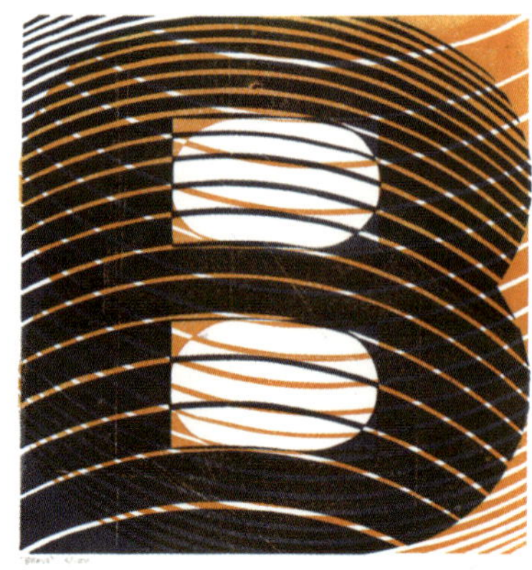

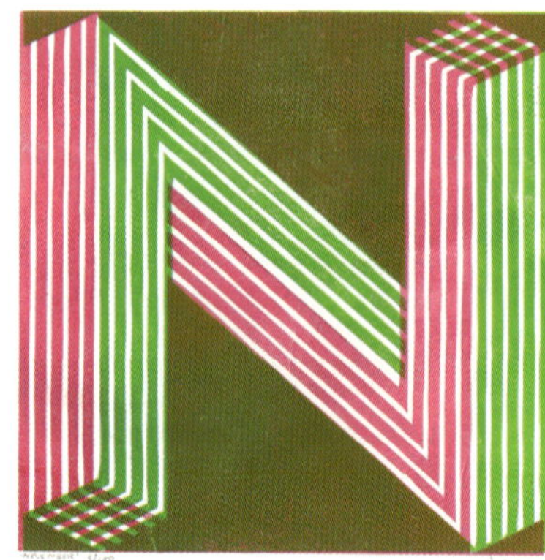

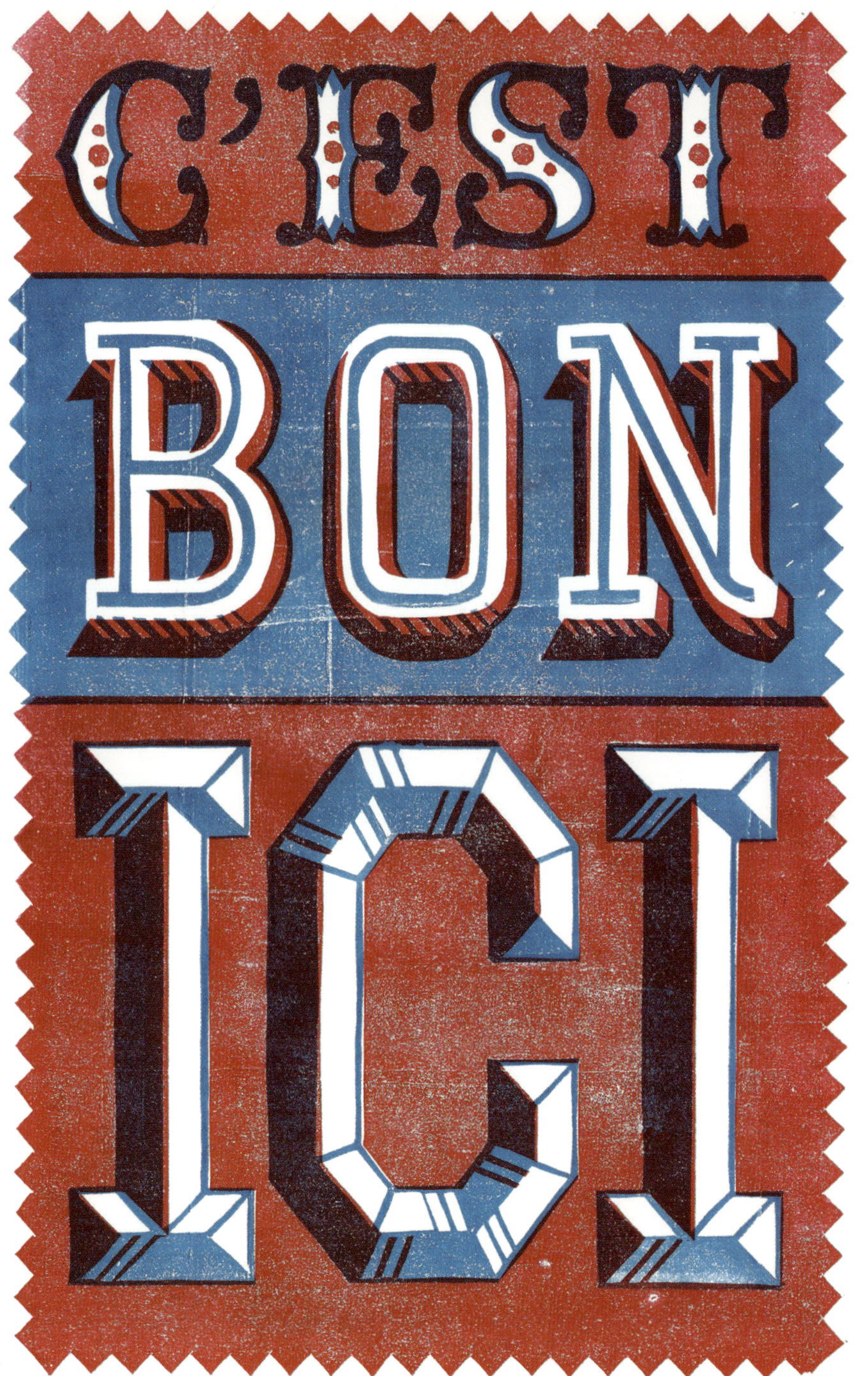

C'est Bon Ici / It's Good Here, James Brown, 29.7 × 42cm, linocut.

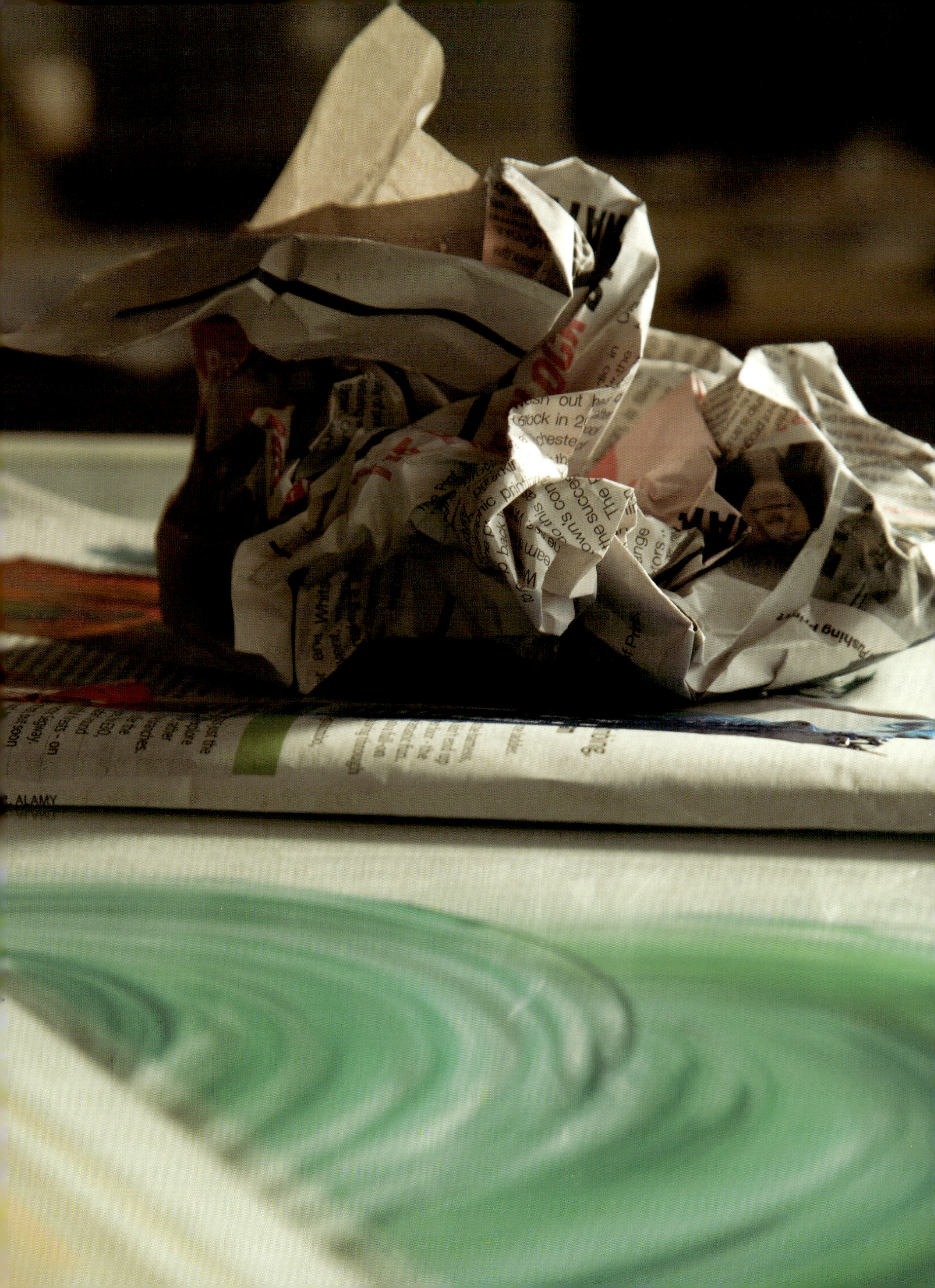

ALAMY

CHAPTER 7

FABRIC PRINTING, PAPER PRODUCTS AND ARTISTS' BOOKS

So far we have looked only at printing linocuts onto paper: an ideal substrate, as it is flat, even and partially absorbent. Prints can also be made on a variety of other surfaces, including fabric, card and wood. This gives rise to numerous possibilities for creating printed objects: cushions and curtains, T-shirts and tote bags, greetings cards and notebooks. Once a surface has been printed it can be cut, folded, sewn or glued. Each surface will print differently, according to its properties, so do some test prints to find out how the ink sits, as well as how long it takes to dry and how well it adheres once dry. Be adventurous, the possibilities are endless.

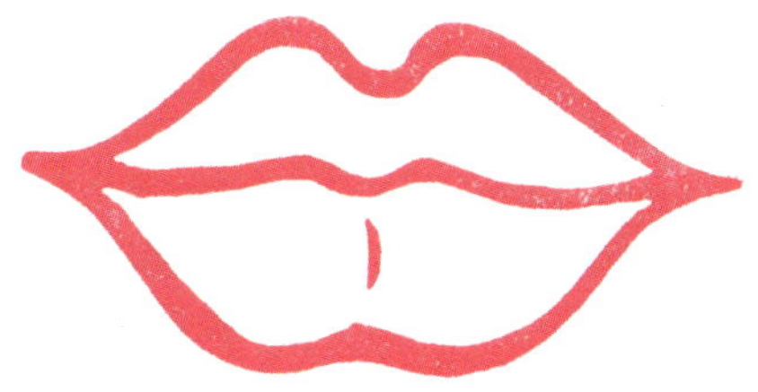

Fabric printing

Block printing on fabric has a long tradition in many places around the world, from Rajasthan to England. It is a fast and simple way to print a repeat pattern across a large surface. Usually wooden blocks are used but a similar stamping technique can be adopted for linocuts. Alternatively you can print onto smaller pieces of fabric as you would on paper, using a press. Hand printing larger designs can be done by pressing on the back of the fabric with a clean roller.

Suitable fabrics

Depending on what inks you use, most fabrics can be printed onto successfully. Natural textiles like cotton work well as they are more absorbent. When printing with water-based inks, avoid printing on nylon and water-repelling fabrics as the ink will not adhere properly. Take care with very stretchy fabrics as your printed design will distort as the fabric stretches. Thin and loose-weave fabrics will allow ink to pass through so you will need to protect surfaces with a backing material. For the best results, buy a variety of samples and make some test prints.

Heat setting

Most inks will need to be heat-set to make them permanent on fabrics. This can be done with a hot iron. Follow the instructions and always iron on the reverse of the printed fabric or through an old cotton tea towel, never directly onto the ink. This process drives out all the moisture from the ink and is known as curing. As the ink is cured it gives off a distinctive, not unpleasant, smell which will tell you it's working. Some inks will change colour slightly when heated so make sure you do a test first.

Washing

If you are printing a design onto fabric which needs to be washable, for example on T-shirts, use an ink which will not fade in the wash. In addition, the fabric should remain flexible after printing. Some ink brands will dry more rigid than others, as will some colours within the same range. After laundering, ink will soften to some extent. To prolong the strength of the ink colour, printed items should be washed at a cool temperature with a mild detergent.

Texture

As with paper, the texture of the fabric you are printing onto will directly affect the look of the print. Closely woven fabrics will pick up more detail than rougher weaves. Bear this in mind when you are creating your design.

Flexibility

Because fabric is flexible it is best to lay the block face-down on top of the fabric when printing. If you try to lay the fabric over the block you will find it difficult to position correctly. The fabric should be laid out flat on an even surface and the edges secured with tape so it doesn't move. Make sure you protect whatever surface you are working on with newspaper or an old bedsheet to catch any ink that goes through. Gently pull the fabric tight and smooth it out to get rid of any wrinkles. Do not overstretch it as it will shrink back when you release it, distorting what you have printed.

Absorbency

Fabric is usually more absorbent than paper. Some inks will sit on the surface of the fabric and others will soak in and penetrate the fibres. In the case of the latter, more ink will be needed. If possible, print a test piece first to check for absorbency and assess how much ink to apply. When new, many fabrics are coated in a chemical which creates a barrier for the ink. It is a good idea to pre-wash new fabric to remove the chemical and then iron it flat. You can buy pre-washed items like T-shirts from wholesale suppliers. Buy organic cotton if you are eco sensitive.

Printing blocks

Traditional linoleum can be used but may not work as well as the more rubbery materials like Softcut. If printing with a stamping technique, these will give a cushioning effect as you push down on them, resulting in a more even print. Mounted blocks are easier to hold and help to spread the pressure evenly as you press down on them. You can buy premounted blocks or mount them yourself by glueing the lino to a piece of wood. For repeat patterns and other designs where accurate printing is required, mount the block onto a piece of clear acrylic or perspex. This will allow you to see exactly where the edge of the block is going as you place it down.

Flocked lino

You can buy lino coated with a layer of flocking which is sold for fabric printing. Flocking consists of tiny fibres which are glued onto a surface, closely packed and all standing on end to give the feel of velvet. A flocked surface will hold more ink, giving a more saturated print. This may be useful if printing onto a particularly absorbent fabric or if you want to print repeatedly without re-inking the block. A flocked block is difficult to carve with gouges, however, as the flocked layer tends to tear. Instead it can be cut into shapes with a craft knife for printing blocks of colour. It should be avoided for any design where fine detail is required.

Inks for fabric printing

You may be able to use the same relief printing ink on fabric that you have used on paper. Oil-based ink prints well and will give a strong colour. It tends to sit on the surface of the fabric and if applied in a thick layer will dry fairly rigid. Oil-based inks will take around a month to set permanently and be washable. Avoid water soluble inks for any fabric that is likely to get wet as even a splash of water could make the ink run. Caligo Safe Wash inks work well on fabric but they do take a lot longer to dry than on paper. The addition of cobalt driers to the ink will help, as will heat setting the print with an iron. This can be done after a week or so.

There are a limited number of specialist inks for relief printing onto fabric. Speedball Fabric Block Printing Ink is an oil-based ink, available in a small range of colours, which washes up in soap and water. It cures at room temperature and is ready to launder after one week. There is no need to heat set it and it also prints well on paper. Speedball Fabric Ink is much more opaque than the Caligo inks and has an almost grainy texture. It dries quite fast on the roller so you have to work quickly.

Gamblin, a US manufacturer, recently created a black ink in collaboration with artist group Drive By Press which is called Drive By Black and is an oil-based relief ink specially formulated for printing onto textiles. Drive By Black produces a good dense print, but is best suited to printing on a press.

It is possible to use screenprinting ink with lino, but results may vary. Generally screenprinting ink is much less viscous than relief ink, making it difficult to apply with an ink roller. The roller will tend to skid, resulting in an uneven layer of ink on the block. In addition, runny ink tends to pool in the carved out areas, filling in any detail. Instead of an ink roller, use a brush, sponge or sponge roller to apply the ink, taking care only to apply it to the raised parts of the block. If the ink is very runny it can be thickened by allowing it to air dry for a while before applying. One brand which is sold as suitable for both screenprinting and block printing onto fabric is Versatex, made by Jacquard in California.

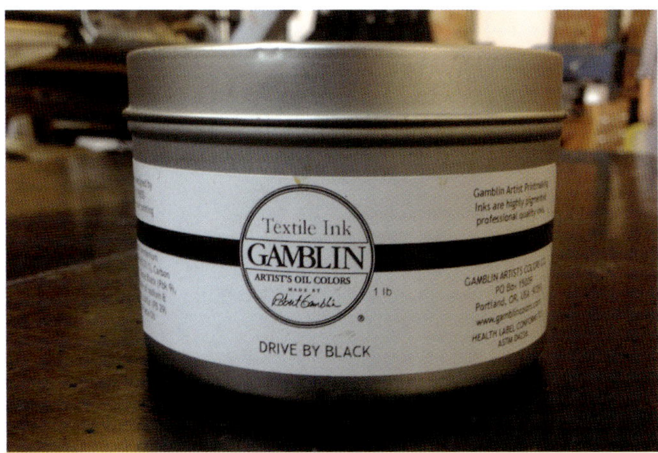

Project: printing a T-shirt or tote bag

The graphic nature of linocut translates brilliantly to T-shirts and tote bags. It is possible to print with multiple blocks to create a design with two or more colours; however, due to the flexible nature of the fabric it will be tricky to get accurate registration. If you have a press big enough to fit the whole T-shirt or bag this will give you the best results although it is possible to print by hand. The same technique can be used for printing tote bags, tea-towels, napkins and scarves. Avoid printing on the seams of sewn items as you will get an uneven print due to the difference in thickness and this may damage the block if using a press.

Printing on a press

T-shirts can be printed on an etching press, a platen press like an Albion, or a large screw or book press. Other types of press may be more difficult or not suitable at all. Note that due to the soft nature of the surface being printed on, more extraneous details may be picked up from the carved out areas than would happen on paper.

Before printing, iron your T-shirt in the area to be printed to remove any wrinkles. Next, put a sheet of thin board or card inside it to prevent any ink bleeding through onto the back. Place the T-shirt on the press and tape it in position. Before you ink the block, place it on the T-shirt where you want it to print and mark its position with masking tape. If you are printing more than one T-shirt the same size, make a note of the distance from the neckline to the top of the block so you can get them all the same.

Ink the block and place it ink-side down in position. Run it through the press and peel the block away carefully. Hang the T-shirt to dry in a warm place with moving air for the fastest drying time.

Printing by hand

Prepare the T-shirt in the same way as for printing on the press. Ensure the surface you are printing on is flat and even. The easiest way to apply pressure to the back of the block is with a clean ink roller (a hard one works best) or a rolling pin. If using a small block you may simply be able to press down on the block with your hand.

Unlike printing on paper, it is not possible to lift a corner to check the printing so practise first on some old T-shirts until you are happy with your inking and printing technique.

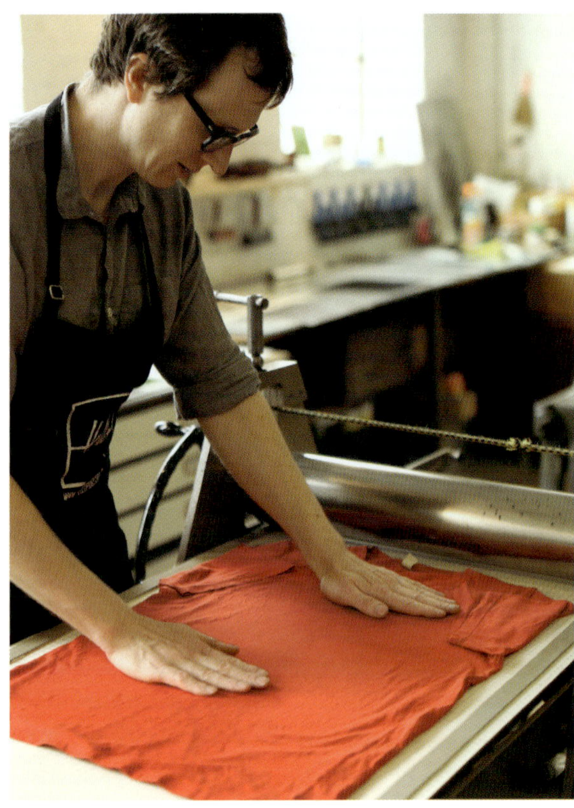

Position the T-shirt on the press, avoiding wrinkles.

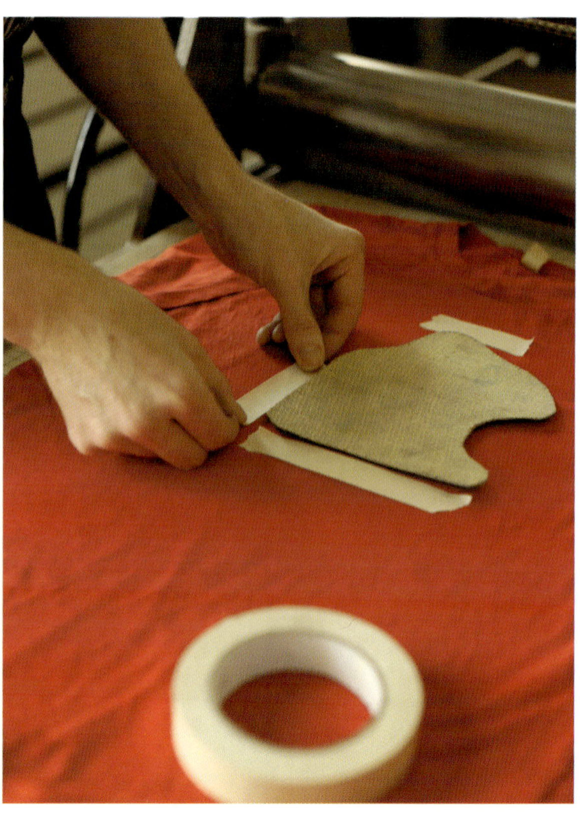

Place the uninked block in position and mark with tape.

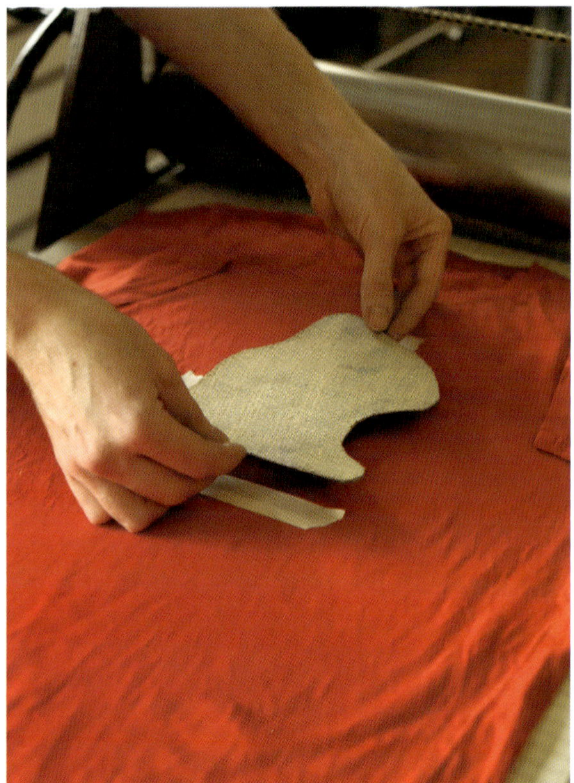

Ink the block and place it face down to print.

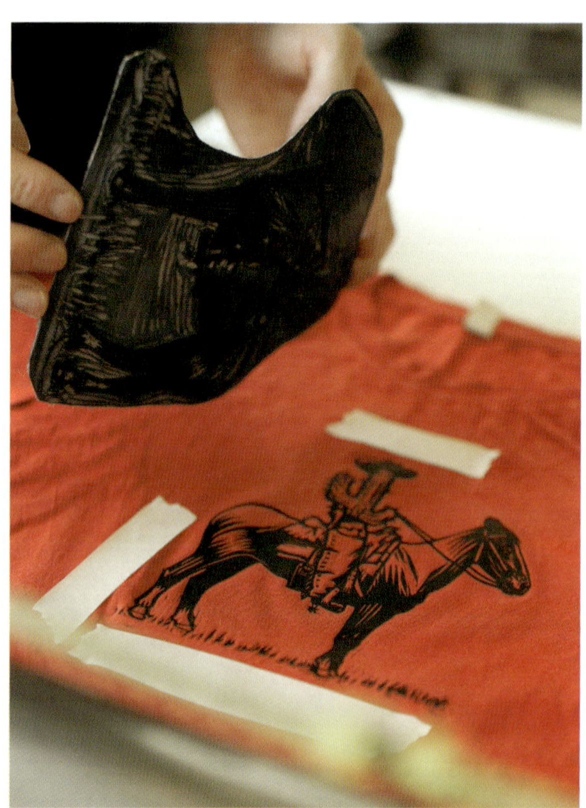

After printing, lift the block carefully.

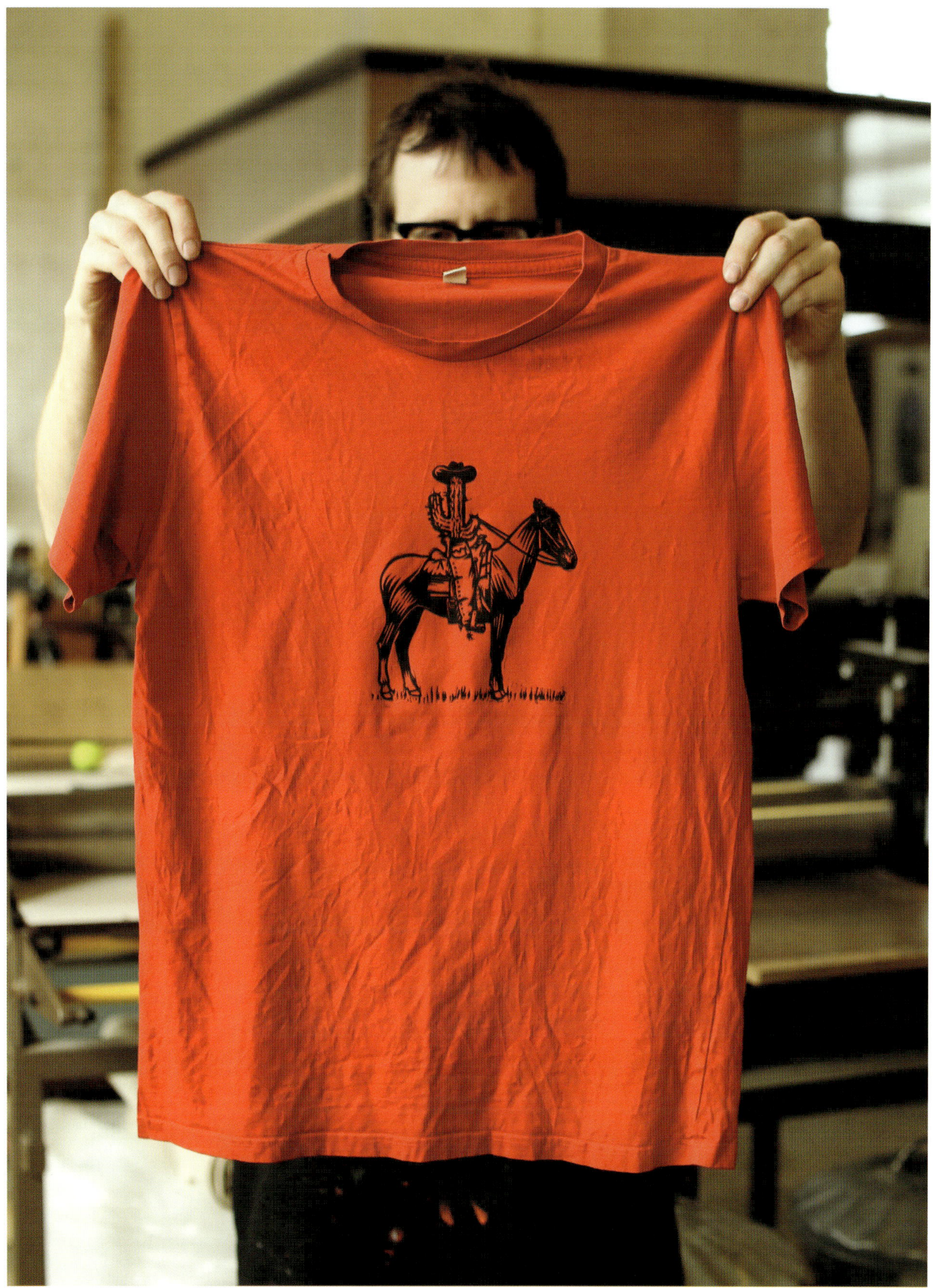

Stamping

If a block is small enough it can be inked and printed by hand, simply by pressing it onto a surface. Rubber stamps can be bought with an existing image on them or can be made to order mechanically using your own design. Many commercial print shops or repro houses will provide this service or you can order online and have them shipped to you. The blocks are usually made from rubber mounted onto a block of wood or clear acrylic for support. You can also carve your own block for stamping, using an eraser and a craft knife or gouges. Instead of applying the ink to the block with a roller, it is inked up from a stamp pad.

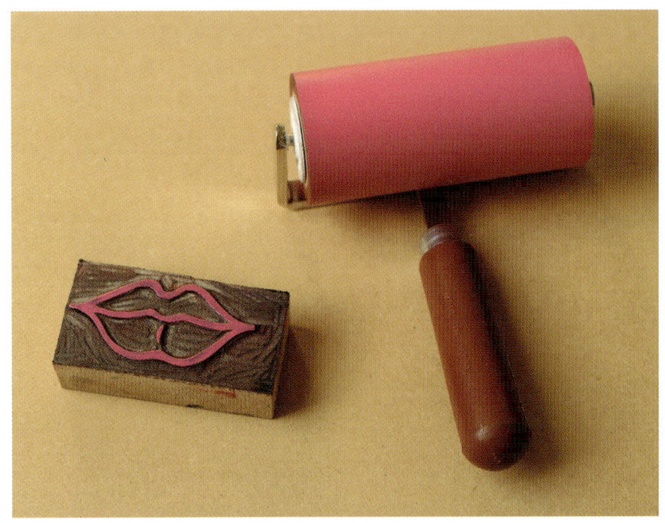

Mount your lino on wood to make a stamp.

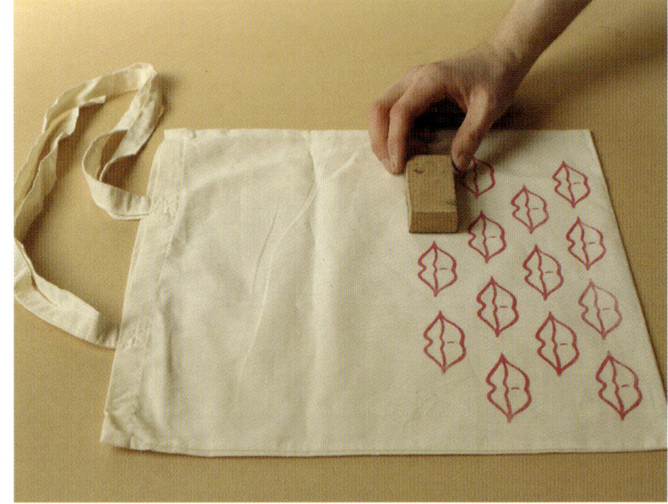

Print a pattern on your tote bag.

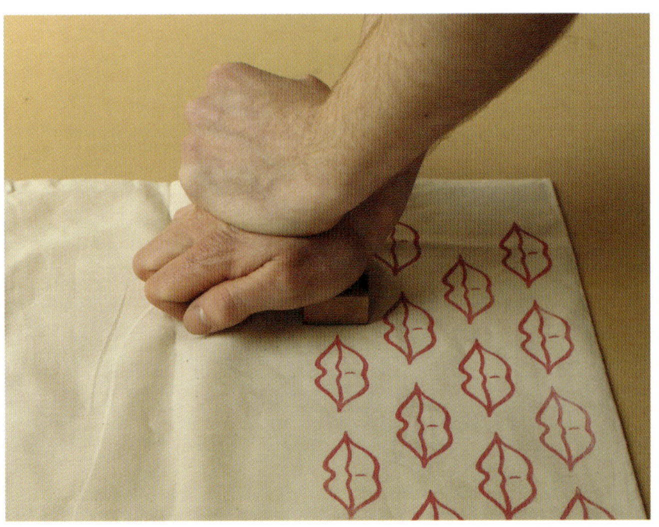

Press down hard on the block using your weight.

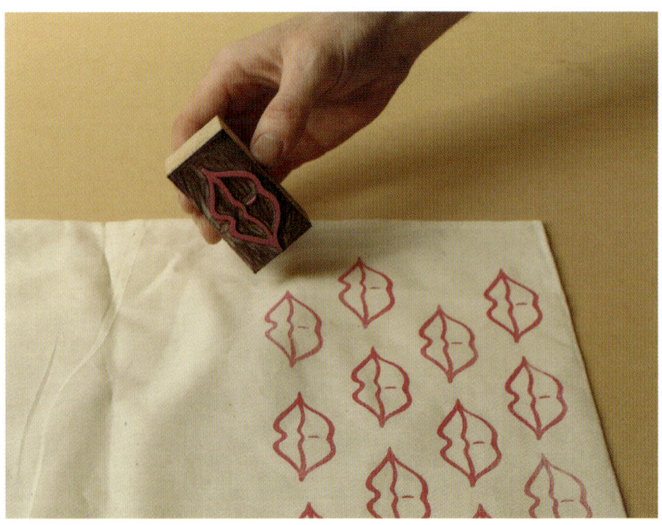

Try a number of different patterns and colours.

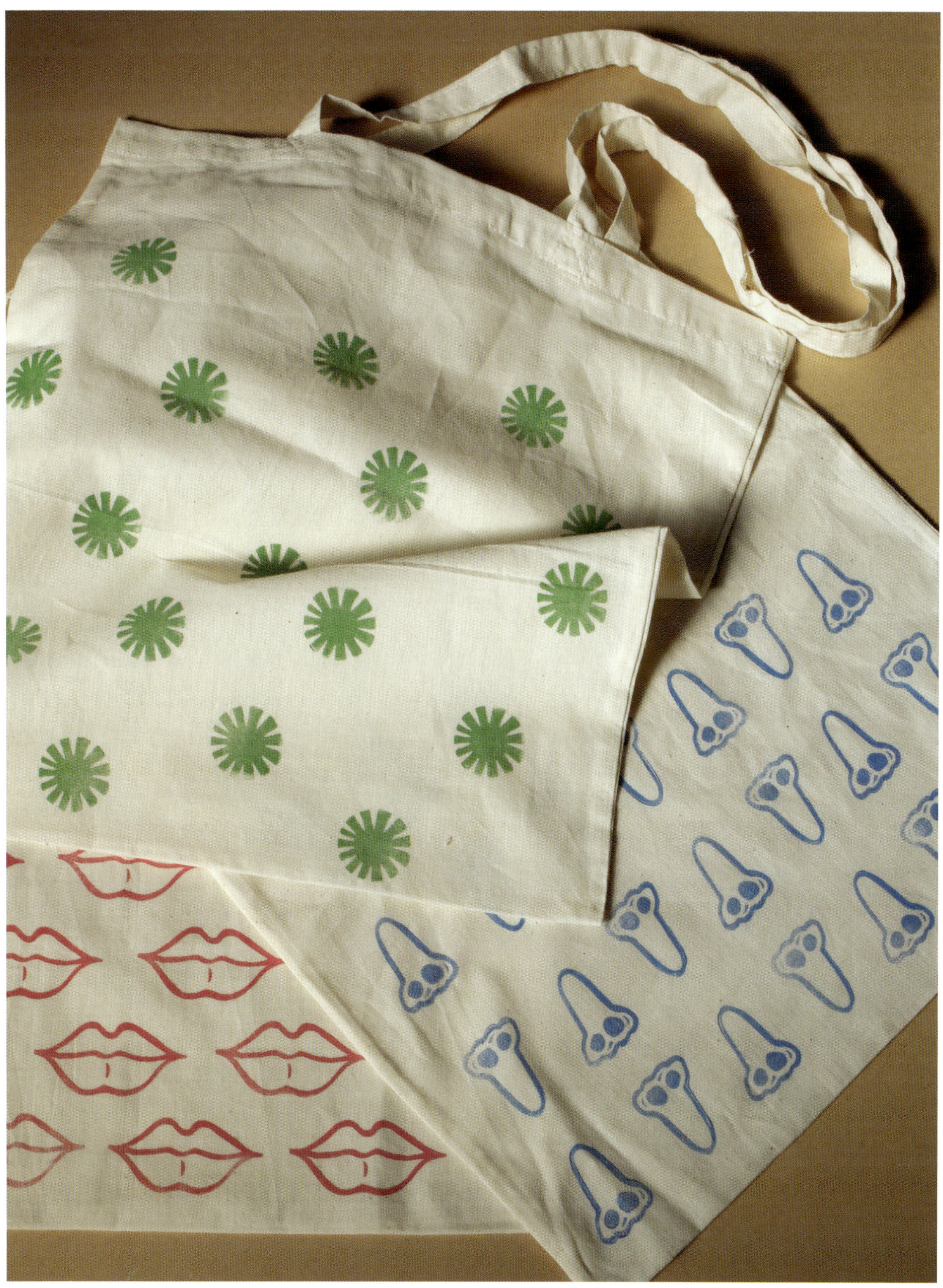

Almost any design will look good printed in a repeat pattern. These tote bags were printed using Speedball Fabric Block Printing Ink which washes up with water but dries waterproof.

Paper products

Greetings cards

Printing your own greetings cards is fun and the personal aspect will be appreciated by the recipient, whether you are making them for your own use or to sell. Printing cards is a great way of using up scraps of paper left over from other projects. Alternatively you can buy packs of blank cards, ready creased, with envelopes. These are available from craft suppliers online with the option of envelopes to fit. If you are printing cards to sell you can also buy self-seal cellophane bags to put them in.

Printing greeting cards to sell can seem like a lot of work for not much return financially but you may consider it worthwhile if you see them as a promotional tool. Make sure your contact details or website are printed on the back of each card so the recipient can look you up. You can get a rubber stamp made up for this or make your own with one of those printing kits with little rubber letters.

Because they are small, postcards and greetings cards are ideal for printing on a small letterpress machine like an Adana. This is a much quicker way to print with the potential to print several hundred in an hour.

Bookplates

A bookplate, also known by its Latin term Ex Libris (literally: from the books), is a small piece of printed paper which is pasted into the front of a book to indicate who owns it. Linocut is perfect for making bookplates, either with a space to write the name or with the name incorporated into the design. If given as a gift, the block can be kept to print more plates in the future if needed.

Use a thin paper for bookplates, like Japanese Hosho, otherwise it will look too heavy. If you give a set of bookplates as a gift you can put them in a box with a tube of rice paste glue to attach them. Keep the block and let the recipient know you can print more if needed in future.

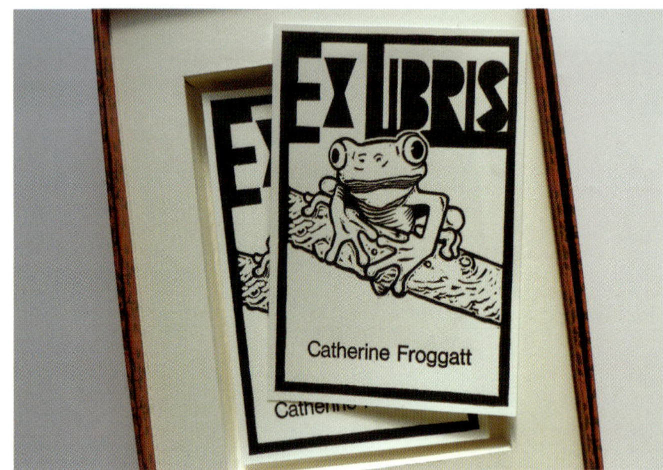

Personalized bookplates make a very special gift. The name here was printed with letterpress.

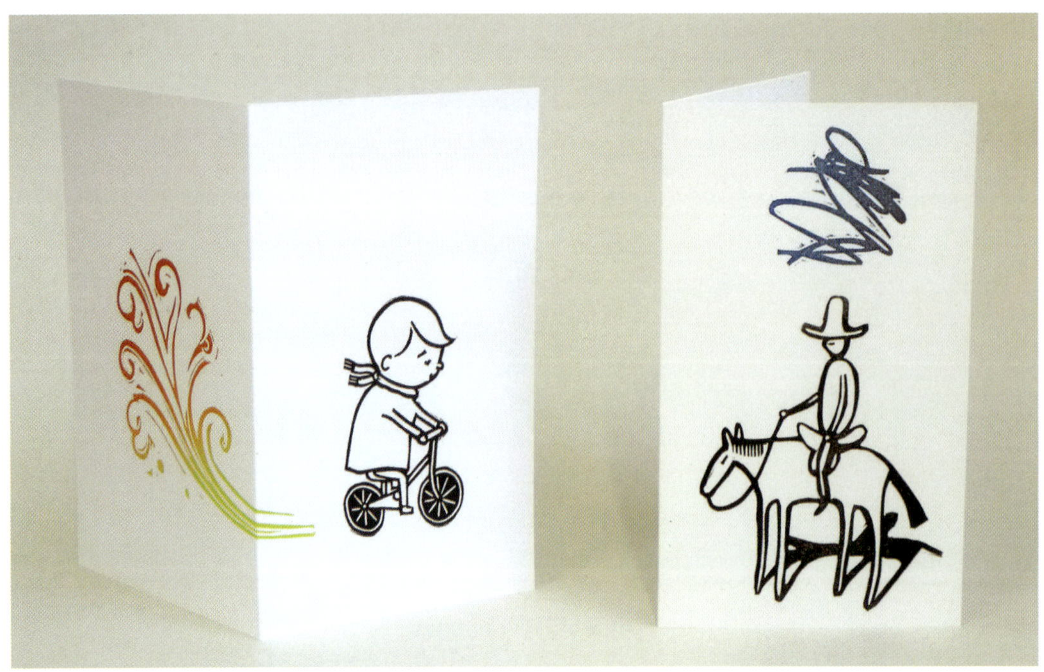

Hand printed greetings cards. Each of these was printed from two blocks.

Artists' books

Artists and designers have been playing with the format of the book for many years. Books can contain any combination of text and image. They come in myriad shapes and sizes, from the traditional idea of pages bound together, to sculptural folded objects. Books can be made from many materials, from the traditional paper and leather to more modern materials like acetate, laser-cut. They can be mass-produced or one-off.

What is common to all books is that they are meant to be looked at from different angles. They need to be manipulated in some way to fully appreciate their content: opened, closed, flicked through, rotated, turned over. Part of the joy of a book is its tactile quality. Unlike a fine art print, books are meant to be held and touched. The weight, density, surface texture, softness or rigidity of its materials is experienced through the hands.

Incorporating linocuts and other printed elements into books gives you an opportunity to explore new aspects and applications of the technique. The printed surface will look and feel different according to how much ink you use, how many layers and what type of ink and paper you use. The ink layer can be almost undetectable by touch or it can be built up thickly until the paper feels like leather. You can print on a press with blankets to create an embossed texture, or print on very smooth paper to give a glossy finish.

This book can only touch on the possibilities of artists' books. If you are interested in making your own or just want to see what's being made by others there are regular artists' book fairs in many countries around the world, as well as zine and illustration fairs which attract a different crowd.

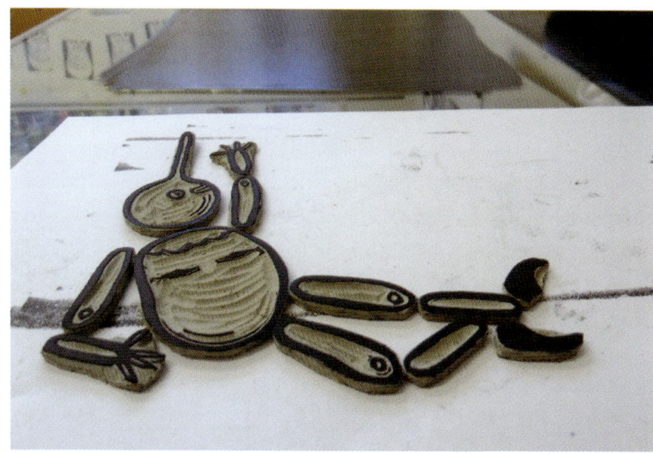

Individual lino pieces were made for Pinocchio's body parts. These were then inked up individually and arranged into a different shape for each letter of the alphabet.

ABC with Pinocchio, Nick Morley. This book was printed on Chinese calligraphy paper which is thin enough to let the light through, even at double thickness.

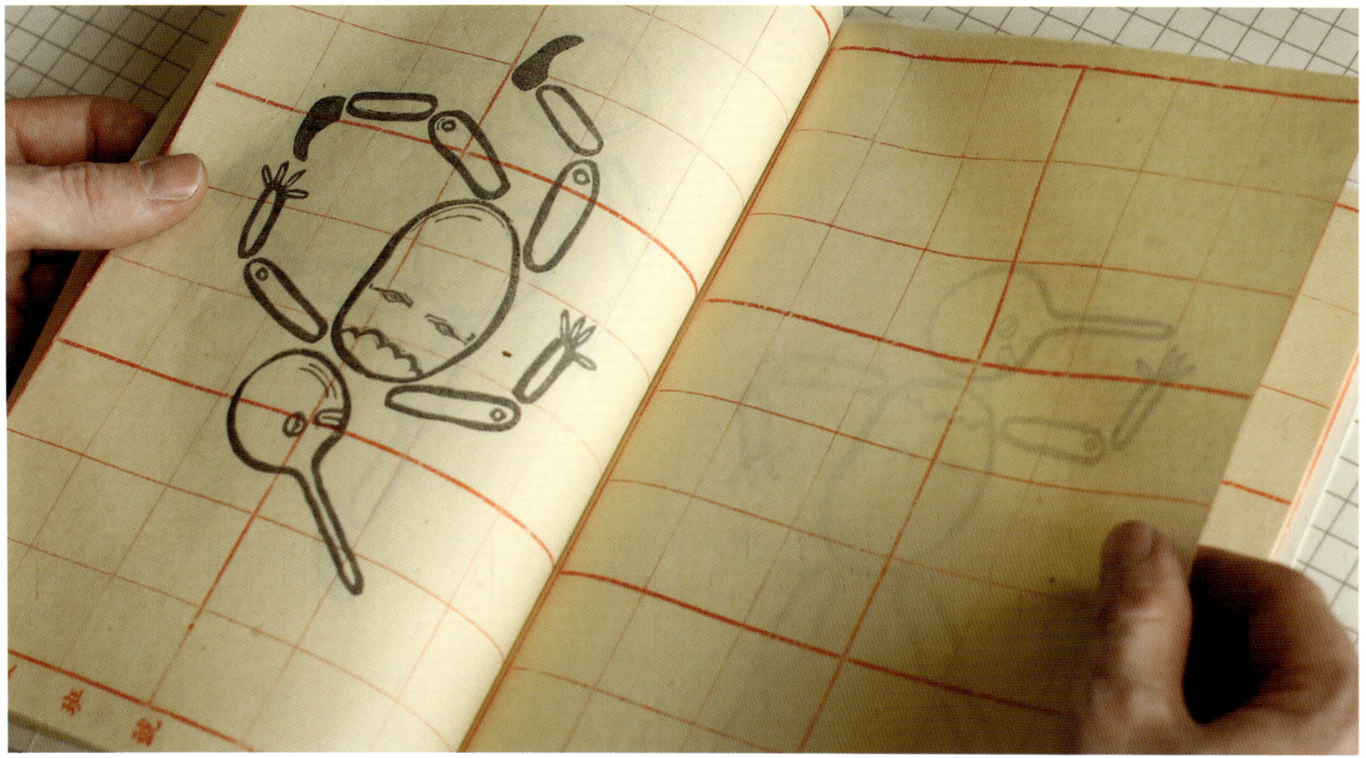

Project: concertina book

A simple but versatile way to make a book is the concertina. This is made from a single piece of paper folded one way and then the other to make a zigzag. The folded pages can be turned and viewed like a standard book or pulled out to their full length to view in their entirety. Both sides of the concertina can be printed onto. The book can also be displayed standing on its edge like a sculpture, giving it an advantage over books that have to be taken down from a bookshelf to be viewed.

Ideally your book should be made from a single sheet of paper or card. If necessary, you can glue a series of sheets together. Work out the format of the book before you start printing so you will know where to position your designs. Remember that if you are printing with the paper on top of the block the start of the book will be on the right.

Paper grain

Most machine-made paper has a grain which allows it to bend more easily in one direction than the other. Ideally the paper for your concertina should be folded along the grain, so it creases easily. You can determine which direction the grain lies by folding the paper first one way, then the other. When you fold along the grain there will be less resistance.

Make a 'dummy' (test) book before you start carving your blocks so that you know you are happy with the shape and size of the book. The paper you choose will determine not only the look of the printed elements but also the weight and thickness of the book and the stiffness and strength of the pages. Make a template on a sheet of paper which is a little bigger than your printing paper and mark where each page will fold. You can then use these marks to score each book before you fold it.

The paper should be printed and allowed to dry fully before folding. This way the paper will be easier to handle and, if desired, your design can be printed across the page fold. You may even want to print from a single block the same length as the paper.

Remember, if you are printing with the blocks ink-side up and the paper on top, the first page of the book will be on the far right end. It is easy to forget this and end up with your pages in reverse order.

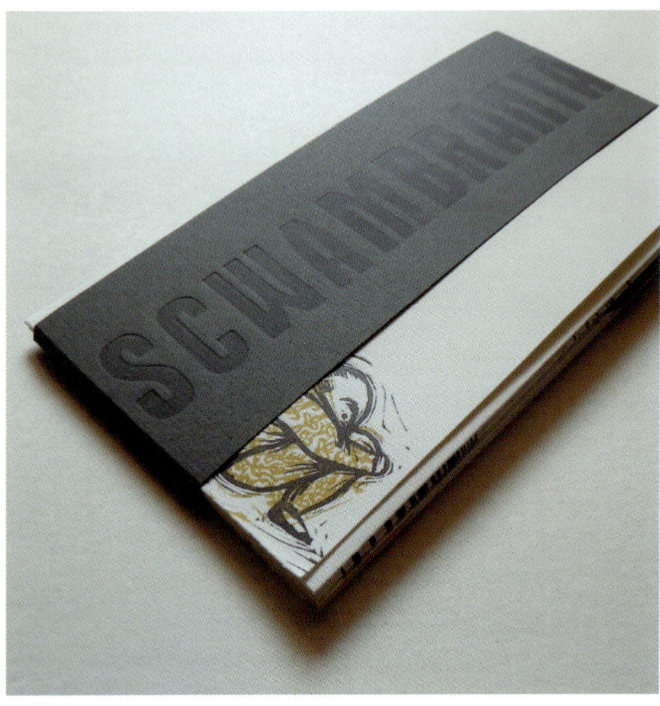

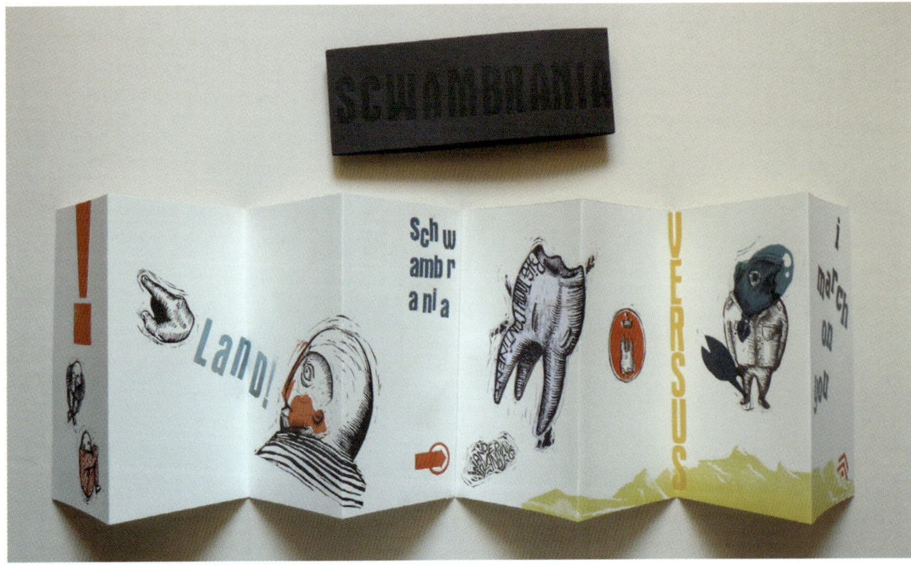

Concertina book by Giulia Semprini, made at a workshop at Opificio della Rosa, Italy. This book was made using linocut, letterpress and collage elements.

The Lion and the Ox and the Boar and the Bear, Nick Morley. Published by KALEID Editions. This book allows the reader to create a number of combinations of text and image to give different readings.

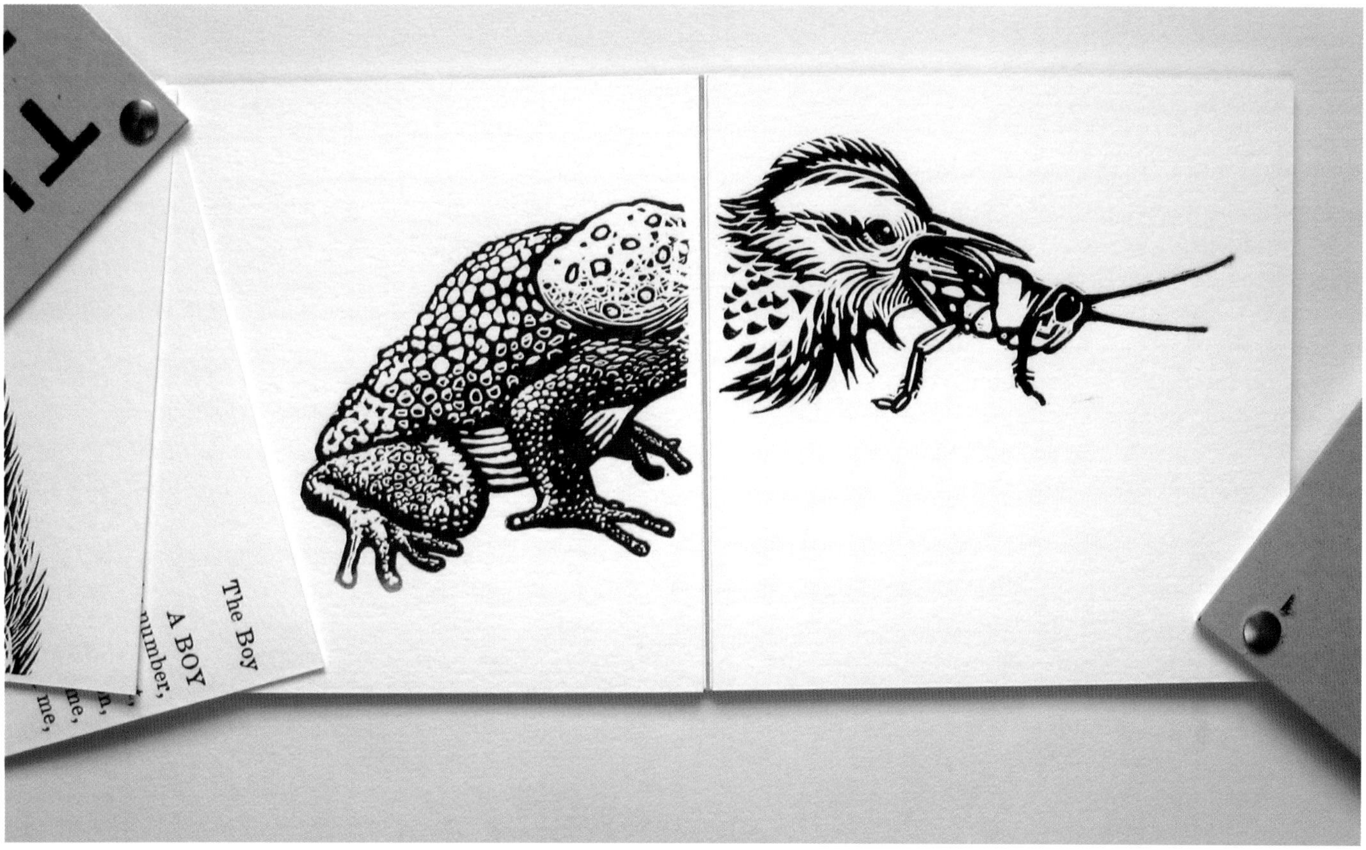

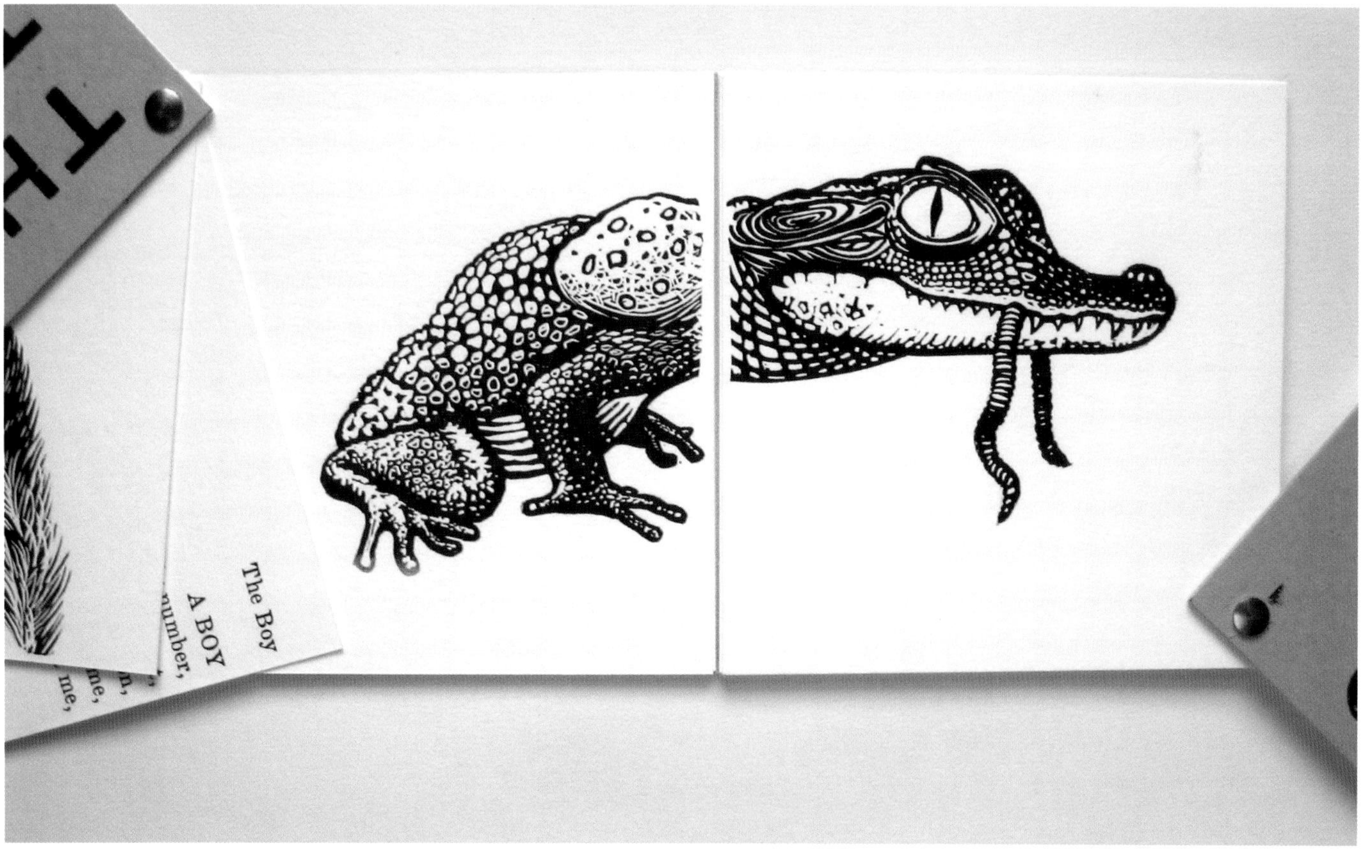

Jesse Breytenbach (South Africa)

www.jessebreytenbach.co.za

Jesse Breytenbach is an illustrator and printmaker based in Cape Town. She makes prints, textiles and sewn products using linocut as well as pen and ink illustrations. Jesse has been making linocuts since about 2007. She chose linocut because she wanted to design textile prints, but didn't have the space for screenprinting and didn't want to invest a lot of money in having them printed by someone else. Her work is available through her website and various online shops, and in local Cape Town shops.

My mother printed linocut T-shirts for us when I was small, and my father did intricate woodcarvings, so I feel as if I've always known the basics. I did an MFA in printmaking, focusing on linocut and woodcut prints, and learned a lot there. When it came to textile printing, I couldn't find much information, as the older oil-based textile inks are hard to come by, so I experimented and taught myself.

In my textile prints, I explore and exploit the limitations of the medium, and try to make things that are perfectly suited to block printing. For instance, I've designed prints for screen printing, and found that there's a limit to the fine detail that can be used, so I do a series of designs based on botanical drawings that celebrates the fine lines and hatching linocut can deliver.

I have a long-running series of limited edition textile prints created from modular blocks that I combine in different ways to create new patterns. The idea was sparked by the way rotating a block can change the character of the repeat printed with it, and the surprising new patterns that can be created by overprinting with another block – literally improvising repeats on the printing table, in a way that's difficult to do with screen printing.

I have a studio that I share with other artists and designers. I have a printing table, a drying rack, and an old manual book press. I do all the designing, cutting and finishing of the prints at home, where I have a small space that serves as illustration studio and sewing room. It's great to be able to mix with people working in other disciplines, and to be able to leave my work out and ready to be picked up at the next session, and have a reason to get out of the house.

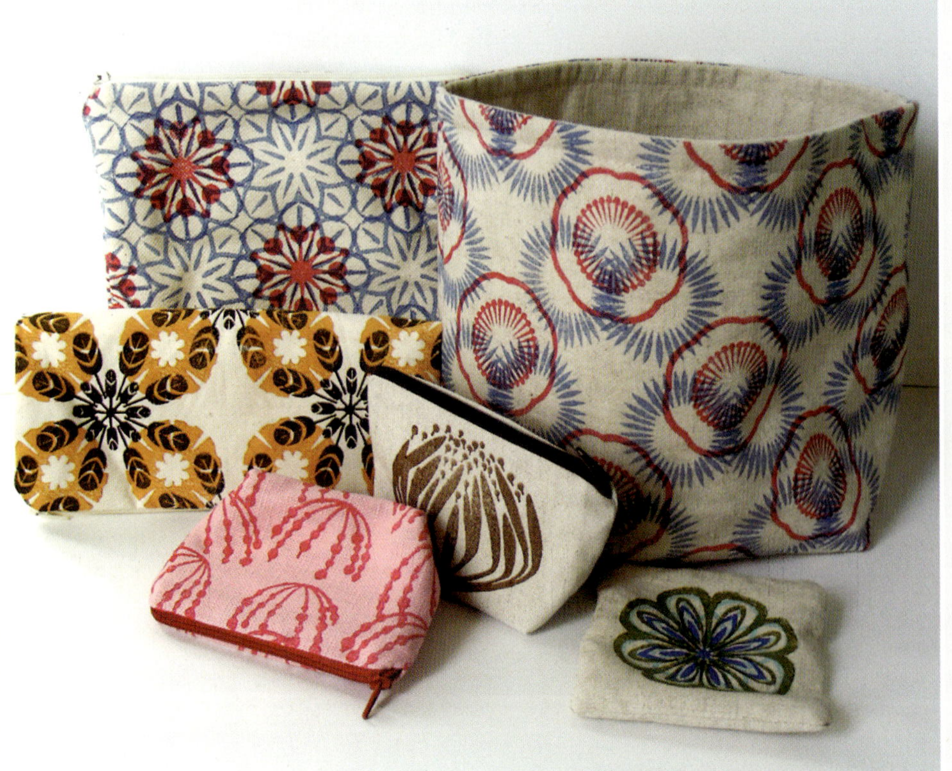

Hand printed bags by Jesse Breytenbach. Jesse sources her fabrics locally, and uses cotton, linen, or hemp blends. Everything is printed by hand, either by burnishing or on an old book press.

Four of Jesse's patterns: Coconut Ice, Icy Plum, Star Anise, Tarragon.

I use a pretty standard linocut set, I don't think it's even branded. I tend to use the V-gouge most, as it's almost like drawing. I found, quite by accident, a holder that's more like a straight woodcut blade holder than a lino one, and hold it almost like a pencil when cutting. I inherited all my father's woodcutting tools, and among them was a tiny chisel, which is one of the most useful tools I have. It's perfect for cleaning up corners and small details.

For my textile prints I use Dala Fabric Paint. It's waterbased silkscreen ink, made in South Africa and easily available at most art shops here. I add Dala Cold Cure Medium to my ink, and then iron it as well. I did a few wash tests and found that combining the two curing methods worked best. Textiles made from natural fibres work better, simply because they're able to withstand the heat needed for proper curing. I prewash everything, as I have sometimes had bad experiences with fabric which is supposed to be 'prepared for print'.

I use vinyl blocks, as I use water-based ink for textile printing, and traditional lino doesn't hold up well to repeated wetting. For textile prints, I cut away as much of the background as possible. I print by placing the blocks face down on the fabric (rather than paper on top of the block, as I would for paper prints) so it's important, for registration, to be able to see where the edges of the print are. I glue the lino to a thin piece of perspex, and mark the perspex with any registration marks I'll need.

> *I like the immediacy and simplicity of linocut. The tactile qualities: when experience has taught you to know just how much ink to use and just how much pressure to apply, so that you think with your hands as much as your mind.*

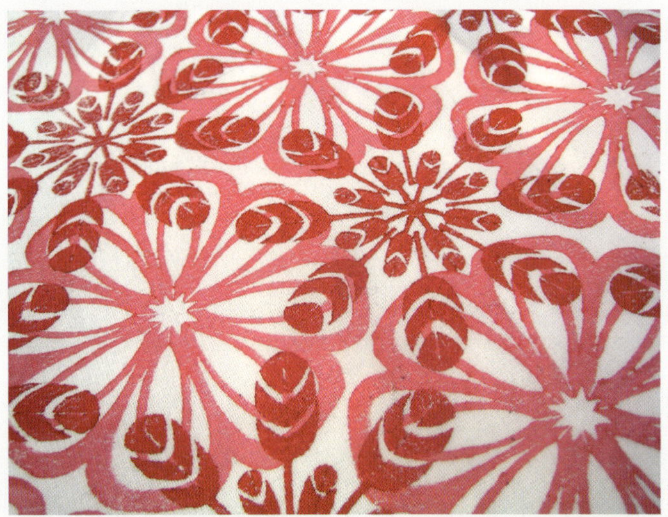

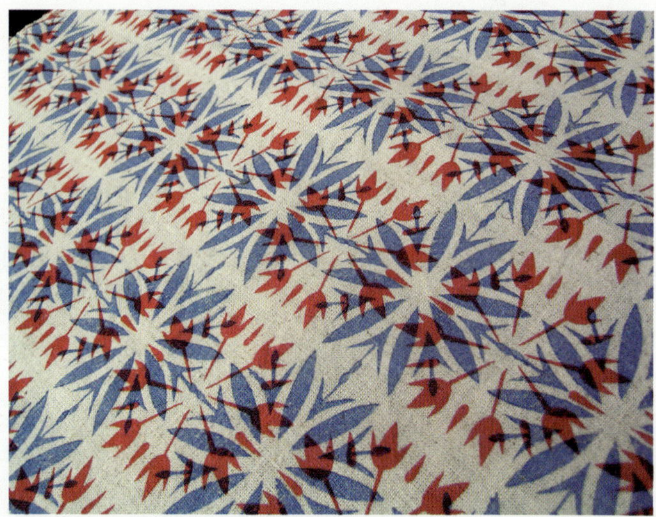

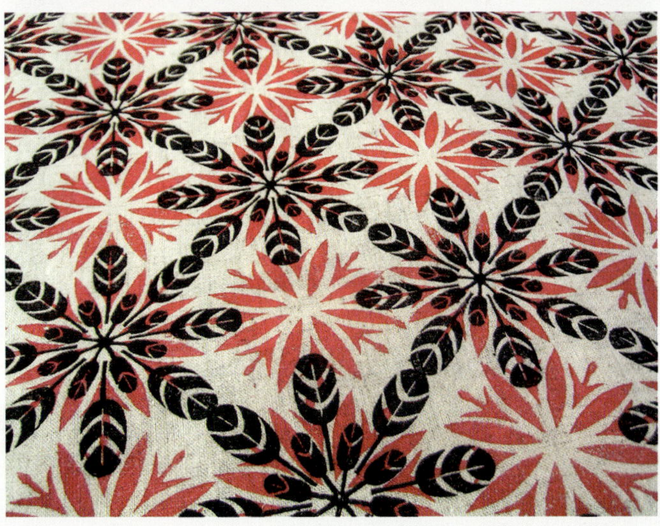

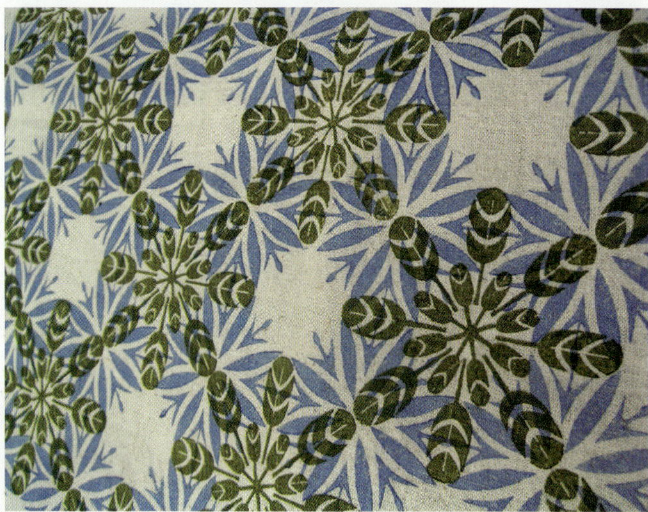

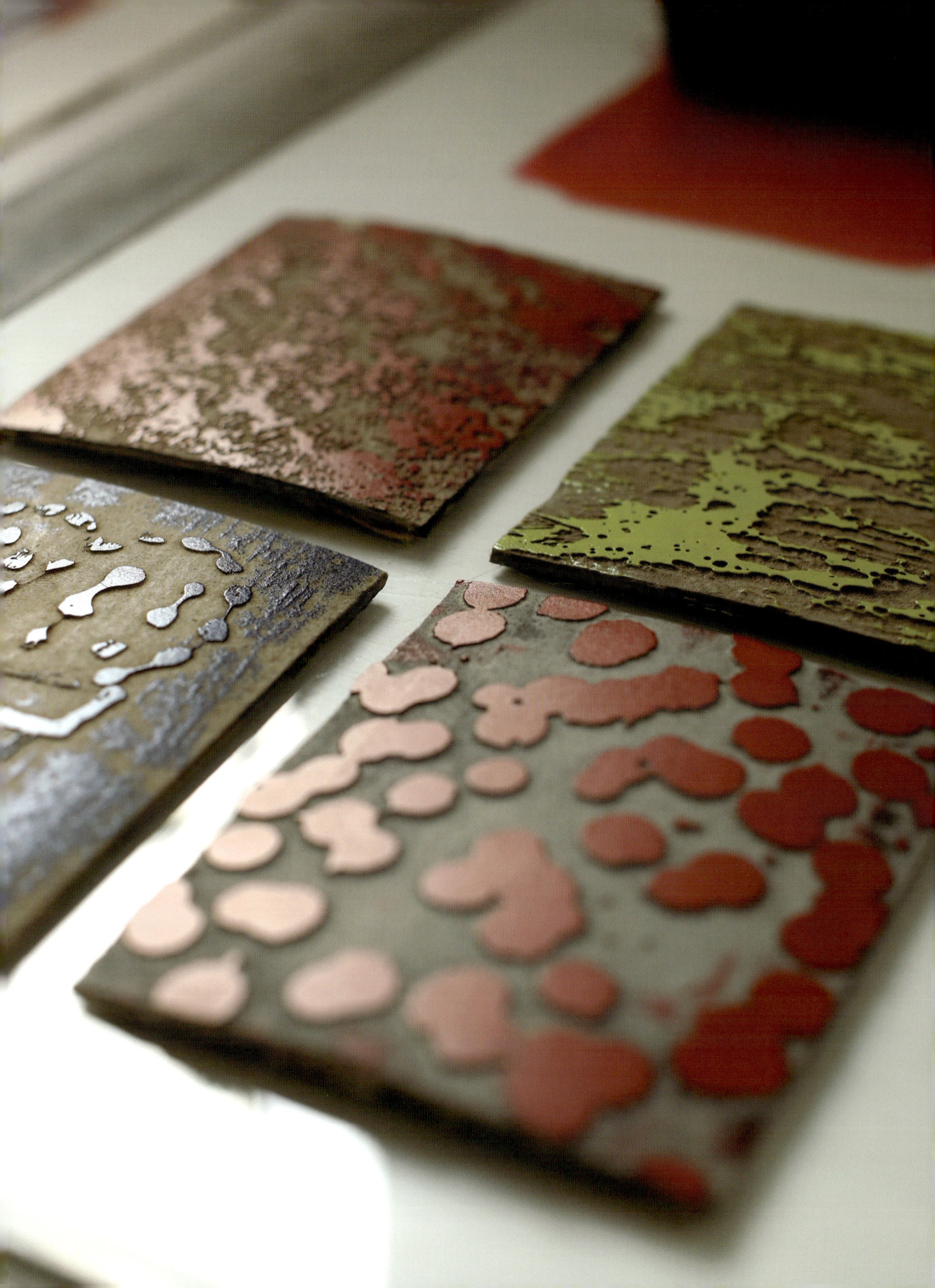

CHAPTER 8

ADVANCED TECHNIQUES

By now you will no doubt be an expert at carving and printing linocuts on paper and fabric. This may well provide enough variety and challenges to satisfy your hunger for many years. If you are still feeling peckish, however, there are a number of other ways to use lino, which perhaps go beyond the traditional idea of the linocut. The following sections include such delicacies as monoprint, etched lino and printing with a steamroller. Where you take it is really only limited by your imagination.

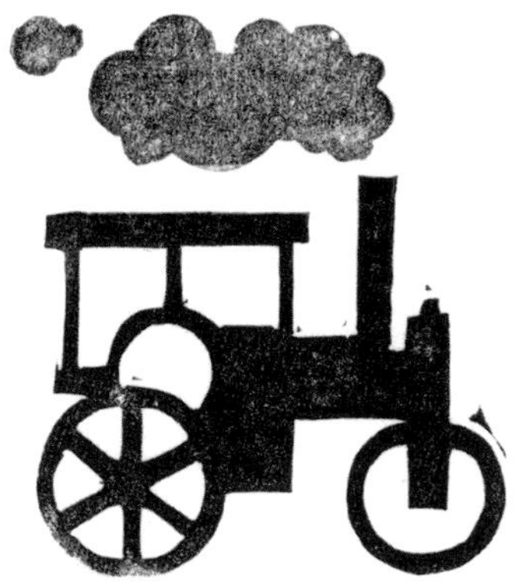

Beyond relief

There are several more ways to make prints from a block of lino beyond the relief printing techniques looked at so far. In many cases two or more techniques can be combined to produce images of great sophistication and complexity. Be adventurous and try your own combinations.

Some of these techniques (monoprint, etched lino) can be printed by hand or with a relief press. Others (intaglio) require an etching press to create enough pressure to push the paper into recessed areas of the block.

Monoprint

Monoprints are prints which cannot be repeated; they are one-offs. Ink is applied by a variety of means to the surface of the block: roller, brush, finger, sponge, dabber etc. This painterly approach allows for expressive and gestural marks to be made. Use a paper or plastic sheet with holes cut out to mask off areas, or to create patterns. Ink can also be removed from the block, making it possible to edit and change bits as well as to make negative marks. Try wiping with a rag, or use a brush soaked in water or solvent to dilute the ink.

Another way to make monoprints is to ink up an uncarved block with an even layer of ink. Place a piece of paper on top and draw onto the back of the paper with a pencil or ballpoint pen. Where the paper is pressed into the ink layer it will pick up the ink resulting in a beautiful, soft line. Pressing harder with the pencil will result in a heavier line. To get soft areas of tone rub the back of the paper with your hand.

Monoprint made by painting a design onto the block with ink.

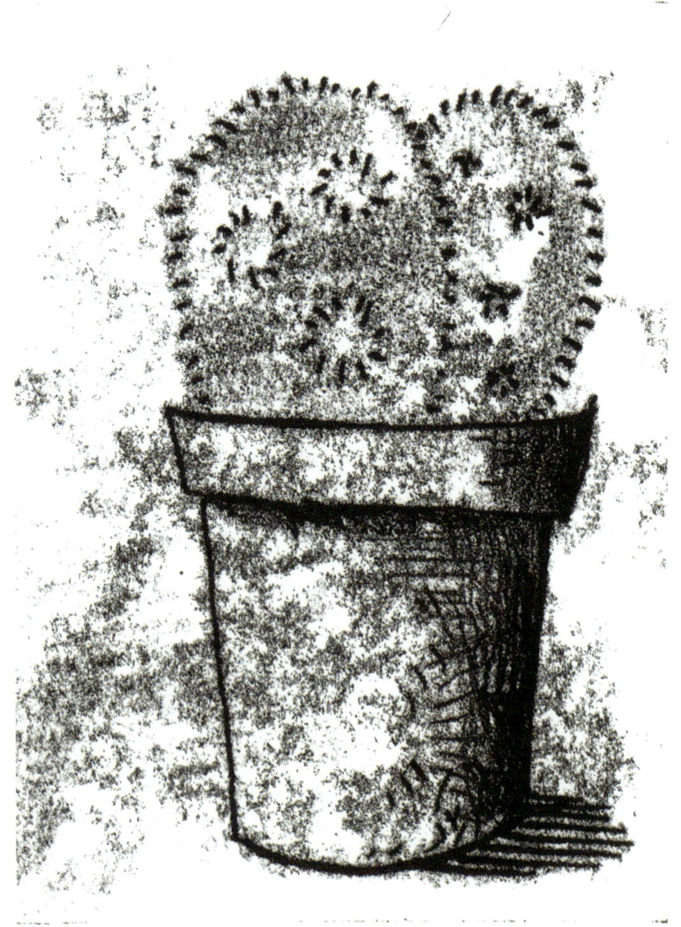

Monoprint made by drawing onto an inked block through paper.

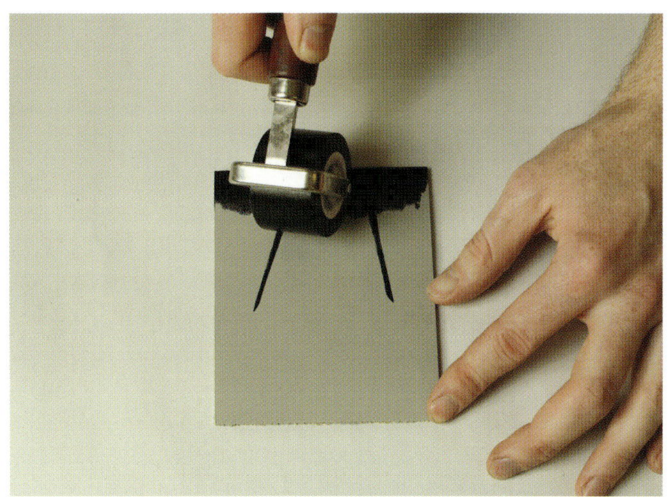
Use a roller to block in areas and the edge to draw lines.

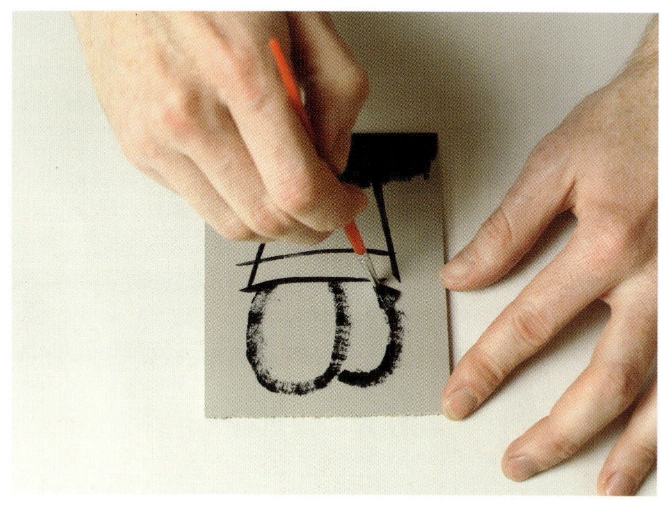
Ink applied with a brush gives a softer mark.

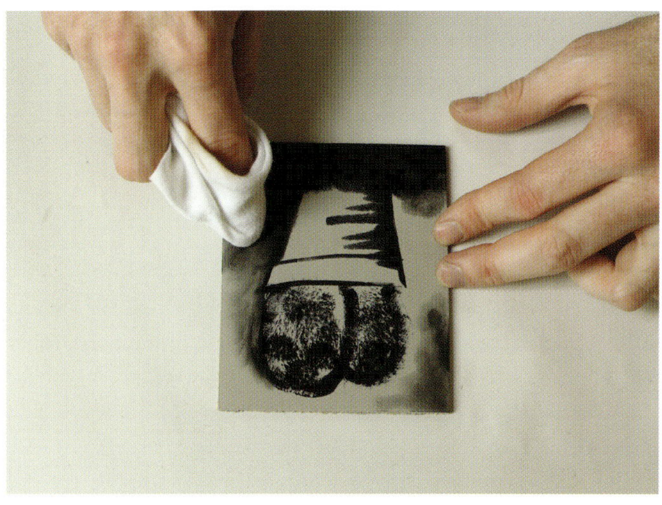
Use a rag to wipe away ink and lighten areas.

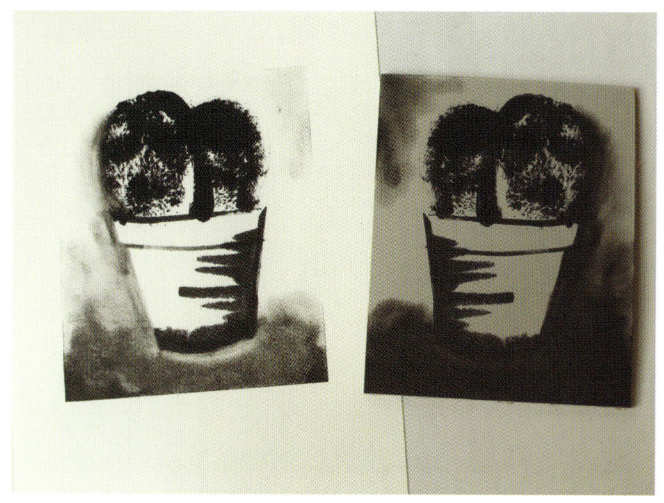
For best results use an etching press.

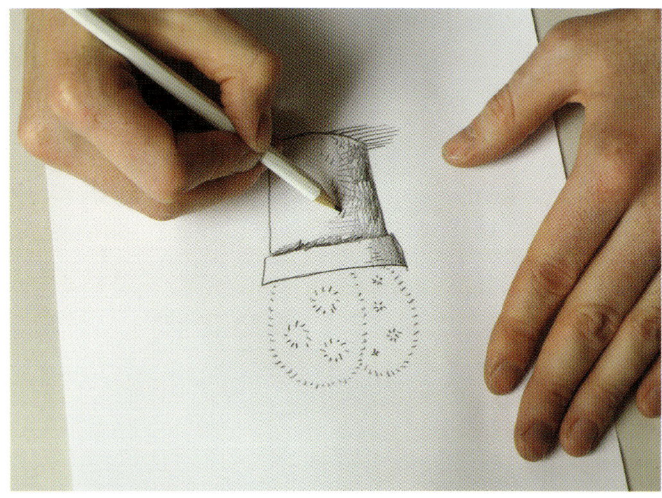
Drawing through paper on top of an inked block.

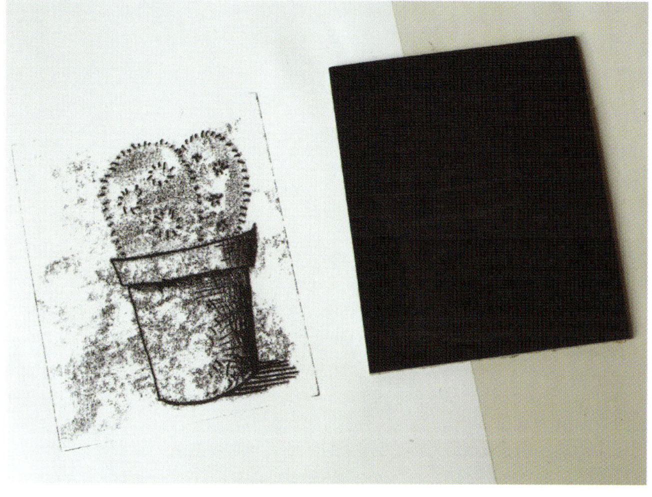
Subtle marks, areas of tone and soft lines are possible.

Distressed lino

A new piece of lino can be inked up and printed in a number of ways to bring out different textures. If you want you can explore this further by distressing the block. Use as many ways as you can find to mark, scratch, dent, roughen and break down the surface. Try hammering it, scraping it with sharp tools, dragging it along the floor, driving over it, throwing it out of the window – whatever takes your fancy. Build up as much texture as possible.

Ink up the distressed block and print it as a background colour, cut it into shapes to make an abstract composition or carve a design into it with gouges. Try printing it with different amounts of ink and pressure to bring out the most detail.

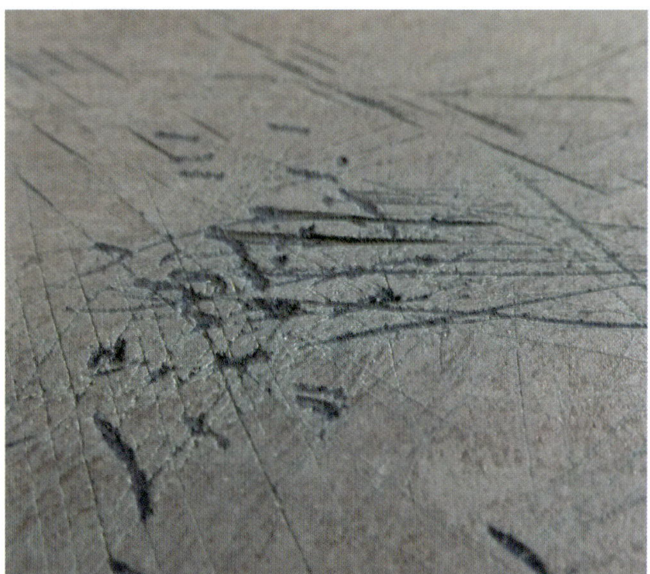

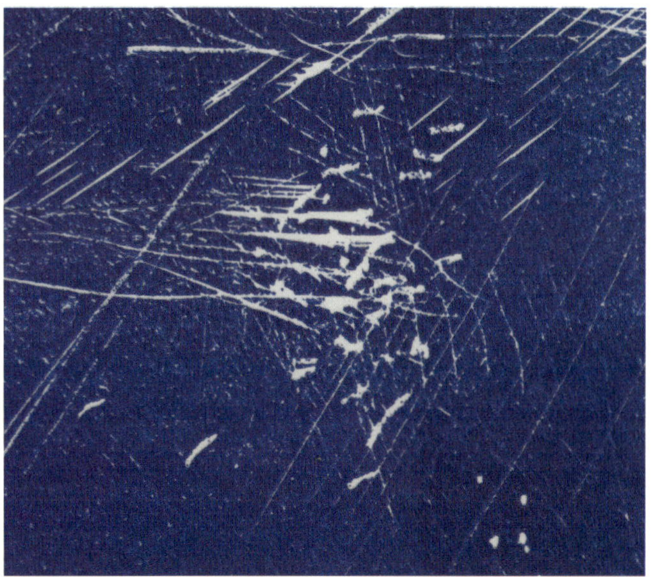

Top: the surface of this block was attacked with vigour using a variety of things, including screws, sandpaper and a saw. Bottom: the resulting print has interesting marks and textures.

Intaglio

Intaglio is an Italian term which encompasses etching, drypoint and metal engraving. It can be applied to any print process where the ink sits lower than the surface of the plate or block. Instead of applying ink to the surface, as in relief printing, ink is applied to the whole plate or block and wiped off again, leaving it only in the recessed areas. When printed under very high pressure, the paper is pushed into the grooves of the block and picks up the ink.

A linoleum block can be carved in such a way as to be successfully inked up and printed like an etching plate, resulting in a print which looks very different to a normal linocut. Instead of carving out the non-printing areas, this time the areas you carve out will hold the ink. The block is printed using an etching press. This is really the only way to exert enough pressure. The paper is dampened to soften it so that it can be pushed into the carved lines to pick up the ink.

Project: intaglio linocut

You will need:

A piece of Japanese relief printing vinyl, a sharp V-gouge, etching ink or oil-based relief printing ink, heavyweight printmaking paper suitable for etching, an old credit card, scrim or newsprint for wiping, rubber gloves, blotting paper, etching press, a water bath to soak the paper.

The intaglio linocut technique works best with a smooth material so that the ink can be wiped from the block easily. Japanese vinyl works brilliantly. This is blue on one side and green on the other. Both sides can be used for carving. The core of the vinyl is black, making it easy to visualize what your design will look like printed as any lines you carve will look black. This type of vinyl is relatively stiff, which is also good because it doesn't buckle under the very high pressure of the etching press.

The paper you use for printing must stand up to being soaked. The best paper for this is one designed for etching, and 100 per cent rag, like Somerset or Rives BFK. The paper will need to be soaked in a water bath for 20 to 30 minutes to soften, and be blotted to remove excess water before printing.

The best ink to use for this project is etching ink, but oil-based relief ink will work almost as well. Water-based inks will not work.

Carving

Draw your design out on the block with a ballpoint pen. A linear design works well. The lines you carve out will become positive marks in the print, so this is the opposite way of working to normal linocut, where you are removing the white areas.

The lines you carve must be fine and not too deep, ideally between 0.25 and 2mm. You will need a sharp V-gouge for this. You can also carve lines using a scalpel. Hold the scalpel at 60–70 degrees to the block and carve one side of the line and then the other to remove a V-shaped section. Larger gouges will make marks which don't print cleanly but may make some interesting textures.

Inking and wiping

The printing process is the same as if you were printing a metal etching plate. Tear the paper down to size and soak it for around 20 minutes to half an hour. Leave it in the water until you are ready to print.

With gloves on, ink up the block using etching ink or oil-based relief ink. Use a piece of plastic like an old credit card or a piece of rigid card to spread the ink over the surface and work it into the lines. Use the card to scrape off the excess ink from the surface of the block. Next, using scrim or a piece of newsprint, wipe the block, being careful to leave the ink in the lines. At this point you can make a judgement about how much ink to leave on the block. You can also wipe away areas of ink using a rag and chalk. These will print as light areas on the print; the cleaner you wipe the block the lighter it will print.

Printing

If you have an etching press where the top roller can be raised, set the pressure as if you were printing an etching plate, but print without the blankets. If the top roller cannot be raised, use runners on either side of the block to support the roller.

When the block is ready to print, with clean hands, remove the paper from the water and blot it two or three times in the blotters until there is no more surface water visible on the paper. It should be slightly damp, but not wet. Lay the block on the etching press, ink side up, and place the damp paper on top, followed by a sheet of tissue paper. Turn the handle of the press to pass the block through. Make sure the paper has passed right through the roller. Remove the tissue and carefully peel the paper back from the block.

The prints should be dried flat between boards with a heavy weight on top (you can use a pile of heavy books) until the ink is dry. This will take two or three days depending on atmospheric conditions.

Multiple inking techniques

A block which has been inked as intaglio can, before printing, be rolled up with relief ink in another colour. This is called a surface roll. The second colour will sit on the raised surfaces of the block. A soft roller will go further into the depressed areas, depositing more ink, whereas a hard roller will only leave ink on the highest part.

Case Study: Wuon-Gean Ho

Artist Wuon-Gean Ho often uses linocut techniques in combination with other processes like screenprint. Over the following pages she demonstrates a combination of intaglio, selective wiping and surface rolling to produce one of the prints from her *Sleeper* series.

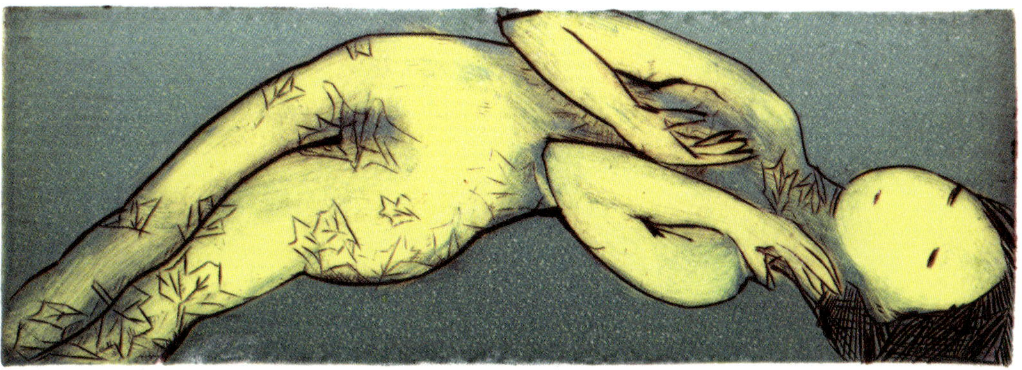

Sleeper Curve Mini, Wuon-Gean Ho, 3 x 10cm, intaglio linocut.

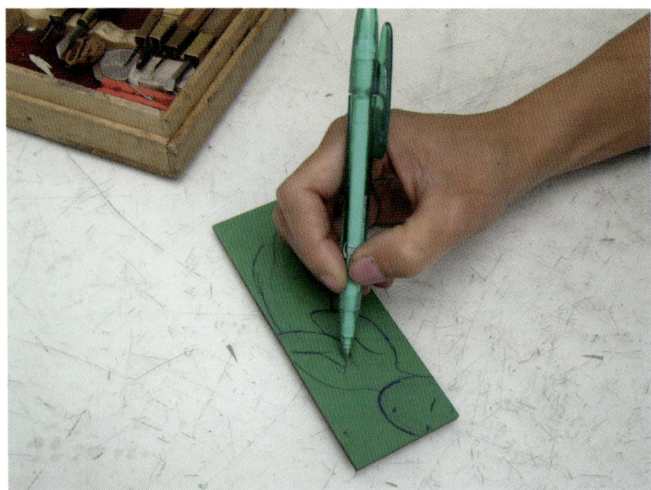

The design is drawn onto the vinyl with a ballpoint pen.

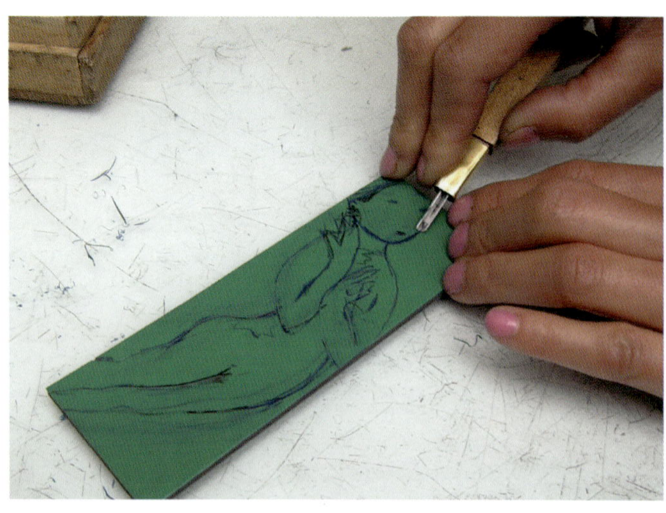

With a sharp V-gouge, the lines are carefully carved.

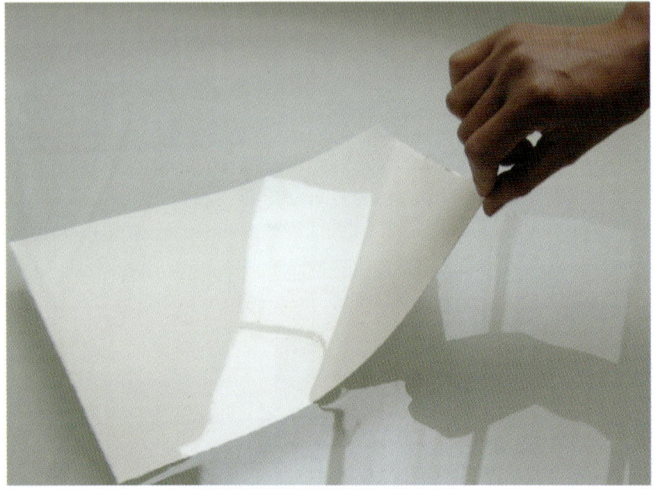

Before inking the block, the paper is soaked in a water bath.

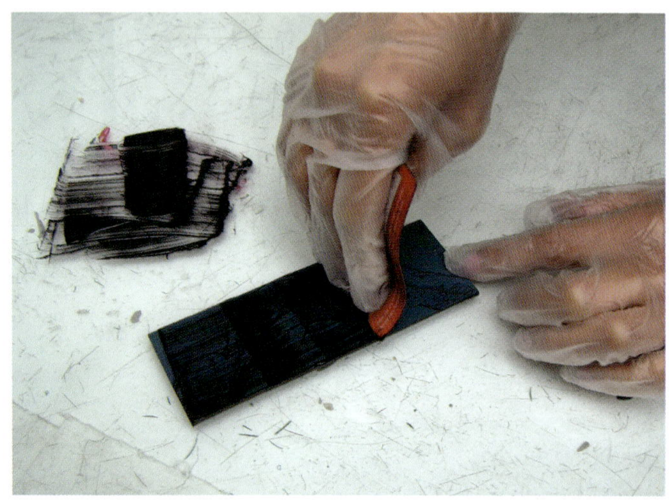

Ink is applied and worked into the lines with a card.

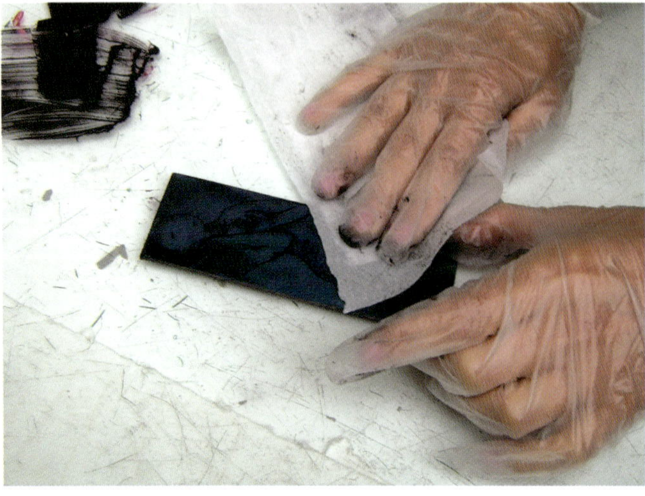

The excess ink is wiped off with newsprint and tissue.

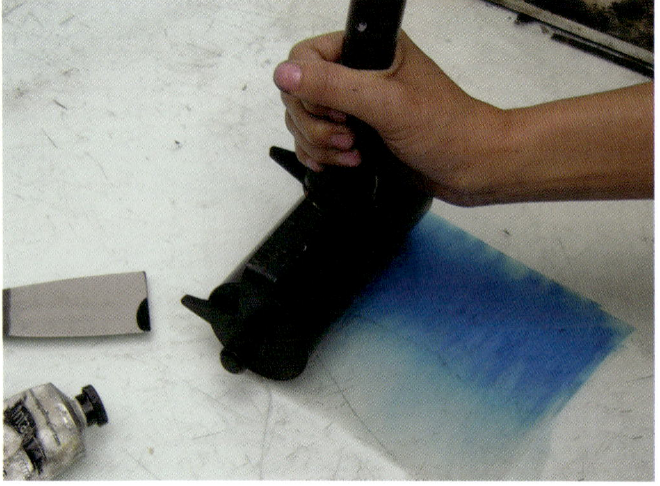

A blue colour blend is prepared for the first surface roll.

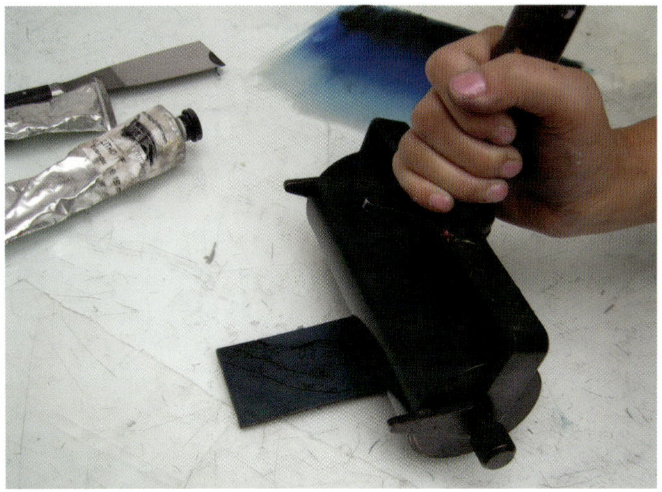

The ink is rolled carefully onto the block.

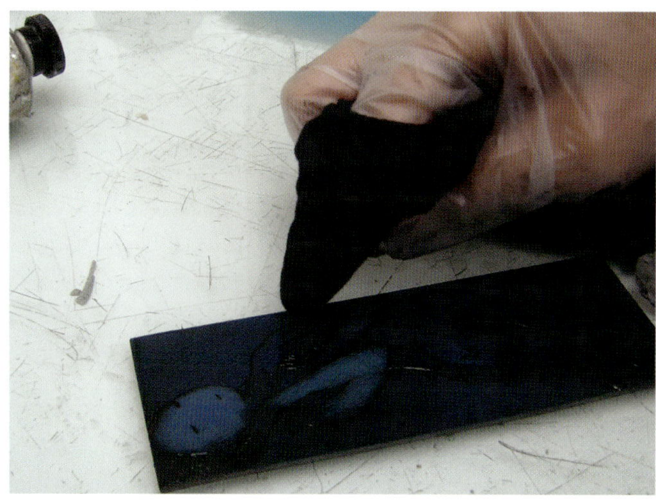

Highlights are lightened by wiping with a rag and chalk.

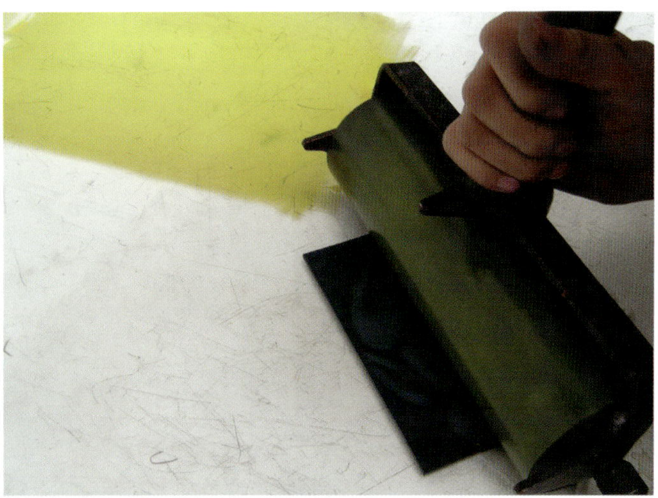

A second surface roll is applied in yellow ink.

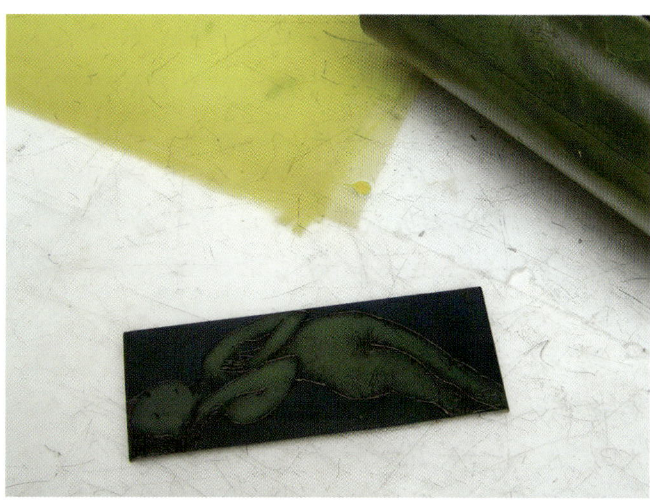

The inked up block is ready to be printed.

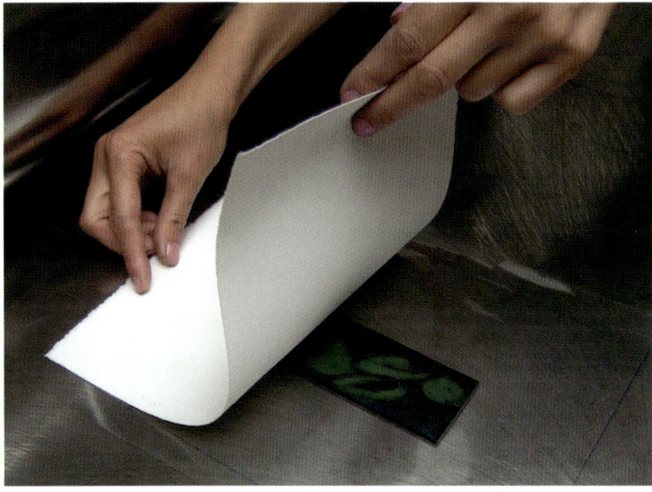

The paper is blotted and laid on the block before printing.

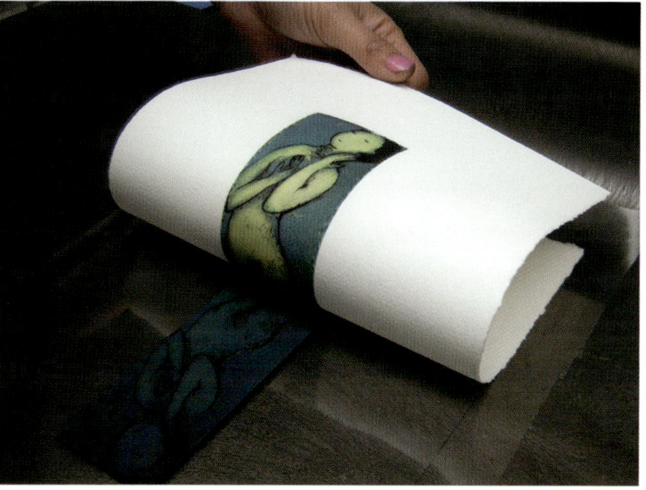

The paper is lifted to reveal the finished print.

Etched lino

Health and safety

Caustic soda, also known as lye or sodium hydroxide, is sold in flake or pellet form as drain cleaner and is widely available from hardware stores. It is highly corrosive and will cause burns to the skin and eyes on contact. It should be handled with extreme caution, wearing thick rubber gloves, goggles for eye protection and an apron. As well as attacking the skin it will damage many surfaces such as paint, metals and clothing. When mixed with water to make a solution there is a vigorous reaction and a lot of heat is produced, together with some fumes. It should only be used in a well ventilated space, preferably outside.

If you get caustic soda on your skin, wash it off with plenty of water and continue to wash with running water for ten minutes. Always follow the instructions on the label. Do NOT swallow and store safely, clearly labelled and away from children and pets.

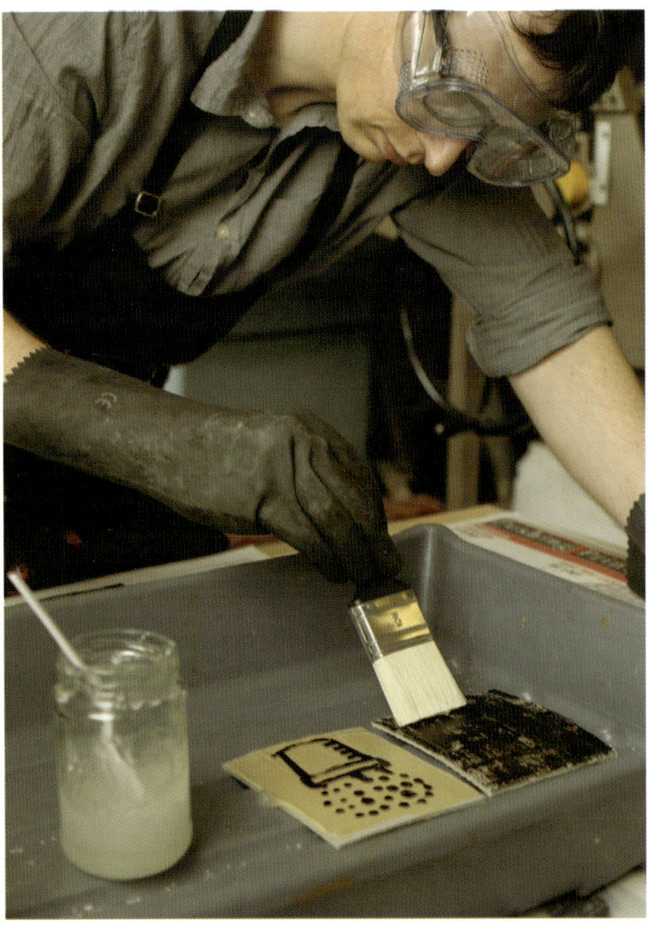

Always wear goggles and gloves when working with caustic soda.

General principles

Traditional linoleum (but not vinyl) can be etched using caustic soda to create painterly, expressive marks and rich and varied tones. The process of etching lino is somewhat unpredictable and should be approached with an experimental attitude.

The chemical is first dissolved in water and wallpaper paste or wheat paste is added to thicken it. This caustic paste is then poured onto the surface of the lino or applied with a brush and left for anything from several minutes up to several hours before washing off. During this time it will eat away at the lino, etching deeper and deeper into the surface. When the etched block is inked up the raised areas will pick up ink and print. The etching process can be used on its own or in conjunction with carving to create a wider range of marks.

Resists and stopping-out

Before etching, the lino can be protected from the caustic paste by applying any substance which will resist it. This process is known as stopping-out and the substance used is called stop-out. Good stop-outs include varnish, bitumen, oil pastel, vegetable oil, vaseline and wax. Areas can also be protected to some degree with plastic parcel tape. Some substances will resist the caustic soda for longer than others. Thicker layers will also resist the caustic for longer, so apply multiple layers if you want to prevent an area being etched at all.

Varnishes which can be used include Charbonnel's Lamour stop-out varnish, Brunswick Black (a bitumen-based varnish) and yacht varnish. All contain solvents to help them dry and should only be used in well-ventilated areas away from sources of heat and naked flames.

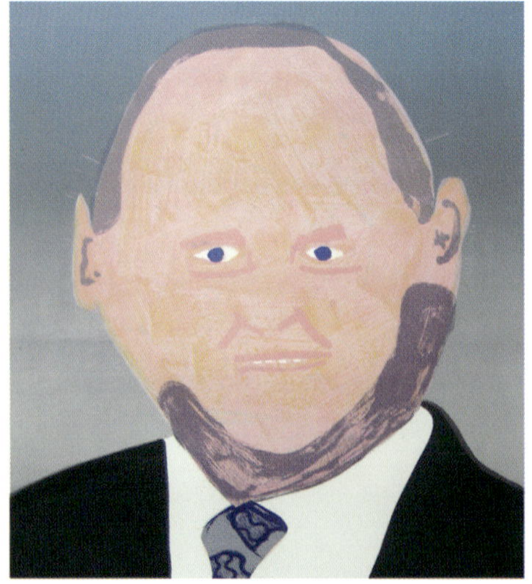

Bigface (detail), Steve Edwards, 87 × 62cm, etched and cut linoleum.

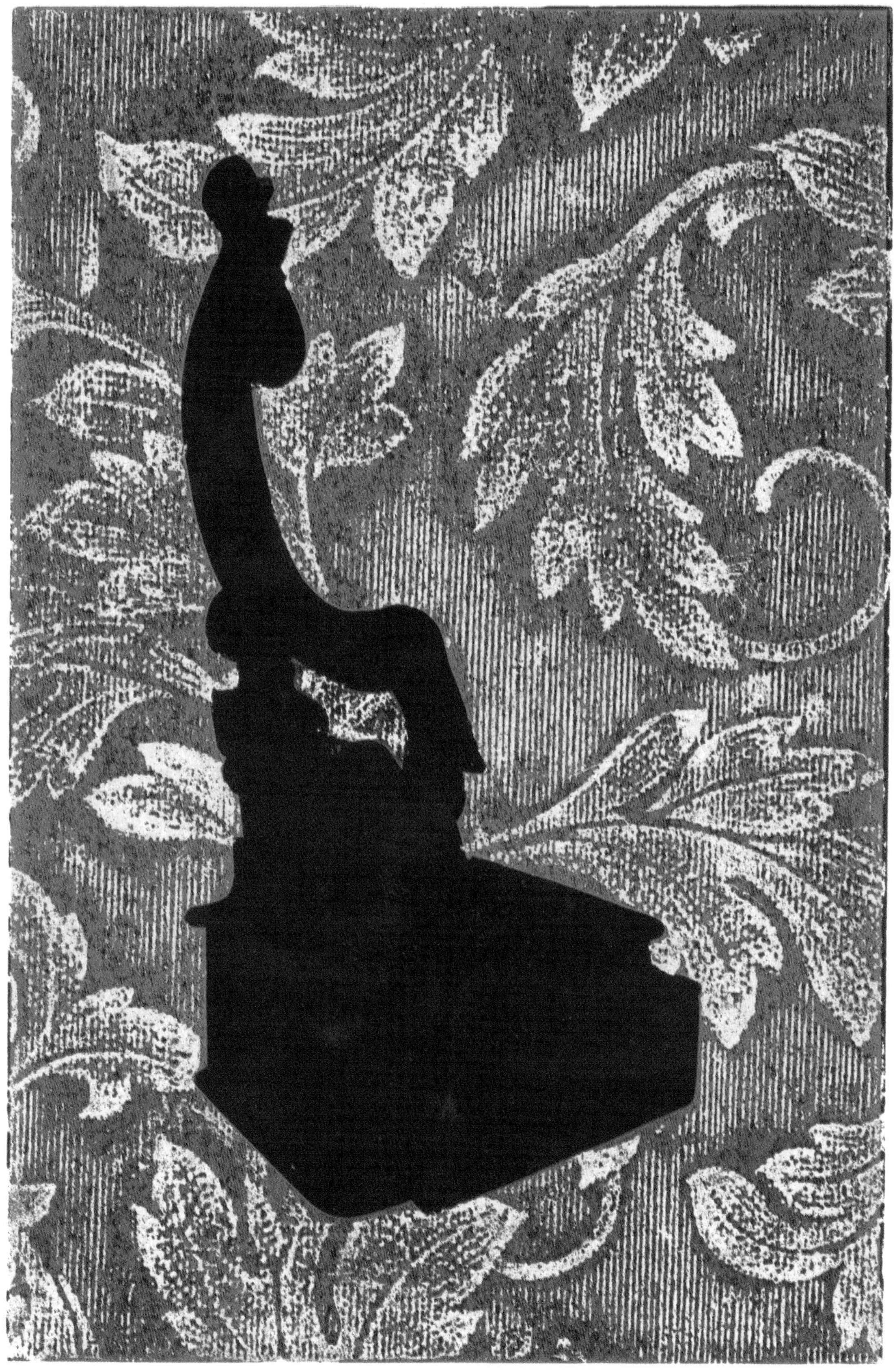

Small Drawer, Helen Brooker. The background texture was transferred to the block by applying Vaseline to textured wallpaper and pressing it onto the block as a stop-out before etching it.

Project: etched lino

Before you start, make sure you have somewhere safe you can leave the blocks while they are etching, as the caustic paste takes several hours to etch deeply. As with other etching processes, the longer you leave the caustic paste to react with the lino, the deeper it will etch. A test block can be made by etching different sections for progressively longer times. There are some factors that will affect the speed of the etching process, including temperature and how strong and fresh the solution is. Remember this is an inexact science and results are unpredictable.

You will need:

Three pieces of traditional linoleum (ideally grey), caustic soda flakes or granules, water, wallpaper paste or cornstarch, measuring jug, two large clean jam jars, plastic or wooden spoon, stop-out varnish, candle, brown plastic parcel tape, old brushes, sponge, plastic scrubbing brush, goggles, thick rubber gloves, apron, plastic tray to contain spills and newspaper to protect surfaces. Optional: methylated spirits, wet and dry (fine) sandpaper.

You will use one of the pieces of lino to apply the caustic paste to directly and the other two to explore stopping-out. The areas which you have stopped out will end up being the un-etched, raised areas of the block.

Stopping-out

Use the stop-out varnish on the first block. Try applying it with a brush and a sponge to get a range of textures. Build up some areas with several layers of varnish, allowing each to dry well before applying the next. Also try dribbling the varnish from the brush to create blobs and drips.

On the second block use candle wax, wax crayons or oil pastels to draw onto the block. Again, use a variety of marks and build up some areas more thickly. Use a lit candle to drip wax onto the block. Take great care with naked flames and keep well away from flammable materials like varnish and solvents.

The third block can be left blank. It may be degreased with methylated spirits or lightly sanded to make it more receptive to the caustic paste. This will make the paste lie flatter on the block, resulting in a more even texture.

Preparing the caustic paste

Work in a well ventilated area or outside. Only use plastic or wooden implements, never metal. Protect surfaces with plenty of newspaper or plastic sheeting. Wear goggles, an apron and rubber gloves at all times when handling the caustic soda and caustic paste. Working on a plastic tray will help to contain any spills. These can be washed down the sink with plenty of cold water.

First you are going to mix up a caustic paste. You want a fairly runny mixture for painting onto the first block and a thicker paste to apply to the other two blocks, which have the stopped out areas.

Measure out 200ml of cold water and pour it into the first jam jar. Fill the other jam jar with water to keep your spoon and brushes in when not in use.

Taking care not to spill any, add 3 tablespoons of caustic soda pellets to the water and stir. The solution will heat up and give off fumes. Take care not to breathe these in.

IMPORTANT: Always add the caustic soda to the water, never the other way round.

Add one or two tablespoons of wallpaper paste flakes or cornstarch to the solution and stir well with the plastic or wooden spoon. Leave to sit for ten minutes. Put the spoon in the jar of water and put it where it won't get knocked over.

Applying the caustic paste

Place your pieces of lino in the plastic tray. Using an old brush, paint a design onto the blank block using the caustic paste. Don't worry if nothing happens immediately. After a while the lino will start to go brown so you know it's working. Try making a range of marks with the brush. Leave some areas unpainted if you want solid areas in your print. Put the brush in the jar of water.

Next, add two more tablespoons of wallpaper paste flakes to the paste, stir it in and let it thicken again. It should now have a thicker consistency which allows you to apply quite a thick layer to the block. Apply to the two stopped-out blocks, covering the whole of their surfaces with a generous layer. Avoid getting any on the back of the lino if possible.

Wash all implements, work surfaces and gloves well with plenty of cold water. Any unused caustic paste can be washed down the sink.

Leave the blocks somewhere safe for several hours, preferably overnight. They should end up looking a bit of a mess – all brown and gunky.

Cleaning the blocks

Wearing goggles and gloves wash the blocks under gently running water (try not to splash yourself) and scrub them well with the plastic scrubbing brush. Keep going until you have removed all of the brown, etched lino. If it turns brown again after you've washed it there is still some caustic soda on it so wash it again. This can take a little while, so be patient and persevere.

Dry the lino in the sun or on a radiator or hotplate on a low setting. It will probably be curled up at this point as the water makes the hessian shrink on the back of the lino. Dry it flat under weights to help flatten it.

Once it is dry, clean off the varnish and other stop-outs with white spirit or a similar solvent in a well-ventilated area, wearing gloves. Again, this can take some time. Scrubbing with a brush can help, as can soaking the varnish. If it is being stubborn, apply a generous amount of white spirit to the block and wrap it in a plastic bag to soak for five minutes then wipe. Candle wax can be removed by gently scraping it off. Once the block is dry it is ready to ink up and print.

Printing

Ink up and print the block as usual. This works best on a press but is possible by hand. When printing, some of the recessed areas will pick up ink and will print. This can be reduced by using a pair of lino runners and a large roller. The runners will hold the roller up and prevent it rolling into the lower sections. Using a soft roller will pick up more ink in the recessed areas, as will printing on the press with blankets.

Taking it further

Etching lino is an unpredictable process but can produce beautiful results. As long as you embrace this you can develop your repertoire through experimentation and apply the technique as you wish. Etched blocks can be cut down to smaller sizes or areas carved into with gouges. An etched texture might make a good background for one of your existing linocuts or you might prefer to layer different textures by printing them on top of each other.

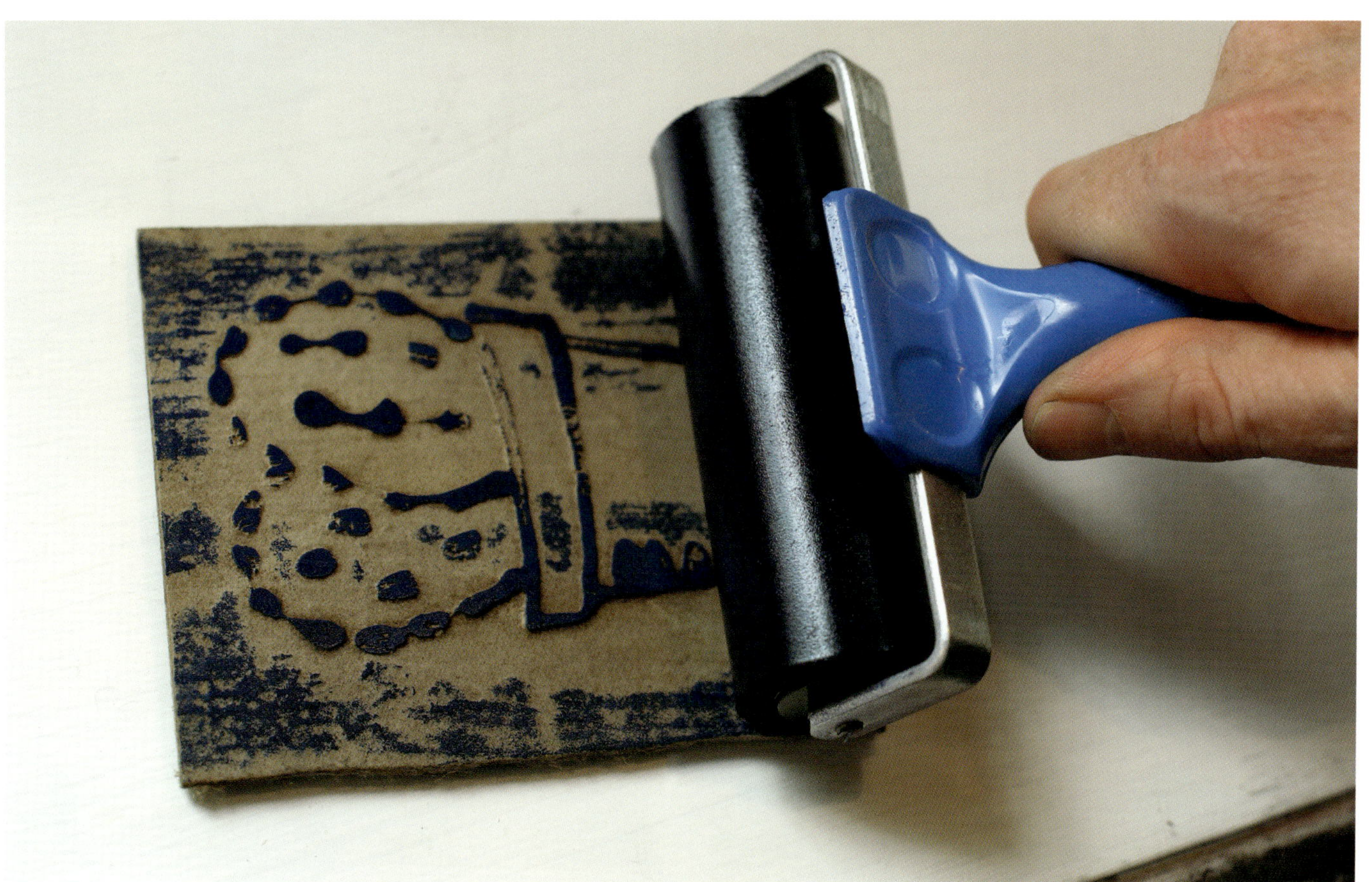

Inking up an etched block. Note how the ink is picked up in the etched areas.

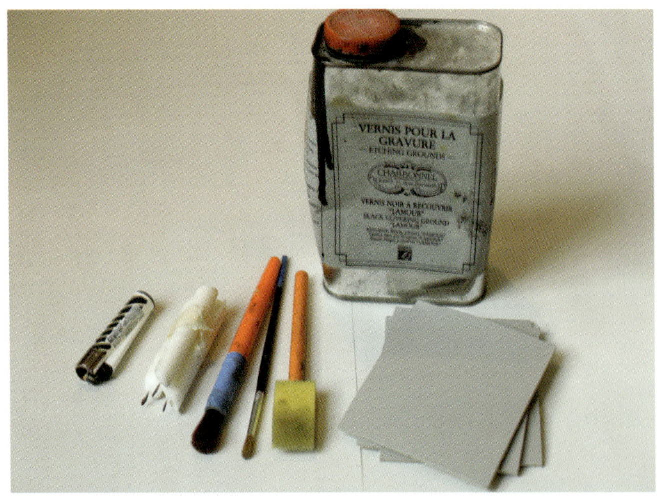

Use a variety of ways to stop out areas of the block.

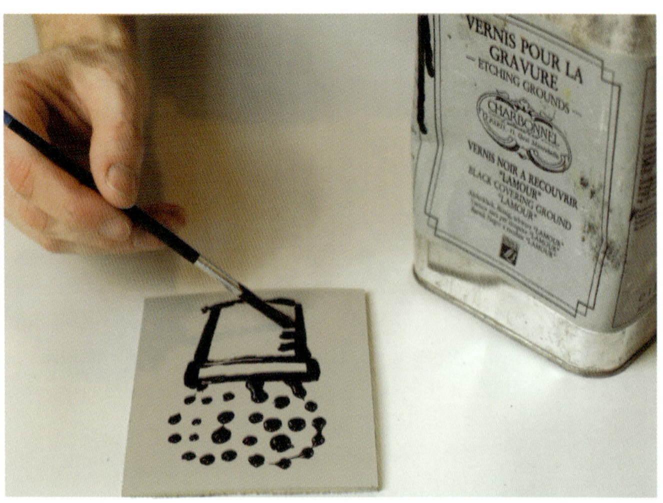

Apply stop-out varnish with a brush.

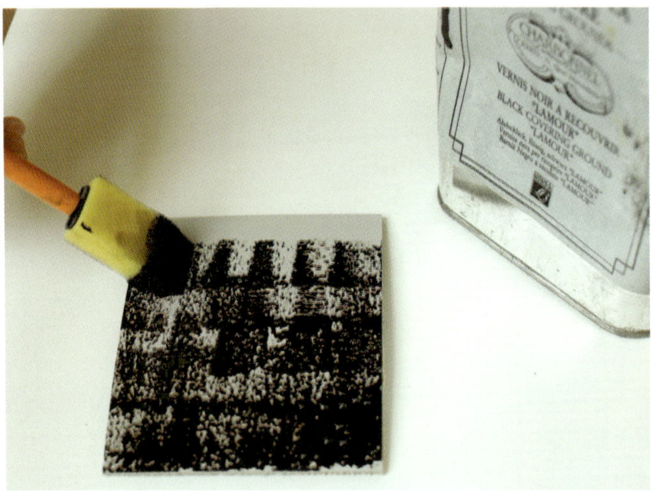

Use a sponge to create texture.

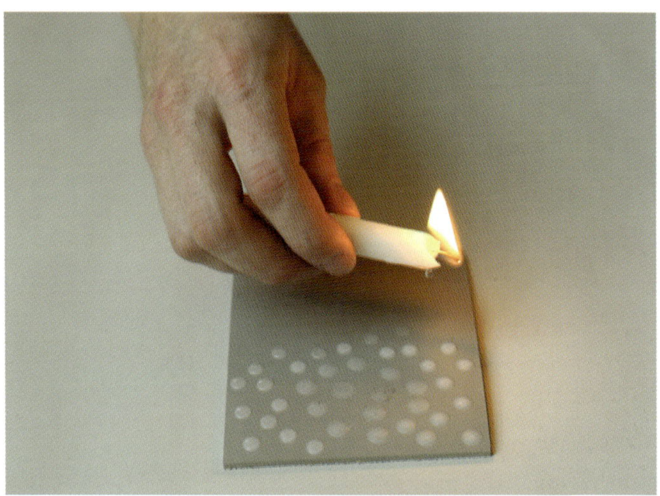

Drip candle wax to create spots.

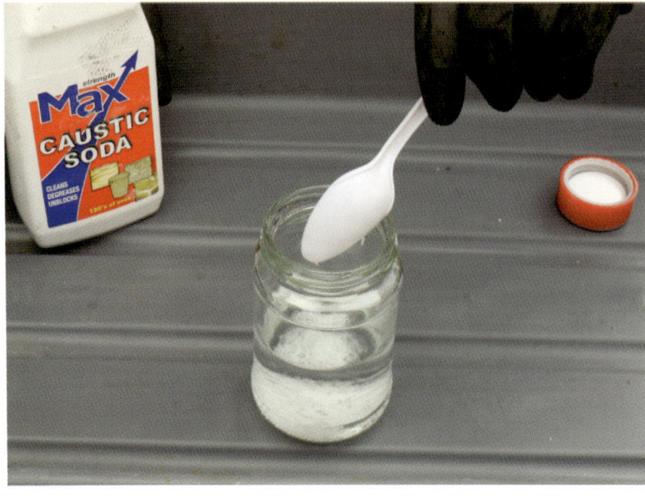

Carefully add the caustic soda to water and stir.

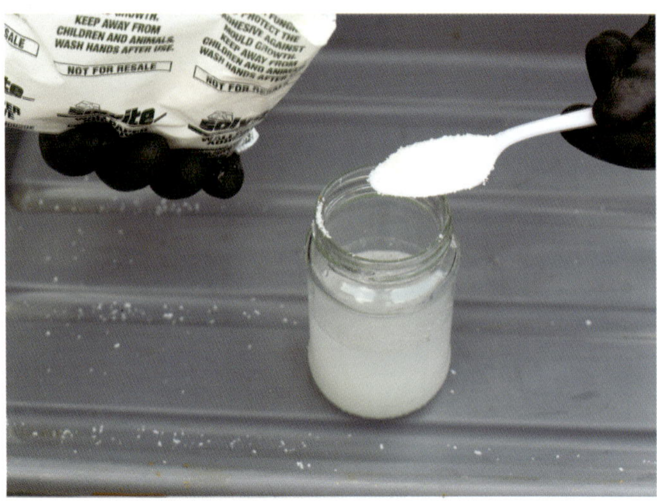

Add the wallpaper paste flakes and mix well.

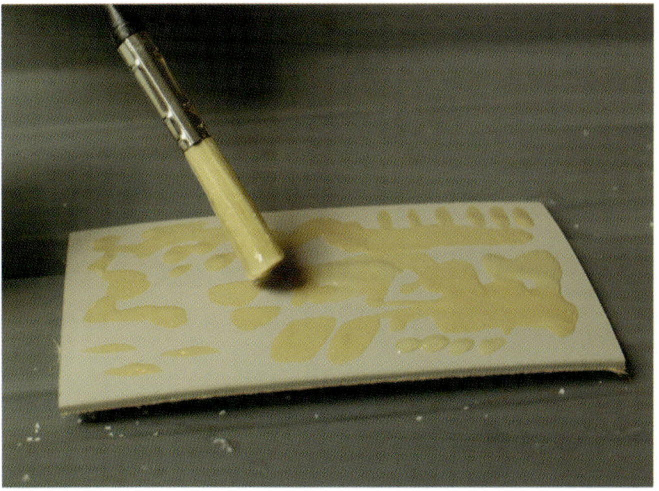

Use a brush to apply the caustic paste to the block.

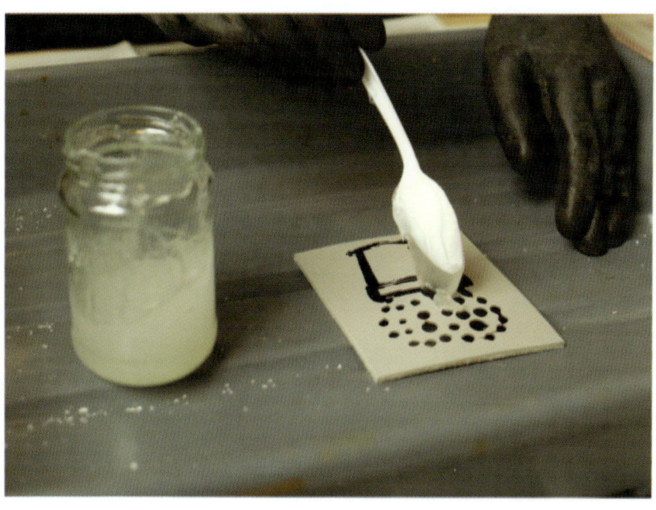

Use the thicker paste for the stopped-out blocks.

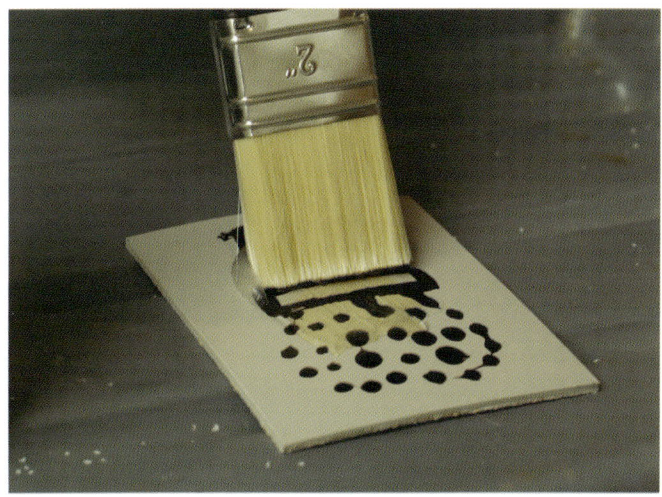

Spread the paste over the entire surface of the block.

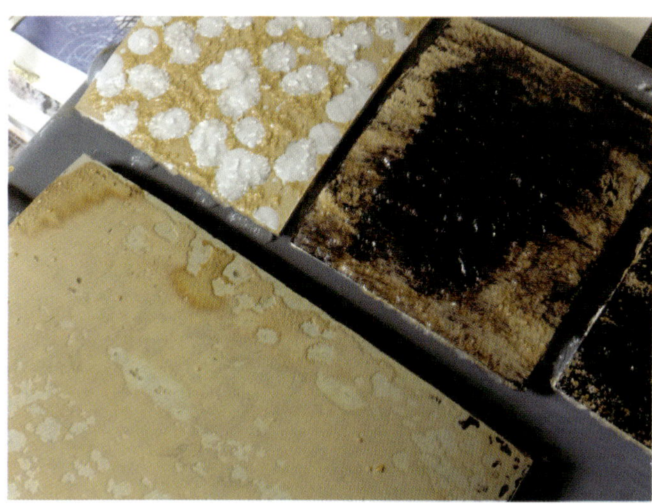

Leave the blocks to etch for several hours.

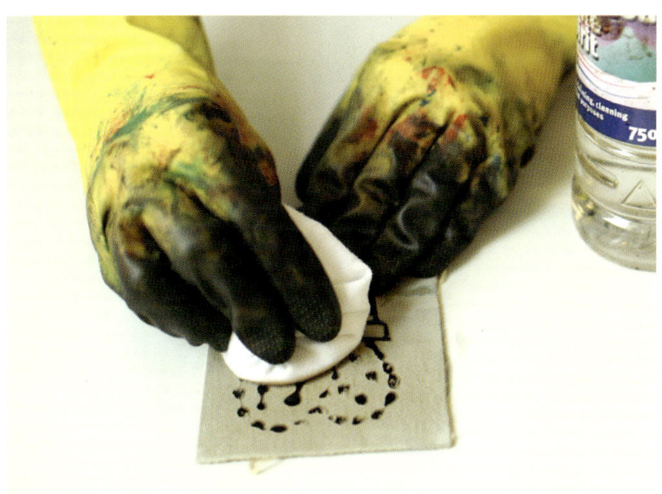

After etching, wash the blocks and remove stop-out.

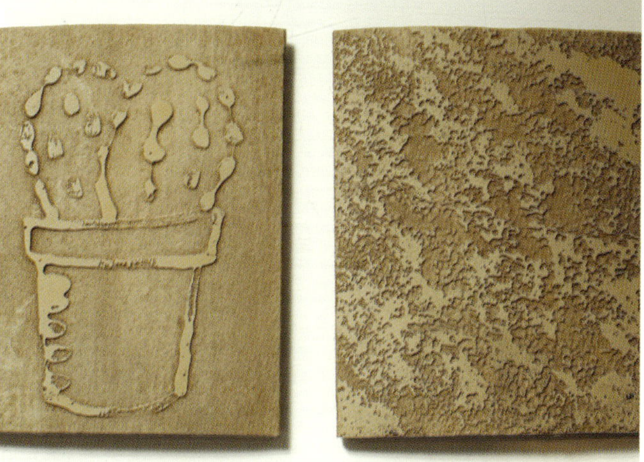

The etched blocks ready to be printed.

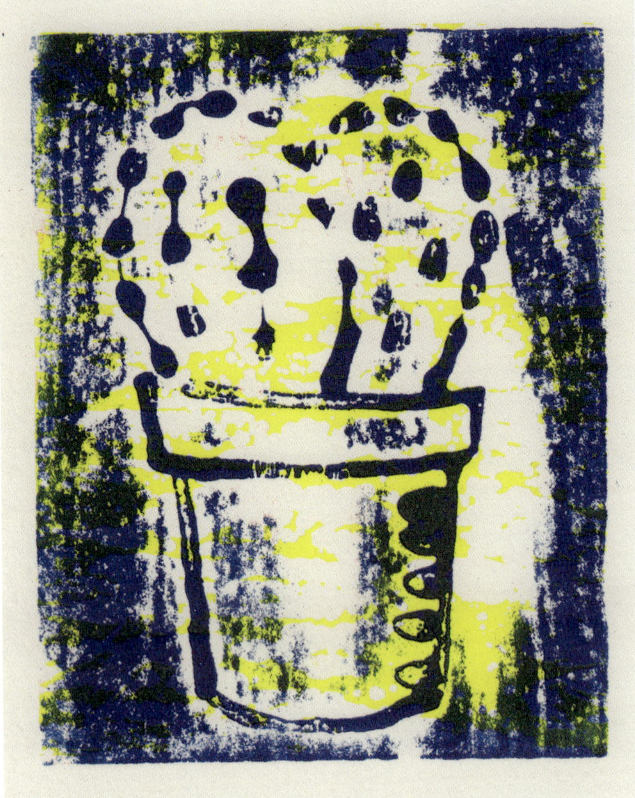

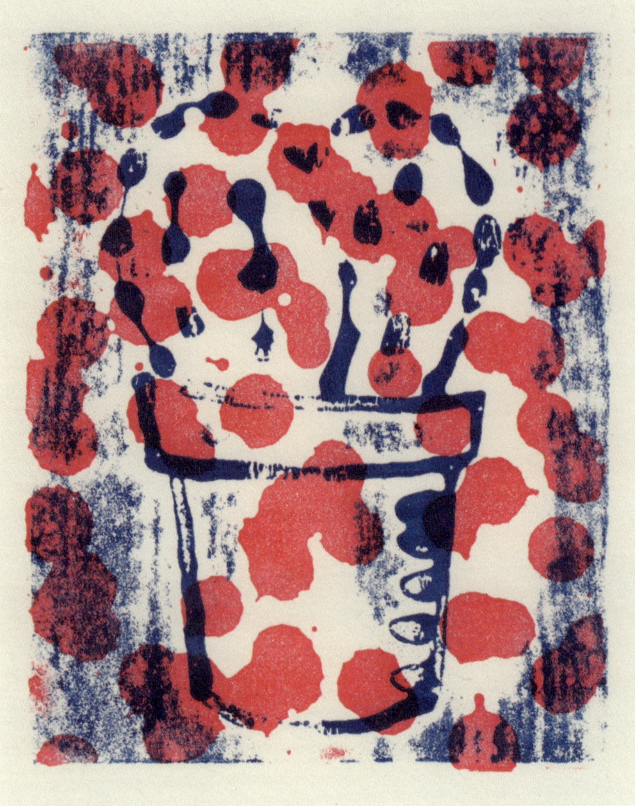

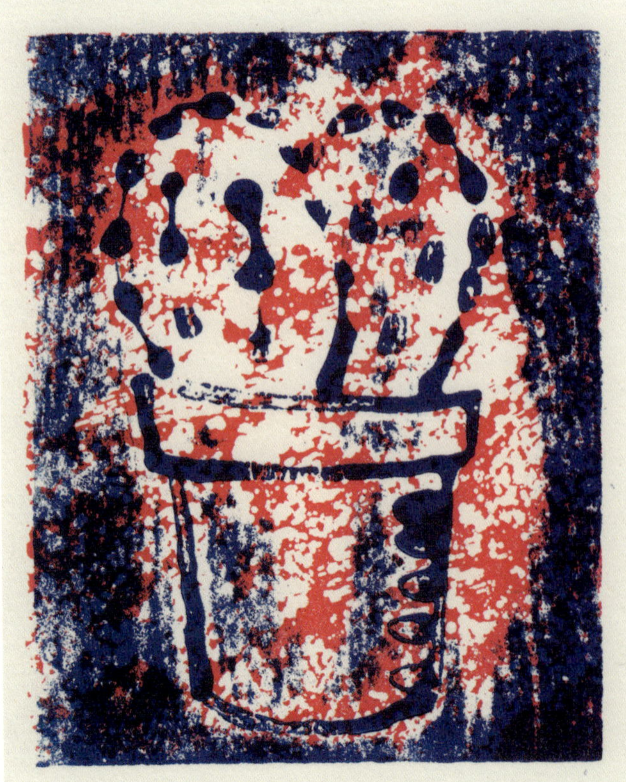

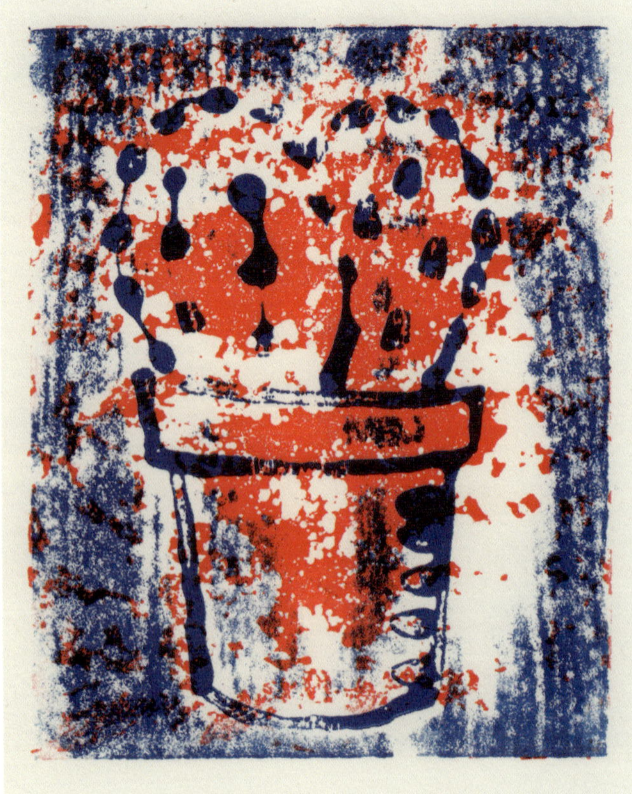

Etched lino: finished prints. Each of these was printed from two blocks.

Combination printing

Linocut can successfully be combined with a number of other print processes including etching, screenprint, monoprint and, of course, other relief print processes like woodcut and letterpress. Bear in mind that certain printed surfaces may be uneven in places, for example a print from a deeply etched plate or an embossed letterpress print. This will affect subsequent layers being printed on top.

Screenprint

Linocut goes very well with screenprint, which can add an extra dimension to your prints. There is a wide range of hand-drawn marks, photographic and computer-generated imagery which can be printed with silkscreen but is impossible with linocut. In addition, images can be screenprinted onto the lino block as a guide for carving.

One particularly useful way of using screenprint is to print backgrounds of flat colour and to fill in large areas. A transparent screenprinting ink is made by adding a high percentage of screen-printing medium/paste. This thin ink can then be printed over a black outline without obscuring it. This has the great advantage of being easier to register than multiple lino blocks.

Woodcut

Wood has a grain to it which comes through in printing and can be brought out even more by brushing the block with a wire brush. It is the grain which differentiates wood from lino and when combined in one print can add an extra dimension.

Collage

Once your prints are dry they can be cut up and collaged. This is a good way to try out new compositions and generally free things up a bit. The destruction of your work can be a liberating experience, allowing for new possibilities to emerge. If you don't want to destroy your best work, use the test prints that went wrong. Cut them up, reposition them, stick them onto new backgrounds, try them in new combinations.

Letterpress

Relief printing and letterpress go hand in hand. In fact, letterpress is a form of relief printing. As long as all the printed surfaces are at the same height, lino and letterpress can be printed simultaneously, side by side. This works best on a press designed for printing type. The lino blocks can be brought up to the correct height (type high) by placing blocks of wood and sheets of card under them.

Much fun can be had printing with larger, wooden, type. When treated purely as geometric shapes these can be used to create pictograms, faces, trees, clouds and so on. By combining this with linocut the possibilities are endless.

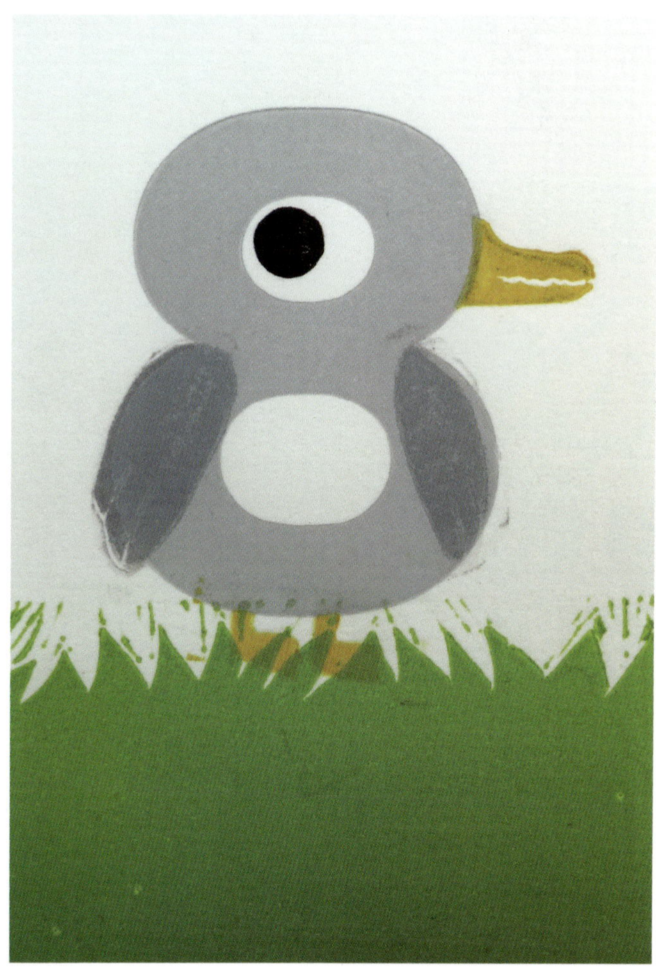

The Ugly Duckling, Alessandra Giardi. Linocut and letterpress. This required careful placement of pieces of lino to make the beak, wings, eye and feet of the duckling.

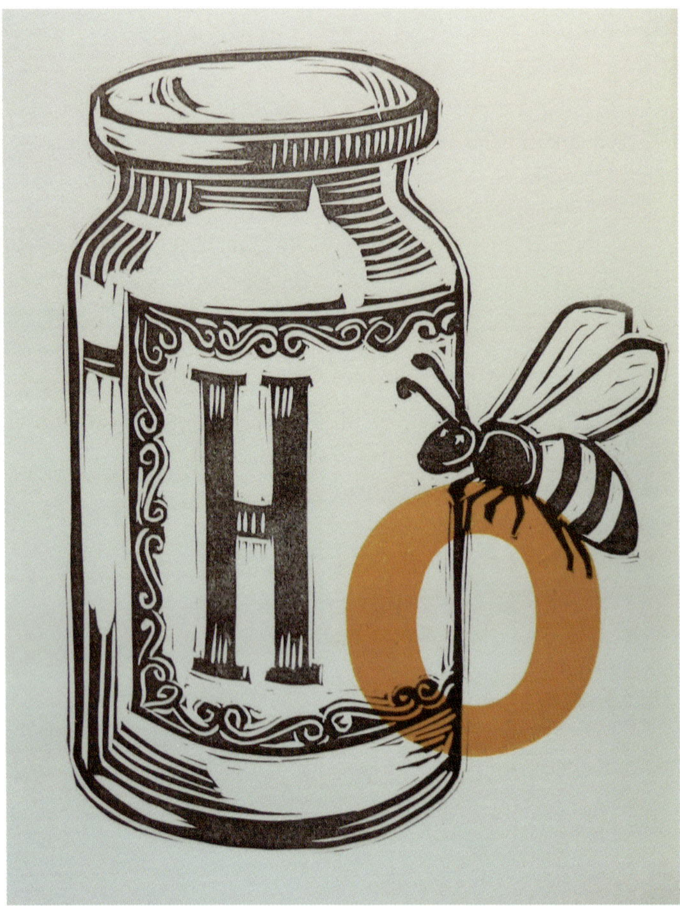

The Owl and the Pussycat, C.J. Whitlock.
Linocut and letterpress.
In this composition the linocut element forms the majority of the design while the yellow letter O creates a splash of colour.

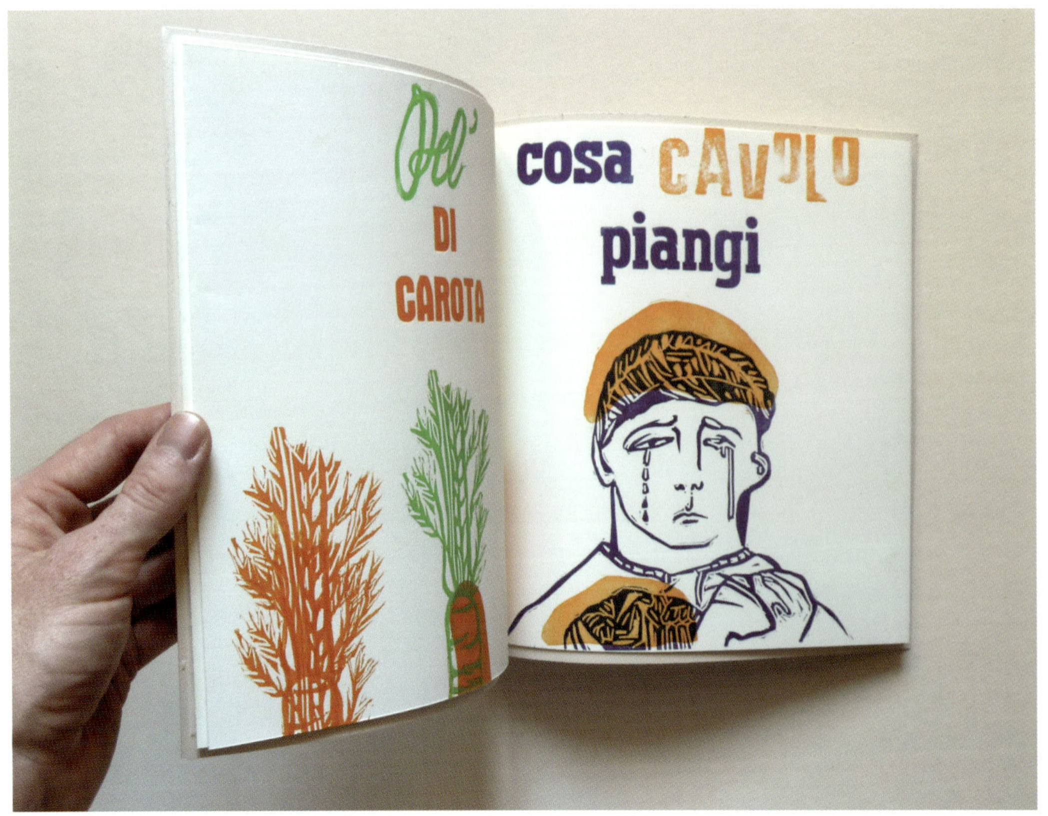

Quando Siamo Frutta, Chiara Leto.
Linocut and letterpress.
Each page uses two ink colours, which helps to give it a strong identity.

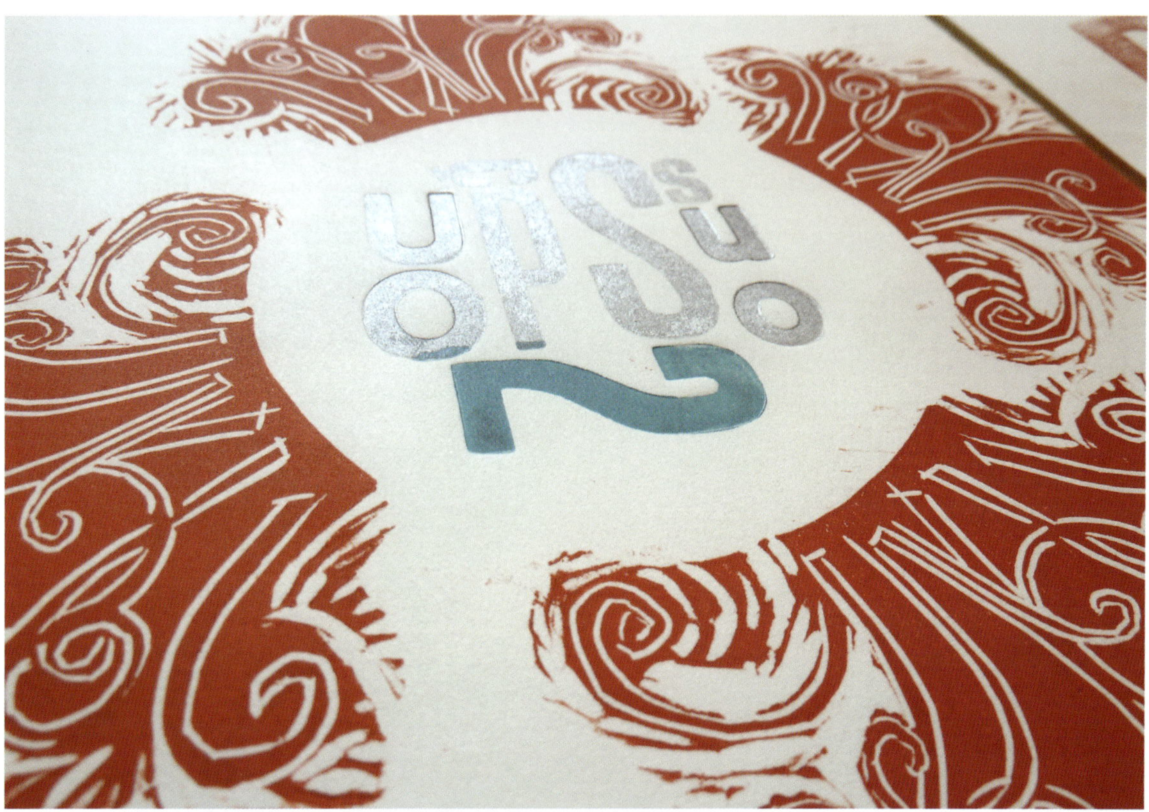

Too Much Paprika, Sarah Joseph. A linocut and letterpress book made on a workshop at Opificio della Rosa, Italy. The same lino block was printed repeatedly to create the shape around the letterpress design.

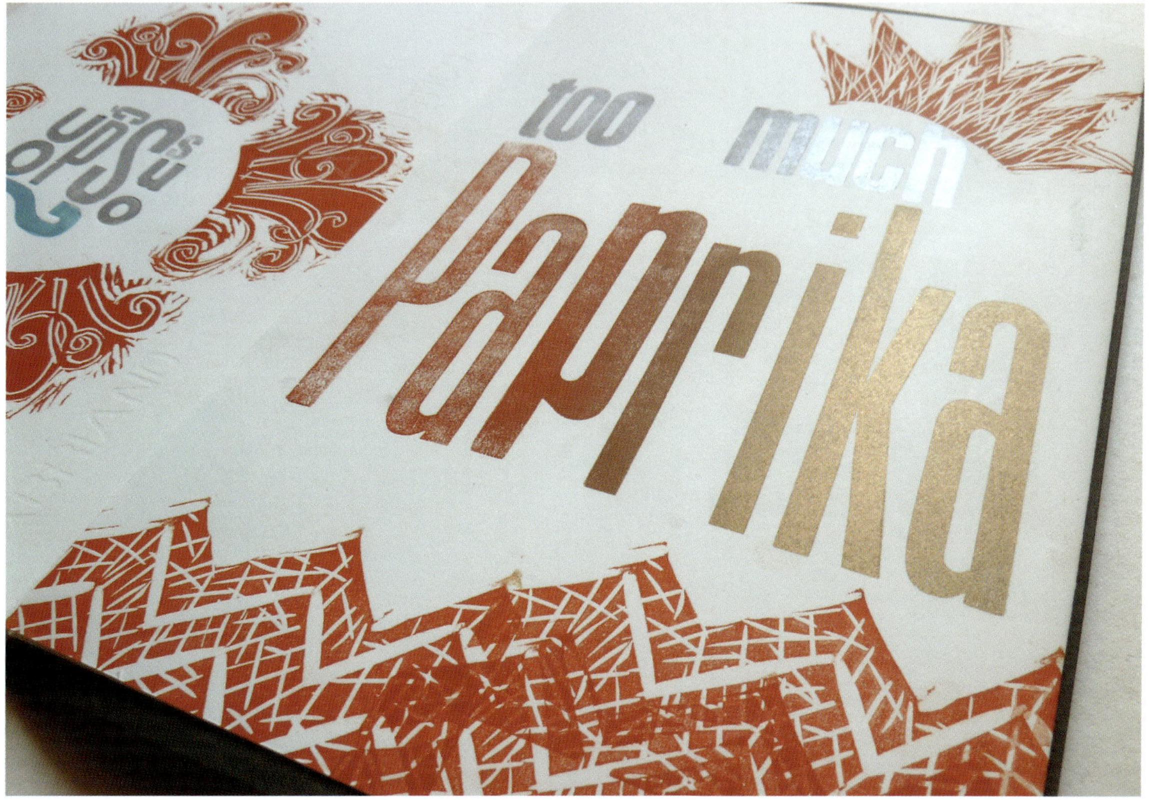

The linocut and letterpress elements are printed in harmonious colours which ties the composition together.

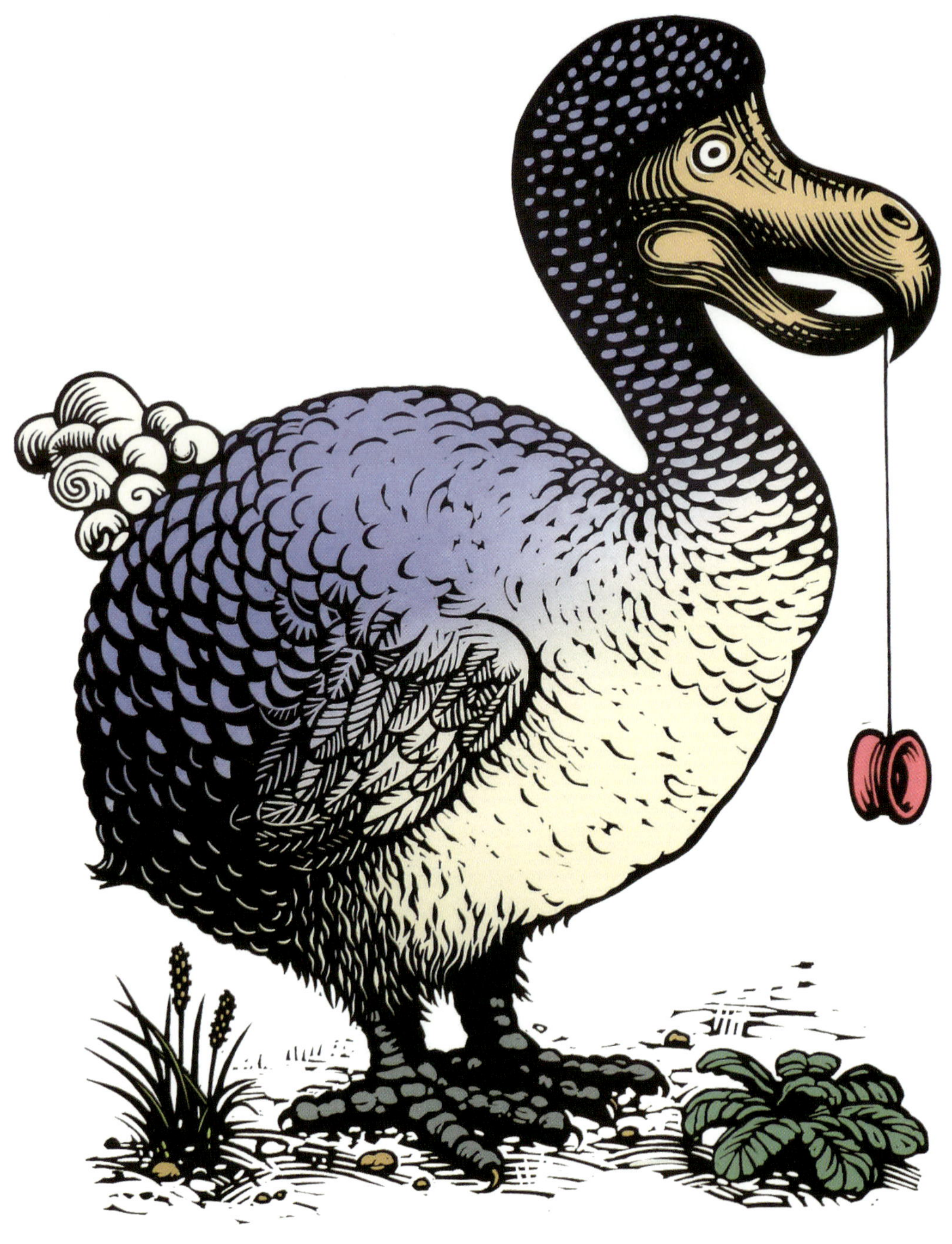

Yoyo, Nick Morley. Linocut and screenprint.
The black key block was carved and printed in black ink first.
The colours were added by screenprinting a thin layer of ink over the top.

Laser etched lino

Linoleum can be successfully etched with a laser in a similar way to wood or paper and the level of detail you can achieve is incredible. There are many businesses offering a lasercutting service and it is growing in popularity. Traditional linoleum can be laser etched but it gives off fumes which should be removed by an extractor fan. Vinyl should be avoided.

You will need to provide an image file (usually a vector file) in black and white. Photographic images will need to be converted to a halftone image made up of dots. Remember to tell the laser operator that you want the white areas of the photograph etched away.

The block can be inked up and printed in the usual way; you will need a good quality, tacky ink to pick up the fine details without filling in the white areas. Use a thin layer of ink on your roller and build the ink up gradually.

The printed image will look very precise and not at all like a hand carved linocut. Do not be afraid to carve into the block after it has been etched. The etched area may only cover one section of the block, forming part of a larger design.

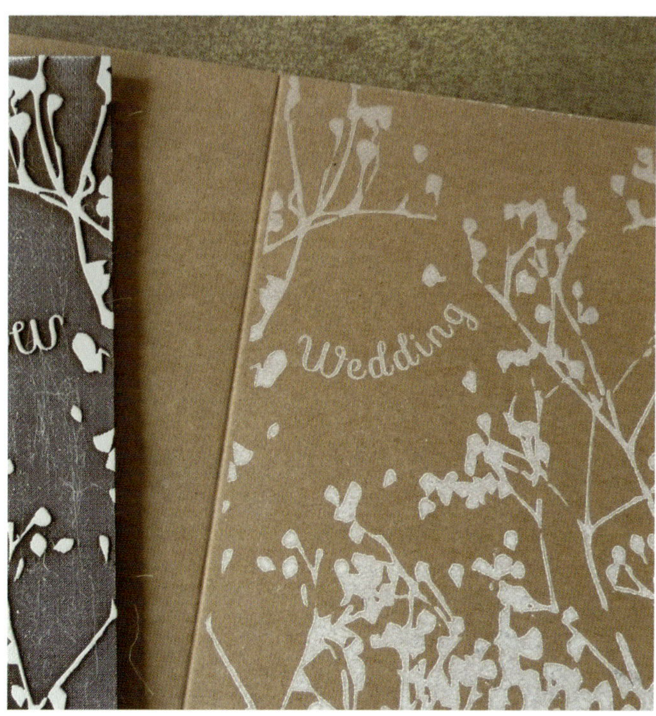

Wedding invite, Lasercraft Creations.

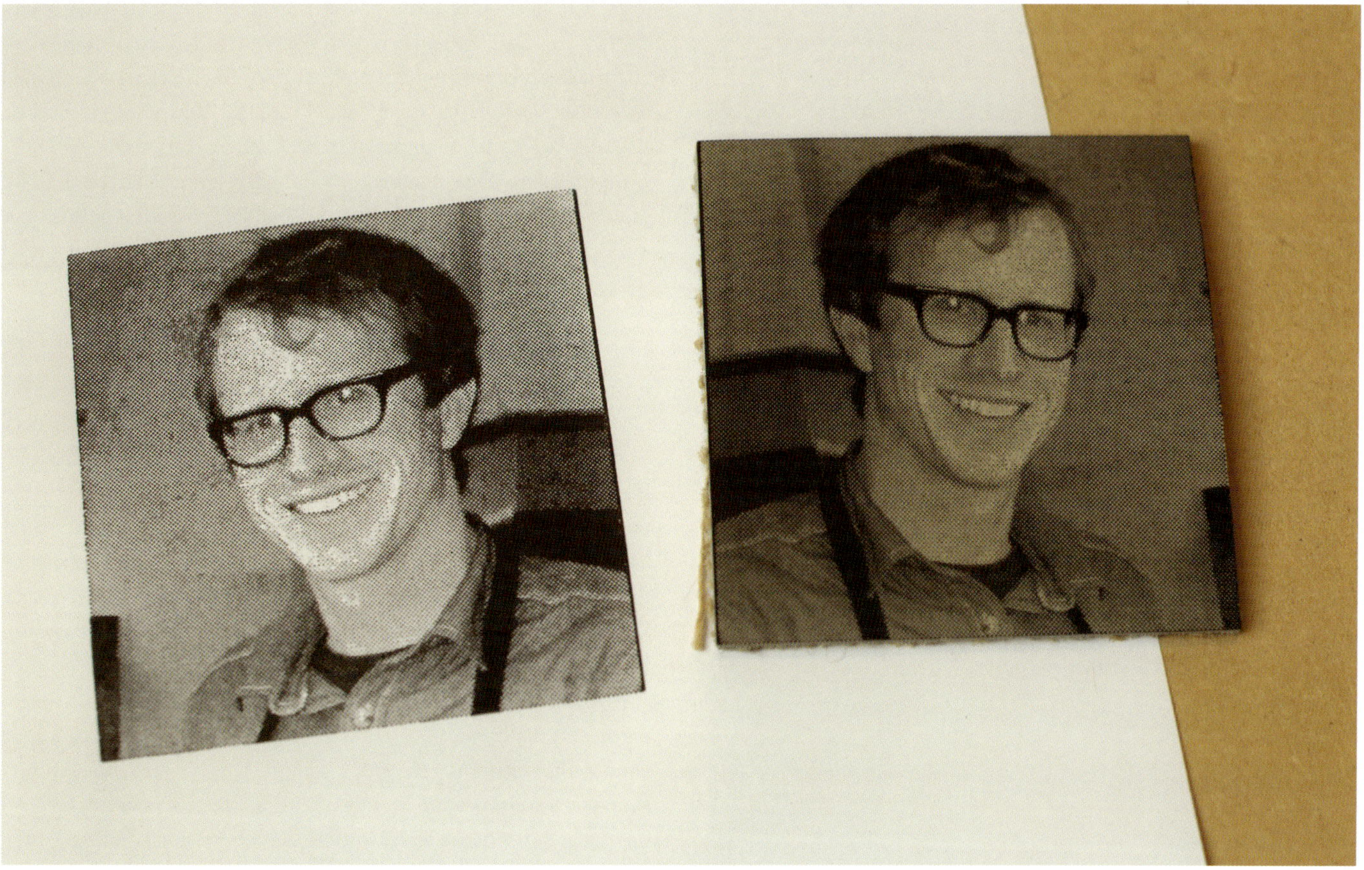

Laser etched lino created by Lasercraft Creations.
An incredible amount of detail can be achieved. This block is only 3in (7.5cm) square.

Large scale linocuts

Working on a large scale can be a good way to push yourself beyond your comfort zone. Grey linoleum is available on rolls up to 3 feet (1 metre) across and several feet long. Working on a sheet of lino which is bigger than you are presents a considerable challenge, not only physically but psychologically. Unless you want to spend several years of your life carving a single block you will have to work with energy and speed, or elicit the help of others. Carving a large block can be a fun communal activity, as can printing one.

Scaling up

One of the challenges of working on a large scale is getting the design onto the block. If you are working from a smaller image you can scale it up to the size of the block in a few ways:

Grid system

Draw a grid on your image, and a bigger grid on the block, with the same number of squares. Copy the image square by square.

Projection

Project your image onto the block and trace the outline.

Digital print-out

Many copy shops will print out digital files up to A1 or even A0. You can then use these to trace down onto the lino. If you have facilities for photo silkscreen, you can expose your digital printout onto a screen and print it onto your block.

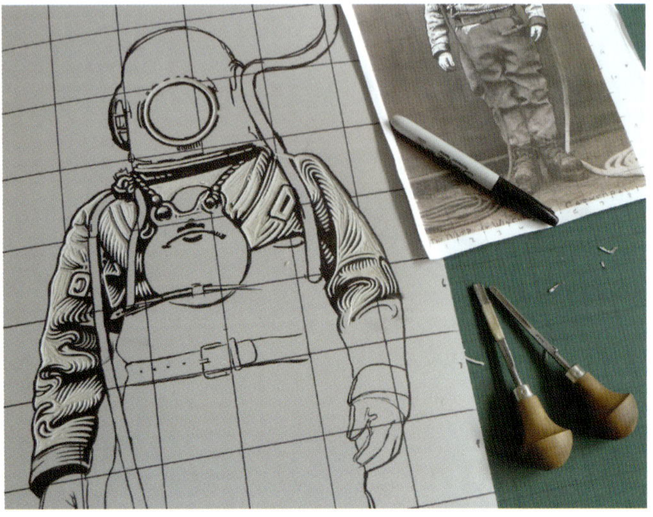

Enlarging an image using a grid system.

Printing with a steamroller

Possibly the most spectacular way to take a print from a linocut is by driving over it with a steamroller. If you can't get a real, old-fashioned steamroller a modern road roller will do. Many print studios have performed this feat and it is sure to attract a crowd. In principle it works like a cylinder printing press; the giant rollers of the machine exert a large but even downward pressure. In practice your prints won't be perfect but who cares when you're witnessing a great hulking machine bearing down on your paper.

If you want a genuine steam-driven steamroller you will need to find an enthusiast who is willing to help you. Bear in mind that these machines are heavy, move slowly and take several hours to fire up before they can move. Even if they have a license to drive on the roads it is unlikely the driver will want to travel very far to get to you. However, people who own working steamrollers tend to enjoy showing them off and it will likely be the first time they have used one to print with.

If you can't find the genuine article you should be able to find a local business which hires road rollers. These are modern machines which run on diesel and are fairly easy to operate. You should find they can be driven with a regular driving licence, but you will need to get extra insurance and probably stick to driving it on private land. As they are relatively small, road rollers can be delivered on the back of a truck. Make sure you have plenty of room for access. Some road rollers have a vibrating action, to help compact the new road surface. You don't want this, so make sure this function can be switched off.

Best results will be obtained on a hard, flat surface like concrete. To protect the paper and block, boards should be placed on bottom and top. A piece of old carpet can also be used to cushion the pressure.

Health and safety

Obviously, precautions must be taken when operating a large piece of moving machinery designed to flatten things. The printing area should be clearly marked out and kept clear of spectators. At large events stewards should be appointed for crowd control. Particular attention should be paid to preventing anyone from standing directly behind or in front of the roller at any time. The vehicle should not be left unattended whilst running or with the keys in the ignition.

It is likely that the use of a steamroller will allow you to print bigger blocks than usual so take advantage of this. Blocks can be as wide as the roller and almost any length. This is a great opportunity to make a collaborative artwork, with several carvers working on one large block or a series of smaller ones which join together. Wood blocks can also be used, including the 8 × 4 foot sheets of plywood or MDF available from timber merchants.

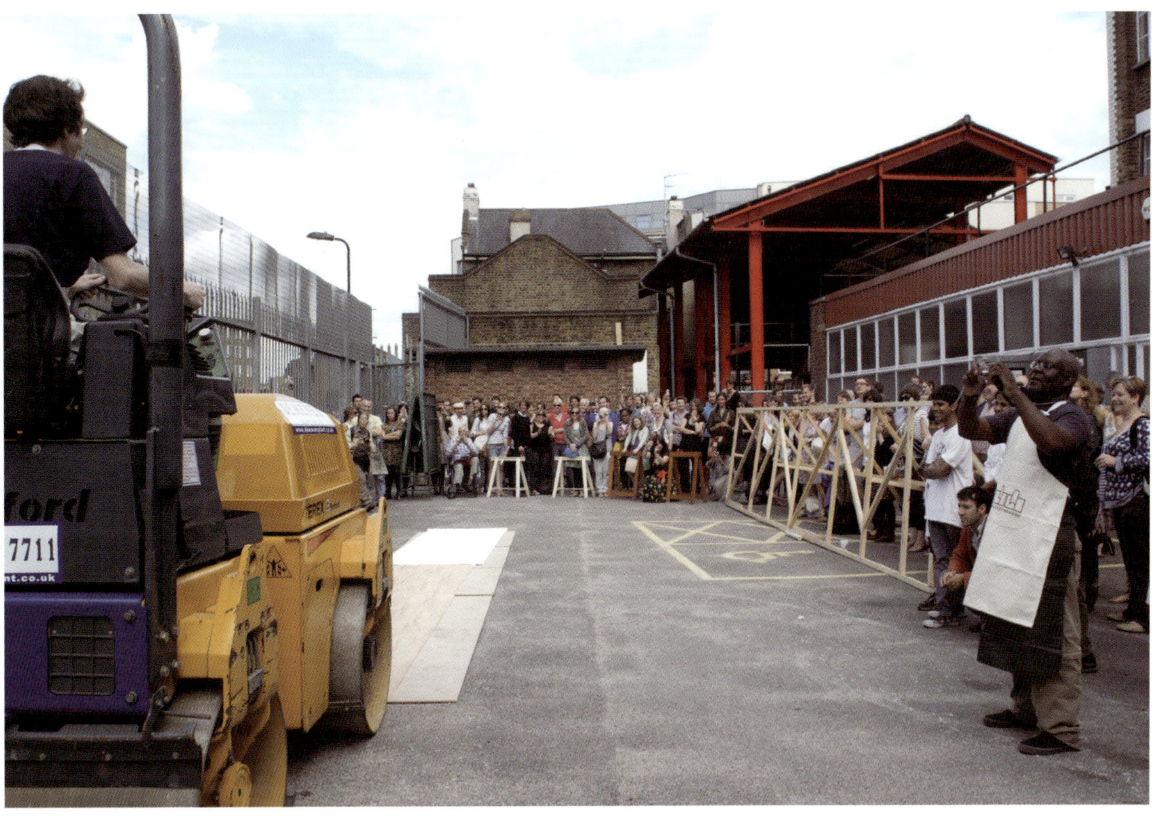

The author driving a road roller at a giant print event at East London Printmakers. (Photo: Teresa Eng)

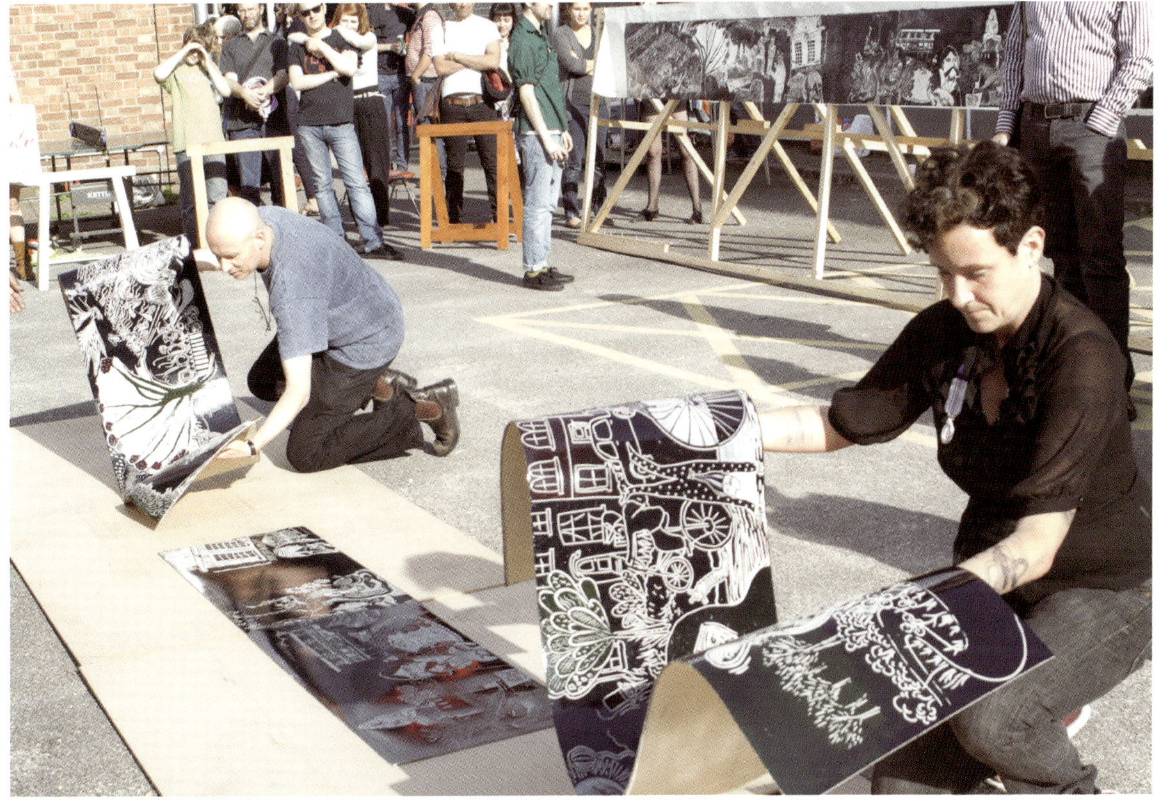

Laying out the pieces of lino ready for printing.
The total length was 24 ft and was printed on one roll of wallpaper. (Photo: Teresa Eng)

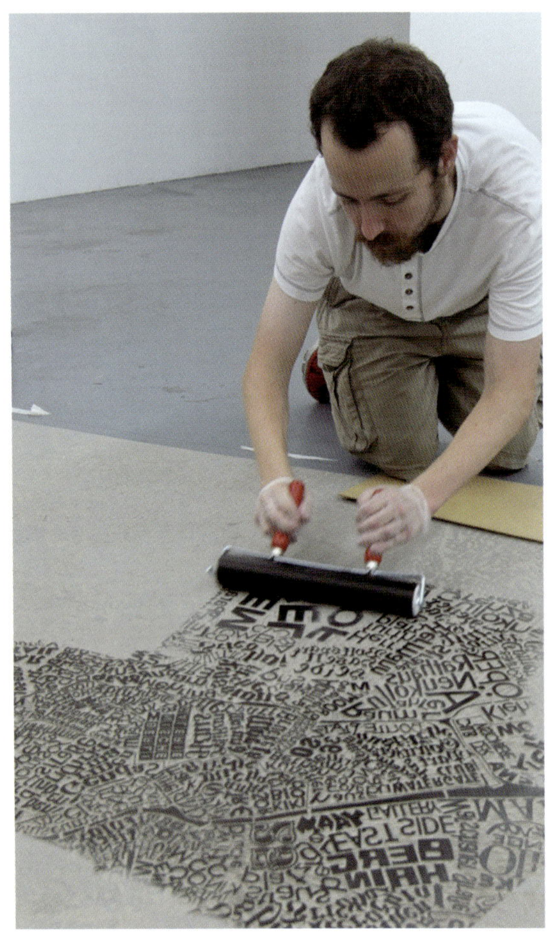

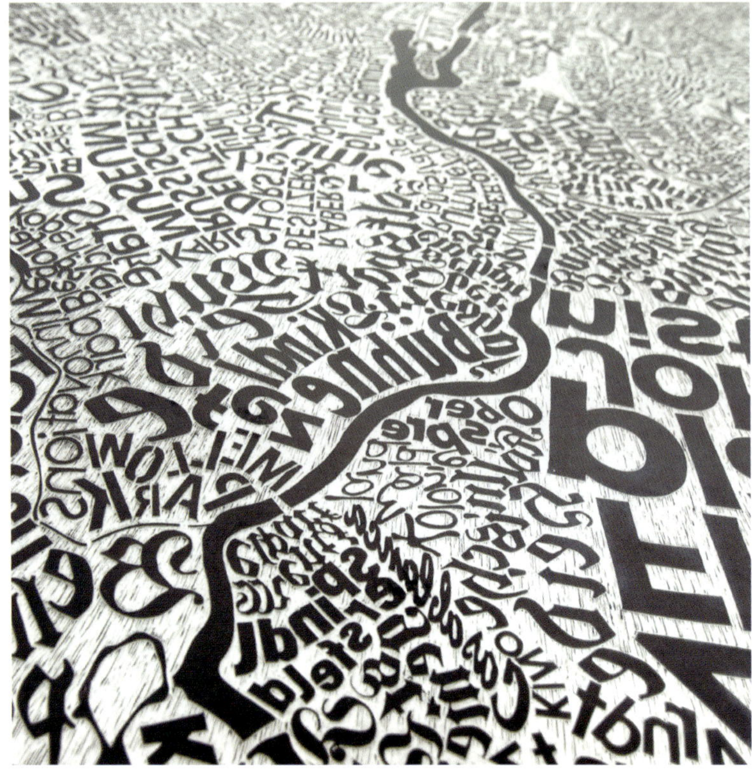

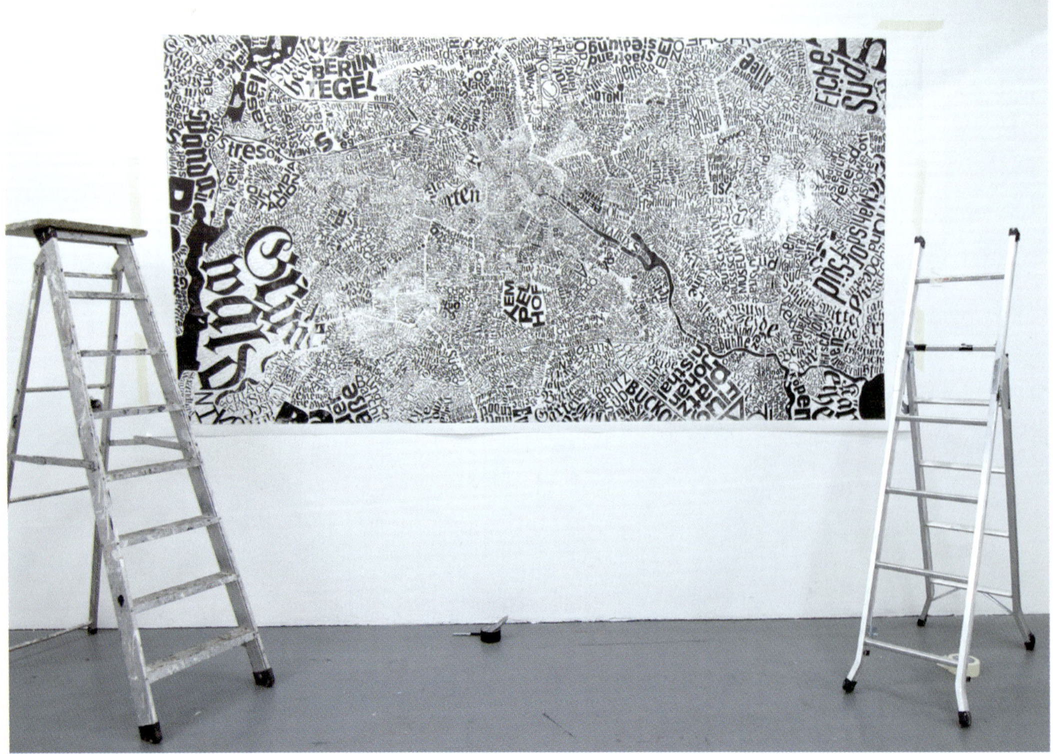

Berlin Map,
Mark Andrew Webber.
This enormous linocut took Mark five months to carve, working for 14 to 16 hours a day, every day. It measures 1.7 × 3.4m (5½ × 11ft). It was printed by hand with a team of helpers using metal spoons. (Photos: Ed Bartlett, The Future Tense)

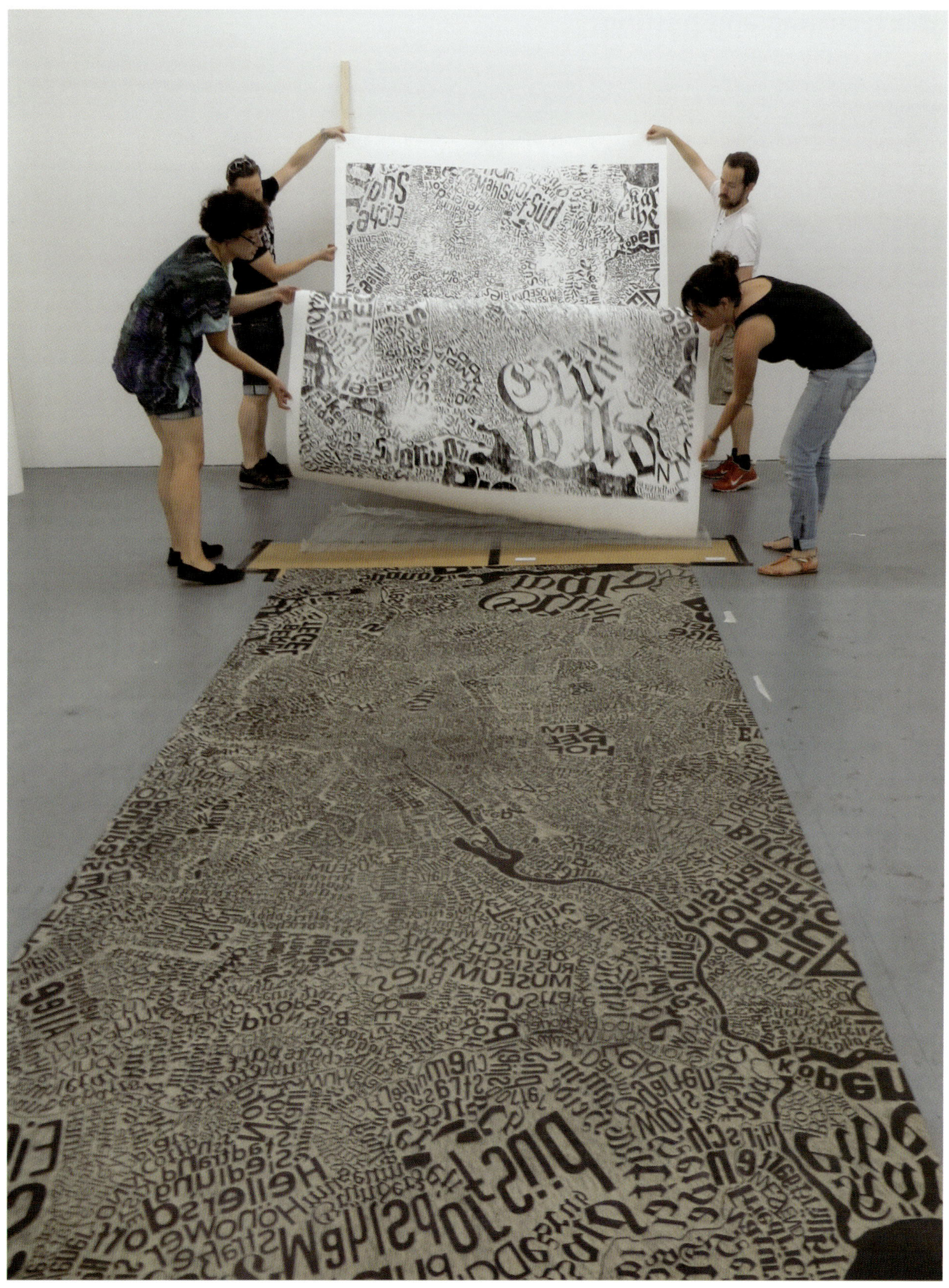

Printing Mark Andrew Webber's *Berlin Map* at his Wonderlust exhibition, Londonewcastle Project Space, 2014, curated by The Future Tense.

Street art: cutting and pasting

Paste-ups are a form of street art where a ready-made artwork on paper is pasted up in a public space using wheat paste or wallpaper paste. The artwork is exposed to the elements and the authorities and is more-or-less temporary. It could last hours or weeks, becoming worn by the weather, obscured by other artworks or faded by time. For the street artist this temporary nature gives the work an extra frisson as he or she never knows how long it will last. The audience is random and transitory. Whether the artwork is seen by a passer-by depends partly on chance, partly on their awareness of their environment. In contrast with art in the gallery, street art exists in the real world, free of trappings. Often street art is site-specific, being made for a particular nook or prominent wall.

There are several artists who use linocuts as paste-ups. It is really not worth investing in good quality paper so cheaper options like newsprint are usually employed. Thinner papers have the advantage of moulding to the shape of the surface they are stuck to; external walls are rarely flat. Because of their strong graphic qualities, linocuts stand up well to being seen outdoors, yet they are subtler than most spray-can art, often merging into their environment in a more natural way.

Birds on a Wire,
Zach Medler.
Wheat pasted linocut,
Lafayette, IN, USA.

Never Stop Searching,
Zach Medler.
Wheat pasted linocut,
Lafayette, IN, USA.

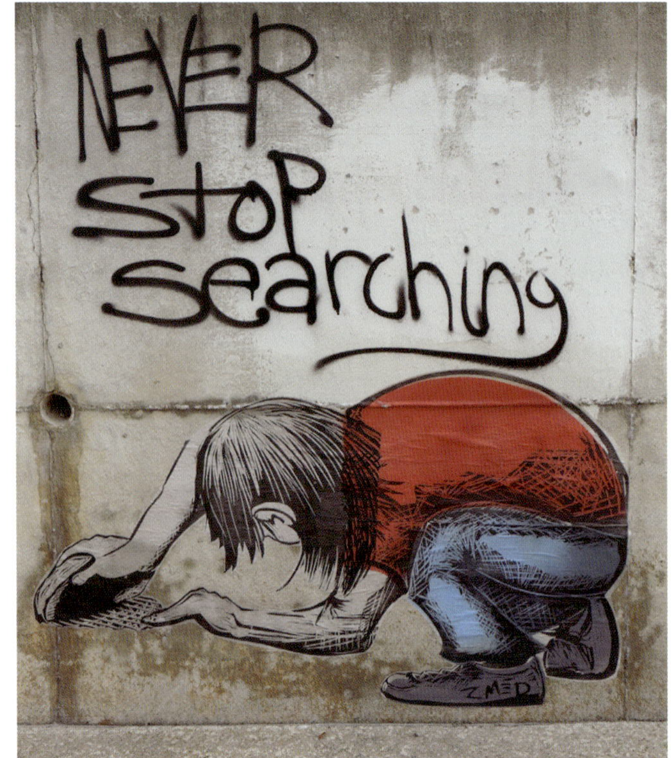

Project: flickbook

A simple animation can be made using linocut very easily, by printing the same image in a slightly different position in successive frames. These can then be scanned or photographed to make into a computer animation. Alternatively you can make a good old analogue animation in the form of a flick book. This is made of a series of pages of thin card bound at one edge. By flicking through the pages quickly the image appears to the eye to be moving.

More than one block can be used, each block moving independently. The trick is to plan the movement of the blocks beforehand. Bear in mind the action will only last a short time so you won't be able to tell an epic tale. As a rule of thumb you will need 25 to 30 frames per second. The maximum length of the animation will be determined by the final thickness of the book.

You will need to choose a paper or card stock with a good thickness and a bit of spring in it; if you bend it and let go it should snap back into position quickly. A weight of 200–400 gsm works well.

When printing the pages of your flickbook, you will need to leave a good sized gap at one side, where they are to be bound together. Anything printed here will be hidden. It is a good idea to make a dummy book before you start planning the animation so you can see how large an area of each page is lost.

Once the individual pages of your flickbook are dry you can bind them together. The easiest way to do this is to punch a hole on each page and fix them together with a nut and bolt or book screw.

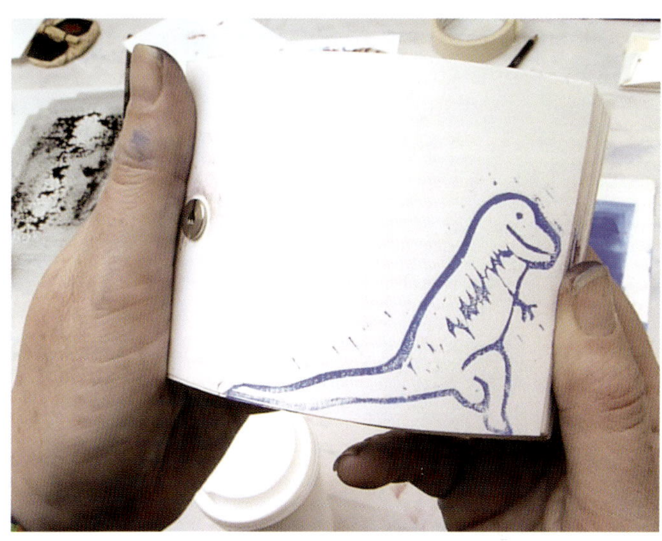

The pages of the flickbook are fixed together with a book screw.

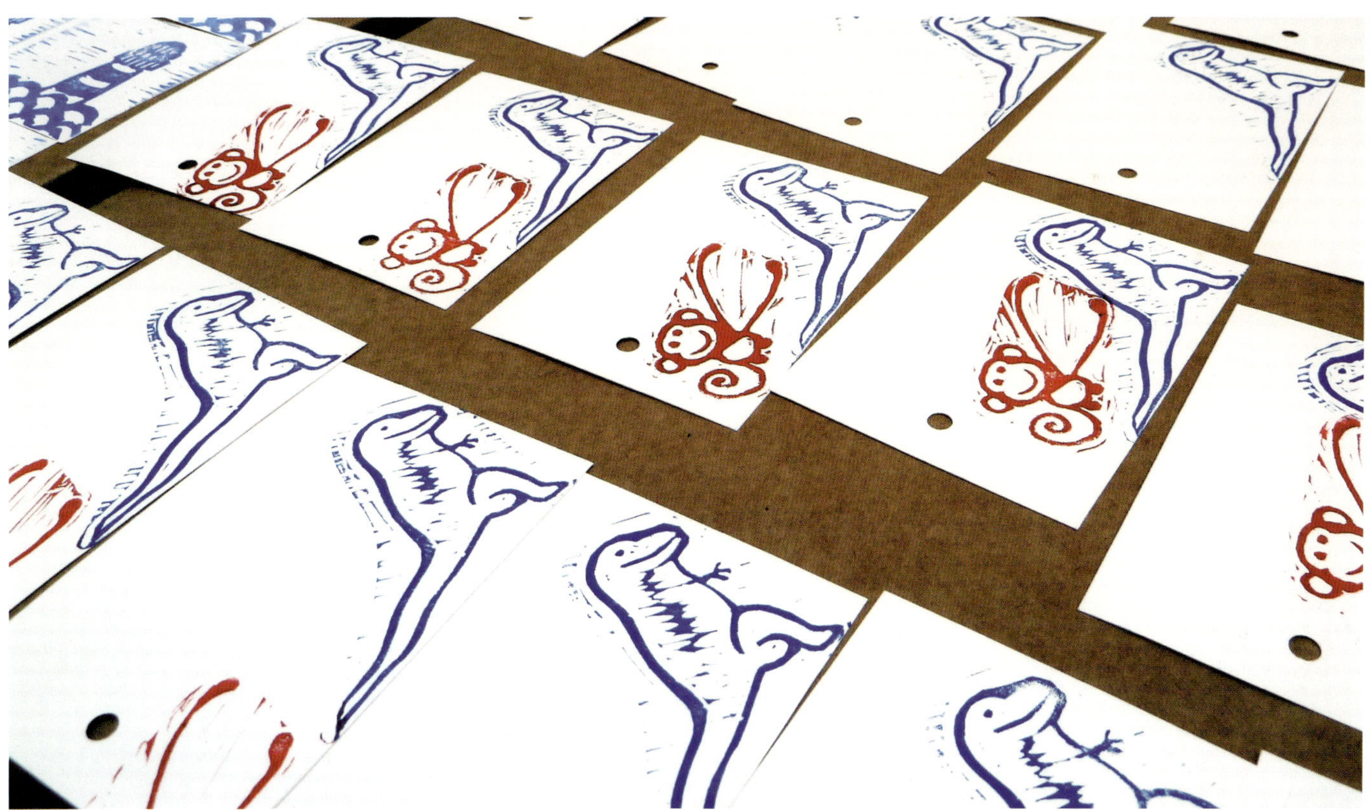

Making a flickbook. Individual pages drying during a workshop with Jotta in London.

Steve Edwards (UK)

www.steveedwardsart.com

Steve Edwards is an artist printmaker who makes large-scale landscapes and portraits using a combination of etched and cut lino. He works at East London Printmakers, an artists' cooperative. He is also a member of Greenwich Printmakers, who run a gallery in London. He regularly shows at the Affordable Art Fair and has work in a couple of commercial galleries.

I started making linocuts about ten years ago. Before that I was an etcher, but craved more colour in my work, so turned to lino. I also realized that it was a cheaper medium than etching, so my work could get bigger. The main draw of linocut for me was colour. I love the richness and strength of colour you can obtain with lino, as well as the complexity you can build when you overlay transparent colours.

The creation of the image and the carving away of the lino has a completely different and unique conception and mark-making process than other printmaking techniques. I use both carving and etching to make my prints. For etching the lino I use caustic soda mixed with wallpaper paste. I'm always on the lookout for substances that will resist the caustic etch. I have also used monoprinting combined with linocut in several prints, which I find very exciting.

My current subject matter is landscape/cityscape. I have been photographing London and other places for many years and have built a large library of photos that I can translate into images. I particularly like the Thames and its bridges. From these vantage points London becomes dwarfed by the surrounding elements, and the inclusion of big skies and the river makes the cityscape more emotional and elemental.

I use Photoshop to break down the photographic source, separating out elements that I can then transfer to lino. I either trace onto the lino with tracedown/carbon paper, or I transfer more complex images by using chemicals to break down photocopies or laser printouts and 'print' them onto the lino.

By the time I get to the lino I have already decided how many blocks it will take and how they could be layered. Colour references are taken from the original photo. What I want when I start transferring the various aspects of the image to the blocks is a mixture of control and freedom. So, if I want a recognizable location in my work I will carve and cut the lino accordingly to create the cityscape.

Once I have one or two blocks prepared I proof them, scan them into the computer, layer them in Photoshop and use this as a reference as I cut/etch the other blocks. Once the required number of blocks have been cut and etched and proofed, I print them and play with the colour variables whilst still referencing the original concept or mood of the piece.

I buy my lino and inks from T. N. Lawrence. I usually get my lino in big rolls which I cut down. I do not warm the lino, as I like the hardness to push against, and chip away at. Then I will use the etched lino technique in a very gestural and free way to create textures, which can represent water or clouds. I like this combination of control and uncontrol.

> *The juxtaposition of the marks that I use to create the buildings and bridges and those that I use to create the sky and water excites me, as does the capturing of the light and atmosphere of the particular view.*

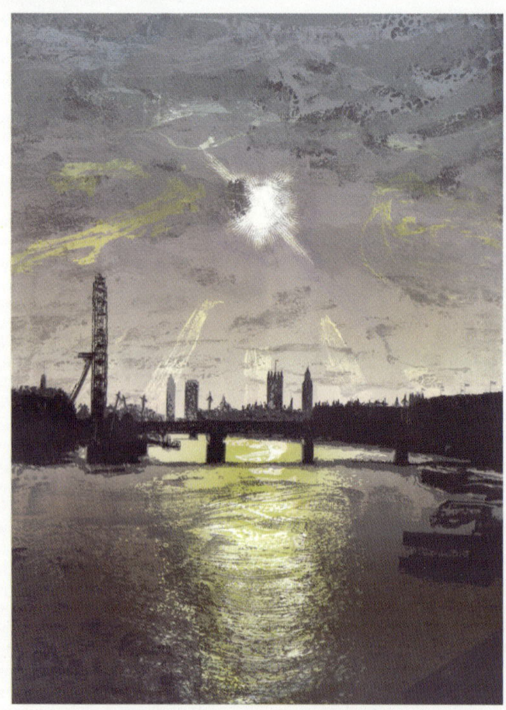

Sunburst, Steve Edwards, 95 × 67.5cm, etched and cut linoleum.

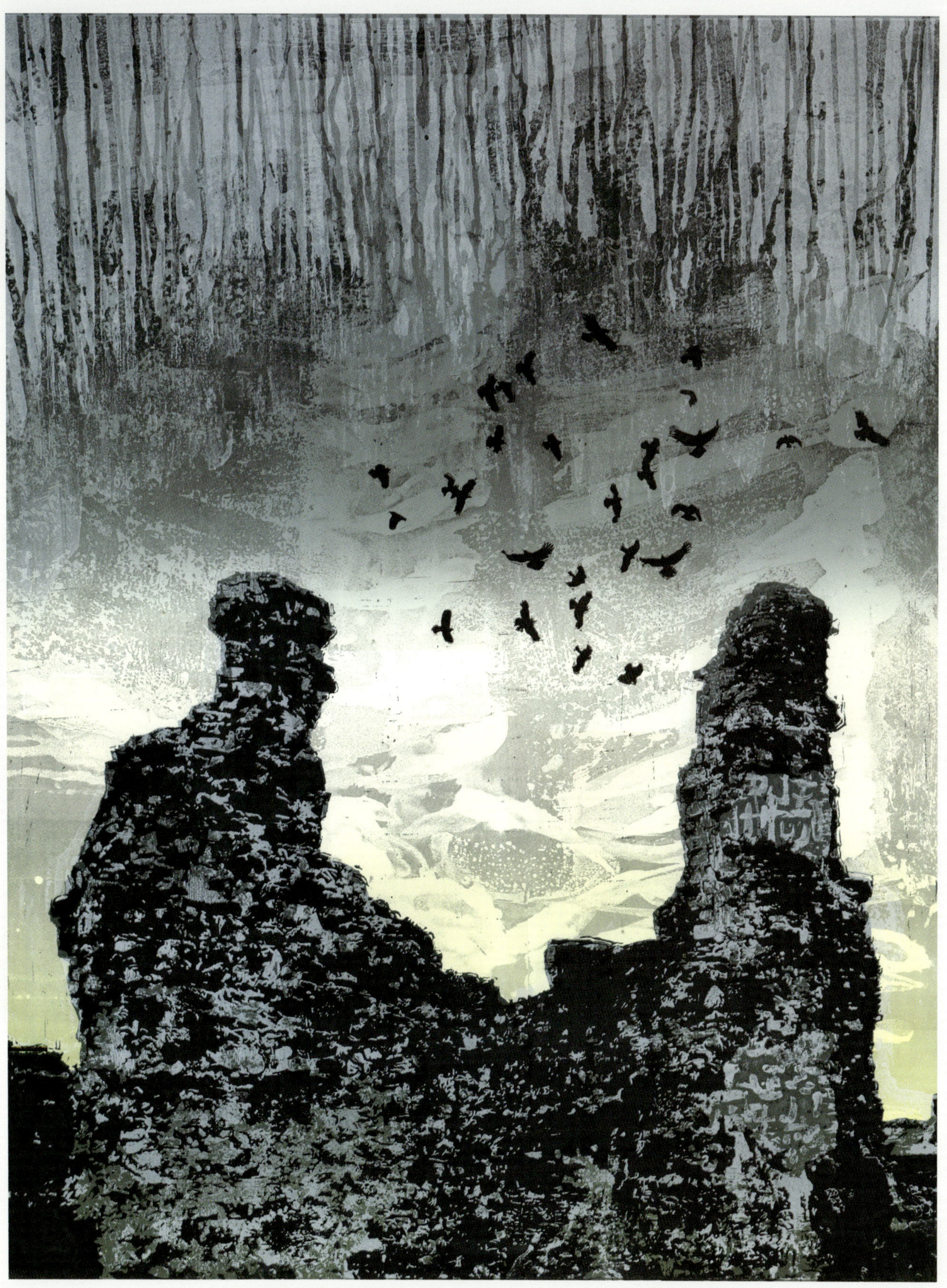

Dialogue, Steve Edwards, 90 × 71cm, etched and cut linoleum.

SUPPLIERS

UK

INTAGLIO PRINTMAKER
9 Playhouse Court, 62 Southwark Bridge Road, London SE1 0AT
www.intaglioprintmaker.com
Wide range of specialist tools, rollers, inks, paper, lino, printing presses.

JACKSON'S ART SUPPLIES
1 Farleigh Place, London N16 7SX
www.jacksonsart.com
Tools, inks, paper, lino, printing presses.

T. N. LAWRENCE
208 Portland Road, Hove BN3 5QT
www.lawrence.co.uk
Tools, rollers, inks, paper, lino.

HAWTHORN PRINTMAKER SUPPLIES
Moor Lane, Murton, York YO19 5UH
www.hawthornprintmaker.com
Presses, rollers, inks, lino.

JOHN PURCELL PAPER
15 Rumsey Road, London SW9 0TR
www.johnpurcell.net
Wide range of papers for drawing and printing, including specialist papers.

SHEPHERDS
30 Gillingham Street, London SW1V 1HU
www.bookbinding.co.uk
Wide range of specialist and decorative papers and bookbinding materials.

GREAT ART
www.greatart.co.uk
Printing presses, tools, inks, paper. General art supplies.

HARRY F. ROCHAT
15a Moxon Street, High Barnet, EN5 5TS
www.harryrochat.com
Manufacture, restoration and removals of printing presses.

CASLON
Caslon House, Lyon Way, St. Albans AL4 0LB
www.caslon.co.uk
Restored Adana letterpress machines and parts.

Germany

GERSTAECKER
www.gerstaecker.de
Presses, inks, paper, tools. General art supplies.

Netherlands

POLYMETAAL
www.polymetaal.nl
Printing presses, rollers, inks, paper.

Australia

SILK CUT LINO
www.silkcutlino.com
Lino, inks, rollers, presses.

USA

MCCLAIN'S PRINTMAKING SUPPLIES
www.imcclains.com
Specialist supplies, including Japanese tools and papers.

DICK BLICK
www.dickblick.com
Inks, papers, presses, rollers (brayers), lino.

GRAPHIC CHEMICAL & INK CO.
www.graphicchemical.com
Inks, papers, rollers (brayers), tools, lino.

INDEX